Thinking, Language, and Experience

Thinking, Language, and Experience

Hector-Neri Castañeda

University of Minnesota Press *Minneapolis*

Published by the University of Minnesota Press
2037 University Avenue Southeast, Minneapolis, MN 55414.
Published simultaneously in Canada
by Fitzhenry & Whiteside Limited, Markham.
Printed in the United States of America.

Library of Congress Cataloging-in-Publication Data

Castañeda, Hector-Neri, 1924–
    Thinking, language, and experience.

    Includes bibliographies and index.
    ISBN 0-8166-1672-8
    1. Thought and thinking.   2.Semantics (Philosophy)
3. Languages—Philosophy.   4. Experience.   I. Title.
B105.T54C36   1988   128'.2   88-17293

Part of Chapter 2 was published as "The Semantics and the Causal Roles of Proper Names,"
in *Philosophy and Phenomenological Research* 46 (1985–86): 91–113, Ernest Sosa, ed. It will
also appear in Klaus Jacobi and Helmut Pape, eds., *Das Denken und die Struktur der Welt:
Castañedas epistemologische Ontologie in Darstellung und Kritik* (Berlin: De Gruyter, 1989).

The following chapters are reprinted with permission of the publishers and editors: Chapter
9, sections 1–5 published as "Omniscience and Indexical Reference," in *The Journal of Philos-
ophy* 64, no. 7 (April 13, 1967): 203–10, Michael Kelly, managing ed., Columbia University.
Section 6 published with permission of Robert M. Adams. Chapter 10, published as
"Metaphysical Internalism, Selves, and the Wholistic Indivisible Noumenon," in *Midwest
Studies in Philosophy* 12 (1987): 129–44, Peter A. French, Theodore E. Uehling, Jr., and
Howard K. Wettstein, eds. (Minneapolis: University of Minnesota Press). Chapter 11, pub-
lished as "Fiction and Reality: Their Fundamental Connections," in *Poetics* 8 (1979): 31–62,
North-Holland Publishing Co., Amsterdam. Chapter 12, published as "Indicators and Quasi-
Indicators," in *American Philosophical Quarterly* 4, no. 2 (April 1967): 85–100, Nicholas
Rescher, ed., University of Pittsburgh. Chapter 13, published as "Thinking and the Structure
of the World," in *Philosophia* 4:1 (1974) (philosophical quarterly of Israel), Asa Kasher, ed.,
Tel Aviv University. Chapter 14, published as "Method, Individuals, and Guise Theory," in
Agent, Language, and the Structure for the World, James E. Tomberlin, ed. (Indianapolis:
Hacket Publishing Co., 1983), pp. 329–53. Chapter 9, section 6 was published in this *Fest-
schrift* with the same title, pp. 293–309.

The University of Minnesota
is an equal-opportunity
educator and employer.

Contents

Part III. A Semantic and Ontological Theory for the Language of Experience: Guise Theory

Preface

Our major concern is the structure of the human mind – that unified hierarchy of powers from which issues human experience. Here we study the chief patterns of experience. Since the fundamental type of experience is that of cognizing the world we find ourselves in, we investigate the grand structure of the world accessible to us.

After gathering and exegesizing a large collection of data, we propose a general semantics of thinking that accounts for the total personal unity of experience: Guise Theory. This fine-grained theory provides an account of the diversity of thought contents. It grounds a solution to current problems in cognitive psychology and sheds light on projects in artificial intelligence. We focus on the main connections among experience, thinking, language, and reality. These connections pivot on the fundamental unity of a person as a unitary subject of experiences of diverse types: perceptual, scientific, technological, moral, administrational, political, esthetic, literary, ludic, and so on. Thus we pursue a general theory of the structure of experience. Since the unity of experience is the unity of the language through the use of which the person lives her experiences, our main topic becomes the general structures and ways in which a natural language functions as a means of thinking and communicating, whatever the experienced contents may be. This sets us into a *semantico-pragmatics of thinking*, in contrast with the standard default doxastic semantics, which focus on the default experience in which we aim at gaining true beliefs about the physical world. We concentrate on the mechanisms of reference to individuals *qua* individuals.

A central presupposition is that the *content* of a thinking episode embodied in the production of a token T of a piece L of a language is, precisely, the representation built on that token by the appropriate semantics governing that L and the pragmatic rules regulating the connection between L and T. This presupposition is completely neutral with respect to the process of acquisition of a language, and the materials of linguistic tokens. Hence, whether thinking requires brains, or an evolutionary history, or social interaction are causal matters that must be discussed in their respective contexts. Thought content is, however, a phenomenon fully determined in the *present*; it is not fully *occurrent*, but stands on a complex hierarchical pedestal of dispositions and propensities. Besides, thought content is precisely what the thinker thinks: what she is aware of—even if unreflectively with no self-consciousness. Furthermore, the content of a thinking is in principle immediately accessible to the thinker. A mature thinker must have at least the capacity to access what he is thinking and thereby gain self-consciousness. Thus, to the extent that these features of thinking and content being thought of obtain, there must be *within* the thinker's reach, and perhaps within the thinker herself, a full determination of the content she is thinking of.

Strong versions of mind-reductive physicalism have attended to the preceding desideratum by identifying the thinking episode including its content with a brain state or a more inclusive bodily state. But I have never been a reductionist.[1] Yet I am tempted by a *methodological epistemological physicalism*, namely, the hypothesis for the purpose of guiding research that every mental state or episode has some distinctive physical manifestation. The rationale is simple: However subjective mental states and episodes may be, they are part of the total causal order of reality and should manifest in physical effects. Moreover, the subjective mental states or acts we can attribute to others must have an attribution basis in the shared common world of physical objects and events. Methodological epistemological physicalism is daring only in the methodological positing of a distinctive sign for each mental state or episode.

Combining the occurrence/access features of mental episodes with methodological epistemological physicalism, we are led to postulate that every episode of thinking has a content fully determined within the thinker's body and accessible surrounding environment. This result seems to be under attack by recent arguments against semantical individualism.[2] These arguments have been spearheaded by Hilary Putnam's Twin-Earth arguments. It may not be amiss to show that their success is more a matter of faith than of proof. Consider the following situation—*Putnam's Ruritanian Example*:[3]

In Northern and Southern Ruritania they speak English, but in the North they use the sounds *s-i-l-v-e-r* to talk about the metal silver, whereas in the South those sounds are used to talk about the metal aluminum. It so happens that in Northern Ruritania, silver is abundant and most utensils are made of silver, but aluminum is unknown, except to some travelers. In Southern Ruritania the reverse occurs: Silver is known only to some travelers, but aluminum is the standard material for utensils. Elmer in Northern Ruritania and Oscar in Southern Ruritania are two boys so much alike that they look like identical twins, and have been brought up in twin environments. Their parents look alike, their houses and their contents are indistinguishable, and so are their neighborhoods—except for the presence of silver objects around Elmer and of aluminum objects around Oscar. They have lived twin biographies. One morning at the very same moment Elmer and Oscar say, "Silver is shiny." Clearly, they are having different thought contents, Elmer about silver but Oscar about aluminum. The story is supposed to show that because of their twin biographies they are in exactly the same psychological state, which because of the presupposed physicalism is conceived to be a brain state. Hence, it is concluded, thought content is not a brain state. Since the meaning of the tokened sentence is part of the content thought of, it is also concluded that meanings are not in the head.

I am not impressed with the conclusion. Undoubtedly, Elmer and Oscar have been exposed to the same words and sentences (presumably with the same pronunciation, intonation, and pitch) in their confrontations with the same objects—except for those made of silver, or, respectively, aluminum. It is not obvious to me at all that these dealings with different metals, which look somewhat differently, feel differently, and have different causal properties, could not make any difference in the boys' brain states and propensities to act with respect to, say, the pots in their kitchens. The argument seems to me to assume an *atomistic* view of objects, meanings, and thought contents. Only if we take each material by itself in a row of unconnected items can we suppose that in Elmer's and Oscar's brain and body there are the same patterns as on a row having silver in place of aluminum. But we must be *holistic* about both the world and the mind. We must take into account the *differences* between the differences between silver and the other materials in Northern Ruritania and the differences between aluminum and the other materials in Southern Ruritania, not to mention the higher-order differences between these differences among themselves. Thus, it is obvious to me that Elmer and Oscar differ in their abilities to compare what they call "silver" pots with their respective brass, iron, wooden pots. In fact the story is too vague to allow semantic or psychological conclusions. Observe, for instance, that Elmer's pots and plates are supposed to be so similar as to create in them similar brain traces. Similar in weight? But then they must be different in size. In fact given the essentially hypothesized differences between silver and aluminum, two complexes of objects, one containing silver replicas of the aluminum objects of the other, are bound to be different. The physical differences between silver and aluminum are bound to make themselves present in any alleged twin rooms, houses, cities, planets, worlds. This transitivity of the differences in metals is part of the holistic character of the physical, and it demands a corresponding semantic holism.

Hence, when Elmer and Oscar thinkingly say "Silver is shiny," they are thinking different thought contents and on a strong view of epistemological physicalism their bodily states are different in that they have different propensities to engage in comparisons of their stuffs in their environment. Some of these different propensities are activated, put in a state of readiness, when one thinks of silver and the other of aluminum. It is not far-fetched to suppose that propensities, which involve counter-factual truths, have nevertheless distinct occurrent signals or manifestations. Some of these are the ones that in a general way can be accessed by a person who thinks that something is silver as a crucial part of her being capable of reflective consciousness that she is so thinking.

Whether thought content is determined by the community or the history of the thinker or the future of the world is not crucial for most of the investigation of reference. But it is helpful to be free of very restrictive presuppostions in the study of the semantics of the means of thinking. Let us proceed.

Notes

1. For my reasons see "Supervenient Properties, Emergency, and the Hierachy of Concrete Individuals," *Proceedings of the 1987 Meetings of the German Semiotic Society* (forthcoming). For a different approach see Jaegwon Kim, "Concepts of Supervenience," *Philosophy and Phenomological Research* 45 (1984): 153–76.

2. Hilary Putnam, "The Meaning of 'Meaning'," in Keith Gunderson (ed.), *Language, Mind, and Knowledge*, (Minneapolis: University of Minnesota Press, 1975). For a revised view, see "Meaning Holism and Epistemic Holism," in Konrad Cramer, Hans Friedrich Fulda, Rolf-Peter Horstmann, and Ulrich Pothast (eds.), *Theorie der Subjektivität* (Frankfurt: Suhrkamp, 1987. See also Tyler Burge, "Individualism and the Mental," in Peter French, Theodore Uehling, and Howard Wettstein (eds.), *Midwest Studies in Philosophy* 4 (1979): 73–121.

3. "Meaning Holism and Epistemic Holism," pp. 268–69.

Acknowledgments

This very much revised collection of some of my studies on reference, perception, thinking, and the structure of the world as we experience it has been in the works since 1982. The chief promoter is Lindsay Waters, who wanted to add this collection to the series of philosophy books he was editing for the University of Minnesota Press. He requested advice from: Roderick Chisholm, who praised the idea, gave some suggestions on what to include, and urged that my papers should be published as they were; Peter French, who worked hard at preparing a series of suggestions for dividing my papers into readable pieces to be combined in valuable chapters; and William Alston, who offered many suggestions including that someone be contracted to write a long introductory summary of my views and a guide to the papers. I am most grateful to Waters for his personal interest in my work and for his management of the project. To Chisholm, French, and Alston, I present my sincere appreciation for their splendid advice, which I have taken pains to accommodate.

For additional suggestions on which essays to select, I am grateful to Lynne R. Baker, James E. Tomberlin, Ricardo Gomez, Ernest Sosa, Jorge Gracia, and Francesco Orilia. Further editorial assistance was provided by Christel Fricke and Adriano Palma. Fricke suggested the title.

Toni Good has earned my gratitude for her patient and painstaking efforts at improving my style and grammar. I thank John Erwin and Terry Cochran, of the University of Minnesota Press, for sustained support of this project.

I also wish to thank the institutions that have financially and otherwise offered support, which has led to the results expounded here. Under a grant from The National Science Foundation I did my research on indexical and quasi-indexical reference and wrote Chapter 9, "God and Knowledge: Omniscience and Indexical Reference," and Chapter 12, "The Language of Other Minds: Indicators and Quasi-indicators." Under a National Endowment for the Humanities Fellowship I studied perceptual reference and the language of perception; only some of the results obtained appear in Chapter 6, "Perception: Its Internal Indexical Accusatives and Their Implicit Quasi-indexical Representation." At the Center for Advanced Study in the Behavioral Sciences, with the support of both the National Endowment for the Humanities and the T. Andrew Mellon Foundation, I wrote the Replies contained in James E. Tomberlin, ed., *Agent, Language, and the Structure of the World: Essays Presented to Hector-Neri Castañeda With His Replies* (Hackett Publishing, 1983). One of them is Chapter 14, "Philosophical Method, Individuals, and Guise Theory" (Reply to Alvin Plantinga). Wayne State University (to 1969) and Indiana University (since 1969) supported the research underlying the chapters of this book.

Thinking, Language, and Experience

1

Introduction

1. Major Objective, Grand Strategy, Chief Topics

The ensuing reflections and theorizations focus on the interaction between experience, thinking, language using, and reality. The core of each experience is a flow of thinking episodes with interconnected contents. The fundamental, default form of thinking is oriented to reality and aims at the acquisition (and rehearsal) of true belief; the primary thought contents are thus piecemeal representations of the thinker's conception of reality. In other types of experience, however, thinking represents possibilities or even impossibilities. But thinking is always representational and, hence, symbolic or linguistic.

Our major objective is to understand the large structure of the world and the major structures of our different types of experience. Our grand strategy is to study *singular reference* as this is diversely carried out in natural language, that is, reference to individuals *insofar as* they are thought of as individuals. This is a fundamental phenomenon lying at the root of every exercise of our thinking powers.

The primary individuals we refer to are existing components of the world. But we also think of possible worlds and non-existent objects, as when we hallucinate, fail in our intentions, pursue unsuccesful plans, contemplate alternative scientific theories, or immerse in literary experiences. Dealing with the non-existing, even the impossible, in variegated ways, is at the heart of living in the biographical sense. We are doomed – by evolution, or by God – to think and to act from our beliefs and intentions, and we possess our shares of false beliefs, even deeply-seated contradictory ones. Thinking is the biological equipment we have inherited through evolution to construct our own biographies in the midst of the surrounding objects of the world, themselves surrounded by sweet mists, or acid rains, of possibilities. Each episode of singular reference is an arrow typically aimed

3

at an individual in the world—yet one that often does not reach, and sometimes overshoots, its target.

The world is partitioned into categories of individuals, and the heads of the arrows of reference, through their composite pointing, silhouette the contour of that partition. Thus, a thorough investigation of referential pointing can give us insight into the basic structure of the world.

The arrows of reference emanate from inside the depths of the referrer's nature. Hence, a delving exploration of the tails of reference can reveal the structure of the mind from which reference issues. The success of reference witnesses the attunement of mental structure to world categorial contour—or vice versa.

The arrows of reference are, like all thinking, representational, embodied in symbols. The more sophisticated our thinking, the more sophisticated its symbolic medium must be. Natural languages are, by admirable evolutionary economy (or divine design), at once sophisticated means of thinking and powerful means of communication. They embody a shared conception of the world and of our types of experience. Thus, to ascertain the categorial profile of the shared world we must engage in a deeply delving, patiently detailed, and comprehensive investigation of the mechanisms of the shared language, by means of which *we* execute our references.

To the extent that there is interlinguistic communication, we may assume that a common core is shared by the world views deployed in the languages involved. That common core is at least a shared view of the structure of the world. This structure must be somehow embodied in the syntactico-semantico-pragmatic structure of a language capable of representing the world. Hence, languages involved in intercommunication contain at least partially isomorphic syntactico-semantic structures.

Consequently, English, though not better, is as good as any other language as our operating linguistic framework. Since we are communicating in English this provides our exegeses of semantico-syntactic phenomena with a special hue of self-knowledge. This is fine. We have a vested interest in our world, therefore, in our language, indeed in our very own idiolects. As Oscar Thend has repeatedly said, philosophy is genuinely done in the first person, and done for the first person.

2. The Four Mechanisms of Singular Reference: Our Chief Topics

A quick perusal of our experiences reveals four main mechanisms of singular reference, deployed in English in overlapping grammatical categories. They are: indexical reference, quasi-indexical reference, descriptive reference, and reference by means of proper names. Let us discuss briefly their roles in experience.

(1) We make *indexical reference* to items present in our experiences as so present; this is the fundamental mechanism for finding one's place in the world by confronting crucial objects in one's environment. There is, thus, in demonstrative reference an *executive* function of *placing* items, so to speak, as confronted in

person, in experience. The English mechanism for making references of this type is composed of a grammatical mix: demonstrative expressions ('this', 'that', 'now', 'then', 'here', 'there'); personal pronouns ('I', 'you', 'he', 'she'); verbal tenses, especially those used in direct speech constructions.

(2) The most revealing way of *attributing* indexical references to others is by means of our making *quasi-indexical references*. These are NOT indexical references, but depictions of others' indexical references. This is a type of vicarious presentational way of referring to objects not necessarily present to us through a representation of their presence to others. Quasi-indexical reference, thus, discharges also an *executive* function of putting before one's eyes a *replica* of the others' indexical references. Quasi-indicators are, thus, a most extraordinay and important mechanism of reference in natural language. The clearest English quasi-indicator is the pronoun 'he/she (him/herself)' in indirect speech constructions with an antecedent not in the same construction. But other expressions, particularly those used to make indexical reference, have quasi-indexical uses. Consider, for instance:

(1) A year ago watching the depression next to the huge oak tree planted by his great-great-grandfather, the Editor of *Soul* thought that
(S) a treasure WAS hidden THERE and that HE (HIMSELF) WOULD BE wealthy if HE (HIMSELF) dug *it* out THEN.

This sentence allows many interpretations. Among them one natural interpretation deserves full attention: Sentence (1) describes a perceptual situation in which the Editor of *Soul* confronts objects, and he confronts them in the way, not so much described, but *depicted*, by the subordinate clause (S). But this is *our* depiction, intended to capture The Editor's own confrontation through indexical references in our terms, rather than by quotation:

(2) A year ago watching the depression next to the huge oak tree planted by his great-great-grandfather, the Editor of *Soul* thought thus:
(D) "A treasure IS hidden HERE. I WILL BE wealthy if I dig *it* out NOW."

The subordinate clause (S) of (1) re-presents *within* the whole context of sentence (1) the Editor of *Soul*'s corresponding indexical references signaled by the matching capitals in (2):

Indicators in (2)(D)	quasi-indicators in (1)(S)
IS	WAS
HERE	THERE
I	HE (HIMSELF)
WILL BE	WOULD BE
NOW	THEN

Of course, we must NOT claim that the expressions in the first column are always indicators or that the expressions in the second column are always quasi-indicators. Obviously, the adverbs 'then' and 'there' are sometimes used as indicators, and we will see that the first-person pronoun 'I' is sometimes used as a quasi-indicator. Likewise, the verbal tenses have non-indexical uses; this is especially true of the present tense. Moreover, the italicized *it* in "if I dig *it* NOW" is obscure. Even within the natural interpretation, this '*it*' may represent the Editor's use of '*it*' as a pronoun tied down to his use of the quantifier 'a treasure'; but that '*it*' may, on the other hand, originate in a use of an indexical phrase like "this treasure."

Clearly, it is a purely parochial feature of English not to have a distinct repertory of purely lexical quasi-indicators. This may show something peculiar about the way the world looks to English speakers when thinking in English. This is a topic suitable for the general anthropology of the English language. For us, the main point—which we will take up—is that conceptual, philosophical data do not lie in words or even clauses in isolation, indeed, not even in syntactic structure, but in pragmatico-syntactico-semantic contrasts. Furthermore, we need the following:

TERMINOLOGICAL CONVENTION. When we speak of indicators—quasi-indicators, proper names, definite descriptions, verbs, nouns, or any other pragmatico-grammatical category—we are speaking of *types of uses* of expressions under consideration. Words and phrases belong to categories only in the context of a discourse.

(3) A minimally rich life requires that we think of and refer to items not present in experience. This allows planning and cooperation with others. This is precisely the role of *descriptive reference* to objects identified and segregated from all others through their properties, expressed by means of locutions of the form *the [thing that is just] so-and-so*. This is the central mechanism for thinking of objects absent from one's experience, but it can be used to think of objects present in experience, in mixed *indexical-descriptive reference*, as, for example, when we think *THAT huge bird approaching THAT tree on the left*. Undoubtedly, some absent objects are accessible to experience; perhaps all objects to which we can refer singularly, that is, as individuals, must be in principle accessible to our experience. If so, all singular reference to objects absent from experience is attained through a path built on their connection to objects present in current experience. Thus, all singular reference involves an explicit, or tacit, connection to items referred to indexically, or to objects indexically available to current experience, or to the experience itself.

(4) *Reference by means of proper names* is a marvelous phenomenon: pedestrian, yet mysterious. All of chapter 2 is devoted to it.

The four mechanisms of singular reference interact. Not only do we have indexical descriptions, for example, "That round building over there," but descriptions and names conjoin, for example, "John, the Baptist," and descriptions and quasi-indicators combine, as in "Mary believed that she herself, the most senior member of the group, should be the first to speak." Indicators and quasi-indicators can combine only in one special case: Indicators are devices for *one*'s making indexical references, whereas quasi-indicators are devices for attributing indexical references to others; thus, only when the speaker (thinker) is the same as the person spoken (thought) of in the mind of the speaker can indexical and quasi-indexical references intermesh convergently — for this contexts of first-person reference are required.

One of my guiding principles has been that the four mechanisms of singular reference should be studied on their own merits, without any preconceived idea of reducing one to the others. Rather, the investigation was always receptive to the discovery of new mechanisms of reference. This is why quasi-indicators could appear in their full range in the first place.

3. The Hierarchical Web of Reference

We have always located thinking reference, or, as others prefer to say, purporting to refer, at the center of a network of intimately connected phenomena discussed under the heading "reference." As we see it, those phenomena belong to a hierarchical web, the strands and elements of which should not be conflated — at least not at the beginning of the investigation, and later only in the presence of a good theoretical account. In particular we must distinguish thinking reference from the communication of reference, and thinking reference from doxastic reference. Again, the goal has not been to achieve reductions of some phenomena to others, but to understand their joint pattern through their interconnecting implications.

One crucial connection we must contemplate is that between language and thinking. There must be positive connections between episodes of thinking and acts of using a language that is a means of thinking. They have to do with the way the symbolism functions in presenting to the thinker his or her thought contents. The general idea is this: there must be a convergence between what the symbols mean and denote and what the speaker thinks. To put it succinctly: *Effective linguistic representation is psychological presentation.* More specifically:

(T-S.C*) The representation built into an occurrent, or token T of a piece of language by the semantic principles and pragmatic rules under which the speaker-thinker S has produced T is the thinking *presentation* for S, that is, is the thought content of S's thinking episode embodied in the episode consisting of S's producing T.

Given the two levels of rules pertaining to linguistic representation, we have as special cases:

(T-S.C*1) In a situation of the type described in (T-S.C*), S thinks the qualities, properties, and relations that are denoted by the predicative expression tokens that compose T.

(T-S.C*2) In a situation of the type described in (T-S.C*), S refers thinkingly (or purports to refer) to the entities strictly denoted by the tokens of singular referring terms composing T.

This convergence between thought content and semantico-pragmatic meaning and denotation should yield a flexible *thinking semantics* – rather than a coarse doxastic semantics. In the rest of this study we concentrate primarily not in the meanings of predicates, but on the phenomenon of reference. That is, we focus mainly on the semantico-pragmatic convergence between linguistic denotation and thinking reference, as postulated by (T-S.C*2). The topic is better demarcated when it is seen in its full setting within the large web of reference.

Some philosophers shiver when they hear expressions like 'thinking reference', not to mention 'first-person thinking reference'. These phrases tend to be associated with private languages, which are supposed to have been shown to be impossible by Ludwig Wittgenstein, or John Dewey. Thus it is worth observing that the above convergence between thought content and semantico-pragmatic reference, required for a language to be both a means of thinking and a means of communication of thoughts, may be a public language like English – which we have explicitly made our subject matter.

In brief, the classical private language issue can be set aside.[1] There has, however, been a current revival of some Wittgensteinian theses. One, promoted by Hilary Putnam, is this: Reference is not a personal matter for a thinker (speaker) to decide. What a speaker refers to is determined by others, the experts.[2] Another thesis, propounded by Tyler Burge, is that the content of a person's thinking episodes is in part external to the thinker's mind and body, and that part belongs to the community.[3] The arguments for these theses seem to imply that the meanings of expressions are not contained within an individual's speech dispositions and acts, but within the community of speakers. These arguments, especially Burge's, have focused on crucial and important data about the use of language which must be considered seriously by *any* theorist of reference. We will discuss these matters later on, after we have built a useful comprehensive reservoir of data. Just one general remark here – those arguments assume that language is a social reality, and that the individual speaker's speeches are partial manifestations of that reality. There is a powerful important truth in this, one that must be highlighted in a study of the role of natural language in ordinary experiences, which involve or presuppose a surrounding community. It lies at the bottom of the activities we carry out and the institutions we belong to. That truth is fundamental to understand how language has evolved and how we have learned it. Yet it must not be allowed to blur certain other important truths, among which are:

(L.1) A language exists *in* the dispositions of each speaker to use it as a means of thinking as well as means of communication.

(L.2) A natural language is not only a family of dialects, but also a family of intersecting idiolects.

(L.3) A mature speaker of a language must be able to use language to think of the world and his experiences by herself and for herself, autonomously, independently of other speakers' control: Her idiolect is her basic linguistic reality.

In summary, the social nature of language must be understood in the context of the reality of language in each individual speaker's nature, since there is no other human nature except the one realized in individual humans. Here we are concerned with language used by mature, autonomous speaker-thinkers, who, of course, are capable of communication.

It seems, then, that to understand fully the phenomenon of reference we must distinguish within the web of reference the following strata from one another:

A. The hierarchy of speaker's first-person thinking references
B. The hierarchy of speaker's doxastic reference, as a convergence of thought of individuals with individuals the speaker has beliefs about
C. The hierarchy of speaker's communicational referential intentions
D. Each hearer's hierarchy of thinking references
E. Each hearer's attribution of references to the speaker
F. Composite audience's references
G. The denotation, if any, built into the shared language

The schedule A-G is not exhaustive. For instance, the problem sometimes heatedly debated whether or not terms in conflicting scientific theories have the same referents may be considered a separate problem, or may be considered a special case of G. Regardless of how broad the web of reference may be taken to be, the order A-G is a logical order of the greatest importance. Recent work on indexical reference has shown that we cannot in general equate G with any of the others. Some recent philosophers have contrasted speaker's intentions to refer with some concept of reference that seems to lie somewhere between D and F, but sometimes seems to be a combination of F and G. We must make the distinctions *wholesale* and keep our minds fastened to the multiply hierarchical structure of reference.

The hierarchical structure of reference and intentions to refer has been a stumbling block in many essays on reference and the unknown culprit of some debates on reference. The role of secondary intentions to refer has been noted very seldom[4] – let alone the roles of tertiary and higher referential intentions.

4. Some Data: A Pentecostal Miracle in Reverse

By way of collecting some useful data that brings forth some of the distinctions made above, let us recall the miracle of Pentecost. It is a purely empirical and contingent – technological – matter that it happened, or didn't happen. It exhibits a grandiose case of successful communication of reference through a miraculous cooperation of many diverse local embodiments of our central mechanisms of reference. As explained above in section 1, however, our concern lies beyond the parochial linguistic embodiments. For us, failures of communication and conflicts among the mechanisms of reference are more fruitful because they separate elements that could be easily assumed to go necessarily together. Consider the following:

(PMiR) *Pentecostal Miracle in Reverse*. Ruth, in some appropriate physical circumstances at a Conference on David Kaplan at the Stanford Silicon-Mirror Auditorium, a marvel of architecture, pointing to and looking at the person some of us know as Joseph Almog, apparently confusing in *my* nomenclature Almog with Paul Benacerraf, who is holding up a copy of *American Philosophical Quarterly*, vol. 4 (1967), bound in a lovely blue jacket, proffers into the microphone:

(3) Paul, the man over there, with the martini-colored copy of *Naming and Necessity*, is the author of *The Nature of Necessity* published by Oxford University Press.

It so happens that the light and the physico-chemical environment surrounding Ruth and her audience cause each hearer to perceive Ruth's pointing, but subjected to a deflection, and hear the sounds "Paul" she pronounces transformed in their auditory perceptions into "Van," "Rog," "Dave," "Rod," and so on, respectively, so that one hearer sees her point to, and *takes* her to be referring to, the person she and I both call Van Quine, another to the person we both call Rogers Albritton, another to the person she calls David Kaplan but I call Nathan Salmon, another to the person she and I both call Roderick Chisholm, and so on.

To whom did Ruth *actually*, *really*, refer?

Neither the semantic rules nor the pragmatic practice of English can decide which one from among the distinguished philosophers mentioned is the individual Ruth referred to. The question is moot. There is a plurality of references: Ruth's thinking references (demonstratively to Joseph Almog, by proper name – whatever this may really be – to Paul Benacerraf and two celebrated books, by definite description to Alvin Plantinga), and each hearer's thinking reference to his own thought of person; there are, to be sure, composite references built up from convergencies of some of the hearers' thinking references. Obviously, there are different ways of computing and combining such convergencies.

Ruth is clearly distinguishing the two books from one another and from persons. Although she is confusing a demonstrably referred-to object, which we know to be *APQ* vol. 4, with *Naming and Necessity*; but is she confusing *APQ* vol. 4 with Saul Kripke's first book? These are *our* references, and we need a theory to connect them to Ruth's. On the other hand, some (but not Ruth) will say she is confusing Paul Benacerraf with Joseph Almog and with Alvin Plantinga. Thus, as I understand the "logic" of confusions of individuals, Ruth must: (i) be referring thinkingly to each one of the persons she is confusing, (ii) have some true beliefs about each one of them, and (iii) have some false beliefs about their identities, as (3) itself shows. Here we need the hierarchy of referential intentions. Her statement (3) taken as a whole *discourse* may be said to contain a primary reference to Benacerraf, a secondary reference to Plantinga, and a tertiary reference to Almog. But this parsing is not binding on the containing paragraphs and sections that constitute Ruth's larger encompassing discourses. It all depends on the themes of these discourses, which may not even reveal the main topic of her lecture. She may be confusing Plantinga with Krikpe.

In (PMiR) we merely have a dramatization of the need to distinguish the strands of the above web of reference. We must take the linguistic unit of both thinking and communicational reference to be *not* a sentence, but a *discourse*.

5. Strategic Plan and Major Methodological Focus and Constraints

Our strategic plan is to immerse ourselves in an investigation *au fond* into the basic four types of reference through the exegesis of the ways the English versions of those mechanisms function in experience.

Our strategic methodology demands that we examine abundant and abundantly rich and diversified specimens of experience that can reveal the large semantico-syntactic patterns. The operative principle is that experience, some would say pragmatics, is the key to semantics and syntax: Syntax, particularly, is arbitrary and has been invented to serve our conceptual and other needs. We shall always keep in mind that syntax needs exegesis. For one thing, syntactical constructions serve different semantic purposes. Furthermore, some syntactic constructions are parochial in their semantic or pragmatic aspects. Moreover, and this is necessary to maintain a catholic interlinguistic perspective, for our purpose it does not matter how English, or any other language, assigns a given semantics to a certain syntactic construction; what matters are the syntactico-semantic *contrasts*. These are intertranslatable across different languages.

The last methodological point is of the greatest importance and deserves an illustration. A fundamental distinction within mental states is that between intending and believing. This difference is so crucial to life that, because of a multitude of reasons,[5] I hold that the difference between the contents of contemplative thinking, built on believing, and the contents of practical thinking, built on intending, is also a fundamental human universal feature, hence, one to be expressed in ALL natural languages. The contents of believing have been called *propositions* (which nominalists have equated with classes of appropriately equivalent sentences). I have called the contents of practical thinking *practitions*, intented contents being first-person practitions. Naturally, English expresses the proposition/practition distinction very neatly. In direct speech the difference for the case of second-person thoughts is expressed by means of the syntactic indicative/imperative contrast. In indirect speech the semantic contrast is, regardless of grammatical person, basically embodied in the contrast between indicative and infinitive subordinate clauses. Here the semiotic function of syntax is of gigantic and dramatic proportions: on the one hand, we confront here the major ontological divide between the ways in which what is intended and what is believed enter in or relate to the world; on the other hand, we face also the major psychological and epistemological difference between believing and intending. For the sake of concreteness let us ponder the following reflective declaration by Professor John Shearle:

I'll go to the Faculty meeting! . . . Yes, *I* intend *to go*. But . . . I don't believe I WILL GO. Barbara will most likely succeed in keeping me away from that meeting.

The two italicized clauses formulate the same intention, but with a difference: First it is presented by itself, in direct speech, then it is presented as the content of Professor Shearle's state of intending. The capitalized clause expresses the corresponding prediction as the content of Shearle's believing. The intention is neither true nor false; the prediction is true or false. Intending and believing differ by their characteristic causal properties, but also by their accusatives. This difference is beautifully signaled by the contrast between the infinitive clause *I* . . . *to go* and the indicative clause *I WILL GO*, subordinated, but to verbs denoting the appropriate mental states involved. Yet the syntactico-semantic constructions themselves are of little moment. What counts is the abstract *contrast* they together represent. We can conceive of another language, say Renglish, very much like English, except for a reversal: In subordinate clauses like the above, Renglish pairs the infinitive with beliefs, and the indicative with intentions. Patently, this is utterly immaterial.

Some empirical evidence may not be amiss. For the case of first-person propositions and practitions, Spanish uses, like English, the semantico-syntactic contrast between indicative and infinitive subordinate clauses. But for the second- and third-person case it uses the contrast between indicative and subjunctive clauses, thus highlighting syntactically the practical role of first-person thinking. Latin had its own way: It used infinitive clauses to express propositions as accusatives of thinking or believing, but used the subjunctive to express subordinate practitions.

In sum, syntactical structure itself is of little philosophical value; pragmatico-semantico-syntactic contrasts are of vital significance. The ensuing essays focus on such contrasts and exegesize them to reveal the roles of language in experience. This is what I have sometimes called *phenomenological linguistics*.

6. Some Major Theses Developed in the Ensuing Studies

The studies in this volume contain a multitude of claims of several sorts and types. The most pervasive claim is a many-pronged *methodological creed*, which has been followed deliberately and at great pains—but rewardingly so. In abstraction the creed seems obvious; notwithstanding, it is most demanding, because, as Oscar Thend has iterated, philosophical method has the *anti-Augustinian* property: When one is asked what it is, one knows what it is, but when one is not asked and one is doing philosophy, one tends to forget how it works.[6]

This anti-Augustinianly trivial creed includes these tenets: (1) Even though in a clear Kantian sense every experience and belief we have issues from a manifold of theories, mostly unconsciously held, there are degrees of theoreticity. (2) We must, in trying to understand the world and our experience of it, examine the data at a certain level and then carefully move up to higher, more comprehensive theories. (3) Philosophical data include EVERYTHING we experience and do in daily life as well as in scientific activity, and also the semantico-syntactic contrasts in the languages we speak. (4) The data collected and exegesized should be abundantly diversified and as complex as we can handle, so that they can exhibit the conceptual patterns we are investigating. (5) Philosophical theorizing aims at the most comprehensive theories. (6) Perhaps several master comprehensive theories, though mutually incompatible, may be feasible, and *all* should be developed as alternatives jointly elucidating their common data. (7) Hence, I regard all the data I have gathered, as well as the data other philosophers have gathered, and the many results of my exegeses of the referential phenomena, as *binding* on ALL scholars working on the same problems, but my theories are individually, and together, no more than a unified point of view deserving of comparisons with equally comprehensive alternative points of view. (8) Theory comparisons are more illuminating and worthwhile, the more comprehensive the compared theories are, provided, of course, that they cater to exactly the same data.

Because of that creed I turned, in Husserl's lovely phrase, away from theories to the things themselves. At the beginning there were not many theories to turn away from. I set myself to contemplate the phenomena of reference, especially the syntax of indicators and quasi-indicators. The set of data collected and exegesized is large, and includes some exciting specimens. Thus there has been little time for polemics against theories. Besides, our methodology implies that opposite theories, rather than being strangled, *must* be helped to mature into comprehensive theories and thus become suitable for dia-philosophical comparison.[7]

A good part of the data on indexical reference I have collected has been used by other philosophers in developing accounts of their own. This is due primarily to John Perry's excellent propaganda.[8] He has added valuable data and has developed with Jon Barwise[9] an impressive theory of reference, which by being so well received has further publicized some of the data. However, not all of my data on indexical reference have been fully used, for example, the data pertaining to the embedding of indicators in chains of psychological or linguistic prefixes, or the experiential features of indexical reference.

Some philosophers have been duly impressed by the peculiarities of first-person reference; some have been recently pressing the need to treat reference to oneself and to time on equal footing.[10] This is welcome. Yet the jump must be taken to appreciating that underlying the peculiarities of the first person and the kinship between *I* and *now* lies a structure undergirding *all* indexical reference as one category vis-à-vis nonindexical reference; furthermore, when the jump is taken the glance must be kept firmly on the experiential roles of all indexical reference, namely, as constituents of a hierarchical framework for the contents of experience: Not only *I* and *now* (and *then*), but also *here*, *this* and *that*, the demonstratives *he* and *she*, and the indomitable *you*, must be given full treatment. The issues reach deeply.

In this regard, some pertinent results of "Indicators and Quasi-indicators" (still the main tract on the topic) are these: (1) Indexical reference is required for a person to have experiences. (2) Quasi-indexical reference is required to conceive in some detail of other subjects of experience. Hence, (3) even a solipsistic language needs indicators, whereas a language of other minds requires quasi-indicators as well. (4) Indexical reference is irreducible to nonindexical reference, first-person reference is irreducible to demonstrative reference to oneself, second-person reference is not reducible to demonstrative reference to the person addressed to, and second- and first-person are mutually irreducible. (5) Quasi-indexical reference is also irreducible. This paper introduced a contrast between *neutral* and *perspectival* properties. The notion of perspectival properties foreshadows and flows into the concept of *propositional guises*, developed in "Perception, Belief, and the Structure of Physical Objects and Consciousness" *Synthese* (1977).

Likewise, the data concerning quasi-indicators have been used sparingly. For instance, quasi-indicators of degrees of higher order are crying out for alternative attention. The same holds for the tacit quasi-indicators in attributions of perceptual experiencs and intentions to others. I hope this anthology will spur wider and systematic use of all the indexical and quasi-indexical data. We need, for diaphilosophical enlightenment, other theories, comprehensive theories.

Following the above methodological creed, I have attempted to develop a theoretical account only *after* there was available a very large mass of results of data exegesis on and for which to develop a unified comprehensive theory. This theory, Guise Theory, was first publicly presented in 1972 at the University of Victoria, in "Thinking and the Structure of the World." It is a general theory of reference that provides an ontological semantics for singular reference, with matching views of the structure of the world and of the referring mind. Its finely grained semantics supports the above Fundamental Desideratum (T-S.C*). This bestows on language an important epistemic transparency – important because it allows thinking to connect to the world directly. Furthermore, by separating semantics from doxastics, the theory is able to deliver a unified structural account of ordinary, historical, scientific, and literary experiences.

Guise Theory incorporates a sort of "bundle" view of individuation, but in two levels; it has been referred to as a bundle-bundle view. The units of individuation are called individual guises. It turned out that guises share some properties of Frege's concepts of individuals and of Meinong's incomplete objects. The chief novelty and flexibility of the theory lie in its account of predication. On another side, the theory has a formal resemblance to phenomenalism, and I have occasionally, for the purpose of quick communication, referred to it as a generalized phenomenalism that shuns sense-data.

In 1973–75 (see "Perception, Belief, and the Structure of Physical Objects and Consciousness"), all the data under Guise Theory, the huge collection of linguistic data on indexical and quasi-indexical reference, the enormous amount of psychological data on perception, and some data on the physics of perception, were drawn together. The outcome was Indexical Guise Theory, which by introducing indexical guises adds a theory of perception, self-consciousness, self, and so on. This extended theory conforms further to the methodological creed by unifying data from different sources. The theory posited *Super-propositions* or Super-states of affairs in analogy with ordinary massive physical objects, as well as *propositional guises* alongside individual guises. Propositional guises provide a unified solution to both the Paradox of Analysis and the phenomenon of knowledge increase by mere discriminating perceptual attention or intellectual reflection. Another important side consequence is a view of the distinction between perceptual and nonperceptual cognitive states. The main result there is called "Miriam's Law" (see p. 336).[11]

The examination of reference, not only reference by proper names, reveals the need of a careful allocation of roles to the language system, its embodying idiolects, and its rehearsing speechs acts. A new unified account of the semantics and the pragmatics of proper names turned up. This account opens up crucial semantic questions, to which Guise Theory provides a satisfying answer. This is a bit of ex post facto confirmation, which makes Guise Theory look fruitful. Other manifestations of fruitfulness have turned up in the papers discussing it.[12]

The table of contents and the index may provide overall guidance on cross-references and development. Let us now proceed to the pleasurable details.

Notes

1. The literature on the classical private language issue is enormous. Besides Ludwig Wittgenstein, *Philosophical Investigations* (Oxford: Blackwell, 1952), a most influential paper was Norman Malcolm, "Review of Wittgenstein's, *Philosophical Investigations*," *The Philosophical Review* 63 (1954): 530–59. A useful collection of some of the main earlier papers is O. R. Jones, ed., *The Private Language Argument* (London: Macmillan, 1971). A summary of the main issues involved is "Private Language Problem," in Paul Edwards, ed., *The Encyclopedia of Philosophy*, vol. 6 (Glencoe, Ill.: The Free Press, 1967). The topic has risen again. The most controversial recent study is Saul Kripke, *Wittgenstein on Rules and Private Language*, (Cambridge, Mass.: Harvard University Press, 1982). The most spirited and detailed response to Kripke is G. P. Baker and P. M. S. Hacker, *Scepticism, Rules & Language* (Oxford: Blackwell, 1984). Paolo Leonardi's review of this book appears in *Noûs* 22 (1988): 618–24. My own involvement in the early debates is assessed in the exchange between Carl Ginet's "Castaneda on Private Language" and my "The Private Language (Response to Cark Ginet)," both in James E., Tomberlin, ed., *Agent, Language, and the Structure of the World*, (Indianapolis: Hackett, 1983)—hereafter referred to as Tomberlin 1. I discuss both the intrinsic significance of the antiprivate language arguments and their significance for my philosophical development in "Self-Profile. II. *De Dicto*," in James E. Tomberlin, ed., *Hector-Neri Castañeda* (Dordrecht: Reidel, Profiles No. 6, 1986)—hereafter called Tomberlin 2.

2. Hilary Putnam, "The Meaning of 'Meaning'," in Keith Gunderson, ed., *Language, Mind, and Knowledge*, (Minneapolis: University of Minnesota Press, 1975), and for a revised view, "Meaning Holism and Epistemic Holism," in Konrad Cramer, Hans Friedrich Fulda, Rolf-Peter Horstmann, and Ulrich Pothast, eds., *Theorie der Subjektivität*, (Frankfurt: Suhrkamp, 1987).

3. Tyler Burge, "Individualism and the Mental," in Peter French, Theodore Uehling, and Howard Wettstein, eds., *Midwest Studies in Philosophy* 4 (1979): 73–121.

4. A lucid use of secondary intentions to refer appears in Michael McKinsey, "Names and Intentionality," *The Philosophical Review*, 87 (1978): 171–200.

5. Hector-Neri Castañeda, *Thinking and Doing: The Philosophical Foundations of Institutions*, (Dordrecht: Reidel, 1975), still contains the largest collection of data for a general theory of human action. In chap. 6 there is an inventory of the data spread about in chaps. 1–9 supporting the proposition/practition distinction; additional causal data appear in chap. 10. The data are rich and variegated: linguistic, semantic, logical, pragmatic, psychological, institutional, etc. Yet the theory is extraordinarily simple, e.g., armed with the proposition/practition distinction the theory solves all the paradoxes of intentions and of deontic logic in a unified way in one fell swoop. The distinction allows for a more comprehensive and explanatory account of weakness of will. See Hector-Neri Castañeda, "Deontic Truth, Intentions, and Weakness of the Will (Response to Michael Bratman)," Tomberlin 1.

6. For a discussion of the perplexing anti-Augustinian property and other aspects of philosophical method see Hector-Neri Castañeda, *On Philosophical Method*, (Bloomington, Ind.: Nous Publications, 1980.)

7. For a discussion of dia-philosophy and sym-philsophical pluralism see *On Philosophical Method*.

8. John Perry, "Frege on Demonstratives," *The Philosophical Review* 86 (1977):474–97, and "The Problem of the Essential Indexical," *Noûs* 13 (1979): 3–21.

9. Jon Barwise and John Perry, *Situations and Attitudes* (Cambridge, Mass.: MIT Press, 1983).

10. Because of the special features of the quasi-indicator 'he (himself)', which expresses reference to oneself as oneself, e.g., in the old example "The Editor of *Soul* believes that he (himself) is a millionaire," Roderick Chisholm (*The First Person*, Minneapolis, University of Minnesota Press, 1981) and David Lewis ("Attitudes *De Dicto* and *De Se*," *The Philosophical Review*, 88 (1979): 513–43) have proposed variants of the view that the accusatives (in my neutral terminology) of believing are attributes or properties, as contrasted with the traditional view that takes them to be propositions, or sentences as in recent nominalistic views. The proposal is fascinating and merits development. Lewis's expression 'belief *de se*' has caught on; one often sees belief *de se* added to the customary pair belief *de re*/belief *de dicto*, without the writer endorsing Lewis's or Chisholm's view. I have argued that the pair is not exhaustive and exclusive because quasi-indexical constructions have both *de re* and *de dicto* features, regardless of whether they represent first-person or other indexical reference. (See "Reference, Reality, and Perceptual Fields," Presidential Address, in *Proceedings and Addresses of the American Philosophical Association*, 53 (1980):763–823.) One problem for the Attribute View — not an objection, for given my methodology, this can be just a problem posed in the spirit of cooperation to see the view become more comprehensive — is this: The main divide is not between the first-person and the other types of reference, but between indexical (experiential) and nonindexical reference; this requires a basic germane treatment of all forms of indexical reference. Thus, it we are to treat the quasi-indicator 'he himself' in belief sentences as a special *de se* belief, as involving attributes, i.e. as a special kind of free variable, we should treat all the other quasi-indicators similarly, as free variables, denoting a higher polyadicity of belief: *de te* (second-person), *nunc* (now), *hic* (*ibi*) (here-there), and *de hoc* (*de illo*) (this-that) belief besides *de se* belief. In "Self-consciousness, Demonstrative Reference, and the Self-ascription View of Believing," in James E. Tomberlin, ed., *Philosophical Perspectives* 1 (1987): 405–54, I examine Lewis's and Chisholm's attribute views.

Ernest Sosa noticed and proposed a way of handling the *now* problem ("Consciousness of the Self and of the Present," in Tomberlin 1. Myles Brand has applied the Attribute Theory to intentions ("Intending and Believing," in Tomberlin 1). I have raised some problems, other than the needed indexical enrichment discussed above, in my responses to them (also in Tomberlin 1).

On the other side, Esa Saarinen, after commending me for my early discussion of the first-person pronoun, rebukes me for obscuring my insight when I generalized to indexical reference in general, ("Castañeda's Philosophy of Language"), in Tomberlin 2.

11. Also moved by the problems of indexical reference, David Kaplan restored Bertrand Russell's view that there are singular propositions, i.e., propositions that have as their constituents existing individuals in their totality. In principle there is nothing wrong with such complexes as *targets* of epi-

sodes of thinking. But, as Frege observed to Russell in a letter, such objects are too massive to be the internal accusatives of thinking. Frege asked: "The whole of Mont Blanc, with its snowfields?" There is also a tremendous obscurity about what to count as the whole individual. Are the vermin and bacteria therein, and the bushes, rocks, and corpses buried in Mont Blanc included? We must distinguish between external targets and internal accusatives of mental states and acts. I discuss Kaplan's theory in "Direct Reference, Realism, and Guise Theory: Constructive Reflections on David Kaplan's Theory of Reference," in Joseph Almog, John Perry, and Howard Wettstein, eds., *Themes in David Kaplan's Philosophy* (Oxford: Oxford University Press, 1989).

12. For major critical discussions of Guise Theory see the essays by Romane Clark and Alvin Plantinga, and Hector-Neri Castañeda's responses in Tomberlin 1; the studies by Jay Rosenberg, David W. Smith, and Jeffrey Sicha in Tomberlin 2; Jig-Chuen Lee, "Guise Theory," *Philosophical Studies* 46 (1984): 403–15; and James E. Tomberlin, "Identity, Intensionality, and Intentionality," *Synthese*, 61 (1984): 111–31. For a most interesting semantic theory related to Guise Theory see William Rapaport, "Meinongian Theories and a Russellian Paradox," *Noûs* 12 (1978): 153–80; "How to Make the World Fit our Language: An Essay in Meinongian Semantics," *Grazer Philosophische Studien* 14 (1979): 1–21; "Meinongian Semantics for Propositional Attitude Networks," *Proceedings of the Association for Computational Linguistics* 23(1985). See also the papers by Friedrich Rapp, Klaus Jacobi, Guido Küng, Paolo Leonardi, Wolfgang Künne, Tomis Kapitan, Hans-Dieter Heckmann, and Castañeda's replies in Jacobi/Pape 1989.

Rapaport has been introducing some of my data on quasi-indicators in the computational analysis of belief and knowledge. See his *Belief Representation and Quasi-Indicators* (Buffalo: SUNY Buffalo Dept. of Computer Science Technical Report, 1984), and William J. Rapaport, Stuart C. Shapiro, and Janyce M. Wiebe, *Quasi-Indicators, Knowledge Reports, and Discourse* (Buffalo: SUNY Buffalo Dept. of Computer Science Technical Report, 1986).

Part I
The Language of Singular Reference

2

The Semantics and the Causal Roles of Proper Names in Our Thinking of Particulars: The Restricted-Variable/ Retrieval View of Proper Names

1. The Intriguing And Most Revealing Story of Greta Bergman and Oscar A. A. Hecdnett

Some years ago, Lars Bergman of Norris, Minnesota, a second-generation American of Swedish descent developed a successful vacation resort on a network of five small lakes. Because of their varying depths, these lakes harbor different types of fish, and thus provide a rich and truly satisfying fishing experience—as even the most demanding connoisseurs acknowledge. When Lars died, his young daughter, Greta, inherited the resort. A brilliant entrepreneur, she developed it into *Summer Paradise*, famous all over the world. But vacation business in Minnesota is seasonal. Seven months of the year, Bergman's lakes are covered by ice. Thus, in the winter, Greta herself vacations in Europe. She loves Italy, in particular, as a contrast to her ancestral Sweden. One day she was observed at a restaurant by Klaus Eberhard, the Munich film director. After some negotiations, Greta agreed to star in one of Eberhard's films. It was a great success in Europe. Since then Greta has been acting in one film every year. She has, however, made it a point of honor to maintain her two careers fully separated.

A year ago, at a reception in Paris given in her honor by Eberhard, she met Oscar A. A. Hecdnett, a distinguished film critic who by the power of his weekly column has made the *Old Republic* the most widely read magazine among the educated. Hecdnett had written very flattering columns about Greta's acting. At the reception he was so struck by her beauty and charm that he studied every feature of her behavior and her appearance. He sculpted in his memory a series of vivid and faithful images of Greta.

This summer Oscar decided to take his first vacation since his freshman year at college. He joined other friends and after some discussion, they decided to go fishing at *Summer Paradise*.

One evening Manager Bergman visited her guests at *Paradise*. She entertained them, and she met Oscar again. Oscar was struck by one of those "reality is stranger than fiction" experiences when he saw the incredible similarity between the famous actress he adored and the charming manager of *Summer Paradise* he quickly came to admire. She had the same expression in her eyes, the same complexion, the same hair color, the same smile, the same figure, the same step, the same voice, the same charm. Or is this Greta even more bewitching than the other? Even the same name! This was just too much for Oscar.

Another evening the Manager of *Summer Paradise* introduced to her guests her grandaunt, also named Greta Bergman, who was visiting the United States for the first time. This lady was also as charming as her niece. All in all, Hecdnett and his friends enjoyed the most wonderful vacation they much needed. So they left with the promise to return.

Two months later Hecdnett is driving through Cleveland. Since his summer experience, his thoughts had often been on the *Summer Paradise* manager-owner and on the famous actress. Then he suddenly sees a hitchhiker on the road. He stops quickly, thus avoiding a womanslaughter. The hitchhiker is wrapped up in rainwear. But Oscar sees in those pleading eyes a glance that feels familiar; indeed, it reminds him of the haunting Greta Bergman from Norris. He offers her a ride. The hitchhiker accommodates herself in the front seat, and removes her hat. Her resemblance to Greta Bergman, the actress, is stunning. They make conversation. The woman declares to have a cottage on St. Clair lake and had been driving to a convention of gardeners in Cleveland when her car had broken down. The more she speaks, the more tantalized Oscar becomes. He almost collapses from unbelief when she says that her name is Greta Bergman.[1] [We must interrupt the story for a linguistic and a psychological commentary – in preparation for our philosophical discussion.]

2. Oscar Hecdnett's World: Exegesis of the Data

Greta Bergman is Oscar A. A. Hecdnett's mysterious heroine. But Hecdnett himself is our crystalline philosophical hero. We are interested in both the state of his mind and the state of his world right after his experience with the hitchhiker. That experience has enriched perceptibly both his world and his language.

Hecdnett's English idiolect includes a new name, 'Greta Bergman', or a new use for *this* name if you so desire. Here is a verbal issue we must sidestep. Let us for convenience stipulate in this exegesis of data that a *proper name in a person P's idiolect* is a label together with the network of mechanisms, which P has the power to exercise for the unified use of the label, in segregating and reidentifying a certain object (the name's *nominatum*) in his/her world. Thus, after talking with the hitchhiker, Hecdnett possesses four homophonic names in his idiolects. (We allow that names remain constant through transliterations in other idiolects of the same person.) We shall continue to refer to a label as a name *simpliciter* meaning that the label belongs to a language and is possibly a name in the idiolect of some speaker of that language.

Hecdnett's world has four persons named Greta Bergman. This is not, however, what bewilders him. He is, like all of us, wholly resigned to the elementary fact that manifolds of homophonic proper names are an unavoidable part of life. What perplexes Hecdnett is that his world has, yet it could still have more than, three different persons that resemble each other so much and so minutely even to the apparently irrelevant point of having the same name. As if all those likenesses depended in some metaphysical way on the very irrelevant name! His affectionate relationship to the actress is most special. He has developed a similar but distinct affection for the businesswoman, and this affection is partly inherited from the one he feels for the actress. But the uniqueness of each relationship is threatened with confusion and fuzziness by the broad spectrum of likenesses between them. This is deeply annoying to him. And then this new hitchhiking Greta Bergman enters the scene!

We are considering Hecdnett's idiolect from *within*. Evidently, Hecdnett's English idiolect belongs to a language common to millions of English speakers. This is of great importance for his communicative intentions. But the fundamental fact is that, precisely as a mature native speaker of English, Hecdnett is able to use his English idiolect with personal autonomy. In order to do that he has to possess the necessary competence to use his idiolect as a means of thinking, whether or not he is interested in communicating what he thinks. Therefore, in the interior of his experience, he connects his thinking symbolism with what he thinks. Thus, the semantics of his thinking symbolism is internally open to the world that his experience reveals to him: To use a language as an instrument for thinking is to use an idiolect of that language, which idiolect is internally connected with what is thought. To count on the help of others is to trust in the semantic internality of the uses of the other's idiolects. Sometimes this is necessary, but then the help of others is effective only when we internalize what they say to us.

In any case, Hecdnett's state of mind at that time is partially characterized by the following crucial doxastic facts:

(1) Hecdnett believes that Greta Bergman [the one he met in Paris] is a great actress, not a Minnesotan businesswoman.

(2) Hecdnett believes that Greta Bergman [the one at Norris] is a fantastic businesswoman, not an actress.

(3) Hecdnett believes that Greta Bergman [the businesswoman] is not (the same person as) Greta Bergman [the actress].

(4) Hecdnett believes that Greta Bergman the businesswoman is not the same as Greta Bergman [the actress].

(5) Hecdnett believes that Greta Bergman [the aunt] is not the same as Greta Bergman [the businesswoman].

(6) Hecdnett believes that Greta Bergman the hitchhiker is not the same as Greta Bergman the actress.

(7) For any two of the four Greta Bergmans he has met, Hecdnett believes that they are not the same person.

(8) There is NO internal inconsistency in Hecdnett's beliefs about the Greta Bergmans in his life.

Undoubtedly, some of Hecdnett's beliefs are false. Nevertheless, the set of his beliefs about his Greta Bergmans is internally consistent. So far we do not yet know whether or not the hitchhiker is the same as the actress. But even if the *real* world has only two Greta Bergmans, the fact is that Hecdnett's world at that time has consistently and coherently four Greta Bergmans. This is a key feature of the data. Let's ponder these data.

Consider facts (1) and (2). What Hecdnett believes according to (1) and (2) is compatible. Yet it would not be if his use of 'Greta Bergman' in (1) denoted (picked up, hooked up with) for him, in *his* experience, EXACTLY THE VERY SAME ENTITY his use of 'Greta Bergman' in (2) denotes (picks out or hooks up with): That is, there is no contradiction in what Hecdnett believes, only if *one* entity is the subject of *his* predications were he to assert what he believes according to (1) by saying: "Greta Bergman is a great actress, not a Minnesotan businesswoman," and *another* entity the subject of *his* predications, were he to assert what he believes according to (2) by saying: "Greta Bergman is a fantastic businesswoman, not an actress."

Let us call the individual entity denoted, or picked out, or hooked by a *particular use* of a proper name by a person who possesses the name in his/her idiolect, the *strict referent* or *strict nominatum* of that use. Clearly, then, Hecdnett's uses of his different homophonic names 'Greta Bergman's recorded above have *different* strict referents (or nominata)—regardless of whether in the (real) world two, and perhaps three, of those homophonic proper names are in *some* inter-use sense coreferring. But what exactly is coreference here?

Evidently, the label 'Greta Bergman' exemplifies in sentences (1)-(7) different homophonic proper names in the idiolect of the person who asserts those sentences. If this speaker believes that the actress and the businesswoman, but not the hitchhiker, are the same person, then this speaker has three homophonic names 'Greta Bergman's in his idiolect.

In sentences (1)-(6), there is a *cumulative semantic aspect* on the names in the scope of 'Hecdnett believes'. On the one hand, tokens of the label 'Greta Bergman' represent, as we have noted, potential uses by Oscar Hecdnett: As philosophers often say, the name occurs de dicto. On the other hand, those occurrences of 'Greta Bergman' stand *also* for uses of proper names in the idiolect of the speaker of such sentences, who is attributing more or less definite beliefs to Hecdnett. This cumulative character of the so-called de dicto occurrence of a singular term in a belief sentence has not been generally attended to (see chapter 5). In any case, because of this cumulation in the speaker's *view*, or representation, of Hecdnett's world, there are also four Greta Bergmans: Indeed, the speaker distinguishes them very effectively by means of the bracketed expressions he attaches to each occurrence of a homophonic name 'Greta Bergman' in sentences (1)-(7). Hence to the extent that the speaker can efficiently represent Hecdnett's consistent world in sentences (1)-(7), he also has four homophonic names 'Greta Bergman's in his idiolect. He differs from Hecdnett, not in language, hence, *not* in semantics, but in *doxastics*. He has the belief, not shared by Hecdnett, that:

(S.1*) Greta Bergman [the actress] is (the same as) Greta Bergman [the Norris businesswoman].

But then the speaker has in his very own idiolect one name. It seems better to treat all homophonic names as applications of one and the same name. To the extent that the speaker of (1)-(7) can communicate most efficiently with others about what Hecdnett believes concerning his Greta Bergmans, these others need also (so far) four different homophonic proper names 'Greta Bergman's. Therefore, it appears that, whatever ontological unity our *doxastics* about Greta Bergmans may require, our *semantics* of Greta Bergmans demand that the four uses of the name have different strict referents or nominata.

Problems

The stipulation that Oscar Hecdnett has four homophonic names of the form *Greta Bergman* assimilates his situation to our common garden-variety experience of one name having several broad denotata. We all possess in our idiolects many so-called proper names that we apply to several persons or objects, for example, the several John Smiths, Mary Browns, and Washingtons we have dealt with. That stipulation is an excellent move in allowing a unified account of singular reference through the use of sentences containing proper names

In fact, all proper names are in principle open to multiple applications. Nothing in the language forbids the varied uses of proper names for different objects. Just the opposite, there are in each language and in the culture built on it entrenched procedures for some inheritance or spreading of some proper names. This is done without the sense that such spreading, or a new application to a different object, counts as a semantic change. This clearly contrasts with ordinary common nouns. Doubtless, we can introduce a new use for a common noun, say, 'green' to talk about a collection of new political ideas advocated by a splinter of a dominant party. But it will be clearly recognized as a semantic act, which introduces ambiguity. Thus, to better understand the connection between language and reality we must elucidate the *semantic openness* of proper names to new applications without semantic change.

The semantic openness of proper names seems to run against their grain as *proper* names, namely, that they seem to be used for singular reference, that is, as means of pinpointing uniquely an object for consideration. This is the feature of their use that has been popular with linguists and philosophers. It needs elucidation, partly because this singularity feature of proper names has to be placed against semantic openness. This semantic openness reveals that the singularity of the references we make with proper names has to come from *outside* the proper name. To appreciate this let us ponder *Oscar Hecdnett's Lecture on "Fiction and Reality In and Around Contemporary Cinema."* Part of it includes his reading some citations from his reviews of Greta Bergman films, and showing some slides of *Summer Paradise.* After some show-and-tell, pointing out some extremely subtle differences, he freezes two slides and declares in three steps:

(Th)   This [pointing to one figure in one film frame] is not the same as this [pointing to a photo of our businesswoman].

(GB.1) Greta Bergman is not Greta Bergman.

        I mean:

(GB.2) Greta Bergman the actress is not (the same as) Greta Bergman the businesswoman. [His pointer is now idling.]

Evidently, on the normal semantico-pragmatic conventions governing their use, neither sentence (Th) nor sentence (GB.2) expresses a contradiction. On the other hand, (GB.1) may do so, though it need not. It expresses a contradiction if the name 'Greta Bergman' is supposed to be unambiguously referentially sufficient to secure uniqueness. But this supposition is foreign to the name's semantic openness. Clearly, (GB.1) may also be self-contradictory if the name merely represents at each occurrence one and the same singular reference whose singularity arises from *without* the name and even the sentence. This is fine and harmonizes with the use of (GB.1) in which it does not express a self-contradiction. In the latter case, which interests us, we can from outside the name find different singularizations, rather than just one. Thus, in the noncontradictory interpretation of (GB.1) each token of the name 'Greta Bergman' is not a complete referring term but only a part thereof. What can the rest of that singular term be?

One answer is to assimilate (GB.1) to (Th). If we do so, we construe (GB.1) as used in the context under consideration as short for:

(GB.1Th) This Greta Bergman is not (the same as) this Greta Bergman.

Then the uniqueness of the reference is in this case secured *not by the proper name* 'Greta Bergman', but by an underlying demonstrative reference, implicit in (GB.1), explicit in (GB.1Th). We may even construe the pointings in the case of (GB.1) as being those of (Th), but we need not go that far. We can concede that the pointings in the case of (GB.1) have the semantic role of expressing a demonstrative, and claim that in the case of (Th) the pointing accompanying each use of 'this' does not have a semantic but only a communicational role. In later chapters we will engage in very detailed study of indexical reference; in this chapter we discuss Tyler Burge's demonstrative view of singular reference by proper names. For the moment it suffices simply to record both that (GB.1Th) is definitely one interpretation of (GB.1) and that on this interpretation proper names function as mere adjectives of demonstratives.

(GB.2) may be another interpretation of the contradictory version of (GB.1). In fact, (GB.2) exhibits a form that other interpretations of (GB.1) can have: *Greta Bergman the one who is F is not (the same as) Greta Bergman the one who is G*. Now in all these cases the singular terms, if there really are any, are not the occurrences of the proper names, but the complex expressions of the form *Greta Bergman the one who is X*, for example, 'Greta Bergman the actress' and 'Greta Bergman the businesswoman' in (GB.2). In these sentences the proper name functions as a predicate, expressing not the uniqueness of singular reference, but the universality of a *shared* property! The actress and the businesswoman certainly share the same proper name. But what can such shared property be? The answer to this question is the backbone of the elucidation of the semantic openness of proper names.

The problem remains of how uniqueness is gained in the singular reference that permeates sentences with proper names. The problem is not about belief, but about the semantics and pragmatics of proper names. Clearly, the problem we are discussing, of how the uniqueness of singular reference is secured, is more basic than, and independent of, Hecdnett's and our beliefs about how many Greta Bergmans there are in the world, or, for that matter, how many Greta Bergmans are real and how many mythical or fictitious. The problem is one about the way proper names connect with the individuals, whatever these may be, that we think about. Hecdnett's beliefs may be consistent, and if so, regardless of how fast and far-reaching his logical powers may be, there is no deduction through which he could find a contradiction. The problem here is the more basic one about the general rules governing the sentences whose use one must master to be able to have or express any beliefs at all.

Palpably, the statements, or propositions—(Th), (GB.1), and (GB.2)—are not really of the form *Not(a=a)*, but rather of the form *Not(a=b)*, more specifically, of the form *Not(N the F = N the G)*, where N is a proper name. The problem of the semantics and pure pragmatics of proper names is precisely the problem of what roles the proper name N is required to perform in such statements in general, and in particular in those cases in which the statements are true: What is the contribution to the truth of the statement that what N denotes makes? This problem is a pressing one when we fasten to the fact they do not function to express the uniqueness of singular reference. It makes no difference if we parse the sentences of that form as: *Not(N[the F] = N[the G]*, where the bracketed expressions are said to be merely indices that signal that we have two names. We need an account of the signaling role, and how the indices contribute, or not contribute, to the uniqueness of the singular reference made in sentences with proper names.

Yet that is not all. Hecdnett's problem is graver than what the preceding paragraph formulates. The above problem is in part what each component, the shared proper name N and the distinctive index or differentiating factor of singular terms built on proper names, contributes to what a person thinks who uses sentences with such expressions as means of thinking or communicating his/her thoughts. Hecdnett's predicament goes beyond that. He can certainly believe not(a=b), for two entirely different terms "a" and "b," when in reality not(a=b). This is the typical case that promotes the illusion that the name picks out a *whole massive individual*. But Hecdnett, the cleverest logician and most perfect deductionist, believes without any possible contradiction he can detect something of the form *Not(a=b)*, when in reality a=b. What in the world can "a" and "b" pick out *for him?* After all, we are concerned with the use of language as a means of expressing thought and belief. That is the general problem of reference, which Frege took seriously.

The problem is not alleviated by our focusing on special terms "a" and "b" sharing a common expression—and it is further assumed that that common expression hooks on to something. More specifically, not only is there a problem about what the two terms 'Greta Bergman the actress' and 'Greta Bergman the businesswoman' can really pick up for Oscar Hecdnett, but there is also the further, graver problem as to what the term component, the proper name 'Greta Bergman', can pick up *for* him who thinks that *Not(Greta Bergman the actress = Greta Bergman the businesswoman)*, when in reality they are one and the same.

Actually Hecdnett's predicament is even more perplexing. It happens that our pliable and ever innovating Greta Bergman has started another separate film career in Stockholm. Whereas the Greta Bergman of Munich has played her roles with extraordinary realism, the Greta Bergman of Stockholm has acted with a staccato impressionism that has flabbergasted the best film critics—including Oscar Hecdnett. Thus, based on many powerful reasons, Hecdnett believes consistently that:

(S.2*) Not (Greta Bergman the German actress = Greta Bergman the Swedish actress).

To be sure the whole terms of (S.2*) as well as their common component terms do converge outside Hecdnett's experience and world. But that convergence has to do with his beliefs being false, not with the contents of what he thinks with those terms. The semantics of these terms allows him to use the terms correctly to formulate his false beliefs, indeed, even to think the falsehoods he need not believe. Our problem is the *thinking semantics and pragmatics* of sentences containing proper names.

3. Some Exegetical Morals of the Bergman-Hecdnett Story

Let us register some important results of our reflection on the consistency of Hecdnett's beliefs about his four Greta Bergmans. Results PN.4* and PN.9 are valuable for their polemical force. PN.5 and PN.6 are crucial constraints on both the semantic theory of proper names and the ontology of their strict nominata. The other results pertain to the cognitive psychology of reference and the management of one's beliefs through the use of proper names. We will clarify them in the subsequent discussion, especially in the theoretical proposals to be put forward. Here are some immediate exegetical results:

PN1. Proper names *simpliciter* are MERE potential parts of a language, even of a dialect: By themselves they refer to or denote nothing. Proper names in a person's idiolect may perhaps denote something. But what? Particular *uses* of proper names in a person's idiolect are bearers of reference: They *strictly* refer to or denote in the primary sense what the speaker means (or purports) to refer to. Derivatively, such uses of proper names denote the entities the hearers construe the speaker to be referring to, in accordance with the appropriate speech conventions.

PN2. By occurring de dicto, each actually used token of a label or a string of marks (for example, the label 'Greta Bergman' in sentences (1)-(6)) represents cumulatively both an exercise by the speaker of a mechanism of singular reference, and the speaker's attribution to the persons mentioned as subjects of psychological states (for example 'Hecdnett" in sentences (1)-(6)).

PN.3. Some tokens of proper names converge in representing the same mechanism, as signaled by the expressions within brackets attached to the occurrences of the label 'Greta Bergman' in (1)-(6).

PN.4*. No two actually proffered tokens of different, though perhaps homophonic, proper names in a person's idiolect need pick out the self-same entity. Otherwise, there would be an internal contradiction in Hecdnett's beliefs. Hence, such tokens *cannot* internally pick out:

   (a) the very same external massive chunk in the (real) world that we *believe* to be associated with the same label;
   (b) the very same set of essential or identifying properties of such massive chunks;
   (c) the histories of those massive chunks in the world that one believes to be associated with proper names in one's idiolects;
   (d) the biological, genetic, chemical, or quark structures of named particulars.

PN.5. An actual use of a proper name N seems, then, to pick out or hook up with, so to speak, an *individual slice* of a massive chunk in the world we *believe* to be associated with N. The general areas from which the Greta Bergman slices in Hecdnett's world come are indicated by the expressions within brackets attached to the label 'Greta Bergman' in sentences (1)-(6).

PN.6. The individual slices that the uses of proper names pick out can be *very* thin. This is strongly suggested by the possibility that the fourth Greta Bergman in Hecdnett's world may, in fact, be the same in the (real) world as Greta Bergman the actress, and also the same as Greta Bergman the business woman. Obviously, there may very well be additional Greta Bergmans in Hecdnett's world, all of whom happen to be one and the same person in the real world.

PN.7. There is no reason to suppose that all the uses of one and the same proper name in a person's idiolect pick out exactly the very same slice of reality as *the* strict referent (nominatum) of the proper name in the person's idiolect, whether she is using the name or not. It may very well be that the general referential unity of a proper name (*not* of a use of it) in a person's idiolect does not issue from the name being connected to just one individual slice of reality. That unity may arise from the unity of a structure that unifies a manifold of possible and actual individual slices severally allocated to the possible uses of the proper name in question.

PN.8. The referential unity of a proper name in a person's idiolect cannot be determined externally: It must be accounted for from *within* the person's doxastic and thinking resources.

PN.9. The preceding morals, especially PN.5, have salutary, though surgical, effects. They raise problems for all those theories that fix the strict referent (the nominatum) of a proper name in terms of a single individual slice or a single object, or of a set of (essential) properties, or whatever *one* thing (for example, something called *haecceitas* or thisness) is supposed to establish the referential unity of the proper name.

4. Some Crucial Problems for Any Theory of Proper Names

The above results of exegesis immediately pose the following questions:

(Q1) How does each *use* of a name N by a speaker having N in his idiolect pick out as strict nominatum one individual slice from the huge number of (possible) slices making up the massive chunk of the world we *believe* to be associated with N?

(Q2) How are the different *uses* of a proper name in a person's idiolect united together as uses of the very same proper name? This is the problem of the unity of a name in a person's idiolect.

(Q3) How do the possibly different individual slices that are strict nominata of the uses of a proper name in a person's idiolect relate to one another as the unitary general referent of the person's proper name, that is, what is the unity of the general nominatum (if any) of a person's proper name as such?

(Q4) What exactly are those individual slices that can function as strict nominata for the uses of proper names in a person's idiolects?

(Q5) How do those individual slices that can be strict nominata relate to the massive chunks in the world we *believe* to be associated with proper names?

(Q6) What exactly is the sameness of the nominata of coreferring uses of a proper name in a person's idiolect? And what is the sameness of the strict nominata of different proper names in a person P's idiolect, that others, but not the person P, can claim to be coreferring?

(Q7) How does the meaning, or the semantic aspects, of a proper name N in a person P's idiolect relate to P's beliefs about the nominata of his uses of N?

5. Theoretical Tasks

The above questions constitute different sides of the problem of understanding the functions of proper names in our experience. They pertain to the structures relating the meaning of proper names to our beliefs about named objects, and to what we refer when we express our beliefs by using sentences with proper names. Here we have a knot of problems at the intersection of semantics, cognitive psychology, and ontology. We will not tackle the ontological problem. We shall limit ourselves to the general issues in the semantics of proper names and the psychology of thinking or communicating with sentences containing proper names. Thus, we aim here at a *preliminary* or surface account of singular reference by proper names. We concern ourselves with the most general aspects of the causal, epistemic, and semantic roles of proper names insofar as they are actually used as mechanisms of singular reference. These are the aspects exhibited in the ordinary management of our beliefs and in our communication of beliefs.

The preliminary account must, of course, be mounted on deeper theories of the mind and of the world, which in their turn must be coherently unified. Clearly, we do not fully understand how a use of proper name, or for that matter, the proper name itself as a mere part of a person's idiolect, connects with its strict nominatum, until we know what sort of entity the strict nominatum is. One such deeper theory of the world, conceived in full view of the problems of the mind's access to the world, is Guise Theory (see chaps. 13 and 14). The data on which the preliminary account of singular reference by proper names is erected constitute, however, data for Guise Theory.

6. Some Logical and Semantical Aspects Of Proper Names

Let us exegesize some points that have emerged from the Bergman-Hecdnett story in order to both specify further criteria of adequacy for any fruitful theory of proper names and be guided by them in the construction of such a theory.

a. Names are count nouns. The Bergman-Hecdnett story underscores this fundamental characteristic of proper names. In Hecdnett's world there are four Greta Bergmans. Some of us are inclined to say that given the told segment of the story, in reality there may be just two Greta Bergmans, but perhaps there are three. More correctly, we should say that in reality there are *at least* two Greta Bergmans – for of the huge majority of objects in the real world we know nothing, let alone that they are named Greta Bergman.

The most elementary, and, therefore, theoretically binding, extralinguistic fact is that proper names can be assigned most freely to objects, there being but exiguously few conventions that govern their introduction into our idiolect – and this only because idiolects are part and parcel of a language we use to communicate. That elementary fact is the root of the (intra)linguistic fact that proper names are count nouns both in the language system and in speech acts. This syntactico-semantical fact and the semiotico-pragmatic fact that sentences containing proper names are used to make singular reference to definite and well-singled-out individuals constitute together the fountainhead of the other aspects of proper names and their uses: the semantic, syntactic, logical, psychological, and even ontological aspects. The world has to be of a certain kind, and we must be put together in a certain way, for us to be able to use proper names efficiently the way we do, and, hence, to think and to communicate about the particular objects and persons we find in our experience. Let us scrutinize some of these aspects in useful detail.

   b. *Existential generalization on proper names: a paradox about proper names.* The backbone of the counting role of proper names is the rule of use that yields the following constitutive implication, where we use Quine's concatenating corner quotes tacitly:

(PN.Gen) For any proper name N:
          N is F → Some N is F.

This implication and the syntactico-semantical rules supporting it belong to the language system. They are part of the framework within which the uses of proper names secure their referents in given speech acts.

   (PN.Gen) seems to be a true case of existential generalization. In applying it we seem to be moving from a genuine singular premise to an existentially quantified conclusion. If this is so, then in moving from the singular term N of the premise, we *seem* to be introducing an *ambiguity* in the symbol N. Either the two uses have nothing in common, and the ambiguity is maximal, or they share something semantical in common. At first sight, the latter disjunct seems to be the true one.

   Undoubtedly, something is present in the premise *N is F* – and it is present somehow at N or in connection with N – which is not present in the conclusion *Some N is F*. That something is the distinctive feature that makes the premise the vehicle for a singular or unique reference to an individual, namely, to the strict nominatum of the use of N in the premise. For convenience let us stipulate:

   N is a *genuine singular term*, if and only if that distinctive feature of singular reference, which secures the uniqueness of the nominatum is *semantically* built into N.

If N is used in the premise as a genuine singular term, then it contains a semantic component that drops out from it in its transfer to the conclusion. Hence, the two occurrences of N in the above implication schema do not have exactly the same meaning. This is the *Ambiguity Datum* of the semantics of proper names.

   An illuminating theory of the semantics of proper names must resolve or explain the Ambiguity Datum. Patently, thet implication schema (PN.Gen) lies at the very core of the whole of our experience, since reference by proper names is central to our thinking and to our communicating with others.

   c. *Reference by proper names is always contextual, but it is not always indexical.* If N in the premise of (PN.Gen) is a genuine singular term, then the distinctive feature that drops out in the transfer of N to the consequent of (PN.Gen) is precisely what makes N in the premise a genuine singular term. That distinctive feature is undoubtedly what secures for N a unique nominatum. As we have seen in the Bergman-Hecdnett story, the uniqueness of the nominatum does not belong to the name as a label, or as a part of a language, a dialect, or even an idiolect.

It is the *use* of the name, not the name itself, that denotes and connects with its strict referent. Strict reference by name is, thus, not a matter of the language system, not even of the idiolect of the person who possesses the proper name in question. The language system provides a basis for reference by name; but the reference with its secured uniqueness of the nominatum is attained in a speech act or in a thinking episode. The context of assertion and the speaker's intentions secure the uniqueness of the strict nominatum referred to internally by the speaker with the use of a proper name. This is so, independently of whether or not a proper name is a genuine singular term in a sentence that conveys singular reference.

A fortiori, if a proper name N in a used premise of an inference that compiles with (PN.Gen) is a genuine singular term, then in the context of the use of the premise, and from resources within that context, the name N gains that distinctive feature that promotes it to the status of a genuine singular term.

The contextual nature of singular reference by proper names suggests the view that perhaps every proper name used to make a singular reference contains a covert demonstrative. Views of this type are put forward in attempts to explain how proper names are, or can be used as, genuine singular terms. For example, the name 'Greta Bergman' would on such view be conceived as being covertly something of the form "This F," where 'F' stands for the predicate expression that a particular view of that type deems appropriate. The simplest and most natural view of this type is to take 'F' to be the very proper name 'Greta Bergman' itself. This view is built on the insight that proper names are count nouns. It is a brilliant view: It has simplicity and power. A staunch defender of this *demonstrative* view of singular reference by proper names is Tyler Burge. We examine his view in section 15 of this chapter.

Here, in the light of the forthcoming outcome of the examination of Burge's view, we simply record that *contextual-dependence* is one thing, and *demonstrativeness* or *indexicality* is another thing. They are related, but must not be equated. I have discussed indexicality in abundant detail elsewhere (see chaps. 4, 6–9, 12).

d. The problem of differentiation and segregation of the nominata. That proper names function as count nouns is a representation of the fact that many objects can be, and in fact are, given the same proper names, that is, the same label. This raises the problem of differentiating one object from another. It is another datum of experience that we proffer sentences containing proper names with the intention of making, and most of the time apparently we succeed in making, singular references. The case is vexing when a speaker uses homophonic proper names in his idiolects to discourse about different individuals. For instance, Oscar Hecdnett has stated that Greta Bergman is not the same as Greta Bergman (see example (3) in section 2 of this chapter). Yet the problem is equally pressing, albeit less obvious (as is typical of simple examples), in those cases in which we think of, or talk about, just one person named N, and even when we have no different homophonic names. How is it that when Oscar thinks (out loud, let us assume) that Napoleon Bonaparte was a very destructive person, he is thinking and communicating about a certain individual, fully segregated in his mind from all others—and in the minds of those who are listening to him?

We succeed in making singular references by singling out the strict nominata for the proper names we use with the resources available within our *beliefs* and in the circumstances in which we proffer the appropriate sentences. That we do differentiate in context is a fact. The problem is to ascertain how we do it, and, especially, whether the mechanism of doing it is semantic or not, that is, whether the differentiation involves tampering with the meaning of the names involved, and if so, in what way and to what extent.

  e. *The problem of the unity of the classes determined by proper names.* Proper names are count nouns. Hence, each proper name determines a class of objects. What constitutes the unity of one such class? Naively one inclines to say: "Well, the property of having the name N is what constitutes the unity of the class determined by the name N." Yet this looks awfully circular. We have some explaining to do.

7. The Restricted Variable View of the Semantic Roles of Proper Names

A chief desideratum is to provide an account of the natural semantics of proper names as they function in our experience. The account must be comprehensive enough to illuminate the unity of all the types of uses of proper names. In particular, the aim is to erect an account that threads a unitary solution to both the Ambiguity Datum and the Differentiation and Segregation Problem. These are the major stumbling blocks for standard theories of proper names—as the studious reader can verify by himself or herself. To confront the issue squarely, we ask:

(Q*) How can we maintain the strongest possible semantic unity of the uses of proper names as subjects of predication (for example, in "Greta Bergman is a great actress, and not the same as Greta Bergman") and their uses as specifications of quantifiers (for example, "One Greta Bergman is a film actress" and "All the Greta Bergmans I know are charming")?

Let's reflect on this question. An expression *used* as a proper name has *referential uniqueness*: The use of a proper name represents a unique subject of predication. This uniqueness is precisely what the proper name must leave behind when, in accordance with (PN.Gen) above, it moves to the position of specification of a quantifier. Obviously, if the two uses are semantically on par, the singularity of reference MUST *not* be included within the semantics of the uses of proper names as representing subjects of predication. This is just it!

Where, then, is the singularity of reference to be located? This question immediately springs forth. The coherent answer to it is as follows:

(PN.Prag1) *First Pragmatic Thesis about Reference by Names*: The singularity of reference by proper names does *not* belong to any particular expression. It belongs at most to the whole sentence, but it is more properly allocated to the whole speech act or thinking episode.

(PN.Prag2) *Second Pragmatic Thesis about Reference by Names*: Proper names are NEVER used as genuine singular terms.

These have two obvious merits. *First*, they allow a thorough semantic unity of the two main types of uses of proper names we are discussing. Since the singularity of reference does not belong to the proper name as subject, then the proper name can migrate to a quantified position without any semantic loss. Of course, the singularity of reference is lost from the *sentence* (for example, of the form *N is F*) when this is embedded in a quantificational frame (for example, the corresponding form *Some N is F*). *Second*, the contextual dependence of singular reference by names on the context of assertion, discussed above, suits well the allocation of the singularity of reference to the *uttered* sentence as a whole. And it goes even better with the allocation of the singularity of reference to the whole speech act, or the thinking episode, in which the speaker makes singular references with sentences that contain proper names.

In short, by adopting the above two pragmatic theses, we shun the inveterate dominant linguistic *atomism* that operates under the program of assigning to the parts of a sentence S the different parts or aspects of what a speaker means in a speech act by proffering sentence S. We also jettison a less widespread tendency to, so to say, semanticize pragmatic aspects of speech acts. The main point is, therefore, that:

(Ref.Prag*) Reference, whether accomplished by sentences with proper names, with definite descriptions, or with indicators, is primarily a pragmatic (or semiotic) phenomenon that occurs within a semantico-syntactic framework.

Let us return to the two main uses of proper names we have been discussing. By (PN.Prag2), proper names always have exactly the same semantic roles, whether they are being used as subjects of predication (which includes uses as objects or accusatives of actions), or as qualifications of quantifiers. Clearly, the latter use is less charged with other nonsemantic roles. Hence, a natural simplifying hypothesis is this:

(PN.Sem1) The semantics of proper names is wholly contained in their role as specifications or qualifications of quantifiers.

Now we must ask: What constitutes the role of a specification of a quantifier? Consider, for instance, the sentence:

(2.1) Some Greta Bergmans are excellent businesswomen.

How does the expression 'Greta Bergman' function in (2.1)? Patently, it functions in exactly the same way in which common nouns function in quantified sentences, e.g.:

(2.2) Some gazelles are beautiful.

The standard view of quantification under which we have been reared is that common nouns are simply predicates. On this view the two predicates 'gazelles' and 'beautiful' are on equal footing and are linked by a conjunction as the standard formalization of (2.2) shows: $\exists x[\text{Gazelle}(x)\&\text{Beautiful}(x)]$. To come to dominate the scene, this standard view had to fight earlier views, which assigned different roles to the expressions 'gazelle' and 'beautiful'. Of late, attempts have been made to include the earlier view within more sophisticated accounts of quantification. The idea that (2.2) must be treated as a special form of restricted quantification, in which 'Some gazelles' is the special quantifier ranging over gazelles, is gaining terrain. The formalization of (2.2) is on this view representable as $(\exists_{\text{gazelle}}(\text{Beautiful}(\text{gazelle}))$. I believe this is correct. In any case, whatever the ultimate diagnosis of (2.2) may be, the sorted-quantification view of (2.1) has seemed to me gospel truth for the last fifteen years. Hence, in (2.1) we must acknowledge the sorted-quantifier 'Some Greta Bergmans'.

In brief, the fundamental *semantic* role of proper names, as illustrated by 'Greta Bergman' in (2.1), is characterized by the following principles:

(PN.Sem2) Proper names used in singular reference are free variables of quantification.

(PN.Sem3) A proper name used as such is a variable with a range of quantifications, which is, roughly, the class of all individuals that bear the name in question.

These two theses go hand in hand with the earlier ones. But they are somewhat schematic, awaiting a theory that explains both (i) what an individual is, and (ii) what it is for an individual to bear the name N. Problem (i) will take us to Guise Theory, which lies beyond this essay. But we tackle (ii) in the next section. One corollary of the preceding theses is this:

(PN.Sem4) A sentence containing a proper name *not* in the role of a specification of a quantifier is simply a schema, a representation of a so-called *propositional function*, which is neither true nor false, rather than of a proposition, or whatever, that is true or false.

The nonquantified occurrences of proper names are, therefore, *free variables of quantification with a restricted domain*. This is a most significant principle and has exciting consequences. For one thing, it demands that a thorough investigation be made into the nature of communication of thoughts. Even an unskillful canvassing of what happens when we communicate reveals that for the most part we impart information, or compare views, by exchanging sentences containing proper names. Consequently, on the view being put forward, thanks to (PN.Sem4), in such cases of communication we simply pass from one to another arrays of schematic information through propositional functions. All the singular truths we communicate with sentences with proper names do *not* quite manage to be semantically encoded in those sentences. How then do we manage?

8. The Sortal Properties of the Type Being Called Such and Such

Linguistic labels, or proper names as parts of a language system (whether a general language, a dialect, or an idiolect) are sortal variables. The sort denoted by a name N is unified by the property being called N. Let us discuss this type of property.

To begin with, we must be absolutely clear about our claim. Kripke has argued that the property being called N cannot be the *individuating* or *identifying* property that assigns to N a nominatum. He adduces that this would be circular. And he is completely correct on this, as well as on his use of that fact against the Attribute theories of reference (which we discuss in section 15). But this dispute does not concern us here. We have seen how proper names are not genuine singular terms; hence, their meaning should not be equated with the meanings of any singular descriptions. Our claim is that a proper name stands for a general property, and that this property is of the form *being called such and such.*

The charge of circularity does not apply to our general thesis. It may not be entirely amiss to see this in detail. Let us consider the issue at two levels: ontologically and epistemologically.

Ontologically, it might be argued that the sort denoted by a proper name N is simply the class of those individuals to which the name N has been given; hence, that there is no N-sort independently of the name N. However, this is not an objection at all—unless one is committed to *Thorough Platonism*. By this I mean the view that *every* sort has an ontological status independent of, and prior to, both the expressions of any language denoting it and the class of entities that belong to it. But this is absurd. The fact is that proper names are at once both the standing counterexample against Thorough Platonism and the paradigm case of Nominalism. Of course, the truth of a thorough Nominalism does *not* follow. We must simply acquiesce to the truth of Minimal Nominalism—the nominalism of the sorts determined by proper names.

The introduction of a proper name N is the creation of both the objective property being an N, and the meta-linguistic property being named (called) N. Like any other objective property, the properties of the form being an N do not belong to a language, but belong to the world. This is exhibited by the fact that proper names, though often transliterated, are not translated. Consider the Spanish proper name 'Linda'. Every Peruvian woman having this name is in every language a *Linda*, not a beautiful, or a bella, or a Schöne. Transliteration is an adjustment to the local phonetics; translation is a semantic correspondence. Being an N is a nominalistic property tied down to the phonetics of the name N. Thus, many names, as is the case with 'Linda', are not even given official transliterations. In brief:

(PN.Ont*) Properties of the form *being an N* transcend both the acts of christening or baptism, in which the name N is introduced, and the language, in which the ceremony introducing N is carried out: being an N is an objective property in the world at large.

Epistemologically, there is no circularity in knowing that, given a proper name N, an individual belongs to the N-sort through knowing that it is named N; nor is it circular to classify an individual as belonging to the N-sort at the same time that one calls it N, indeed, the classifying is done through the calling.

The significant issue concerning proper-name sortals is the nature of the properties of the type being called such and such.

Consider the property *being an Edmund Gettier*. I know one person who has this property. He appends 'III' to his name; hence, by inference, I believe that there are or have been at least three members of the Edmund Gettier sort. What does this property that determines this class consist of? Manifestly, it consists of the behavior, psychological responses, and behavioral and psychological dispositions among the users of the name. To have the name in one's idiolect is to have a manifold of networks of such dispositions in one's repertory. Each such network is an organized family of interrelated dispositions oriented toward one of the objects that belong to the Edmund Gettier sort.

The properties of the form *being named such and such* must be carefully distinguished from the properties expressed by locutions such as 'my name is . . . ' or 'I'm called . . . '. These latter properties include dispositions to think and act that connect with *first-person* thoughts, among which intentions deserve a special mention. That is, among other things, on hearing one's name one tends to think thoughts of the form "I. . . . " There is nothing circular in responding with thought, emotion, or behavior to a token of the label 'Edmund Gettier' in English sentences—or to its transliterations in sentences in other languages. Recall that 'Edmund Gettier' is a sortal variable of quantification. Hence, whatever individual one thinks of on hearing a sentence containing it, for example, 'Edmund Gettier discovered the unbridgeable gap between knowledge and true belief', one simply has to pick out that individual through identifying resources that are not semantically included in the name 'Edmund Gettier'; but some are available within one's beliefs and some lie within perceptual reach in the context of thought or of the speech situation.

The properties of the form *being an N* are, of course, very special. We have noted their nominalistic character. Being called N depends on there being objects that have been given the name N. Now, to be given the name N an object must be thought of through a singular reference. This pinpoints the object through a set of traits capable of singling it out from all others in the world (*of* the name giver). Hence, it would be utterly circular to use the property being named N in the initial singling out of an individual to be named N. Yet once the object has received the name N, it has the property of being named N. This property can certainly be used in further identifications of the individual in question. Indeed, it may very well be the only object named N in a certain context. Identifying by name can both precede and epistemically justify believing that the object has some other property we are very much interested in.

To sum up, the property *being an N*, for a proper name N, determines a lightly and nominalistically unified sort. It is not an independent property. It rides "piggyback" on identifying properties of *each* one of the individuals that receive the name N. Objects just cannot be primarily identified through any of the properties of the form being called such and such. Names are not individuating devices. Yet they function in communication as if they were, so much indeed, that for most philosophers they are the paradigms of singular-referring terms. How do they manage to project such a pervasive appearance?

9. A Complementary View of the Semantics of Proper Names

Proper names are, palpably, common nouns actually used to predicate the corresponding properties of the form *being named such and such*. These most interesting properties are truly nominalistic: They are created by linguistic fiat. To give the name N to an object, whether there is a formal ceremony of baptism or not, is at once to *create* or re-create, perhaps unknowingly, a predicate N and the corresponding property *being an N*. Typically the act of baptism secures one instance of the property in question. Hence, it would seem that a fundamental use of a proper name N should be clothed with the define article in locutions of the form *the N*. Thus, we may view the singular uses of naked proper names as uses of tacit definite descriptions. For example, a singular-referring use of 'Ronald Reagan' is then a use of the implicit term 'the Ronald Reagan'. Since there are, or may very well be, many Ronald Reagans, the implicit 'the Ronald Reagan' functions in discourse in precisely the same way as definite descriptions like 'the table' or 'the president'. That is, the uniqueness meant by the definite article 'the' is supplied by the speech context (see chap. 3). More precisely, this view treats the semantics and pragmatics of proper names as recorded in the following three theses of the *double contextuality of proper names*:

(PN.Abrev)   *Thesis of Implicit Abbreviation*: A token T of a proper name N used to make a singular reference denotes an individual named N, and T is an abbreviational token, contextually determined, of the definite description of the form *the N*.

(PN.ConSing) *Thesis of Contextually Determined Singularity*: A token of an implicit definite description of the form *the N*, for any property name N, used to make a singular reference—just as each similarly used token of an explicit definite description of the form *the F*, or *the P one*, for any noun phrase F or an adjectival phrase P—has a strict denotatum determined jointly by both the semantics of the description and a uniqueness furnished by the context of thought and speech.

(PN.Freedom) *Thesis of Contextual Freedom*: Because of the speaker's total semantico-pragmatic freedom to give anything any name whatever, that is, to create by fiat any property of the *being an N* type, the speaker can always manipulate in principle his speech context so as to insure the contextual uniqueness of the referent of the relevant definite description of the form *the N*.

These theses agree with the view sketched out above in *not* locating the singularity of a singular sentence of the form "N is F" on the name N, but on the *whole* sentence. It is "N is F" as a whole that abbreviates the sentence "The N is F." This claim is fully compatible with the view that the proper name N *itself* in singular use is literally a specially sorted free variable ranging over the subdomain of objects named N. I hereby adopt this complementary semantic view.

Some English readers may protest that it is utterly ungrammatical to put the definite article before a proper name, precisely when an ordinary singular reference is intended. Extraordinary references are all right, as when I was once asked in Alberta: "Castañeda? Are you *the* Castañeda?" The question clearly assumes that I am *one* Castañeda. Equally clearly to me, and to the chagrin of the questioner, excited about the prospect of visually devouring Carlos, I was not, and am not, *the* one.

The protest is too parochial. Other languages allow articles before proper names, like Italian and Ancient Greek. In the colloquial Spanish of middle and lower classes in some Central American areas, it is almost mandatory to use the definite article before the names of women ("La Marta . . . "), and in some cases even before the names of men ("El Alfredo . . . ").

A glance at other languages helps dispel a parochial attitude toward English. However, our complementary semantic view sprung forth, rather, as an abstract deduction from the way proper names function in experience. The first paragraph of this section is of the sort Kant labeled *transcendental* deduction. The actual finding of languages that use the definite article before proper names has a similarity to what Kant called the *metaphysical* deduction of the categories.

Sophistication enters, of course, in the use of proper names without definite articles. It is a sophistication rooted in efficiency in communication. We can appreciate it better judged against the background of the Contextual-Abbreviational View of proper names.

Yet proper names do not function as genuine singular terms. They function as artificially made and always available definite descriptions. This is a powerful function. But in order to discharge it they must be inbued in the speech habits constitutive of an idiolect. Then they can play their requisite causal roles. Let us turn to these.

10. The Causal and Epistemic Roles of Ordinary Proper Names: The (Causal) Retrieval View

The semantic roles of proper names we have ascertained force us then, to raise these questions:

(Q.ThPN*)   How is it that a thinker, whether thinking out loud or not, whether intent on communicating or not, connects the individual i that is the strict nominatum of his use of a certain proper name N, with the propositional functions expressed with sentences containing N, through which sentences he is thinking of i?

(Q.ComPN*)   How does a hearer of a sentence S containing a proper name N come to think the proposition the speaker of S thinks as the one to communicate by uttering S? What counts as successful communication of thought content (whether believed or not by the hearer)?

The full answer to the preceding questions requires a detailed account of how thinking is produced and how information is processed in our brains. Patently, this is beyond our present state of knowledge. Here we can furnish only the general conceptual account within which the detailed, complementary empirical answers to those questions have to be formulated. More specifically, we are concerned with the most pervasive structural aspects of the causal and epistemic roles of ordinary proper names in our thinking, and in our informational transactions with others. The ensuing account together with the semantic view of proper names outlined above was developed in the late 1960s.[2] I called it the *Causal View of Proper Names*. But since this name has been widely used for the famous view that Kripke and others have developed (briefly discussed in section 13), I hereby change the name of the former view to the *Contextual Restricted Variable/Retrieval Theory*.

Let us discuss the second component, the Retrieval View of our preliminary account of proper names. Proper names are purely formal devices lacking in content. No property through which an object can be surely identified is part of the meaning of singular reference. What then is the role of proper names in thinking and in the communication of thoughts?

The role is twofold. On the one hand, proper names have a *doxastic*, or (since we aim at gaining knowledge) *epistemic* role: They function as devices by means of which we *organize* our beliefs, that is, the information we possess as belief. To acquire a proper name in one's idiolect is to open a file for the storage of information: To possess a proper name in one's idiolect (in the way in which Oscar Hecdnett possesses four homophonic names 'Greta Bergman's) is to maintain that information file in an open or available status.

On the other hand, proper names have a *retrieval* or *causal* role. They are keys that open the information files for the retrieval of particular pieces of information. This causal role is crucial in our personal management of information, but is equally crucial in the transferral of information in communication with others, whether we believe this information or not. Thus, the thinking, often the perception, of a proper name causes one to have further thoughts about the object, thus mobilizing the information in one's doxastic depository. When one perceives the proper name in new sentences—as, for example, when one reads or converses or engages in any other form of communication – one may confront new information for possible doxastic storage. Here again the episode of apprehending the name causes the mobilization of the contents of the appropriate doxastic file, or may cause the creation of a new file, or the combining and reshuffling of already existing files. The latter is lurking in Oscar Hecdnett's future, given that he has at least two doxastic files labeled 'Greta Bergman' – whereas reality has, so to speak, all that information (and much more) in a huge single file.

The sentence 'Vladimir loves Tatiana' is, therefore, merely the formulation of a propositional form x *loves* y, where the variables 'x' and 'y' are governed by the rule that their instances or *values* come respectively from the nominal sorts being named "Vladimir" and "Tatiana". Such values are individual slices in the worlds of the different parties at the act of communication – like the Greta Bergman, individual slices Oscar Hecdnett picks out every time he uses the free sorted variable 'Greta Bergman'. Some *substituends*, or fillers, of the variables 'x' and 'y' in the general scheme 'x loves y' are, by the rule just mentioned, also substituends of the free variables 'Vladimir' and 'Tatiana'. Such substituends are expressions that *in the context of assertion* denote the appropriate strict nominata, namely, the appropriate values in the speaker's world and the appropriate values in the hearer's world.

The substituends of the sorted variables 'Vladimir' and 'Tatiana' have three crucial characteristics. *First*, most likely they include indexical expressions, probably 'I', 'here', 'now' and perhaps others, for example, 'you' and 'this' or 'that'. These indicators, as explained in detail elsewhere (see chaps. 4, 6–9, 12), help to identify individuals by these individuals' places and roles in the experience of each party at the act of communication, whether this experience is perceptual or a merely intellectual one of simply thinking. *Second*, and this is of the greatest importance (see section 16), the thinker, whether the speaker or the hearer, need *not* produce substituends that would represent the way she thinks of the nominata in question. *Third*, for the success of the speaker's communicational intention (and, perhaps, also the fulfillment of the hearer's communicational desires), it is not necessary that the substituends of the variables 'Vladimir' and 'Tatiana' that would represent the speaker's strict nominata, be self-identically the same as those that would represent each hearer's apprehended strict nominata. It is required only that the substituends be, in the standard jargon, *coreferring*. That is, more fundamentally, the strict nominata the speaker thinks, when he issues his sentences with proper names, must correspond to one another, and to the nominata the hearer thinks on perceiving the sentences in question, in the way that is described in standard parlance as *contingent identity* (or, *sameness*).

The second point is the falsity of the thesis we call below the Formulable Local Definite Description View. Given that it has received a good discussion, let us dwell on it. It is a well-established fact that a person who is thinking of an object O and expresses his thought of O with a name N often cannot, when asked, offer a definite description uniquely true of O. This is an important fact that any theory of names must account for. Naturally, it is *also* part of the data that the inability of a speaker to offer either an individuating trait of O, or a description to be equated with N, does *not* establish that that speaker did not think of O through thinking an individuating trait. The basic datum here pertains to the connection between what one thinks and the external language one uses to communicate what was thought, but it says *nothing* about the contents of the consciousness of the thinking in question, or about the events involved in the required inner "speech."

There is a variety of reasons why a person who thinks aloud may not be able to offer a description to be equated with a proper name he uses. But all of them have to do with the difference and the gap between the bodily events that are contingently identical with his episode of thinking and the events of overt articulation. Here is a partial inventory of cases. In some cases, (1) the gap is unbridgeable, as when a person is thinking of objects at least partially individuated by determinate properties, or *infimae species*, for which the language does not have expressions. Examples are the fully determined specific shades of color. In other cases, (2) the gap is, in principle, bridgeable, but the time required for the necessary search for words is not available. This is often the situation when a person individuates objects through traits he thinks by means of fugitive images. In other cases, (3) the only verbal formulation is by means of demonstrative descriptions, or even simple demonstratives. This happens when a speaker individuates objects through demonstrative properties pertaining to the relations among the objects in the speaker's perceptual fields. Moreoever, (4) there is no reason to suppose that the speaker's verbal mechanisms connecting a name to definite descriptions may not be temporarily jammed. Indeed, the very fact that a speaker is asked to give a description can produce a disturbance in his brain mechanisms, which disturbance can prevent him from offering a definite description to be equated with his use of a name. Slips of the tongue are examples of short-lived articulatory disturbances.

11. The Restricted Variable/Retrieval View of Proper Names: A Summary

On the Restricted-Variable/Retrieval View of proper names, proper names as parts of the language system are sortal variables of quantification. They are *never* genuine singular terms. The sort determined by a proper name is a nominalistic sort of the type being called such and such. The central roles of proper names are their pragmatic and semiotic roles of organizing beliefs and causing revisions, expansions and combinations of memory files. They are used in the retrieval of believed information. That is the reason why proper names are *not* synonymous with definite descriptions. Definite descriptions connect primarily to proper names only in particular thinking or speech acts. Hence, this connection does not even belong to the speaker's idiolect, which at most connects a manifold M of descriptions to a name N via a mechanism that embodies a selection function — freely used by the speaker in his/her speech acts — that maps types of speech contexts in whith N can be used on to M. In actual speech the speaker exemplifies a given speech context and produces a token of N through which tokening he/she thinks a member of M. (Semantico-pragmatic functions are *psychologically* realized in speech and are vital for the connection between language and thought content: The speaker instantiates an argument of one such function and is caused to think the corresponding value assigned by the function. See the appendix to the study mentioned in note 4.) But the language system, which encompasses each one of us who has a subservient idiolect, cannot, if it is to be at once both an efficient means of thinking and a useful means of communication, be burdened with either dangling or fettering definite descriptions that hang uselessly from proper names.

The *freedom* of a proper name to serve as a focal point for gathering information is at bottom the freedom of an unbound variable of quantification together with the freedom to create properties of the *being named N* type. The efficiency of proper names in our doxastic management requires their enormous freedom. This freedom also bestows on them a piggyback character: They have to ride over identifying traits, which can be expressed in genuine singular terms. These terms are the substituends of proper names, and their values are the slices of individuation determined by the identifying traits they represent.

Evidently, the preceding causal account of the role of proper names in thinking and in communication can be only preliminary. It has eventually to be mounted on the appropriate ontological foundation that explains what contingent identity is.

12. Some Types of Semantic Theories of Proper Names

In the preceding discussion we have plunged directly into the problems of singular reference by means of proper names, without attempting to refute alternative theories already in the market. We have preferred to gather rich and reasonably complex data that can show the main conceptual patterns of our use of proper names in experience. Certain theoretical hints have sprung from our exegesis of the data, and we have already followed some of those hints. It is part of my metaphilosophical stand that it is extremely hard, if not impossible, to refute a philosophical approach. *All* theories within each approach *should* be both internally developed in full detail and externally subsumed under more comprehensive theories. We can, of course, refute particular theories representative of a given approach. But the theory can always be revamped and the approach developed further. Yet comparison of approaches can be illuminating. Each approach gains in clarity and scope by comparison with alternatives. (See the discussion of diaphilosophy in my *On Philosophical Method*. Again I see my mission to develop views not in the mainstream in order to help secure a plurality of views for contrastive study.) The ensuing discussion is meant in part to raise problems and queries for the further development of the views within the alternative approaches. Let us, therefore, take a look at approaches to the semantics of proper names alternative to the Restricted Variable/Retrieval View.

From very early on, philosophers studying the workings of proper names real-ized that there were two *boundary conditions* for any theory. These are: (i) sen-tences or utterances containing proper names are used to make singular reference to particular individuals; and (ii) it is the use of the (sentence containing the) proper name that picks out a thinking, or even communicational, denotation or referent. One consequence of (ii) is that even if nominata are assigned to proper names insofar as these are parts of the language system, reference belongs not to the language system but to the speech acts. The theory of reference by names pertains, thus, to pragmatics, and semiotics. The distinction between speech acts and the language as a system has not always been put to service, and there has always been a strong pressure to move the phenomenon of reference up to the semantics of proper names in the language system. We shall discuss some efforts of this sort.

Seizing upon the primary phenomenon of reference, then, depending on how one views the connection between a proper name and the properties or attributes by means of which a speaker identifies the name's nominatum, one can naturally adopt one of the following main approaches to the semantics of proper names.

Direct-Reference Approach: Proper names are directly referential, that is, on each occasion of its use a proper name picks out its nominatum *without* the media-tion of a property (or attribute, or trait) through which the speaker identifies the nominatum in question. This approach may be called *Millian*, because of John Stuart Mills' dictum that proper names have no connotation, but only denotation. This dictum includes, besides, a claim about the language system.

Attribute Approach: Proper names stand for attributes (properties or traits): On each particular occasion of its use a proper name *represents* a characterization of its nominatum through which the speaker identifies this nominatum. This ap-proach may be called Fregean-Russellian.[3]

These two approaches can be pursued in one of two forms, depending on a grave *presupposition* about the connection between thinking and language-using. The dividing fork in the road is this: whether an episode of thinking, say, of state of affairs S consists of, or at least requires, the thinker's production of a token of an overt sentence, or a sentence-analog in her brain, that is a full representation of the state of affairs S. Thus, focusing on the case at hand, the issue is whether in order to think of a particular Greta Bergman as characterized by certain traits, Oscar Hecdnett has to think of her by means of a phrase that has a predicate ex-pression for each of the traits used by him to segregate a Greta Bergman from the rest of the individuals in his world. Thus, the following theses have been debated:

Local Description View: On each occasion of its use as a singular term, a proper name *stands for, and abbreviates*, a definite description of its nominatum.

Local Nondescription View: A proper name used to make singular reference does not stand for any definite description of its nominatum.

The Direct-Reference Approach implies the Local Nondescription View. But the Attribute Approach does *not* require the Local Description View. This important point is often neglected.

Sometimes the Local Description View is confused with a significantly different thesis, which we have refuted, namely:

Formulable Local Description View: If a speaker uses a sentence with a proper name N to make a singular reference, and N stands for a definite description of N's nominatum, then the speaker should be able to *produce* the definite description in question on demand that he do so.

Undoubtedly, the connections between the language system one uses to perform certain speech acts and these acts is a profound topic of the utmost urgency. It is, therefore, understandable that a theorist of proper names attempt to connect her view of the referential roles of proper names with the language system. We shall discuss some representative efforts of that sort.

Before turning to some specific alternatives to our Restricted-Variable View of proper names, let us emphasize that any useful theory must provide accounts of:

(1) The semantic roles of proper names as parts of a language system.

(2) The main structure of the phenomenon of singular thinking reference carried out in a speech act or a mere thinking episode by means of a sentence containing a proper name.

(3) The main structure of the communication of singular reference from the speaker of a sentence containing a proper name to the hearer of such a sentence.

Obviously, any theory of proper names worthy of our attention must cater to, and illuminate, the data contained in the Bergman-Hecdnett story. At this juncture in history, we should NOT have much patience with theories that restrict the data beyond necessity. In particular, we want theories that face squarely the facts that:

(a) Proper names are count nouns. Hence,

(b) Proper names as labels can apply to any number of objects.

(c) The ordinary massive objects of the (real) world can have different names.

(d) The ordinary massive objects of the (real) world can be carved out in different ways by the very same proper names *qua* labels; hence,

(e) A proper name, either as a label in the language system, or as a referring device in a particular speech act, does NOT harpoon the whole massive ordinary object of the (real) world.

(f) Thinking reference to particulars is *internal* to experience: It is always carried out from the *inside* of referring speech acts or thinking episodes.

(g) Proper names in sentences containing them are, indeed, involved in singular reference. (How?)

In (a)–(g) we have powerful criteria. Their application to current theories of proper names reveals very important dimensions of possible development.

13. The Theory of Causal Reference with Rigid Designation

The Direct-Reference Approach fastens firmly to the *singularity* of the singular reference that a speaker makes with a sentence containing a proper name. The approach locates that singularity on the axis formed by both the proper name and the nominatum. One of its strengths lies in the fact that the Local Nondescription View, as explained in section 10, is true. It gains further strength from the fact that the Formulable Local Description View is empirically false. Furthermore, as we have seen, no particular description or set of descriptions can be synonymous with, or abbreviated by, a proper name – this holds for general labels within the language system as well as for ephemeral proper names used only on and for a particular occasion. For instance, a teacher says: "Let us call this triangle ABC." Evidently, the name 'ABC' is not put forward as an abbreviation of, or as synonymous with, the definite description 'This triangle'. It is, as explained in section 9, proposed as the single member of the class of triangles here now called ABC.

The Direct-Reference Approach can easily connect its thesis about reference with a general thesis about the denotation of proper names as part of the language system. It may maintain that once a proper name N has been introduced in an idiolect belonging to a language L with an entity E as nominatum, N is part of L and *rigidly* denotes E. If different speakers of L introduce the same label N for other objects, then N is referentially ambiguous, but it may be said that it connects rigidly with each nominatum. To which nominatum does a speaker S of a sentence containing N refer? This is another matter. There has to be a selection function assigning to S's referential act the appropriate nominatum. Such function will have a special realization in a mechanism through the exercise of which S executes his thinking and referring acts. That mechanism has, of course, to include crucial causal strands that mobilize S's experiences.

The preceding general description of the Direct-Reference Approach can, of course, be instantiated in many different views. One theory of this type has become almost the dogma in the philosophical discussions of the topic in the main stream. Let us call it *The Theory of Causal Reference with Rigid Designation for Proper Names*.

The theory I am alluding to has been extended to nouns denoting natural kinds. But here we shall be concerned only with proper names. There is NO general a priori reason – certainly not at this juncture in the chapter or at this stage in the history of philosophy – to suppose that proper names and natural kind nouns have the same semantics. There is *one reason* to suppose that they are different: In one case we are dealing with particular individuals, in the other with universals – the former are instances of the later, but not vice versa.

The theory has been hailed as having Saul Kripke, Keith Donnellan, and Hilary Putnam as its founders. But the view has spread like a Californian fire in a dry summer. As a consequence, several variants have been propounded. Here we cannot go into the appropriate scholarship to disentangle either the recent genealogy of the view or its parochial variations. We are interested in *comparing* approaches. Therefore, here is *no* claim that the ensuing discussion refutes the tenets of any defender of the approach. (Recall that on my meta-philosophy, views are not so much to be refuted but to be developed. Criticism should be stimulus for development.)

The Theory of Causal Reference with Rigid Designation for Proper Names includes the following theses:

DR1. *Direct or Pure reference.* A proper name *N* connects with, or harpoons, directly its nominatum without the mediation of an attribute.

DR2. *Initial Baptism.* The introduction of a proper name N requires an act of initial baptism through which an individual is segregated from all other individuals and pinned down for the establishment of the direct, not attribute-mediated or guided, harpooning connection between N and its nominatum.

DR3. *Rigid Designation.* The harpooning bond between a proper name and its nominatum is permanent: For any possible world discussed with sentences containing a proper name N, N has the same nominatum.

DR4. *Causal thesis about reference.* A speaker S who uses sentences of a language L with a proper name N refers to N's nominatum O, only if there is a causal chain of events that starts with the initial baptism through which O becomes the nominatum of N, goes through referential uses of N by persons who witnessed the referential uses of N by previous speakers with a referential pedigree to the initial baptism and have adopted the intention to use N with the same referent, and speaker S is one of such users of N. Let us say that a speaker qualified by the appropriate causal chain of witnessing referential uses of N, with the appropriate intention of following suit, has the *N-pedigree.*

Evidently, theses DR1–DR4 need some elucidation. For that reason Kripke has insisted that he has not offered a view, but only a "picture." Let us call it here *The Picture.* David Kaplan has formulated a powerful ontological theory of Direct Reference for demonstratives. It postulates, in the manner of early Bertrand Russell, Russellian propositions, having ordinary massive, infinitely propertied objects as components; the direct reference of uses of demonstratives is their harpooning such components. This theory is not under discussion here.[4]

The Picture does not delineate the requisite relationships between a language system and its idiolects. The initial baptism establishing the direct harpooning of an individual O as a nominatum of a label N is a speech act. It certainly introduces the proper name N in the idiolects of the parties at the initial baptism. But theses DR3 and DR4, of rigidity and causation, *seem* to make the initial baptism an introduction of the proper name N into the language as a system. DR3 seems to be the tenet that *once a nominatum, always a nominatum* (of the same name, of course). This, presumably, holds of both the language system and each of the idiolects. Obviously, rigidity needs elucidation.

Yet we will set rigidity aside. Our concern here focuses on the phenomenon of reference by proper names. This pragmatic phenomenon is fundamental and it anchors the semantics of proper names. Here lie the main hurdles confronting the Direct-Reference Approach. The phenomenon of reference has two sides: the relationship between the person who makes references and what she refers to, and the nominatum. Connecting both is the operation of the mechanism of singular reference it badly needs. This mechanism must, on the one hand, deliver first-person thinking reference. On the other hand, the mechanism must be a viable realization of the functions that assign individuals as nominata to the proper names in the asserted sentences containing them. Thus, we focus primarily on theses DR1 (Direct-Reference Thesis) and DR4 (the Causal Thesis).

Let us consider speaker's thinking reference by proper names. Evidently, The Picture needs complementation. For instance, it should *not* suffice to know the N-pedigree and proffer a sentence with N to be referring to N's nominatum. Obviously, the initial intention to use N in the same referential way as the speakers whose uses one has witnessed is too weak. States of intending are dispositional, and one can have an intention and not act from or against it.[5] Here is a problem. Requiring that the speaker rehearses, at the time of utterance, his intention to refer to the entity referred to by the person from whom he acquired the name N, clearly, looks very much like bringing in an identifying attribute to mediate the reference. This conflicts with DR1.

The Causal Thesis is too weak in the cases in which a speaker uses a proper name that she knows applies to several objects. Most of us often refer to one of the many Johns in our respective worlds. How can we select the John we want to talk about without the mediation of an attribute to segregate that John from the others? Obviously, to require that a name have only one nominatum amounts to refuse to provide a theory of genuine proper names.

Recall Oscar Hecdnett's situation having in his world at least two different Greta Bergmans, who for us (and the real world) are one and the same. His uses of the label 'Greta Bergman' shows—as we have noted—that they do not pick out the ordinary massive object that we *believe* to be in the world, or a nucleus of its essential properties, or its characteristic and peculiar genetic structure, or its history. As we observed, each of Hecdnett's uses appears to pick out a slice of that massive object, which slice is demarcated by identifying or segregating attributes. Thus, to all the lights on the case, it appears that Hecdnett cannot refer to any of his Greta Bergmans without singling her out by means of some identifying attributes.

The problems that confront DR1 (the Direct-Reference Thesis) are not limited to speaker's thinking reference. They have a perfect match in the hearer's thinking reference. When Oscar's friend Olga Marina hears his statements about Greta Bergman, she needs some help in deciphering to whom Oscar is referring to. The causal chain constituting the relevant 'Greta Bergman' pedigree can help. It exemplifies an excellent identifying attribute. On the other hand, if the fact that the name 'Greta Bergman' directly refers to an individual is all that Olga Marina has to go by, then she will be unable to understand fully what Hecdnett says: Her thinking reference on hearing the name 'Greta Bergman' would be blind and so would be her attribution of reference to Hecdnett.

In brief, whatever the details of the causal chain constituting an N-pedigree for a proper name N may be, and whatever the nature of rigidity may turn out to be, there are crucial, inescapable data—like the Bergman-Hecdnett story—that appear to show that proper names are *not* purely, or directly, referential. It seems that no proper name can harpoon its nominatum without the identifying mediation of some attribute.

Let us turn now to the ontological problem of the nominatum. To begin with, an account has to be adjoined as to how the harpooning of the nominatum comes about. Is it the whole ordinary massive object we believe to exist with an infinity of properties that is harpooned? If so, how can we say that the object changes properties using the same name to refer to it notwithstanding its changes? Or is it a substrate at the core of the nominatum that is harpooned in the baptism—the substrate that undergoes all the changes we include in the history of the object? Or is it, rather, a nucleus of essential properties that is harpooned and remains constant in determining the identity of the object through time?

These questions are at this stage somewhat rhetorical. We have seen how the Bergman-Hecdnett story establishes that Oscar Hecdnett—like all of us—used proper names to pick out neither substrates, nor essences, nor core individuals, nor *haecceitates* nor the totalities of their nominata. The story reveals forcefully that a token of a proper name meant to refer to an existent must take as its *strict* nominatum a slice of an ordinary massive chunk in the (real) world we *believe* to exist. We saw how such strict nominata can be very thin. Hence, the urgent ontological problem for any theory of reference by proper names is that of elucidating the nature of such individual slices. What exactly are they? How thin can they be? How do they relate to the identifying attributes that mediate reference to them? (See chaps. 13 and 14 on Guise Theory).

The ontological issues also infect rigidity. If a proper name harpoons an essence, then the connection can be rigid, but in what sense is it direct or pure, that is, unmediated by attributes? In any case, a strict nominatum is neither the total ordinary massive object we *believe* to have an infinity of properties, nor an essence, nor a substrate, nor a history, nor a genetic or quark structure. But then what is rigid about the harpooning bond between N and its nominatum? (Perhaps the transparency of what is thought of by being somehow exhausted by the traits through which it is thought of.)

14. The Attribute Approach

Here we cannot enter into the important historical questions concerning what exactly are the views on natural-language proper names propounded by Frege, Russell, Wittgenstein, Peter Strawson, John Searle,[6] and other philosophers who have adopted the Attribute Approach. In particular, we leave undecided whether these philosophers have endorsed the linguistic theses we have called the Local Description View and the Formulable Local Description View. I am not sure that Frege held these linguistic theses. Apparently, Strawson was at some time committed to them. At all events, we must distinguish sharply the Attribute Approach from the linguistic theses implied by it *together with* specific views about the connection between language and thinking.

We must, of course, avail ourselves of all the data already collected. As we have seen, the unavoidable data contained in the Bergman-Hecdnett story sharply point out that the uses of proper names are *somehow* mediated by identifying attributes, or characteristics, of the nominata. The real issue is simply the specification of how the mediation takes place. One thing is already beyond controversy. The recent proponents of the Direct-Reference views have conclusively established that the mediation in question does not consist in the speaker having a definite description he can reel off on demand (see section 16). Both the Local Description View and the Formulable Local Description View are false. This shows that the connection between thinking and language, that is, the language used in communication and thinking, is much more complex than what these two naive linguistic theses presuppose.

Attribute views of proper names are at present the brunt of drastic castigation. Most of the criticism pertains to the alleged equation of the Attribute Approach with the Local Description View and the Formulable Local Description. These are false. Yet it should not be suppressed that persons who use proper names *are* typically able to satisfy a demand that they offer definite descriptions that represent identifying traits behind their use of proper names. Critics of Attribute Views reply that many definite descriptions that speakers offer when asked whom they are thinking of do not denote anything. This is true, if the definite descriptions are taken as complete. Once again, this is an attack on the subsidiary linguistic thesis, which leaves the Attribute Approach unscathed. The fact is that—for excellent reasons that have to do with the finitude of the mind, but that we cannot go into here—the overwhelming majority of definite descriptions, as noted in section 9, and further discussed in chapter 3, which we offer in communication and use in overt thinking, are elliptical and implicitly indexical. Thus, when in response to "Which Benjamin are you thinking of?" one responds with "The chairman of the committee," this definite description is elliptical, leaving it out to the context of the dialogue to specify which committee is being talked about. This ellipsis will itself connect to tacit indexical properties. The committee in question may be the promotions committee of *our* department.

In short, singular reference by names has normally a contextual, and even an indexical, dimension. This has to be brought forward in a general theory of proper names. The role of indexical reference underlying our use of sentences with proper names has not been generally appreciated. One philosopher who has appreciated it and has erected an impressive and elegant theory of proper names that highlights indexicality is Tyler Burge. His view is discussed in section 15 of this chapter.

The role of indexical reference in singular reference by proper names has not been generally attended to partly because theorists have been preoccupied with language systems, rather than with *idiolects*. A large portion of the arena of this debate about the semantics of proper names is the language system. The debate has concentrated on the refutation of the two linguistic theses mentioned above. The chief underlying reason for this lies on the correct emphasis on the communicational context of reference. Thus, the referential role of names is seen as a social phenomenon and it is, consequently, placed at the center of the language system—the common structure available to all the speakers. The theorists on *each* side of the issues have hung their concerns about reference with proper names on the language system, rather than on speech acts performed with the use of proper names. Now we must see how that idea also guides the work of the Attribute Theorists. Yet, as we have stressed, the locus of the issues is at bottom the interaction between a language system and its idiolects. As a consequence, the discussion of the issues of reference, semantics, the scope of belief, and the dynamics of communication needs relocation; the different problems need a revised schedule of priorities. This is—in my estimate—the most *general* and most *significant* point that has emerged from the debates on the roles of proper names.

The idiolects of a language and their exercise in speech acts play the central part in linguistic activity. *A language exists only through its idiolects.* This elementary truth has slowly and only until recently been entering the stage of the discussion on proper names. On a long diachronic view of the debates about proper names, this is the truth from which each round of debate has removed a veil.

Frege and Russell were quite sure that no ordinary proper name is systematically connected with one description or a set of descriptions, that not even one and the same person would relate his uses of a proper name N to exactly the same set of descriptions. This evinces an awareness, albeit an inarticulated one, of the location of singular reference by proper names at the level of speech acts, that is, at the level of the exercise of an idiolect. Yet the problem was assumed to belong to the language system. The motivation is that proper names lie *in some sense* in the common language with which we communicate. This suggests that we need an account that places proper names in the language system. Since they are already there in the syntax, what remains is to locate their semantic nature. Given that proper names are essentially involved in singular reference, it is hard to resist the temptation to engage in a program of developing a theory that assigns the singular reference of proper names to the language system. The natural way is to connect proper names with definite descriptions. The strongest semantic connection is synonymy. Thus, very naturally, the problem becomes that of finding the right descriptions for synonymy with given proper names.

Strawson and Searle saw very clearly that there was no easy synonymous connection between a proper name and a set of descriptions. But they still wanted a connection with the community of speakers who use the name. This social aspect of the communication of reference exerts a tremendous pressure for linking proper names with definite descriptions available to the members of the community. Then the picture develops of a proper name connected with a network of definite descriptions—and the network is all *there*, in the language system from which we can *all* pick and choose. Of course, all of us cannot have access to those definite descriptions; after all, some of us are less informed than others, and some are less capable than others of understanding complicated descriptions. But a majority of those descriptions, or some especially earmarked set, will do. Once the meaning of the proper name has been anchored to the language system, it is easy to extend a bridge toward the idiolect. One can both allow that from the public network each speaker picks out his own subnetwork and require that this subnetwork be involved in the speaker's acts of singular reference using the name in question. This public network/personal sub-network view is nicely put forward by Searle in his celebrated "Proper Names" as follows:

(a)   . . . I am suggesting that it is a necessary fact that Aristotle has the logical sum, inclusive disjunction, of properties *commonly* attributed to him. [p. 172; my italics]

(b)   Suppose we ask the *users* of the name "Aristotle"to state what they regard as certain essential and established facts about him. [Apparently this 'him' refers to Aristotle.] Their answers would be a set of uniquely referring descriptive statements. Now what I am arguing is that the descriptive force of "This is Aristotle" is to *assert* that a sufficient but so far unspecified number of these statements are true of this object. [p. 171; my italics]

Presumably, the view entails that whoever makes a statement with the sentence 'Aristotle was the teacher of Plato' asserts that a sufficient number of the relevant uniquely descriptive statements are true of—whom? This object? Aristotles? The name again! Here are nice problems. (Note how ontology intrudes into the semantic enterprise.)

What causes me to fret most in the above account, and what the critics object to, is the *shared presupposition*: that the singularity of the reference of proper names must be centrally located in the language system, so that the pragmatic phenomenon of a *use* of a proper name having a nominatum has to be explained by equating the use's nominatum with the nominatum of the proper name itself.

This is one of the deep-seated presuppositions that the Greta Bergman-Oscar A. A. Hecdnett story explodes. The exegesis of the story reveals that the singularity of the reference does not belong to the language system, not even to an idiolect as such, but to a particular speech act. There is NO strict nominatum for a proper name as a mere label in the language system. The language provides *only* a framework for singular reference. Obviously, the identifying traits (*not* definite descriptions), which underlie the singularity of the singular reference to a nominatum attained with a sentence containing a proper name N, belong to the act of referring, not to the language system.

Views within the Attribute Approach are defective chiefly because they misplace the issues and reverse the order of the dependence relations involved between language systems, idiolects, and speech acts.

15. Burges's Demonstrative Variable/Descriptive View of Proper Names

Tyler Burge[7] has constructed an elegant and illuminating theory of proper names, delicately sensitive to many crucial features of our authentic use of proper names in experience. It does justice to important insights of the Attribute Approach and to equally important insights of the Direct-Reference Approach to proper names. Although he does not put it in these terms, Burge appreciates the fact that singular reference belongs in the speech acts, the language system providing only the framework for reference. He wants a unified account of both the singular uses and the quantificational uses of proper names. His semantics assigns to proper names as part of the language system, an implicit demonstrative which functions as a variable. He has the correct conception of the connection between proper names and the characteristics of the named objects, and of how the unity of the extension of a proper name as a count noun depends merely on the fact that the name applies to the objects it is a name of.

Here is Burge's own formulation of his main tenets:

(B*1.PN)   "Proper names, in singular use, are represented as terms containing a demonstrative governing a predicate analogous in form to 'that male' [p. 84] . . . e.g., the linguistic meaning [of the name 'Ossian'] is that of the term 'that Ossian'." [p. 85]

(B*2.PN)   "demonstrative pronouns are represented by terms which are analogous to free variables *both* in taking unique assignments (referents) only in contexts of use, *and* in being INSTRUMENTS OF PRONOMIAL CROSS-REFERENCE." [p. 84; where the capitalization signals my emphasis]

I like this theory. It is simply the best alternative to the Contextual Restricted-Variable/Causal Account that I know of. Manifestly, the main differences between Burge's Demonstrative Variable/Descriptive View and the Restricted-Variable Retrieval View are:

(M-D*)   (a) On Burge's view a proper name includes a demonstrative, whereas on my view a proper name does not include anything demonstrative.
(b) Different views of the referring roles of variables.

This main difference (M-D*) has some important consequences. *First*, in the terminology introduced above, Burge allows proper names to function as *genuine* singular terms in sentences containing them through which speakers make or express some singular reference. On my view, on the other hand, proper names remain free variables even when they occur in sentences with which singular reference is achieved. Hence, *second*, singular reference is for Burge located at the *proper name* of the sentence; for me it is located on the whole sentence, but we could locate it at the *position* in the sentence occupied by the proper name. A *third* difference lies on our different views on the roles of demonstratives.

Momentous consequences issue from Burge's thesis (B*2.PN) about the role of demonstratives. He conceives demonstratives to be, like all variables of quantification and all purely cross-referential pronouns, mechanisms of direct or pure reference.

We must admire the elegance, the originality, and the richness, of Burge's view, and we can greatly benefit from the illumination it irradiates. The covert demonstrative he postulates within each name is his overture to the Direct-Reference Approach. His predicative use of the proper name itself is his olive branch to the Attribute Approach. This is indeed a very slim branch. Because of his view of the use of demonstratives or indicators, his concession to the Direct-Reference Approach is more substantial. What I most admire is his claim that insofar as proper names belong to the language system, they are *not* genuinely referential, because they contain a demonstrative, which, insofar as it is part of the language system, is itself a mere variable of quantification. Burge's view gracefully slides between the Scylla of the Direct-Reference View and the Charybdis of the Attribute Approach.

Why, then, do I not convert to Burge's view? For two main reasons. *First*, I believe that demonstratives are not means for making that kind of direct or pure reference. All thinking reference is mediated through some cognitive content or other. *Second*, it seems to me that each of the mechanisms of singular reference — definite descriptions, indicators (or demonstratives), proper names, and quasi-indicators — has its own characteristic and peculiar roles, which preclude the assimilation, subordination, or reduction of one mechanism to the others. We should attempt no reduction of one to the others, but try, rather, to formulate the different principles and laws in accordance with which they are instruments for organizing our experiences and help us both to conceive the structure of the world and to refer to its contents.

I have elsewhere argued specifically (inter alia) against Burge's contentions: (1) that demonstratives are "instruments of pronomial cross-reference" (second part of thesis (B*2.PN)), and (2) that in their singular use proper names include, semantically (not, obviously, syntactically), a covert demonstrative (thesis (B*1.PN).[8]

Concerning (B*2.PN), I have adduced data that show: (a) The pronomial mechanisms for cross-reference have nothing to do with demonstratives, they being neither demonstratives nor proxies for demonstratives; (b) lone demonstratives have nothing to do with cross-reference, but with co-reference.

Concerning Burge's central tenet (B*1.PN), I have found that ordinary referential mechanisms run in opposition to it. First, (c) the examination of discourses establishes that the replacement of a proper name N with its corresponding Burgean demonstrative definite description of the form *That N* is often incorrect, and when the replacement is appropriate nothing like synonymy or commonality of sense comes forth. Furthermore, (d) because indicators are always alien in indirect speech (*oratio obliqua*), being creatures of direct speech (*oratio recta*), because they express speaker's reference, proper names in indirect speech simply cannot include a covert indicator. Moreover, (e) because quasi-indicators have indirect speech as their exclusive habitat, and have an antecedent in direct speech, whereas proper names need no antecedent, the Burgean view cannot be easily extended to allow proper names to include either a covert indicator or a hidden quasi-indicator without breaking up the semantic unity of proper names (see chap. 6, sect. 5).

We have no room in this essay to go into claims (c), (d), and (e). Fortunately, they should become crystalline after a perusal of studies on indexical and quasi-indexical reference. In any case, the full discussion is available.

We will not treat claim (a) here. Let us, however, briefly discuss claim (b), which is after all the centerpiece of Burge's Demonstrative Variable/Descriptive Theory. Let us examine Burge's thesis that a name N is to be understood as the singular term of the form "that N." Consider the following dialogue, with its translation in its hypothesized Burgese demonstrative original:

QUINE (in his office at Harvard talking on the phone to Strawson in his sitting room at Magdalen College in Oxford):

(4) "Scott is here and sends his best wishes to you."

STRAWSON (who the day before learned that John Scott Jr. was coming to Boston today):

(5) "So soon? How is John Jr.?"

QUINE: (6) "John Jr.' Who is John Jr.?"

STRAWSON: (7) "John Scott Jr. is. . . . He left Oxford. . . . "

QUINE: (8) "The Scott here, my Scott, our Scott, is Dana Scott. He's here at Harvard for this week. But when is that Scott of yours coming to Boston?"

That QUINE (in his office at *that Harvard* talking on the phone to *that Strawson* in his sitting room at *that Magdalen College* in *that Oxford*):

(4) "*That Scott* is here and sends his best wishes to you."

That STRAWSON (who the day before learned that *that John Scott Jr.* was coming to *that Boston* today):

(5)"So soon? How is THAT John Jr.?"

QUINE: (6) "*That John Jr.?* Who is THAT(?) John Jr.?"

STRAWSON: "(7) THAT(?) John Scott Jr. is. . . . He left *THAT* Oxford. . . . "

QUINE: (8) "The Scott here, my Scott, our Scott, is *that Dana Scott.* He's here at *THAT* Harvard just for this week. But when is that Scott of yours coming to *THAT Boston?*"

This translation is very educational. Evidently, some occurrences of some names N can indeed be replaced with occurrences of the corresponding indexical name-description of the form "that N." But others cannot. Interestingly enough, in some cases we can replace a name N with the indexical description of the form "this N". We confront here an intriguing convergence of different mechanisms of singular reference, which must be subjected to careful exegesis before we draw any conclusions. The following chart sorts out the different pieces of the phenomenon:

(I) Indexical name-descriptions headed by an italicized lower-case '*that*': Name N is replaceable neither with 'that N' nor with 'this N'. N seems neither to include a demonstrative element nor to allow the intrusion of a demonstrative element. The Burgese replacement is out of order.

Examples:
   (1) In the reporter's foreword: 'That Quine', 'that Harvard', 'that Strawson', 'that Oxford'.
   (2) In Quine's speech: 'That Scott' at (4), 'that John Jr.' at (6).
   (3) In the reporter's introduction of Strawson: 'That Strawson', 'that Boston'.

(II)   Indexical name-descriptions headed by a nonitalicized but capitalized 'THAT':
   The proper name N is replaceable with 'that N', but not with 'this N'. Yet the token of N is not synonymous with 'that N'.

Examples:
   (1) In Quines's utterance (6) the demonstrative 'THAT' is all right if Quine is referring to Strawson's speech, e.g., by saying something like: (6') Who's that John Jr. You're talking about?
   (2) In Strawson's speech: 'THAT John Jr.' at (5) makes a reference to Quine's utterance (4) and expresses his assumption that the Scott mentioned by Quine is his John Scott Jr. Similar remarks apply to the use of that description in (7).

(III)   Indexical name-descriptions headed by an italicized and capitalized 'THAT':
   The proper name N is replaceable with 'this N', but not with 'that N'. However, the token of N is not synonymous with 'this N'. The Burgese replacement is incorrect.

Examples:
   (1) In Strawson's speech: 'THAT Oxford' at (7); if Strawson believed that Quine believed there were other Oxfords, he could have said, instead, 'this Oxford';
   (2) In Quine's speech: Similarly, 'That Harvard' and 'THAT Boston' could very well have been, respectively, 'this Harvard' and 'this Boston'.

(IV)   Already existing indexical name-descriptions:
   At (8) we find the Burgese name description 'that Scott of yours'. Clearly, this description cannot be simply replaced with the name 'Scott' without introducing ambiguity. The same holds for the other name descriptions 'The Scott here', my Scott', 'our Scott'.

Data (IV) shows how the demonstrative name description 'this N' or 'that N' can be used, at its very *first* occurrence in the discourse, to refer to an object named N, segregating it from the other objects named N, which are not mentioned but are alluded to as part of the background context doxastically supporting the discourse. In the above texts this is particularly evident in the case of the names 'Oxford', 'Harvard', and 'Boston'. Note especially how Strawson can from the very beginning say 'this Oxford' instead of just saying 'Oxford', and Quine can say 'this Boston' instead of just 'Boston'. On the other hand, Quine can say 'that

Oxford', and Strawson 'that Boston'. Which of the two demonstratives a speaker uses is very important: *it helps him to place the object in his world and within his experience as this is structured at the time of speech.*

The data in group (I) establish that proper names do not have the semantics or pragmatics that requires them to have, as Burge's thesis (B.1) claims, a demonstrative covert component.

We have no time to ponder all the morals the preceding (hypothetical) Quine-Strawson exchange and its Burgean translation teach us. But two points, which jump to sight in the previous chart, may be worth underscoring:

(N.Dem*) An indexical name-description of the form "that N," for a name N, rather than introducing an individual named N into discourse serves, instead, both *to place* on the focus of consideration an individual named N previously introduced in the current discourse, and *to segregate* that individual from others also named N.

(D.Dem*) The demonstrative role of a demonstrative description, whether a name description or not, consists of the speaker's placing the described individual in current experience, whether perceptual or merely reflective (see chaps. 4–9).

I conclude that proper names do not include a covert demonstrative, but have their own functions in thinking and communicational economy.

16. Howard Wettstein's Datum

Howard Wettstein[9] has raised some objections to certain aspects of my causal view of proper names. He thinks that objections to Attribute Views apply to my view. Interestingly enough, his objections bring forth a useful datum which is evidence for my view.

The first difficulty Wettstein presents is this:

A main line of their argument [i.e., that of Donnellan and Kripke] has been that in using a proper name, *successful reference* is possible even when the speaker fails to possess any correct (uniquely) identifying characterization of the referent. Thus, I can refer to *a*, assert and apprehend propositions about *a*, even though I do not possess a single, correct identifying *description* of *a*. [p. 149; my italics]

This passage is not incompatible with my causal theory of proper names. *First, in that passage there is no evidence or data against my view: there is only the remark that Donnellan and Kripke have argued in a certain way: but we need the actual arguments to determine how effective they are. Second,* it is not clear what Wettstein's successful reference is. I have explained earlier in this discussion that for the reference I have been talking about both in the paper commented on by Wettstein and here, that is, first-person thinking reference, the use of names is never involved in the reference in question. *Third*, I grant the datum mentioned by Wettstein in his example. I have already explained in section 10 how there can be different ways in which one can think of *a* and yet not be able to offer a description of *a* that uniquely characterizes it. *Fourth*, my account of proper names and of thinking of objects has the virtue of dealing with Wettstein's datum as well as with other data, as explained earlier.

Wettstein puts his second difficulty as follows:

> Consider an assertive utterance of "John was born on March 23, 1976." If the speaker *knows* enough about John, he will possess several (nonequivalent) unique characterizations of him. . . . For each replacement of the name "John" in the uttered sentence by such a characterization (or by a conjunction of such characterizations) [How can we conjoin characterizations, which are substituends of names?] we obtain a sentence which formulates a different proposition. Now if the speaker is asked which of these sentences formulates the proposition he had in mind, he will be often unable to select some one sentence as *the* correct one. "Although I meant to refer to John," our speaker might well reply, "I don't think I meant to refer to him *as* my best friend, as opposed to say, *as* my wife's brother. . . . " If this response is one that we are likely to get, then we cannot suppose that the speaker had a Fregean proposition "before his consciousness." [p. 150; my italics]

The datum Wettstein adduces is of prime importance. Patently, Wettstein is considering a context of communication. To meet me, he is considering speaker's reference. But as I have noted (see chapter 1), speaker's reference in a dialogue is *not* identical with first-person thinking reference. The former includes not only what the speaker thinks but also his intention to communicate about his subject matter. Nevertheless, Wettstein's datum is one that any theory of reference *must* take into account.

Wettstein is too quick to conclude, however, that his datum by itself shows that the speaker did not have before his consciousness a Fregean proposition. In any case, my own theory of proper names can be applied beautifully to Wettstein's datum: it looks as if my theory had been devised just to deal with his datum. I must note, *first*, that I spoke in "Foundations," not just of one but of possibly many propositions before a thinker's consciousness. *Second*, that a speaker knows many truths about a person he is talking about does not imply that he is thinking of all those truths. Thus Wettstein's example requires that his speaker must *think* of several truths about the John of his speech. Then the datum is this:

> (*Wettstein's Datum*) The speaker is thinking of a certain person, called John, and he is thinking that that person is his wife's brother *and* also his best friend, but when he proffers "John was born on March 23, 1976," he is not referring *communicationally* to John as his best friend, or as his wife's brother, or as both his best friend and his wife's brother: He is simply referring to John, without attributing to him any property.

In my causal theory of proper names, Wettstein's datum is forthcoming. The speaker intends to cause his audience to think of a certain person as having been born on March 23, 1976, under *any* individuating traits available to them for Wettstein himself is *not* putting any particular identifying trait in (on, next to, under, alongside) his token of the name "John." The reference (in the communicational speaker's sense of reference) that goes with his utterance *is* deprived of descriptive or characterizing content.

Perhaps it may help to note that if Wettstein had asked his speaker not how he is (communicationally) referring to John, but what he is thinking of John as, then the speaker would not be reporting accurately were he to answer "I am not thinking of him as my wife's brother or as my best friend or as both." The example requires that he think of the person in question *not* only as his wife's brother and as his best friend but also as a person named "John."

17. Conclusion

The Contextual-Restricted-Variable/Retrieval View of ordinary proper names has been supported directly through the rich data in the Bergman-Hecdnett story. It has received additional support from the data involved in the examination of current alternative theories. And it has received the unexpected support from Wettstein's datum. The examination of data strongly points out the need to place that theory on the pedestal of an ontological theory of individuation, identity, and predication. Thus, we have here a route that leads from the semantics and the causal properties of proper names to Guise Theory.

Notes

1. The data contained in this Greta Bergman-Oscar Hecdnett story includes the crucial data contained in Saul Kripke's Pierre story. The former was partially influenced by Kripke. I was absent from Indiana University when in 1978 Kripke gave a lecture in which he presented a version of his "A Puzzle about belief," in Avishai Margalit, ed., *Meaning and Use* (Dordrecht: Reidel, 1979). It created a commotion among my colleagues that lasted until my return. Upon hearing my colleagues' reports I realized that the multiple uses of names for one and the same object, which had preoccupied me, was the substance of the Pierre story, and that the contrast between different languages central to this story is not essential. In 1982 I read Kripke's paper, and I have remained convinced of these points. According to Kripke's story, Pierre is a young Frenchman who having learned nothing but French has come to believe what he expresses by saying, "Londres est jolie"; later on he moves to an ugly section of London and learns English and comes to believe what he expresses by saying, "London is ugly." The puzzle consists in that according to some generally accepted or plausible principles about translation and elimination of quotation marks. Pierre turns out to have self-contradictory beliefs, yet he clearly has no self-contradictory beliefs, for the simple reason that he cannot by mere logical deduction derive any contradiction from what he believes, as long as he does not believe that the city he calls "Londres" in French is the same as the one he calls "London" in English. Told this way the Pierre story constitutes a refutation of the set of principles from which the contradiction is derived. Since we are not here interested in refuting any view, the Bergman-Hecdnett story is told with no attached view to refute, it is told, so to speak, nakedly, as a mere collection of data for exegesis from which we can distill obligatory criteria of adequacy for *any* worthy theory of proper names. (Our procedure here is, thus, not dialectic or polemical, but one of phenomenological linguistics.) The

Bergman-Hecdnett story was first told in Hector-Neri Castañeda, *Sprache und Erfahrung: Texte zu einer neuen Ontologie*, translated by Helmut Pape (Frankfurt am Main: Suhrkamp, 1982), pp. 100–104.

2. See Hector-Neri Castañeda, "On the Philosophical Foundations of the Theory of Communication: Reference," *Midwest Studies in Philosophy* 5 (1977), which was presented at a 1970 conference in the philosophy of language, at Arizona State University, Tempe. The theory of proper names developed by Roderick M. Chisholm in *The First Person* (Minneapolis: University of Minnesota Press, 1981) has important similarities to my account. For the other causal theory see Saul Kripke, "Naming and Necessity,"in Donald Davidson and Gilbert Harman, eds., *Semantics of Natural Language* (Dordrecht: Reidel, 1972), pp. 253–335.

3. For Frege see Gottlob Frege, "On Sense and Denotation" in P. T. Geach and Max Black, eds., *Translations from the Philosophical Writings of Gottlob Frege* (Oxford: Blackwell, 1966). For Russell see Bertrand Russell, "Lectures on Logical Atomism," in Robert C. Marsh, ed., *Logic and Knowledge* (London: Allen & Unwin, 1956), pp. 243–54.

4. I have exegesized Kaplan's theory of demonstrative direct reference in "Direct Reference, Realism, and Guise Theory (Constructive Reflections on David Kaplan's Theory of Reference)," presented at the conference *Themes on the Philosophy of David Kaplan* at Stanford Univesity, March 1984, and published in Joseph Almog, John Perry, and Howard Wettstein, eds., *Themes from Kaplan*, (Oxford: Oxford University Press, 1989). [See pp. 126–130 below.]

5. On the nature of intentions, their logical structure, and their role in practical thinking, see Hector-Neri Castañeda, *Thinking and Doing* (Dordrecht: Reidel, 1975), chaps. 6, 10, and 11; see also the articles by Michael Bratman, Myles Brand, Bruce Aune, and Wilfrid Sellars, and Castañeda's replies to them in James E. Tomberlin, ed., *Agent, Language, and the Structure of the World* (Indianapolis: Hackett, 1983). See also Hector-Neri Castañeda, "Intentional Action, Conditional Intentions, and Aristotelian Practical Syllogisms," *Erkenntnis* 18 (1982): 239–60.

6. See Frege "On Sense and Denotation" (cited in note 3); Bertrand Russell, "On Denoting," *Mind* 14 (1905) 479–93; Ludwig Wittgenstein, *Philosophical Investigations* (London: Macmillan, 1953; transl. by Elizabeth Anscombe); P. F. Strawson, "On Referring," *Mind*, 59 (1950): 175–95; John R. Searle, "Proper Names," *Mind* 67 (1958): 166–73.

7. Tyler Burge, "Russell's Problem and Intentional Identity" in James E. Tomberlin, cited in note 5.

8. See Hector-Neri Castañeda,"Reply to Tyler Burge: Reference, Existence, and Fiction," in James E. Tomberlin, cited in note 5.

9. Howard Wettstein, "Proper Names and Propositional Opacity," in Peter French, Theodore Uehling, and Howard Wettstein, eds., *Contemporary Perspectives in the Philosophy of Language* (Minneapolis: University of Minnesota Press, 1979). It is a comment on "Foundations" cited in note 2.

3

Singular Descriptions

1. Singular Reference and Individuation by
Networks of Differences

To think of an individual, or a particular, *as* an individual is to segregate the individual in question from all other individuals in the world, or from all other individuals we *could* think of, and pin it down before our minds. This is sometimes referred to as the *epistemic identity* or identifiability of the object in question. Now, whatever deeply in their metaphysical innards individuals may be, they must be segregated from one another by virtue of their accessible differences from one another; among those differences lie their properties and relations. On the other hand, the fundamental contents of mental acts or states are properties and relations. Undoubtedly, this harmony of mental content and world content is the result of the vicissitudes of evolution. In any case, the primary way in which we think of a particular as a given particular is by taking it to be altogether a *total* bundle of differences, encompassing all the differences that could in principle differentiate it from any other object in the universe. This is the ontological foundation of the actual identifications we can carry out in practice. Thus, the harmony between world and cognizing mind, given the finitude of our operations, requires, further, that from the total bundle of differences constituting an individual, small sets of differences be sufficient to pin the particular down as *the* individual we are thinking of. Hence, the following principles are a foundation on which our thinking of particulars as particulars rests:

(On-Ep.H.1) *Basic Principle of Ontological and Epistemological Harmony*
  For cognition and belief the individuality of an individual—whether this is finite or infinite—amounts to the exhaustiveness of the complete set of the individual's differences from everything else.

(On-Ep.H.2) *Ontologico-epistemological Principle of Singular Reference*
Since singular reference is confined to finite individuals, the individuals think-able *in propria persona* amount to finite sets of differences bounded by an im-plicit constitutive claim that those finite differences suffice for the total differentiation between that individual and any other.

(On-Ep.D*) *Principle of Differentiation*
Each ascertainable difference between two individuals consists in a difference in properties. Thus, every property possessed by an individual is a principle of difference, and the set of differences characteristic of an individual is tanta-mount to the set of properties possessed by the individual.

Because of these principles, the fundamental experience of thinkingly refer-ring to particulars consists of thinking episodes having as partial contents what the locutions of the form *the so-and-so* express, where the definite article *the* ex-presses individuality and the phrase represented by the locution *so-and-so* represents a completely segregating set of differences. We shall call these expres-sions when they are so used *singular descriptions*; but we shall also resort to the term introduced by Bertrand Russell for very much the same purpose: *definite descriptions*.

An example of a definite description is "The first man." Clearly, the relation of being first differentiates one man from all other men, and the property of being a man presumably differentiates all men from everything else. However, here is a problem. We seldom have the occasion to think of the *very* first man in the whole history of the universe. Even Christians who call that man "Adam" seldom raise their thoughts up to the moment of creation. Nevertheless, in theology, in scien-tific theorizing, and a few other lofty occasions we may perhaps refer to *the* abso-lutely first man.

It is worth remarking that we do not think collectively of *all* men as often as philosophers or logic books suggest. In daily life we are typically concerned only with just *some* men. We are interested in talking about ALL the men of a certain kind, or about some men of that kind, or about *the* man of that kind who is such-and-such. Many times we can specify the kind in question. We say "Everybody came to the party" and only an infantile joker will counter: "So Queen Elizabeth came. Did Mussolini come too?"

The crucial fact is that, presumably at least for reasons of expediency, our typical thinking has to do with our daily actions on objects and to or with persons in our vicinity, and we refer to them within a network of presupposed beliefs about our vicinity. Acts of thinking occur on a small stage supported by a huge doxastic pedestal. Our finitude rules out pursuing all the layers and strands of that pedestal. Thus, thinking occurs within a *context* of beliefs about the vicinity in which our thinking occurs as well as the surrounding world. Let us dwell on this a bit.

2. The Contextual Dimension of the Semantics of Quantification

Let us consider quantification and build a general semantico-pragmatic background for studying singular reference by discussing our practice of quantification statements. In daily experience, typically we make statements like these:

(1) The females are *all* highly qualified: It will be hard to choose from them.

Evidently, the person who proffers (1) does not mean to refer to ALL the females in the world now living—let alone *all* females ever. Most likely we have in mind a very small number of females. Presumably we can elucidate the domain of 'all females' by furnishing a relevant classification of the females under consideration. For instance, the particular use of (1) under exegesis may have been intended as an abbreviation of:

(1.a) All the female applicants are highly qualified: It will be hard to choose from them.

Yet this does not solve the problem of interpretation. The fact is that (1.a) does not demarcate the domain of the quantifier 'all females' in (1): Many, indeed *most* female applicants are not meant—for example, those who have applied for jobs not connected to the company or institution the speaker belongs to. The speaker of (1) in asserting (1) means to refer to all those female applicants for the vacancies existing in his company or institution at the time of assertion.

There are, thus, three semantico-pragmatic views one can adopt:

a. *Elliptical View*: Ordinary quantifier expressions—'all', 'everybody', 'some', and so on—are often used in sentences that are ellipses of sentences containing full specifications of the relevant domains of quantification.

b. *Elliptico-indexical View*: The ellipses mentioned in the Elliptical View are all indexical: The phrases specifying the domains of quantification contain at least one indexical expression, for example, 'the female applicants *we* are *now* considering'.

c. *Contextualist View*: Ordinary quantifier expressions are often used in sentences that do not contain a specification of the domain of quantification, yet they are not ellipses of sentences with phrases, whether indexical or not, denoting that specification; the domain is determined by the context of speech.

I have adopted the Contextualist View. This view allows that in some cases a sentence may be for certain an ellipsis of a sentence that conforms to the Elliptical View, indeed to the Elliptico-indexical View. Whether this happens or not is an empirical matter open for investigation. The Contextualist View claims that ellipsis is not necessary. It aims at accounting for several crucial facts, among which the following two deserve special mention.

One fact of experience is this. Many times we use quantifier expressions without having any particular way of specifying the relevant domains of quantification. Worse, even after reflection, we have no particular locution in mind as the one that was omitted from speech. Here we are touching on a most important fact too often neglected in studies on reference. Before treating it let us discuss the meanings of quantifier expressions.

The Contextualist View of quantifiers involves, thus, the following semantico-pragmatic theses:

(LS.Sem-q) The semantics of the quantifier expressions of the natural language systems is schematic: They have a semantic slot for a domain of quantification.

(LS.Prg-q) The slot is filled in by the speaker in each speech act in which with a view at the speech context he or she assigns a domain of quantification to the quantifiers he or she uses.

Part of the preceding two principles can be formulated by saying that the general meaning of a quantifier Q is a function that assigns to speech contexts functions that assign restricted domains of quantification to Q.

3. The Hierarchical Nature of Thinking

We MUST be able to think entities directly, without having to think that we are thinking of them. Not only is it the case phylogenetically that we learn to think of objects and events in the physical world or physiological changes in our bodies before we learn to think of our mental operations. The fact is that ontogenetically, too, awareness of our mental operations is mounted on the consciousness pertaining to those operations. Here is a problem of an infinite regress that could be vicious, if we lay it down that self-consciousness is presupposed for consciousness. But even if we put it in a nonvicious way by simply requiring that consciousness of something be accompanied by self-consciousness, this can lead to an infinity that runs against the finitude of the mind. Thus, we must deliberately endorse this anti-Fichtean thesis:

(HS.Ref-Th) *Hierarchical Structure of Reflective Thinking*:
Episodes of reflective thinking not only rest on episodes of non-reflective thinking, but characteristically they do not give rise to reflective thinking upon themselves.

Fichte erred in holding that all (episodes of) consciousness are (episodes of) self-consciousness.[1] In the case of example (1) above, or (1.a) for that matter, the speaker must be able to think of the female applicants under consideration without having to think that they are being thought of. The considerer's consideration opens up for her a domain of entities to consider, and she must be able to consider those entities fully as having these or those properties, as conforming to such and such criteria, as satisfying the relevant desiderata, and so on, *without* always having to think of her consideration as well. To suppose the opposite appears to introduce a circularity in every act of thinking. Perhaps a theory can be developed without circularity, but such a theory will have to account also for the fact that the power to think reflectively requires higher order concepts (for example, in the case of (1) the concept of considering) that children seem to acquire later on, after they have become skillful at unreflective thinking. To think, one needs concepts, but not the concept of thinking itself.

4. The Indexical and Contextual Dimensions of Singular Descriptions

To tackle definite descriptions let us reflect on this example:

(2) Please put these books on *the table*.

Very much the same considerations reeled above about the quantifier 'all females' apply to the definite description 'the table'. There are millions of tables in the world; hence, to interpret the definite description as ranging over the total universe is preposterous. In many situations we may be satisfied with the contention that in (2) 'the table' is short for 'the table over there' or 'the table in this [that] room'. Nevertheless, even in the simplest cases we may be in difficulty trying to ascertain what phrase is the one that has actually been left implicit. In brief, for (2) as for (1) we adopt the Contextualist View:

(LS.Sem-the) The meaning of the definite article in the natural language systems has a semantic slot for the specification of uniqueness.

(LS.Prg-the) The uniqueness of what a speaker means to refer to by an utterance of a token of a locution of the form *the so-and-so*, embedded in a token of a sentence S, is determined by the speech context, and neither the locution nor the sentence S nor their proffered tokens need be elliptical.

The uniqueness of a reference to an individual as an individual is, therefore, achieved in two different ways: (i) by a totally differentiating set of properties, which for the case of existing objects may be infinite, and (ii) by contextual determination. The former uniqueness may be termed Leibnizian, because it incorporates Leibniz's idea that the individuation—where he clearly meant differentiation—of an individual belongs to the individual as a whole. In principle it provides an absolute criterion of differentiation, and suggests that an individual may be equated with the totality of its properties (including relations). We may thus speak of *Leibnizian definite descriptions*.

It is not clear that, except for the descriptions of the universe, Leibnizian descriptions are available to us, that is, absolute individuations of particular without reference to any other particular. For instance, we discussed the definite description *the (very) first man* understood as widely as possible. Yet even there the uniqueness of the expression depends on our relating the man in question to the universe, even if not to God. Suppose that we believe that the universe has evolved on its own and has no beginning and has evolved in a circular fashion.

What can we mean then by 'the first man'? We could still speak of the first man as we normally do—for example, the first man of those who registered for a certain class, of those in a certain lineup. We could speak of the first man within the cycle of the universe *we* belong to. If the universe is composed of parallel worlds, some of which have similar histories, 'the first man' could refer to the first man in *our* world.

It seems then that our thinking of particulars presupposes a framework of uniqueness relations to some presupposed particulars. The universe as a whole is one such particular. Yet we seldom need to conceive persons or objects so abstractly as they belong to the universe. We need to conceive of them as connected to ourselves in the corner of the universe in which we act and for which we have plans. We refer to persons and objects as parts of an environment seen from the vantage point of a manifold of assumptions on which our action plans rest. These shifting manifolds of assumptions, in tandem with our shifts of interest, determine the contexts of speech. These contexts determine the particulars we are referring to in terms of presupposed references to ourselves, or to particulars we find in our immediate speech context. How do we refer to ourselves? How do we refer to the particulars we confront immediately? The short answer is: We refer to them indexically. We must try to make this answer longer.

Notes

1. See, for example, Johann Gottlieb Fichte, *Science of Knowledge*, transl. by Peter Heath and John Lacks, 1794 original text, (New York: Appleton-Century-Crofts, 1970). Chisholm with his Self-ascription View of believing produces a dissolution of self-reference as content of thinking, but incorporates self-reference as a a modality of the mental acts and states, thus providing a self-less realization of Fichte's claim that all consciousness is self-consciousness. It seems that the main task for this view is to account for the obvious distinction between nonreflective and reflective consciousness, of which, correctly, Jean-Paul Sartre made so much in *Being and Nothingness: An Essay in Phenomenological Ontology*, transl. by Hazel Barness from the 1943 original. (New York: Philosophical Library, 1956).

4

Indexical Reference
Is Experiential Reference

1. Confrontational Reference

The fundamental reality is that of existing individuals. Thus, to build one's biography one has to deal with objects and persons in one's environment as the individuals they are. One must locate them in the world by finding them in some experience or other, either confrontationally, *in propria persona*, or vicariously merely through their connections to confronted objects. In confronting an object or aspect of experience, one bestows on it a place in present experience thereby constituting it as a present and presented referent. Thus, confrontational reference, the fundamental way of thinking of individuals, is *executive* or performative.

We must fasten to principle (HS.Ref-Th), of the hierarchical structure of reflective thinking, in chapter 3.3. To think of an item—object, time, place, person—as it is present in an experience is NOT to think that one is being presented by such an item. To think the latter is to have a reflective piece of thinking, which must rest on the merely factually confrontational thinking. The executive role of confrontational thinking grounds the second-order classificatory or descriptive thinking of the experience, as well as the description of the experience as undergone by a subject.

To the extent that thinking is symbolically representational, one has to possess symbolic mechanisms capable of representing confronted entities insofar as they are confronted. To the extent that one thinks out loud, whether also in communication or not, such symbols convey to others one's confrontational references. But communication is not at the moment our concern. We are concerned with the English symbols for confrontational reference. These are of a bewildering variety of grammatical types. To oneself as oneself, one refers in the first-person way: as *I*. To each person we find in our immediate speech context as co-dialogants we refer in the second person: as *you*; to the persons we observe without talking

68

to them, we refer demonstratively as *he* or *she*; to observed persons and objects, we confront immediately as *this* or *that*. To the confronted time at which we think of the relations differentiating some individuals from others, we refer to as *now*, and to places we confront immediately as *here* and *there*. We call these fundamental mechanisms of reference to confronted particulars *as such* INDEXICAL.

A little reflection reveals that indexical reference is perforce personal: One refers indexically to what *one* confronts in a given experience. Also, indexical reference is essentially ephemeral: The particulars a person finds in an experience, he better not find in another experience—if one is to have a rich experience capable of sustaining one's life. What one calls by an indexical expression is typically not what one calls by the same expression in a succeeding experience. Palpably, the thisnesses or thatnesses of the objects one perceives are exasperatingly ephemeral: A *this* quickly turns into a *that*, and soon enough it is lost to experience and is not even a remote *that*; a *you* goes away and is replaced by another, and then there is just oneself alone fretting about something or other. Nothing is really an enduring *you*—except God perhaps for the abiding mystic. Nothing is intrinsically a *this*, or a *that*. Likewise, no moment can claim to be a *now* beyond itself—except perhaps the whole of time as confronted by God. And no place can claim a proprietary right to be a *here* or a *there*—except perhaps the whole of the world space as confronted by God. Is there at least an *I* that abides through the vicissitudes of its experiences? If so, which I? Mine? Well, this is the only I I can refer to singularly at this moment by using these tokens of the first-person pronoun *I*, but how enduring is it? How long can *I* exist? I believe, of course, that I *have* lived for sixty years; but doesn't this belief amount to I-*now* believing to have lived, that is, to I-now believing that something, or rather, a sequence of somethings has existed for sixty years and that something or each member of that sequence is postulated to be *dia*chronically the same as I (-now)?

The ephemeral nature of indexical reference creates a serious problem as to how we can refer to the same things again and again, as apparently we must be able to do if we are to carry out plans, indeed, if the world is to have some abiding structure and not be a Heraclitean chaos. On the other side, the personal character of indexical reference raises a serious question about the communication of references, and, hence, about our being able to cooperate and share the world that we both cognize and act on. These are profound questions. Obviously, we need above all to live in a world that allows some communication of indexical references, and immediately next, we must share a language that contains mechanisms (which I have called *quasi-indexical*) especially devised to transmute our indexical references, ephemeral and personal though they are, into interpersonal and enduring representations. This of course requires a harmonious match of world and language: It requires a comprehensive ontology that can be semantically anchored to the sytax of our language.

Patently, the first step in our understanding of such a harmonious match is a descriptive examination of our experience of indexical reference. On the assumption that our references are linguistically mediated, this examination evolves into a patient exegesis of the uses of our English mechanisms of indexical reference, that is, our English indicators. (The structural analysis of the experiential resources of a natural language we call *phenomenological linguistics*. Recall the discussion of semantico-syntactic contrasts in chapter 1.)

One point of clarification. Social action and interpersonal cooperation require a general, shared system of reference that can transcend each person's particular confrontations, a system where our experiences can converge. We need thus some fixed interpersonal and abiding particulars in relation to which we can identify all other particulars. Those privileged particulars form a general and uniform schema of reference. Such schema is precisely physical space-time. Science, concerned with constructing general information about the contents of the world independently of our personal confrontations, sometimes treats the space-time framework as absolute. And it may very well be so, especially when it is considered in the abstract. This fits in well with the fact that natural science deals with structural, general aspects of the universe, and that the universe and some special cosmic events are the few particulars that as such concern science. Nonetheless, in our applications of science, whether technological or experimental, we have to relate scientific results to *us*. Then we have to bolt down that impersonal schema by superposition on some network of particular confrontations. Thus, an account of experience, even of the experience required for testing scientific theories, presupposes the orderly and harmonious functioning of indexical and quasi-indexical references. That order and harmony is what the phenomenological linguistics of indexical reference aims to elucidate.

2. Irreducibility of Indexical Reference

Indexical reference is personal, ephemeral, confrontational, and executive. Hence, it is not reducible to nonindexical reference to what is not confronted. Conversely, nonindexical reference is not reducible to indexical reference. On the other hand, as remarked in chapter 3, singular reference to objects not present in perception often involves relating them to items in experience, at least to the time of the experience. Thus, the objects not present in experience are often singled out as objects thought of by means of a kind of indexical recipe for locating them in possible experiences—in some cases merely possible, contra-factic experiences. For instance, *the man who died next door* is the one who could have been found, in the appropriate circumstances specified in the context of thought and speech, next door. Other terms are not themselves indexical but point to a manifold of indexically anchored recipes for placing in principle certain objects in possible experience. As we observed in chapter 3, many terms are not abbreviations of indexical expressions; as they exist in the speakers' speech habits embodying a language system they have only a schematic claim of uniqueness to be fulfilled in contexts of use. Thus, *The Emperor of France* does not by itself harpoon any person, but in the context of a discussion about Bismarck's wars, or about the unification of Germany, or about the Battle of Sedan, its tokens can be used to fetch an object of thinking, for example, the mustachioed leader of France defeated in 1871 by Bismarck. This fetching does not specify any particular indexical path, but it has to proceed along some indexical route: It includes a time in some way related to the *now* of the speech act and to *I* that speaks. In any case, each member of the following hierarchy of mechanisms of reference has unique functions to perform in our experience:

    I. Pure Indicators
    II. Indexical Singular Descriptions of Presented Objects
    III. Indexical Singular Descriptions of Absent, Nonexperienced Objects
    IV. Contextually Determined Singular Descriptions
    V. Leibnizian Singular Descriptions

These mechanisms must be understood in full before the adoption of any reductionist program on them. At least three mutually irreducible dimensions of reference must be secured: (i) the irreducibility of the confrontational function of indexical reference, (ii) the primitivity of the executive character of indexical reference, and (iii) the special qualitative or relational experiential aspects differentiating thought of entities referred to indexically. We may postulate an overall unity of indexical and descriptive reference by considering indexical reference as the pinning down of items by means of *indexical properties*. Yet not only are indexical properties and relations most peculiar, and their peculiarity must be fully appreciated, but the executive, creative character of the attribution of such properties is an ultimate irreducible constitutive element of indexical reference. Furthermore, purely indexical properties are ephemeral, that is, exhausted in their presence in experience: Their *esse* is *percipi*. Or so they appear to be. More exciting data will be discussed in detail in the ensuing chapters, aimed at developing a crescendo impact of the irreducibility of indexical reference. In section 7 below we discuss a celebrated attack against the irreducibiliyt of first-person reference.

3. The Irreducibility of the Differences in Grammatical Person

Within indexical reference we find three further irreducible dimensions, namely, the differences in the three grammatical persons. Some subtle issues lurk behind these three major experiential theses:

I*.   First-person reference is not reducible to demonstrative third-person reference to an entity spoken of, even if this is oneself.

Y*.   Second-person reference is not reducible to demonstrative third-person to an entity spoken to, even if one is speaking to oneself.

I-Y*. First-person reference and second-person reference are mutually irreducible.

It might be thought that a purely psychological term like 'self' or 'person' may be successfully employed in the analysis of either the first-person pronoun 'I' or the second-person pronoun 'you'. A proposal I read some place is that 'I' can be defined as 'this self', or 'this person', or 'this person now speaking', or 'this thinker'. Some crude examples show that these analyses do not work. Palpably, a man, say Gaskon, can be in the following circumstances. Gaskon believes (perhaps mistakenly) that men with a certain facial appearance have a certain fatal illness Fness. Gaskon sees his own face and body in a very clear mirror, without realizing that he is seeing himself or even that he is seeing into a mirror, and sees the dreaded facial appearance. Gaskon thinks demonstratively, out loud — for our philosophical convenience: *"He* (or *this* person, or *that* man [pointing to the man in the mirror] is F."* For semantic emphasis let us suppose that Gaskon barely has time to finish conceiving his thought, for he immediately dies of a heart attack. Thus, Gaskon never thought the first-person content *I am F.* Thus, tenet I* is established. Obviously, similar circumstances establish Y* and I-Y*. For instance, Gaskon can (before dying, if you wish) think of another person he sees in the mirror *"She* (or *that* person) looks splendid" without realizing that he is referring to the person with whom he has been conversing.

The possible reply that Gaskon pointed to and referred to his mirror image, not to himself, is beside the mark. To be sure, Gaskon points to the image, but even if he knew that he was pointing to an image, he was still referring to a person. We do say things like "The sheriff saw the outlaw in the mirror and shot first, killing him."

Nevertheless, mirror images are not essential to the argument. Since the issue is of great importance, perhaps we should explore other situations, even more bizarre ones, that can reveal the semantic limits of indicators more perspicuously. It is only an empirical fact, though perhaps psychologically necessary for us, that binocular persons see the physical world from the top of their noses as the focus of the perspective they find in their visual perceptions. We can easily imagine a universe — ours after some future technological developments — in which one's focus of visual perspective is located several feet away from one's nose. In that universe, besides, the focus of visual perception changes from time to time, according, perhaps, to certain happenings in one's brain caused by what one has digested. In such a universe one's focus of perspective may be at one moment on the left of one's body, and later on in front, with one's own body among the objects one sees. One would know that a certain body is her own in the usual way, namely, by feeling kinesthetic sensations, pains, itches, and so on, in that body. At moments in which all his bodily sensations were nonexisting, or too dull and unattended, one of two identical twins may be momentarily confused as to which of two similar bodies in his visual field was his. He could solve his doubt by walking or trying to grab something: The body that moved might be his, but certainly the one where he feels the sensations of effort, pressure, muscular tension, and so on, would be his. In a world of that sort, clearly, nothing need prevent Privatus, Gaskon, and the other people talking with them from being very similar to one another in both bodily and vestiary appearance.

One good afternoon, Privatus, Gaskon, and other friends are having a meeting around a circular table in a symmetrically decorated room. Gaskon dozes off for a few minutes. During those minutes his focus of perspective changes from left to right. Also during that time a rash develops on his forehead. Gaskon wakes up and sees his body and thinks, truly: *This person* (or, *here is a self that*) *has a blister on his forehead*. Again, we may nail down the case by supposing that he dies upon conceiving that thought. Thesis I* shines again. It is worthwhile to record that in this case:

(1) Gaskon knows (believes) that *he himself* has a blister on *his own* forehead

may very well be false even though it is true that:

(2) There is a person demonstratively identified by Gaskon, which person happens to be identical with Gaskon, and whom Gaskon believes (knows) to have a blister on his forehead.

The point is this: The italicized locutions in (1) depict Gaskon's potential uses of first-person reference, and the contrast in truth-value between (1) and (2) shows that those locutions are not reducible to the attribution to a person X of demonstrative reference to himself. Those locutions are *quasi-indicators* depicting the first person. They also represent in (1) irreducible mechanisms of reference. We shall say a lot more about quasi-indicators. The above case is fantastic, no doubt, but logically viable. It shows that even in the presence of a very strong criterion of perceptual identification of a person, (2) fails to imply (1). Of course, on weaker criteria of perceptual identification, the disparity between third-person demonstrative reference to oneself and first-person reference is huge. In fact, in many situations, in view of massive contextual assumptions, we are allowed to claim to have seen a certain Mike on merely seeing part of his face, or his hand, or his shoes, or his pattern of dental fillings.

Very much the same considerations, impelled by weak criteria of perceptual identification, create strong discrepancies between demonstrative reference and second-person reference to the same addressee, and between first-person and second-person references to the same person. They establish theses Y* and I-Y* above.

4. Three Hurdles for Reductionism of Indexical References

Some philosophers may accept the irreducibility of first-person reference, and propose instead reducing the other types of indexical reference to first-person reference. For instance, isn't *now* the time at which one has an experience? Isn't *here* the place where one experiences something in an appropriate way of experiencing? Isn't a *this* an experienced object? Isn't a *you* simply a person or personified object one talks to? Why are these patent truths not capable of being developed into analyses of the italicized expressions? Obviously, the word 'one' used throughout the preceding questions represents the first person.

There are three general types of reason why reductions of one type of indexical reference to another, or, a fortiori, to nonindexical reference should always look suspicious. These are:

(R.I) The executive or performative character of indexical reference: A *this* is CREATED as such just in and during the act of its being thought of as a *this*; a *you* is ERECTED by the aiming of a piece of thought (and speech) to an entity being addressed; and so on.

(R.II) The crucial structural principle about thinking discussed in Chapter 3, namely: We MUST be able to think entities directly, without thinking that we are thinking of them:

(HS.Ref-Th) *Hierarchical Structure of Reflective Thinking*:
Episodes of reflective thinking not only rest on episodes of unreflective thinking, but characteristically do not give rise to reflective thinking upon themselves.

(R.III) One must be able to think of an entity of type T without thinking that it is of type T, especially in those cases in which there is an activity oriented to the entity, where one must be able to act on the entity without classifying it.

We have already watched the power and significance of (R.I): We have seen how positing something as a presented *this person* does not posit it as an *I* or *you*. Let us contemplate the force of the (R.II) and (R.III). Consider the following proposal:

(Prop) *I* =   (by analysis) the person [or speaker, or thinker, or self] who is having *this* experience, or is seeing *this* table [book, after-image, or whatever].

Palpably, (Prop) also fails to create a confrontation with one's own I. For one thing, this encounter must be executed for EACH type of indexical reference in EACH particular act of referring. In accordance with (HS.Ref-Th), one must be able to think of something (a table, an afterimage) as a *this* without being able to think of it as owned by oneself. Similarly, once the subject has moved to a higher level of thinking, it can think that the confrontation with the something in question (the table, afterimage) is while confronted—most likely in an encompassing specious present—a *this experiencing*; yet this need not in principle involve the thought that the experience is owned, much less owned by just one self, not to mention *owned by just one present(ed) self*. Even this last proposed analysis fails to bring forth the executive role of indexical reference: To think believingly that something is present *in propria persona* is not to confront that something. Here we find a symbiosis of (R.I) and (R.II).

(Prop) sins drastically against the hierarchical structure of reflective thinking in a way that violates (R.III). The crucial hierarchical fact of noncircularity requires that one must be able to speak, think, experience without having to think that speaking, thinking, experiencing are occurring, and much less that one is speaking, thinking, or experiencing. But the trouble lies not just in the hierarchical order of mental activity, but also in the classificatory aspect brought in by the higher-order thoughts. Let us consider a sophisticated application of (Prop), in which the suggested analysans contains a demonstrative used reflexively:

(3) [a] *I see Peter coming*
    is [proposed to be] analyzable as:
    [A] the self [person] who is experiencing *this* seeing of Peter.

Here (R.III) is being violated. To think (3)[a], *I see Peter coming*, is not to classify oneself as a self, person, or thinker, much less as a speaker. In fact, (3)[a] does not even imply that one is a person, or an embodied thinker, or a speaker.

Perhaps a clarification of (R.III) may not be amiss. (R.III) claims that for the case of mental acts there is a contrast between, say, (i) a very small child or a sophisticated robot separating the apples from the pears mixed up in a basket, without classifying the objects he (it) places on other baskets—because he lacks the relevant concepts—and (ii) an older boy (or a future really thinking robotish humanoid) separating pears from apples through *classifying* them—thus exhibiting his possession of the concepts of apple and pear.

The distinction between doing something moved by presented properties in instances and doing something moved by the classification of those instances is pervasive and of the utmost importance. It applies to thinking, and it is precisely what is involved in higher-order thoughts and in reflexive thinking. It is at the heart of the distinction between:

(4) John believes that the sun is shining

and

(5) John believes that that the sun is shining is true.

John, as described in (4), has an *operative* or executive concept of truth, which allows him to segregate propositions (sentences) as true without classifying them. That is, John has a power to deal with propositions, including true propositions, confrontationally, not classificatorily. The power to deal pragmatically with truth is the foundation of our power to deal with it semantically, as John is doing according to (5). Likewise, indexical confrontation is the foundation of the semantic classification of the items referred to indexically as of this or that ontic category.

Another line of development is to take 'I' to be short for 'this self [person]'. Clearly, we face here the same difficulty: Small children can use the first-person pronoun without having the concepts of self or of person. To be sure, when a speaker uses the first-person pronoun she is placing herself in the class of selves (or persons), but she is *executing* the placing and exhibiting her selfhood without classifying herself as a self (or person). This may be appreciated more fully by observing that the indexical description 'this self [person]' explicitly denotes a contrast between *this self [person]* and others. Now, (a) such a contrast is not a necessary part of what the first-person pronoun expresses, and (b) such a contrast is not sufficient for first-person reference. To see (a) observe that we all use the first-person pronoun correctly, for example, when we think: *I am working hard*, without carrying out an investigation, however trivial it might be, to ascertain that *this* self [or person], rather than another, is the one working hard. In fact, we could investigate that under the question: "Who is the one working hard: that one, this one, I?" The fact is that one is not merely *this self* [*person*], but the *default self* [*person*]. And this default reference is not a conclusion of an investigation, but it is presupposed by an investigation. Situations embellishing the Gaskon story reveal both (b) and the falsity of (Prop). One can hear one's own words without realizing that they are one's own, and can think "The self [person] having this thinking . . . " and "This self [person], who thinks . . . ," without realizing that it is oneself who is thinking that. The sense in which one is *this self* [*person*] requires a very special thisness: a most intimate one that allows no error, expresses always an uncancelable default reference, and expresses the experience of that immediacy and that default feature.

Undoubtedly, we can use the word 'this' as a general indicator schema. We could then define, thus:

(6) I = This-i

where the suffix '-i' is a signal of that immediate and default thisness just described. The issue then becomes: Is this property analyzable, or reducible to some other properties? The executive role of references by means of 'this-i' makes that property irreducible. Then 'this-i' is a demonstrative pronoun that expresses the primitive executive property one attributes to oneself when one uses the first-person pronoun. Hence, the term 'this-i' is merely a verbal substitute for the word 'I', and it expresses equally well the indefinable properties I-nessess the first-person pronoun expresses.

One ontological comment on the property I-ness is essential. The first-person pronoun as a part of the language system denotes a *generic* indefinable property, a *determinable* property. In a given speech act, an utterance in direct speech that contains 'I' expresses a specific property that falls under the generic one. This is comparable to the case of color words. In the language system we have the word 'blue' denoting a generic, determinable property; in a given perceptual judgment to think attentively *That is blue* is to think a determinate property. But there is a difference between color properties and indexical ones. The color *determinate* properties are specific: They are truly un*iversals*: they can have many instances. On the other hand, the indexical determinate properties are *particularized*: They can have only one instance.

5. Perceptual Reference and Vicarious Confrontational Reference

The presently existent divides up usefully between what exists in presence and what exists in absence. Presence and absence are relations between the thinker and her environment through the medium of actual thinking. What is presented is what the thinker thinkingly confronts, so to speak, *in propria persona*, in perception. Patently, the life-preserving and life-enhancing function of thinking is more effective the more useful ways an agent has of confronting what exists. At any rate, a perceptual experience just consists of a thinker confronting a field of demonstrative referents of a type characteristic of the modality of perception involved. The mechanisms of demonstrative reference are thus the tools with which an agent builds a map of his immediate environment. Perceptual maps are as ephemeral as it behooves the shifting environment. Being confrontational, perceptual maps involve somehow an *identification*, or not differentiation, between the represented and its representation: This convergence is the substance of presentation, and because of that, perceptual thinking may be said to be *iconic*. This is crucial for action. To change the environment intentionally is to place change-causing energy on the proper objects at the right places and times: Each of such objects must be thought of as the relevant *this* or *that* for action *here now*, or, in case causation can operate at a distance, *there then*.

By the principle of the hierarchical nature of reflexive thinking, a perceiver need not think that he is perceiving. If this reflexive thinking is not altogether within the power of the perceiver, we have what I have called an *Externus* type of thinker, thinking, and consciousness.[1] Some form of intentional agency is feasible to an Externus. Yet an agent cannot fully exert her causal powers intentionally — especially her powers for complex long-range plans with alternative contingency subplans — without thinking, or at least taking it for granted, that the causation involved is hers. This involves the agent presenting herself to herself somehow, not classificatorily, and certainly without the higher-order reflexive thinking that objectifies experiences as in the analysis of (3) above, as the subject of the currently occurring thinking episodes and as the agent who causes action by thinking volitionally. These roles must be represented as presented as such whatever else the agent may be.[2] This is precisely what first-person reference accomplishes. To refer to oneself as *I* is simply to refer confrontationally to those roles in presented thinking, whether this be merely contemplative of the passing show in the world or creative of changes in the history of that same world.

Thinking is a superb life-enhancing device because it bestows some vicarious presence to whatever is not available for confrontation. To think nonperceptually is to make something absent somehow present through a representation drastically different from what it represents. Because of this drastic difference, nonperceptual thinking is *symbolic*. Here for efficacious thinking we need, on one side, an adequate and rich symbolism. On the other side, we need repeatable properties, universals, through which we can identify the thought of an absent object with one confronted in experience; but we also need repeatable properties to secure the unitary topic of a train of thoughts about one and the same object; moreover, we need properties to differentiate the objects we think in absence. Hence, thinking in (perceptual) absence can reach its objects only if it segregates them from other objects by means of a set of uniquely possessed traits: *The (one and only one*) . . . is, as we saw in chapter 3, the fundamental form of the mechanism of singular nonperceptual reference.

By reflexive thinking over one's thinking episodes, one lives a confrontation, a second-order confrontation, with one's own states and acts. One can thus think of them demonstratively: *This thinking; this seeing*; . . . Now, episodes of thinking in absence are procedures, we have said, for imbuing absent objects with a vicarious presence. Thus, in the confrontation of one's own episodes of thinking, one has a vicarious confrontation of the absent objects thought of: One has in fact a genuine confrontation of their vicarious presence through and in the episodes of thinking subjected to reflexive thinking. Thus, one has a purely intellectual experience in which one demonstratively refers to what one is thinking. One thinks: "The man with a red hat I saw yesterday really disliked talking to the woman who stopped him. *This* [referring confrontationally to the vicariously present object in temporal closeness] was lost and wanted instructions to reach the Conference Center."

Meditation is a form of purely intellectual nonperceptual activity that creates domains of presentation, without having to be reflexive, hence, without having to involve self-consciousness. Each train of meditation creates its own *meditational demonstrative space*. To illustrate consider the case of Madame Curie, who used to while away her time during official dinners by engaging in mental mathematics. She had trains of formulas aligned in the space of her imagination. Consider one occasion, call it M, in which she thought a long train of thoughts, which included this fragment:

(F.M) . . . *this* won't do; perhaps *that* one will work . . . ,

where the tokens of the (French, or Polish) demonstratives she used referred presentationally to some mathematical truths she was then considering. Here the ordering distance thought of here depicted by the 'this'/'that' contrast is purely temporal. Thus, Madame Curie's meditational demonstrative space on occasion M may be equated with a temporal segment composed of selected moments of the time Tm of M. Hence, more perspicuously for us we can represent the fragment of her thinking on M as:

(F.Ma) . . . *This*$_{tm}$ won't do; perhaps *that*$_{tm}$ will work . . .

Many times our meditations are enhanced by our drawing diagrams to represent certain objects or conditions or suppositions. We map the ongoing thinking demonstrative space on a two-dimensional physical space, yet what matters is not the physicality of the map, but the visuality that accrues to the thinking space. If the physical substrate of the diagrams were to vanish, and we could maintain an inspectable enduring, or retrievable, mental picture, the function and nature of the three-dimensional thinking space-time could remain unaltered.

The crucial point is that in nonperceptual thinking, *we* confront successions of experiential spaces of different dimensions in which we have arrangements of *this*'s, *that*'s, *yonder*'s, *beyond*'s, and so on. Some of those demonstrative spaces have a perceptual basis, namely, the perceptual space containing symbolic representations of what one is thinking; but some demonstrative spaces are purely imaginational.

6. Storytelling: Staging the Story and Telling the Story Proper

Nonperceptual experience, as a form of experience, has its own demonstratives, and its context determining uniqueness of reference of definite descriptions. In brief, the discussion in chapter 3.4 applies to nonperceptual experience and its contextual space of reference. Consider a story reported by a gossiper:

(S.1) Socrates has a dog. *This* [dog] bit him very badly. . . .

In (S.1) the opening statement has the contextual force of: "Socrates has *one* certain dog (perhaps out of many other others), which is the dog hero of this part of the story." This is the contextual force, but it is not equivalent to this. The opening statement *executes* the function of introducing the characters of the story, without classifying or describing the performance. Since the uniqueness of the reference to the introduced characters is relative to the story itself, which is yet to be told, that uniqueness involves a *reflexive* aspect. This runs against the hierarchical nature of thinking discussed in chapter 3.3. Hence, the expressions used to introduce the characters of the story must peforce gain their uniqueness of reference *contextually*, pragmatically, by the brute force of the speech act itself. The semantics (as this belongs to the language system, in dialects or idiolects) is indetermined. The story introduction is a text that contains INSTRUCTIONS for *staging the story*. The instructions, abstractly considered, semantically, say indefinitely: "a chair, a woman, a dog, a house, a window, a tree. . . . " The execution of the instructions creates *one presented* chair, woman, dog, house, window, tree. . . .

Once the characters of the story have been introduced, that is, brought to presence, we can refer to them demonstratively. The story proper begins with demonstrative references. This is beautifully illustrated by (S.1). But the story can be told somewhat differently, with an *editorialized* setting, with the editorial comments separated by hyphens:

(S.2) Socrates has a dog—well, he actually has three dogs; in any case: — This dog bit him very badly. . . .

The annotation merely highlights the executive uniqueness of reference bestowed upon by the setting of the story.

Now consider a variant telling of the story:

(S.3) Socrates has a dog. It bit him so badly that . . .

The question here is: What type of pronoun is the 'It' beginning the story proper? This issue has been debated by several philosophers. Given the preceding discussion about stories and their stagings, we propose that this 'It' is a *demonstrative*:

a mere phonetic variant of the demonstrative 'This' of version (S.1). This contextually-executed uniqueness and demonstrative reference accounts for certain insights of Geach and Evans, for example, that the 'It' in (S.3) is referential and not a mere variable bound to the particular quantifier 'a dog'.[3]

7. Boër and Lycan's Waning Attack Against the Irreducibility of First-Person Reference

In a very ingenious and fruitful counterexample, Stephen E. Boër and William G. Lycan[4] have attacked my semantico-syntactic claim that:

(A) The first-person pronoun used indexically is not reducible to other mechanisms of reference.

This is just one thesis of the set of irreducibility theses argued for in the preceding sections and in earlier papers, particularly "Indicators and Quasi-indicators" (see chapter 12).

A consequence of (A) is this: Sentences with an indexical first-person pronoun express different propositions, different truths, or falsehoods, from those expressed by sentences with third-person expressions. Recall the Gaskon examples. This goes hand in hand with the thesis that the truth (or falsehood) expressed by the subordinate clause *he himself is in danger* in (7) below is different from the truth (or falsehood) expressed by any other subordinate clause in which the pronoun 'he himself' is replaced with a coreferring term, as in (8):

(7) Brother John believes that *he himself* is in danger.

(8) Brother John believes that Brother John is in danger.

Hence, thesis (A) is immediately complemented with this other thesis:

(B) Quasi-indicators depicting attributions to others of first-person reference are not strictly reducible to nonquasi-indicators.

In fact, in Chapter 12 ('Indicators and Quasi-indicators') the main argument for thesis (A) runs through thesis (B). For quasi-indicators see Chapter 5.

Now, Boër and Lycan preface their counterexample with a formal argument against (A). But as they point out, the argument is based on a premise they call A, which they acknowledge that (Kripke and) I reject in the way they interpret it. Hence, they correctly think that the argument is not conclusive, and assign greater significance to their counterexample. Clearly, any general argument is bound to have some premise I must reject. Thus, a formal proof of the error of the irreducibility thesis is not easily forthcoming. Nevertheless, the proposals of such proofs can be educational: They help make irreducibilists aware of other negative commitments packaged in the irreducibility theses (A)-(B).

Conversely, my arguments for the irreducibility theses have their own assumptions *within* my approach to the problems of indexical reference. Hence, I cannot refute a view that stubbornly shunts (A) and (B). My counterarguments would only help make explicit to the defenders of such a view some assumptions they cannot take for granted.[5]

Consequently, Boër and Lycan very meticulously proceed to offer an important datum. As they see it, that datum clashes with the irreducibility thesis. Thus, they see themselves as breaking up the opposition to their view and as paving the road to it with the resulting pieces. As I see it, the datum, which deserves careful exegesis, is not only *not* inimical to the Irreducibility Theses, but shows on scrutiny a certain complexity that requires some important distinctions, particularly, something I have already said in other contexts, namely: the distinction between the strict, narrow contents of thinking episodes and the rich doxastic contents of believingly thinking that something exists. The requisite distinctions are fully enthroned in *Guise Theory*. Thus, by being able to account nicely and snugly for the fruitful Boër-Lycan Datum, Guise Theory finds an unexpected corroboration, thus exhibiting thanks to them its fruitful mettle. The datum is the following counterexample, which must be reported in full:

> Now, we may also add positive strength to our case by calling attention to a type of situation different from Castañeda's paradigm, in which intuitions run squarely against the Irreducibility Thesis. Here is an example: Perry Mason has just been approached by a murder suspect, Larson E. Whipsnade. . . . The following dialogue ensues.
>
> MASON: Here are the police now. They will arrest you and ask a lot of questions.
> WHIPSNADE: Oh, God!
> MASON: Tell them that I am your lawyer. And refuse to answer any questions prior to the hearing.
> (Police enter.)
> LT. TRAGG: Good morning, counsellor.
>   (Turning.) You're under arrest, Whipsnade!
> WHIPSNADE (to Tragg): Mr. Mason here is my lawyer. And I won't answer any questions until the hearing.
>
> Mason has issued the order:
>
> (15) Tell them (the police) that I am your lawyer.
>
> Let us legalistically SUPPOSE that "Tell X that P" here means "Say to X a sentence which expresses PRECISELY the proposition that P." Now, in his declaration to Tragg, Whipsnade has told the police that Mason (that very person, etc.) is his lawyer. Thus Whipsnade has obeyed the unuttered command:
>
> (16) Tell the police that Mason (here) is your lawyer.
>
> But if the Irreducibility Thesis is correct, (16) is NOT EQUIVALENT to (15) as uttered by Mason, since Mason "May not know that he himself is Mason," and so on. And, according to Castañeda's view, Whipsnade has NOT OBEYED (15), since the PROPOSITION expressed by the first sen-

tence he uttered to Tragg is not the SAME PROPOSITION as that (if any) expressed by (15)'s complement. . . . But this is absurd. Surely Whipsnade CAN OBEY and *has* OBEYED Mason's order, in as strict a sense of "OBEY" as any non-partisan might care to invoke. So much the worse for the Irreducibility Thesis. ["Who, Me?", pp. 441f; my capitalization.]

Boër and Lycan proceed to refute some possible rejoinders they themselves ascribe to me. I agree with their retorts to those rejoinders. Their example is an excellent datum. It is *much more important* than a mere refutational counterexample: it is a NEW PARADOX OF REFERENCE. Its force lies on the following:

B-L's Datum

(a) There is in ordinary English a good usage of the relevant words to say that when Whipsnade tells Tragg:

(15c) Mr. Mason here is my lawyer.

Whipsnade is obeying Mason's command (15).

(b) Furthermore, there is a use of the words

"what — is the same as what . . . "

according to which it is correct to say that in such a case,

what Whipsnade told Tragg is THE SAME AS what Mason told him to tell Tragg.

This datum must be taken seriously by any theory of reference. I concede this immediately. Obviously, the nuclear force of B-L's Datum lies in (b). It is the use of the word 'same' that provides Boër and Lycan with their exhibited sense of crushing victory. Yet I think we should take things slowly, with full equanimity. Let us start with some methodological points.

Exegesis of the Boër-Lycan Datum

First, after Wittgenstein we should be wary of taking the ordinary occurrences of the word 'same' as semantically crystal-clear. Recall Wittgenstein's remark: "When it is 5 o'clock on the earth it is the same time on the sun." Sameness is such an abstract and structural term that it cannot be used without previous satisfactory specification of sameness criteria — unless it is used in a datum deploying a sort of paradox to be exegesized for hints for an array of solutions. And this is precisely the best interpretation I can put on Boër and Lycan's alleged counterexample: not so much a *counter*example, but an example that cries out for an account of the sameness asserted in (b).

Second, but the sameness claim is puzzling just because it sits on pedestal of enormous DIFFERENCES: (i) as Boëer and Lycan themselves carefully note, Mason quite definitely uttered command (15), but left command (16) unuttered; (ii) the proposition that Whipsnade uttered (15c) *Mr. Mason here is my lawyer* implies semantically (M) *Some (called) Mason is my lawyer*, whereas what Mason commanded Whipsnade to say — *that I am your lawyer* — does not imply (M) (at this juncture the discussion of proper names in chapter 2 becomes relevant, and expands on this difference); (iii) Whipsnade's obeying Mason's command by uttering statement (15c) implies that the commander's name is Mason, yet this may come as a surprise to Mason, who may have temporarily forgotten his name; (iv) Mason did *not* command Whipsnade to use the name 'Mason', yet he did, going, apparently, *beyond* what Mason commanded him to do. Etc. Well, then there is a difference between the two commands, and by (ii) a difference in implications between the propositions involved in them, so by Leibniz's law they are different. *Ergo*, the counterexample fails.

Third, refutation, or refutation of refutations, should not be our concern. We must gain philosophical insight. As often in philosophy (see, for example, Frege's Morning Star/Evening Star, or the Oedipan sieves in chapters 13–14), whenever we have a conceptual tension we can always put it as a tension between a sameness and a difference. Recall how Frege's Sense/Reference Theory catered to the difference between the morning and the evening stars by postulating different senses, and to the sameness between as the identity of the one referent that realize those senses. As we shall see (chapters 13–14), the novelty of Guise Theory lies in taking the sameness and the difference in tension at face value and enthroning different individual guises (analogous to Frege's senses) linked by different kinds of sameness relations, thus throwing Frege's first referents out of the semantic connection.

The Boër-Lycan example is a typical conceptual puzzle: On the one hand, we have the SAMENESS postulated by B-L(b); on the other, we have the enormous differences noted above. We face, therefore, a philosophical conceptual puzzle: a tension between a sameness and a difference. Obviously, the puzzle by itself *cannot* refute any theory. Hence, the Irreducibility Thesis could not conceivably be worse off merely because of this puzzle.

Fourth, the Irreducibility Thesis seems to Boër and Lycan to be worse off after their example only because of the assumptions they make about it. They want to press the sameness we find, and some persons assert in ordinary language. Yet the example of its own force exerts no pressure either way, but shows a tension crying out for resolution.

Fifth, Boër and Lycan are among the most brilliant philosophers now avidly writing, and they realize that their example leaves things exactly as they are. They, in spite of some strong statements along the way culminate their discussion with the more modest claim of a kind of impasse:

> So perhaps our Perry Mason argument begs the question against Castañeda in an extended sense of that term. But [B-L] we take the argument to show that the Irreducibility Thesis' plausible consequences for Castañeda's amnesiac cases and mirror cases are offset as least to some degree by its crassly implausible consequences for other cases. ["Who, Me?", p. 443; my bracketed labeling.]

Given my commitment to the nonrefutability of philosophical approaches and to philosophical pluralism, Boër and Lycan's modest claim of a stalemate is not entirely disagreeable to me. Philosophical stalemates are the normal philosophical state of affairs, and they represent the clash of different underlying presuppositions, it being *wholly open* which ones should be given up in the pursuit of a comprehensive theory.

Sixth, I must register a caveat. Their declaration that Castañeda's Irreducibility Thesis has "crassly implausible consequences" in the Perry Mason-Whipsnade is, as noted, too rash. More important their polemical plan has prevented them from seeing the magnificent force of the B-L Datum: a *new* paradox of reference.

Seventh, Boër and Lycan have found a "paradox" as significant as the one that led Frege to his Sense/Referent View. It requires the development of a theory of sameness. Hence, the problem is unsolved, and the Irreducibility Theorist has an open field as to what to do with this new paradox. Thus, Boër and Lycan were rather premature in suggesting that the said sameness between orders (15) and (16) will overwhelm the Irreducibility theorists.

Eighth, we need a theory that resolves the tension between the sameness established by B-L(b) and the difference between the two commands (15) and (16), the former being uttered, the latter remaining unuttered. Undoubtedly, one theory is to take the sameness to be that of one proposition—in the way in which Frege postulated one common referent for the expressions 'the Morning Star' and 'the Evening Star'— then postulate some other difference between commands (15) and (16). I have no objection to such a theory. Indeed, I urge the interested parties to develop it. I want to insist, however, that so far we have here too small a theory to worry about it by itself. We must consider comprehensive theories that embed it and then compare the resulting embedding theory in richness of data catered to, elucidatory powers, simplicity, and so on, with Guise Theory.

Another approach, the one adopted by Guise Theory, is to continue using the word 'proposition' in its primary use in the traditional sense as referring to the *internal* accusatives of mental episodes, as the truths, or falsehoods, that appear so to speak in person to a thinker, the ones he can represent with his conceptual resources. In this sense, clearly the fact that command (15) was uttered, but (16) wasn't, and the additional implicational and other noted differences, reveal that we are confronting the very representational resources at Mason's *own disposal*: the nature of the accusatives of his thinking episodes. So far, here are both a terminological stipulation as to how to use the word 'proposition', and a theoretical decision to account for the sameness of the B-L Datum in terms of Mason's and Whipsnade's conceptual or representational equipment narrowly understood. In any case, we must say that *just as commands (15) and (16) are different, so are the corresponding propositions*, the one Mason presented to Whipsnade by saying *I am your lawyer* and the one Whipsnade asserted to Tragg by saying *Mr. Mason here is my lawyer*.

Then we must account for the sameness posited by B-L(b) in some other way. To resolve this problem we must concentrate on the the concept of sameness, and keeping fast in mind that in different types of discourse we need different criteria of sameness, investigate our uses of the word 'same' in other contexts in order to gain a useful perspective to judge B-L(b). This way we can propose a fruitful solution.

A Cursory Look at the Background of Sameness Claims

(a) John is standing on a chair looking through an upper window, whereas Mary is scrubbing the floor and sometimes looks through a lower window under the one John looks through. A man passes by. John sees a head; Mary sees a pair of shoes and the end of a pair of legs. Yet they see the SAME man. Do they see the same thing? Yes, of course: They saw the same man. No, indeed, one saw a head, the other legs.

(b) Christopher and Martin were pushing the SAME car—but one was pushing the right side of the back bumper, the other was pushing the left side. Were they pushing the SAME thing?

(c) Paul and Charlotte kicked Anthony, the SAME Anthony, she on his buttocks, he on his shoulders. Was what one kicked the SAME as what the other kicked? (See B-L(b) above.)

(d) Mr. Brown pays a debt to the Whites by paying the money to Mrs. White; and Mrs. Black pays a similar debt to the Whites by paying Mr. White. Did they pay the SAME payee?

To sum up, very frequently X does some action A to an entity Y by doing A to a part of Y, to a representative of Y, to a member of Y, or to some other entity having the appropriate representational relation toward Y. *Synecdoche is a fundamental form of life*: It possesses a tremendous pragmatic value, thanks to its encompassing information at the convergence of classes of entities.

A Glimpse into the Guise-Theoretical Solution to the Fruitful New Boër-Lycan Paradox of Reference

The question we must ask is, therefore, whether, even though commands (15) and (16) are different, there is an entity to which they are related in an intimate way, so that in a broader, typical sense of 'same' to perform certain speech acts on (15) is the same as performing the SAME acts on (16). The answer is ready at hand: For the purposes of action in the world, as contrasted with actions as conceived either in rehearsals of belief or in rehearsals of intention, we generally do *not* care about intensional distinctions, that is, the precise propositions that are the *de dicto* contents of the mental states. In such cases, we *are* interested in the *de re* targets of the mental states or acts. Then coreferring expressions, though denoting different Fregean individual senses (which are akin to Castañeda's individual guises), pick out the SAME Fregean referent (or the SAME unspecified system of guises to which they belong). Here 'coreferring' means referring to items that are said to be empirically and contingently the same (in Guise Theory, consubstantiated). Hence, all those propositions expressed with sentences that differ in having coreferring terms form one system of *broadly* equivalent propositions, in this sense: They are either logically equivalent or materially equivalent, but in any case structurally isomorphic. Two propositions P and Q are structurally isomorphic if: P is canonically expressed by a sentence S, Q by a sentence S', and S' is obtainable from S, and vice versa by the replacement of one or more occurrences of coreferring terms. Let us here call a system of broadly equivalent propositions a *message*. The same applies to commands. As Boër and Lycan tell us, Mason's command (15) is different from command (16); yet they are materially equivalent and structurally isomorphic and are therefore broadly equivalent, and belong (or constitute) the SAME *command-message*.

Clearly, whenever we are interested in the *de dicto* content, or the literal accusative, of a person's thinking episode, that accusative is a proposition, or a command, and this proposition or command may be said to *represent* the message to which it belongs. In those cases in which it does not matter what exactly the internal accusatives of a person's thinking episodes are, we can speak of the messages of those thinking episodes as their targets. In such cases we communicate the SAME propositional messages, and obey the SAME command-messages.

What I am here calling a *message* is what I have called PROPOSITIONS or STATES OF AFFAIRS (*sic*, with capitals all through). They are systems of what I have called *propositional guises* that are broadly equivalent. Systems of propositional guises that are just logically equivalent or analytic correspond to standard *propositions*. This threefold distinction is crucial to Guise Theory and solves in a unified way a series of related problems, of sameness and difference, for instance, the paradox of analysis, the analytic growth of perceptual discrimination by attention, the *de re* phenomenon of extensional communication.[6]

In conclusion, the Boër-Lycan Paradox of reference is a valuable unexpected test of Guise Theory, and it is satisfying to see that it passes the test with flying colors (see chapters 13–14).

The Irreducibility of the Second Person

It is most revealing, even ironic, and of course, a crucial additional datum, which I will call Boër and Lycan's datum (C), that they terminate their paper with the only appropriate answer to the *dialogical* question in the title of their essay:

> But for now it seems to us that the *most reasonable answer* to the skeptical "Who, me?" is "Yes; you." ["Who, Me?", p. 463; my italics.]

The answer to the skeptical dialogical "Who, me?" is, of course, as they say: "Yes, you." It is NOT "Yes, Mason (Lycan, Boër, Wilfrid Sellars, Frederic Chopin, the author of *Self-Knowledge and Self-Identity*, or even *that man*)." The representational mechanisms of what is being referred to require the second person, which, of course, is the subject matter of another irreducibility thesis about indexical reference (see thesis Y* in section 2 above). We face the problem of sameness and difference once again. The answer "Yes, Lycan" is different, because, as they say, it is not the most reasonable, yet it should be the *same* as the most reasonable answer "Yes, you" that Lycan's interlocutor has to give. The problem is, of course, aggravated, because the 'you' seems ineliminable.

To be sure, in a monologue the most reasonable answer to "Who, me?" is "Yes, me (I)," NOT any of the third-person answers. Thus, we have moved full circle: We are exactly where we began—but wiser.[7]

8. Interim Conclusion

Indexical reference is, therefore, the backbone of perceptual reference. Hence the final theory of indexical reference and the ultimate account of the semantics of indicators are to be found in a theory of perception. We try our hand at this comprehensive theory elsewhere (see note 5), but see chapter 6.

Notes

1. For the first time in "On Knowing (or Believing) That One Knows (or Believes)," *Synthese* 21 (1970): 187–203. Externus types of consciousness are perhaps illustrated by animals—as David Schwayder has urged. The concept was already applied to human development in "Consciousness and Behavior: Their Basic Connections," in Hector-Neri Castañeda, ed., *Intentionality, Minds, and Perception* (Detroit: Wayne State University Press, 1967).

2. The production of intentional action is a complex causal matter. The basic case of action at will involves an internal causation in this sense: A thinking involved in the causation of an event that counts as the thinker's performing action A is a thinking of a practical content of the indexical form *I to A here now*. For details see Hector-Neri Castañeda, *Thinking and Doing*, (Dordrecht: Reidel, 1975, chap. 10, sect. 3, "Intentional Actions, Conditional Intentions, and Aristotelian Practical Syllogisms"); *Erkenntnis* 18 (1982): 239–60; and "Reply to Michael Bratman: Deontic Truth, Intentions, and Weakness of the Will" in James E. Tomberlin, ed., *Agent, Language, and the Structure of the World* (Indianapolis: Hackett, 1983). A brief account appears in chap. 7 here.

3. P. T. Geach, *Reference and Generality* (Ithaca, N.Y.: Cornell University Press, 1962), and Gareth Evans, "Pronouns, Quantifiers, and Relative Clauses," *Canadian Journal of Philosophy* 17 (1977): 4670–536.

4. Stephen Boër and William Lycan "Who, Me?" *The Philosophical Review* 89 (1980): 427–66.

5. As argued both in *On Philosophical Method* (Bloomington, Ind.: Nous Publications, 1980) and in "Philosophical Refutations," in James H. Fetzer, ed., *Principles of Philosophical Reasoning* (Totowa, N.J.: Rowman and Allanheld, 1984), there are neither refutations across theories nor genuine refutations of philosophical approaches. Thus, we need all theories. Hence, I am particularly anxious to see their theory developed fully, all the way to all the data for which Guise Theory has been propounded. That larger theory is the one I want to compare with Guise Theory (including its accounts of indexical properties and indexical and quasi-indexical reference; see 'Perception, Belief, and the Structure of Physical Objects and Consciousness," *Synthese* 35 (1977): 285–351, and chaps. 6–7, 13–14 here), which is an abridgement of *Sprache und Erfahrung*, translated by Helmut Pape (Frankfurt: Suhrkamp, 1982), Part 4, pp. 397–497.

6. See "Perception, Belief, and the Structure of Physical Objects and Consciousness."

7. Boër and Lycan have recently come to acknowledge an important linguistic irreducibility of first-person reference, in Stephen E. Boër and William G. Lycan, *Knowing Who* (Cambridge, Mass.: MIT Press, 1986). I am delighted with this development, and my delight is not marred by some reservations about their view of self-reference. See "Boër and Lycan's Sellarsian-Davidsonian account of the Quasi-indicator 'He Himself' of Degree One," appendix to "Self-consciousness, Demonstrative Reference, and the Self-ascription View of Believing," in James E. Tomberlin, ed., *Philosophical Perspectives* 1 (1987): 405–54. For complementary discussion of these issues, see Tomberlin, "Critical Review of Myles Brand's *Intending and Acting*," *Noûs* 21 (1987): 45–55, and Tomberlin, "Semantics, Psychological Attitudes, and Conceptual Role," *Philosophical Studies* (forthcoming)

5

Attributing Reference to Others: The Language of Other Minds

1. Attribution of Thought Content: Cumulation of References and Propositional Transparency

We have been discussing the making of reference by a (mature) speaker of English, that is, a thinker who thinks in English, whether speaking or not, whether conversing or not. In dialogue we have the actual references that each interlocutor apprehends. These are also thinking references; the hearer's references differ from the speaker's references in their causation. Furthermore, a hearer, especially in the case of a dialogue in which he sees himself as the target of a seduction or sale, attributes to the speaker both expressed and unexpressed references. But a dialogue can proceed without the attribution of references to the other interlocutors. One can be caused to express one's thoughts by the apprehensions of other thoughts as interpretations of the other persons' utterances and behavior, without intervening or accompanying attributions of thoughts to them. (Recall the hierarchical nature of reflective thinking discussed in chapter 3.) Yet the highest forms of communication involve attributions of thoughts and references to the other parties at the dialogue, indeed even to persons not involved in the dialogue. All these cases occur within varying doxastic and purposive presuppositions. For the time being, however, we focus on the general phenomenon of attribution of (mature speaker's) thinking reference.

Attributed references need not be involved in dialogue. Indeed important attributions are not of references, but of propensities or powers to refer. When we attribute belief or intention to a person, we are not attributing actual references, but merely potential references, namely, those the person in question would make were she to rehearse internally her belief or intention, or were she to express, or communicate, her belief or intention. In contrast, when we report speech acts or thinking episodes, we refer to actual references made by the speaker-thinker.

The attribution of thoughts to others need not involve the attribution of the power to communicate in a dialogue. It presupposes, however, that the others and we share causal structures within which we believe we can cause the others to have the thoughts we attribute to them.

Attributions of references to others are part and parcel of our attributions to those others of speech acts or thinking episodes, anchored to such references. Likewise, attributions of powers to refer are included in, as central components of, attributions of dispositional mental states, for example, believing, taking it for granted, intending, having a purpose or a plan. All these types of attribution presuppose that *we share one and the same world*. Sharing exactly the same experiences, that is, sharing numerically the very same particular contents or even the same types of experience, does not seem required. (Just a trivial example to fix the idea: We converse with others about the colors of objects, without in the least being concerned with whether they are color-blind, much less whether they see objects under a reversed spectrum, not to mention more drastic changes in perceptual content.) Nevertheless, those others and we must have experiences that have at least the same structural relationships to the shared outer world. These structural relationships place us in relation to one another in the same one world.[1]

In brief, when I attribute to a person P a (real or potential) reference to an object O, the following obtains:

(i) I intimate that O is an object in the world P and I share, or an entity in a shared domain of thinkables;

(ii) I claim that we both have access to O;

(iii) I attribute to P the power — perhaps even the exercise of it as when I attribute to P a speech act — to refer in some way to O,

(iv) which I may reveal in the case of direct quotation or may represent or allude to in the case of indirect speech;

(v) I am myself referring, in my very act of attribution, to O,

(vi) thereby expressing the *convergence* of P's attributed reference to O with mine,

(vii) it being immaterial whether P knows this or not;

(viii) if there is uncertainty as to the way P refers to O, or there is no need to reveal it, I simply allude to it and reveal my posited convergency with my own;

(ix) if there is a disagreement about the existence of O, I may note it;

(x) since no mental state or act is an island unto itself, but is fused with the rest of the person's mental powers, in my attribution I quietly point to my assumption of a background of a larger convergence of potential references, which encapsulates a shared background of beliefs and purposes.

In brief, to attribute to another person references to real objects is to represent, on some assumptions of convergency of references to objects in the shared world or in a shared domain of thinkables, one fragment of that other's view of the world in one's own terms, as *part of one's world or of an extension thereof.* Of course, one can attribute to some persons attributions of references to yet other persons, and so on. These references represent from the speaker's point of view an inter-locking of partial pictures of the world in something like a *set of Chinese boxes.* Yet the crucial point is twofold: the ontological presupposition of sharing the world and the epistemic claim that references converge. In chains of attributions there is a claim of cumulative convergencies.

The perfect case of attribution of thoughts or beliefs to others is that in which the attribution-making statement (and sentence) *exhibits* EXACTLY the other's thought or belief content, or the other's mechanism of doxastic representation. This includes not only the exhibition of the convergence of the speaker's reference with her attributions of (actual or potential) references to the persons she is speak-ing of, but also the revelation of the properties and relations these other persons think. Let us for mere convenience call the content of belief *proposition* (leaving it entirely open whether propositions are to be equated with classes of sentences or linguistic roles or patterns of representational brain or computer events).[2] Thus, the archetypical case of attribution of belief (and related cognitive states) may be said to be *fully propositionally transparent.* But as we shall see, proposi-tional transparency allows of degrees.

Concerning singular reference, propositional transparency is the revelation of how the persons talked about refer to the objects the speaker mentions. One spe-cially perspicuous case is that in which a speaker's attribution of a mental state or act to another reveals the identity between the ways the speaker and the other refer to the same objects. Obviously, propositional transparency allows of many different degrees in the case of attributions of attributions of . . . references, where propositional opacity can creep in at so many different junctures. To illus-trate consider a statement made by an assertive utterance of the following sentence:

(1) Anthony believes that his wife said that the President of the United States holds that the Secretary of State claims that the King of Spain is a cunning statesman.

The ordinary *semantics* of this sentence allows it to have many different interpre-tations. On the most interesting one, given the contextual assumption that the speaker is using language candidly, and is talking about contemporary persons, the sentence is most propositionally transparent, revealing how each person talked about refers to the objects and persons mentioned. On this interpretation there is a maximal convergency of reference among the references attributed to the persons mentioned in the order they are mentioned, and the speaker's refer-ences. The appropriate *syntax* for this interpretation is the *Chinese-Box sentence form,* that is, in which every subordinate clause lies fully in the scope of the preceding psychological verb, as follows:

(1.a) Anthony believes that {his wife said that [the President of the United States holds that (the Secretary of State claims that/the King of Spain is a cunning statesman/)]}.

We shall say that each expression in indirect speech *occurs internally* or has *internal construal* in each bracketed subsentence as well as in the whole sentence (1). In particular, then, each singular term occurs in (1) internally. Hence, each term represents not only a mechanism of reference attributed to each of the persons mentioned before it, but also the *cumulation* of exact convergences of all those persons' references with the speaker's own. For example, parts of the network of referential convergencies are:

(a) speaker's reference to the King of Spain, that is, speaker's exercise of the mechanism of reference in his idiolect, consisting of his possessing the expression 'the King of Spain';

(b) speaker's attribution of that very mechanism to Anthony, to his wife, to the President of the United States, and to the Secretary of State;

(c) speaker's attribution to Anthony of the attribution of such a mechanism to his wife's attribution of it to the President of the United States.

In general, if a sentence S has n psychological or linguistic verbs whose scopes are fully nested, that is, verbs that occur internally, in the Chinese-Box grammar, in all the subordinate clauses in which they appear, there are in S 2^n levels of attribution cumulation. Each expression occurring internally in the innermost subordinate clause can represent a cumulation of $n+1$ referential levels, the speaker's references being of the first level.

Referential cumulation is a most important phenomenon. It is the foundation of human communities and institutions: the whole of human life pivots on it. On one side, it is the backbone of our ability intellectually to share a common world; on the other side, it is the key mechanism for entering into other persons' minds and representing to ourselves the thought contents of those minds. Referential cumulation underlies the flow of thoughts illustrated in the linguistic movement from indirect speech to direct speech, for instance in:

(E.1) Columbus believed that Queen Isabella was the dominant figure in the Spanish politics during the 1490s; but *she* was not, however, all that powerful.

There is a referential cumulation at 'Queen Isabella': The speaker uses the term both to make her own reference and to attribute a potential reference to Columbus. She then proceeds, correctly, to disentangle her own reference maintaining a cross-reference by means of the anaphoric pronoun 'she'. In general:

(Ref-Cum. An) The referential cumulation of a so-called de dicto term T, that is, with internal construal within a psychological sentence of the form X *E's that* (. . . $T-$), grounds the use of an anaphoric pronoun that cross-refers to T with external construal with respect to the psychological prefix '*X E's that*', thus: *X E's that* (. . . *T*–), . . . *he* (*she, it*).

Clearly, even when the person one talks about has (for us) absurd beliefs about nonexisting entities, we must extend at least temporarily our world with those entities in order to accurately represent their beliefs. Accurate representation is best accomplished by attaining the maximally feasible propositional transparency, that is, by depicting those beliefs in internal, or de dicto, construal. Because of the cumulative character of internal construal, the speaker is thus positing those nonexistents in an outer ring demarcated by the attribution of thought content to that absurd believer. The speaker is of course free to extract his own referential strand from that cumulation. He may do so and draw a boundary to what really exists in his world. This illustrated by this example:

(E.2) Jason believes that THE WITCH who attacked A BLUE DRAGON is a friendly one. But, of course, *that witch* and *that dragon* do not exist; in fact, neither witches nor dragons exist.

In (E.2) we have not only an illustration of the disentanglement of the speaker's reference from a referential cumulation. We have also an illustration – in the case of the indeterminate reference to "*a* blue dragon"– of the staging/story-telling phenomenon discussed above in Chapter 4, section 6. The subordinate clause in indirect speech functions as the stage setting for the introduction of the character that acts in the narrator's story. This explains why the speaker's reference-disentangling anaphoric pronouns occur after the reference-cumulation point.

(E.2) illustrates an interesting phenomenon: we must disentangle for *our* personal reference those absurd entities others believe to exist in order to deny existence to them. Apparently, then, we must refer not only to the nonexistents we believe, but *also* to the nonexistents others and only they believe in. This seems to be the price we must pay for sharing our minds. This strongly suggests that the ontology we can think about, which underlies the semantics of the means of thinking, is broader than the ontology of our beliefs. We can be strict and narrow-minded about our *doxastic ontology*, but we must be broad-minded and tolerant about our *thinkable ontology*. This contrast should be elucidated by the theory of semantics and pragmatics of thinking we must eventually construct.

We are not, however, always able to enter fully into another person's mind. Nor do we need to. Often we are just interested in the changes in the shared world other persons can bring about. In those cases we are not concerned with propositional transparency, but with convergence of references, and we settle for propositional opacity. Let us make this contrast more precise.

Let E be a particular occurrence of an expression in a discourse text T, which may very well be just a sentence. We call *candid use of T* a use by which a person who, conforming to the semantic-syntactic rules governing T in a language to which that use of T belongs and conforming to the pragmatic rules that apply to that use of T in the speech context, merely uses T to think the syntactico-semantico-pragmatic denotation of T in that context. (See (T-S.C*), the Fundamental Desideratum about the Thinking-Semantic Connection, in chapter 1.3.) We say that a *competent interpreter of T* is a person who has mastered the syntactico-semantic rules of the language to which the speaker's utterance of T belongs, as well as the pragmatic rules governing the application of utterances of T as of that language to speech contexts like the one in which the speaker uses T. Now, consider a candid use C(T) of T, and let tE be the token of E in C. *Token tE occurs with degree 1 of propositional transparency in C(T)*, if and only if: tE occurs in T in direct speech and a competent interpreter of T, on the assumption that C(T) is a candid use of T, has the linguistic know-how to ascertain, and hence think him/herself, what the speaker of C(T) has thought with tE. *Token tE occurs with degree N of propositional transparency in C(T)*, if and only: tE occurs in T in the scope of M psychological verbs, and a competent interpreter of T, on the assumption that C(T) is a candid use of T, and knowing the scope patterns of T intended by the speaker, has the linguistic and pragmatic knowledge to produce a correct Chinese-Box interpretation of C(T) in which tE occurs in the scope of N-1 psychological verbs, where M $\geq$ N−1.

We shall say that a token tE of an expression E occurs *propositionally opaquely* in a token C(T) of a text T, if and only if tE occurs in C(T) but has no degree of propositional transparency.

As noted briefly in Chapter 1, there are abundant and powerful reasons for distinguishing the accusatives of contemplative and theoretical thinking, that is, propositions, from the accusatives of practical thinking, for example, commanding, requesting, wanting, intending, planning, which have been called *practitions*. Thus, there is a parallel concept of *practitional transparency* and its degrees. Reference is the same in both propositional and practitional thinking.

2. Attribution of Reference: Internal/External Construal of Terms, and Propositional Transparency

Patently, an expression that has internal construal in a psychological sentence occurs with an appropriate degree of propositional transparency. But not all expressions in indirect speech have internal construal. This is an important feature that allows natural English to be more flexible in its applications. Many times we do not need to know or consider exactly how a person refers to certain objects: We do not need to know the exact contents of his or her mental state. Often on such occasions we are exclusively concerned with a person's conduct, and what matters is that the person we talk about acts on certain objects, regardless of how she refers to them. To illustrate consider the following example originated with Roderick Chisholm:

(2) Columbus believed that Castro's island was China.

Clearly, this sentence is ambiguous in many ways. Here we are interested in just one dimension of ambiguity, namely, the semantico-syntactic ambiguity of the logical scope of the term *Castro's island*: We can construe this term in (2) internally or externally, as follows:

(2.A) *Internal construal (Chinese-Box construal)*:
Columbus believed that [Castro's island was China];

(2.B) *External construal*:
Castro's island: Columbus believed that [it was China]

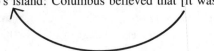

Interpretation (2.A) is anachronistic. It attributes to Columbus possession of the mechanism of reference *Castro's island*, which the speaker certainly possesses and is exercising, but it is utterly doubtful that Columbus had. Nonetheless, a person who believes in Columbus's premonitory prowess may want precisely to assert (2.A). Be this as it may, it is interpretation (2.B) that is most likely to be intended by any contemporary speaker. Its key features are these:

(i) In (2.B) the term 'Castro's island' does *not* represent a referential cumulation point, but simply expresses just speaker's reference; the term really belongs outside the indirect speech clause as indicated.

(ii) Yet the term 'Castro's island' plays in (2.B) an important semiotic role by occurring in indirect speech, namely: It *signals* the convergence, claimed by the speaker, between his own use of 'Castro's island' and some possible, or real, uses of *unspecified* mechanisms of reference available to Columbus at 'it'.

Important Elucidation. In describing (ii) I am deliberately avoiding the use of my own expressions, for example, 'Cuba', 'Jose Marti's country', or 'the country of the poet who composed *La Niña de Guatemala*', so as not to intrude my points of referential convergence. Other philosophers would, however, be happy describing (ii) with a very *special*, but mysterious, use of the proper name 'Cuba'. Such philosophers would say something like this:

(ii.DR) The speaker uses 'Castro's island' to refer to Cuba and attributes to Columbus the use of unspecified terms available to him to refer to Cuba.

The use of the name 'Cuba' is here special in that the philosopher who propounds (ii.DR) suggests that he is NOT intruding his own way of referring to what the speaker refers as "Castro's island," but offering, instead, a neutral, objective and interpersonal description of the semantics and syntax of sentence (2B). Clearly, (ii.DR) is much stronger than, and implies, (ii). The alleged objectivity of 'Cuba' grounds the convergency of the speaker's explicit reference and Columbus's unspecified one. Yet it is a mystery how the proper name 'Cuba' (or any other name) can function like that. In chapter 2 we studied how proper names function in experience, so we need say no more here.

The moral is that there are NO neutral, objective, interpersonal references as implied by (ii.DR). All references are made and conceived from a point of view.[3] The suggested neutrality of the name 'Cuba' in (ii.DR) is fictitious: (ii.DR), rather than being a neutral description of what happens in (2.B), is a positional description in which the philosopher proposing it intrudes his own reference and posits the additional convergence between his use of 'Cuba' and the use of 'Castro's island' by the unknown speaker of (2.B). (See chapter 2 for the personal and perspectival dimension of the use of proper names.)

A crucial point concerning communication is this: Singular terms in external construal introduce some degree of *propositional opacity*. In the case of (2.B) we are NOT told how Columbus referred to what the speaker calls "Castro's island." Thus, external construal does not only represent a point of scope ambiguity, but it is *communicationally unperspicuous*. The unperspicuity is necessary, the ambiguity isn't. In fact, English has the proper devices to express propositional opacity without ambiguity by means of the locutions 'believe of' and 'believe about'. Thus, interpretation (2.B) of sentence (2) may be paraphrased less equivocally as follows:

(3) Columbus believed *of* (*about*) Castro's island that it was China.

3. De Re/de Dicto Occurrences of Terms, and Apparent References to Nonexistents

It is customary to describe the contrast between the internal construal (2.A) and the external construal (2.B), or, equivalently, the perspicuous (3) by saying that in (2.A) the term 'Castro's island' occurs *de dicto*, whereas in (3) and (2.B) it occurs *de re*. The Latin terms contrast a *dictum* (sentence, statement) with a *real* thing. The customary Latin-formulated contrast overlaps with our internal/external construal contrast. The expressions that occur *de dicto* reveal how the person talked about refers to an object, what he or she *says*—modulo translation into other languages. We may very well adopt the 'believe *of*' formulation as a canonical way of making perspicuous which expressions have external construal: Then we may speak of the *of*-components of a belief attribution.

However, the customary *de dicto/de re* contrast differs from our pragmatico-semantico-syntactic contrast between internal and external construals. As urged by the Latin terminology, many philosophers interpret the *de re* or *of*-elements of a belief sentence as denoting existents. In the case of (3) this is undoubtedly correct. Any speaker who proffers (3), or the externally construed (2), assertively claims that Castro's island exists. Notwithstanding, even here our internal/external construal contrast differs. It is neutral with respect to this semantic or ontic claim of existence: This must be *added* to the contrast by the speaker's meaning intention tacitly or contextually or explicitly by the utterance of an appropriate locution. Thus, our pragmatico-semantico-syntactic interpretive contrast does *not* rule out as meaningless sentences like these:

(4) Prof. Irving and Dr. Solera believe *of* Don Quijote many different things, which most contemporary Cervantes experts do not, but the early readers of *Don Quijote* attributed to him.

(5) Mark Shpastin is a fictitious spy invented by the CIA to confuse the KGB, but most Americans know nothing *of* him and what some highly placed CIA agents believe *about* him is staggering, for example, that he is a philosopher at Arizona State educated at Pittsburgh and Harvard who has taught in Detroit, Bloomington, Indiana, and Tucson.

These sentences not merely feel meaningful: They may even be used to express significant truths.

Terms with external construal, we have seen, express speaker's reference without cumulative attribution of reference; this is a most important pragmatico-syntactic role, and it can be put to a very good use in diverse types of experience—provided that it is not indissolubly married to the additional role of packaging the speaker's existential claim. In other words, a comprehensive account of experience as this is lived through the use of language, requires a recognition of the distinctness and separability of those two roles. In example (4) we have a statement of a type needed for the experience of literary criticism, not to mention the literary experience itself. We must not deny to literary critics the use of externally construed expressions when they compare the views and aesthetic judgments of literary critics, without having to commit themselves to the existence of literary heroes. Similarly, literary commentators or critics often speak *of* literary characters outside their original stories, and assess their changes across their migrations into different stories or novels, or even their flight into different art forms, as when Don Quijote appeared in Avellaneda's novel, and when he migrated to opera and to sculpture.

Example (5) illustrates another basic form of experience where our uses of language exhibit a divorce of external-construal syntax from existential *de re* semantics. Evidently, the sort of experience captured in (5) is typical of our mixed dealings with reality and irreality. Dealings with mixtures of existence and nonexistence are of the greatest importance in life, not only as in the sociopolitical case depicted in (5), but also in our daily pursuit of plans in which many of our intentions to build objects and produce events are unsuccessful. To live biographically, not merely biologically, is to transact with nonexistents.

Consequently, it is more realistic to acknowledge that expressions in internal construal, like 'Castro's island' in (2.A), do not express an existential commitment on the speaker's part.

The fundamental reason why an existentially noncommittal understanding of the *of*-elements of attributions of reference is more useful and explanatory is this: A speaker's views of what exist may differ from those of the person she speaks of. One type of case is not problematic: The speaker does, but the person spoken of does not, believe that an entity E exists. Here the speaker may use his terms to refer to E with existential import. But in another type of case the speaker believes that an entity S does not exist and several persons she speaks of believe that S exists. Here too the speaker must be able to think of a convergence of their references, or purported references, if you wish, to S; but she must think of her nonexisting S somehow in order to depict the convergence of the others' (purported) references with her (purported) reference. Clearly, the easiest way is for the speaker to think of the entity S as an *of*-element lacking existential import.

The convergence of references, or purported references, is of the essence of attribution of thoughts (beliefs and intentions) to others. These attributions are built on the common foci in the shared world. Being a focus of reference, or purported reference (if you still wish to hold on to the terminological decision to use 'refer' with existential import), is the fundamental phenomenon of thinking – and of the semantics of the language used to think. The convergence of foci is what the standard uses of the ordinary locutions 'believe of (about, concerning)' seem to have been assigned to represent. (Of course, we can stipulate that 'of' always has existential import, and allow 'about' the flexible generic use. Then the basic data in [purported] attributions of reference lies in the *about*-elements.)

Sometimes the *de re/de dicto* distinction is formulated as the distinction between a term's occurring and its not occurring in a context in a position that can be reached by a quantifier governing the whole context. This syntactico-semantic claim is obviously different from our syntactico-pragmatic characterization of external construal as expressing speaker's reference. Whether they overlap or not depends on the domains of the quantifiers the speaker uses. For instance, on the *existential* use of the words 'there is' or 'there is a person' no one holding (5) should go on to derive:

(6) There is (exists) a person, named Mark Shpastin, who. . . .

On the other hand, if the asserter of (5) does not mind using 'there is' in such a way that she means to cover all her uses of (purportedly) referring terms whether what these denote exist or not, she may derive from (5) the broader quantification claim:

(7) There is (NOT, exists) a person named Mark Shpastin, who . . .

4. Quine's Referential Transparence, and the Crucial Problems of Referential Opacity

In recent times W. V. O. Quine has spearheaded the tremendous development of accounts of reference in attributions of belief to others. Quine has insisted on the crucial distinction between a singular term occurring nonreferentially, or *referentially opaquely* – as 'Castro's island' occurs in (2.A) above – and a term occurring referentially, or *referentially transparently* – as 'Castro's island' occurs in (2.B). It is clear that Quine is formulating in his terminology the *de re/de dicto* contrast. The referentiality Quine has in mind is speaker's referentiality, and referential opacity is precisely the discrepancy between what the speaker believes to exist and what the person she speaks of believes to exist. Quine is not, however, much concerned with the details of the thought content of the person to whom we attribute belief or thought. He is prepared to analyze a belief-sentence like (2.B) as having certain *of*-elements, those carrying speaker's existential reference, and the rest of the sentence as forming one indivisible whole. Thus, believing is conceived as a relation between a believer, a time t, a sequence of individuals in the order in which they enter the thought proposition, and an attribute (or predicate). Quine actually has no truck with propositions and attributes, and these can be conceived for the time being, respectively, as classes of equivalent sentences and classes of equivalent predicates. Thus, where 0 is the null sequence of *of*-elements, (2.A) is parsed as:

(2.A.Q) Believes (Columbus, t, <0>, [Castro's island is China]).

On the other hand, (2.B) is parsed as follows:

(2.B.Q) Believes (Columbus, t, < Castro's island >, [x is China]).

These formulas seem to be correct lists of the elements that enter into the situations. They are useful semantic depictions of the situations if we interpret them in accordance with two crucial semantic rules:

(R1) The phrase within square brackets has *internal* construal and the expressions composing it constitute points of referential cumulation.

(R2) the other elements within the major pair of parentheses represent just speaker's references.

In the case of iterated belief-sentences we must modify rules (R1)-(R2) appropriately. Consider:

(8)   Pinzon knew that Columbus believed that Castro's island was China.

This sentence is multiply ambiguous. For openers, it can be regarded as an embedding of (2.A) or of (2.B). If so, we find, respectively:

where: 'P' abbreviates 'Pinzon'; 't', 'time t'; 't''', 'time t''';

'C', 'Columbus'; and 'CI', 'Castro's island'

(8.A) Knows (P, t, <0>, [Believes (C, t', <0>, [CI is China])])

(8.B) Knows (P, t, <0>, [Believes (C, t', <CI>, [z is China])])

If (8) is interpreted as having 'Castro's island' with wholly external construal, then it is parsed as:

(8.C) Knows (P, t, <CI>, [Believes (x, y, <z>, [z is China])]).

Furthemore, if (8) is meant to have all the terms in (2) with total external construal, it is of the form:

(8.D) Knows (P, t, <C, t', CI, China>, [Believes (x, y, <z, w>, [z is w])])

Now, (8.D) has all its *of*-elements right at the beginning, thus making it perspicuous that they express speaker's (purported) references. What (8.D) says is roughly:

(8.D.Eng) Of Columbus, of some time t', and of Castro's island and China, Pinzon knows at time t that *the first* believed at *the second* that THE THIRD is (the same as) THE FOURTH.

I say 'roughly' because there is an ambiguity of the utmost importance in (8.D.Eng). On the one hand, the terms *'the first'* and *'the second'* depict the *single* convergence of the explicit references by the speaker and the unspecified references by Pinzon, to the admiral and the time *t'* in question. On the other hand, the terms 'THE THIRD' and 'THE FOURTH' exhibit a *double* convergence of references: that between the speaker's and Pinzon's, and that between the unspecified references by Pinzon and the unspecified references by Columbus. But we have no reason to suppose that in general the latter convergence is identity. This requires a theoretical way of distinguishing between a noncommittal double-convergent use of the terms 'THE THIRD' and 'THE FOURTH', and the strong use in which the second convergence is identity. The solution is feasible by means of quantifiers. Thus we can represent the two interpretations of 'THE THIRD' and 'THE FOURTH' as follows:

(8.D.1) $\exists x, \exists y, \exists z, \exists w$ {Knows(P, t, $<x, y, z, w>$, [Believes (x, y, $<z, w>$, [z is w])])}

This says that the ways in which Pinzon and Columbus refer to what the speaker calls "Castro's island" and "China" are identical. In the case of mere convergence, we need to ascribe to Pinzon the power to identify the referents of Columbus's references to what the speaker respectively refers to as Castro's island and China. That is, Pinzon possesses knowledge or belief that Columbus's references, whatever they may be, and his very own (to what the speaker calls "Castro's island" and "China") converge. We can put this by having Pinzon believe or know that there is an object z (as Columbus refers to it) which is the SAME AS v (as Pinzon refers to it). We symbolize this sameness relation by 'S='. Thus, the more general interpretation of (8.D.Eng) is:

(8.D.2) $\exists x, \exists y, \exists z, \exists w$ {(Knows(P,t, $<x,y,z,w>$, [$\exists u, \exists v$ (z S= u & Believes(x,y, $<z,w>$ [z is w])])}

This is fine up to a point. But it raises some semantic and ontological problems. *First*, what are the values of the variables 'x', 'y', 'z', 'w', 'v', and 'u'? The initial movement took Columbus, China, Castro's island to be ordinary objects of the world, persons and countries. These have infinitely many properties. But it is clear that these massive individuals cannot be the values of the variables 'x', 'y', 'z', and 'w' insofar as they represent the speaker's beliefs, namely, that she is considering infinitely propertied objects of the world. But once a need appears to consider these individuals *as* they are thought of by Pinzon, then it is not clear that those variables range in fact unrestrictedly over such objects. It seems, rather, that the variables range over, so to speak, slices of such objects, namely: slices of them *qua* thought of by Pinzon. This is tantalizing. But then the variables 'v' and 'u' are introduced to handle the limited beliefs that Columbus has *as* seen by Pinzon. We seem to need for 'v' and 'u' a thinner slice of the infinitely propertied objects we posit in the world.

Hand in hand with the preceding problem comes, *second*, the problem of determining fully the sense of 'sameness' represented by 'S=', which seems to hold between the slices of the entities the speaker believes to be infinitely propertied as they are cut by Pinzon and Columbus.

We leave these problems here. They are parallel to the problems of the strict denotata and their sameness we found underlying our semantics and pragmatics of proper names in Chapter 2. As we know, many different accounts are feasible, but we want an account that is comprehensive enough to deal with the *total* collection of data at present available—on reference, thinking, believing, intending, and whatever types of experience we are capable of enjoying, or suffering. *One unified solution is Guise Theory, which we discuss in chapters 13–14.*

5. Proper Names: Their Essential Opacity and Their Special Psychologico-Linguistic Attribution Cumulation Role

As we saw in chapter 2, proper names are variables of quantification ranging over a special domain, namely, the domain of the entities called by the name in question. We also saw that when used in sentences ostensibly expressing a singular reference, proper names function as free variables. Thus, except for the presentation of the characterizing trait of the domain of quantification, such free variables are *propositionally opaque*, because they do not reveal the basic way in which the object thought of is referred to. This is true of direct speech constructions. Yet, as we also saw in chapter 2, proper names also appear in internal construal in indirect speech. The very examples we have discussed illustrate this. Consider:

(9) Pinzon realized that Columbus admired Queen Isabella.

Suppose that all the expressions of the subordinate clause have internal construal. Then we seem to attribute to Pinzon the acquisition of knowledge he would have been able to express in English by saying:

(10) Columbus admires (admired) Queen Isabella.

We are not, however, reporting how Pinzon identified the right Columbus, that is, segregated him from all other objects in the world, to attribute to him admiration for Isabella. Presumably Pinzon knew several Columbuses, certainly Christopher, Fernando, and Diego. Perhaps he simply thought to himself, as the culmination of a conversation with the admiral:

(11) So, you admire her!

In an extremely literal sense it would then be inaccurate to affirm (9). Pinzon is really predicating admiration for Isabella of a *you*. Following the idea of belief or thought-of slices we have been toying with, we may say that Pinzon attributes admiration for Isabella to the *you*-slice the admiral presented him with during that conversation. Especially if Pinzon did not believe that the person he was calling "you" was not merely named Columbus, but was the Columbus the speaker has in mind. This is so because, as we have seen, expressions in internal construal are pragmatico-semantic cumulation points of reference.

There is a fruitful wisdom in acknowledging that sentence (9) should perhaps be used with external construal, if what Pinzon thought was (11). This takes the episodic character of realizing seriously. Consider now a dispositional case:

(12) Pinzon believed that Columbus admired Queen Isabella.

In this case we do not attribute to Pinzon any actual episode of referring to Columbus. We may construe 'Columbus' *externally* to capture any unspecified way in which Pinzon can refer to whom we call "Columbus." In that we are not even committing ourselves to Pinzon being able to convey his belief by uttering (10).

On the other hand, we may want to attribute to Pinzon the power to express the belief described in (12) by means of the assertive use of sentence (10). This is precisely the point of the *internal construal* of the proper name 'Columbus' in (12). Of course, Pinzon may always fail to do so. Perhaps whenever he thinks, has thought, or will think of the admiral's admiration for the queen, he will refer to our Columbus in other ways than using the name. In any case, sentence (12), with the internal construal of its subordinate clause, is a perspicuous and canonical means of attributing to Pinzon the *power* to express his belief by means of sentence (10).

To sum up, proper names are *qua* free variables the most propositionally opaque singular terms, because they are in terms of communication not even referentially transparent or perspicuous in that they do not specify their referents by themselves. Yet they possess a certain *psychologico-linguistic transparency*, which includes a *structural propositional transparency*. A psychological context of the form "X E's (N)," containing some occurrence of the proper name N in internal construal, is canonically used to attribute to the subject X possession in his or her idiolect of the referring mechanism represented by N. This means, ontologically, acquaintance and ability to handle both the nominalistic property *being named (called) N* and the sorted variable of quantification *N* ranging over the instantiators of that property. Thus, the person X is being attributed knowledge of a specific propositional structure and even a general procedure for specifying propositions of that structure.

6. The Propositional Opacity of Indicators in Attributions of Mental States or Acts

Let us discuss the role of indicators (personal pronouns, verbal tenses, demonstratives) in attributions of mental states or acts. As observed earlier, the same words can function in many different ways. Thus, when we speak of indicators, we have in mind not so much words like 'I', 'you', 'this', 'that', 'now', 'here', and the like, but the *indexical function*, whatever its means of expression may be.

What in general is the indexical function? Here we face the problem of demarcation of a research topic,[4] which poses a threat of circularity. This threat is undercut by distinguishing levels of inquiry and of definition. We start with a *proto-philosophical* "definition" or initial characterization of (genuine) *indicator*. This delivers a domain of objects to investigate. Then in a series of theoretical stages we propose, if necessary, more delving and illuminating characterizations of indicators.

As a proto-philosophical demarcation of indicators we take our clue from the preceding pragmatic discussions of singular terms.

Proto-philosophical Pragmatic Characterization of (Genuine) Indicator:
(IND*) A singular term *i* is a (genuine) indicator in a sentence S as used in a certain context C, if and only if: *i* expresses nothing but speaker's reference in S as used in C and would necessarily express in C nothing but speaker's reference in *every* sentence E embedding S.

The pragmatic function I have attempted to capture in (IND*) is my undergirding intuition that indicators are by semantic design some sort of *effective* pointers, which is what the word 'demonstrative' was intended to pin down. Clearly, an effective pointer has to be in use. Thus, the pointing role has to belong exclusively to the speaker.[5]

Consequently, whereas proper names and definite descriptions *may* be construed internally, or externally, (genuine) indicators *must* be construed externally. They never express speaker's reference with cumulation of attributed reference or attribution of mechanism of reference. Consider, for example:

(13) Leonore believes that I am happy here now.

Obviously, he who asserts (13) is not attributing to Leonore the very references expressed by the tokens of 'I', 'here', or 'now' composing the uttered token of (13). Leonore may be at that time sleeping, not even making references in a dream. She may not know that the speaker is saying anything at all. Furthermore, (13) does not even attribute to Leonore the ability to use the first-person pronoun, or the demonstrative indicators 'here' or 'now'. These terms express nothing but speaker's references. The indicators do signal, however, by their positions in the subordinate clause, the *convergence* posited by the speaker between his or her indexical references and some possible unspecified references by Leonore.

In brief, in indirect speech constructions *indicators themselves* have necessarily a wholly external construal. Yet *their positions* are internal revealing part of the structure of the content of the mental state or act attributed to the subject.

In any case, the preceding exegetical comments on (13) reveal that the information it conveys given the semantics of the expressions in it has the following schematic form:

(13A) Speaker's own references: I   (now)   here
       Speaker's claim:

                        ‖   ‖   ‖
       Leonore believes that: [alpha] is-[gamma] happy [beta]

Here the schematic letters 'alpha', 'beta' and 'gamma' stand for the unspecified mechanisms of reference attributed to Leonore. Undoubtedly, because of the representational nature of thinking (and believing), those mechanisms are embodied in some linguistic devices. But we must not hasten to conclude that the schematic letters denote expressions. They stand for expressions Leonore would use, that is, stand in the sense that singular referring terms available to Leonore are their *substituends*. But they do not merely stand for such expressions in the sense in which variables or schematic letters have *values*. For instance, the speaker of (13) may say by way of justifying his claim (13):

(14) Leonore said that today she would still believe that her mysterious admirer would be happy here today, and I AM the mysterious admirer. (I am not, however, happy here.)

It does not matter whether (14) justifies (13). This is an epistemological question. What interests us here is this crucial datum: the speaker of (13) and (14) equates, through his use of the capitalized 'AM' in (14), *not* himself with an expression, but *with a person*: (Leonore's) mysterious admirer. Thus, the term 'the mysterious admirer' is a substituend of the schematic word 'alpha' in (13A), but its value is (Leonore's) mysterious admirer. This raises a question that had begun to perplex Aristotle, perplexed Frege and Quine afterward, and has exploded in a general worry: the problem of the identity of objects as seen by others. Clearly, *I* (the speaker) am not the *strict value* of 'alpha' in (13A), since *I* am not as such in the internal scope of Lenore's beliefs about me. This is precisely the point of the referential opacity of 'I' in (13). Of course, in a liberal sense I, for the benefit of all of us, could reason as follows:

(15) *The mysterious admirer* is a [the] value of 'alpha' in (13), but *I* am the same as the mysterious admirer. Hence, *I* am also a [the] value of 'alpha' in (13).

This argument seems to me to be not only valid, but important. Clearly, similar considerations apply to the other terms 'now' and 'here'. The validity of argument (15) and its like hinges on the liberal sense of 'value'. It secures the contrast between strict values and values of the schematic letters in (13). This immediately raises several questions of the utmost importance for semantics:

(Q1) What are the strict values of the schematic letters of (13)?
(Q2) What are the values of such schematic letters?
(Q3) How do strict values relate to values?
(Q4) What is the sameness relation mentioned in (14) and represented in (13A) by the vertical identity sign '//'?

We need a general theory of the semantics of reference to deal with this. But at this stage some preliminary remarks may be helpful. *First*, the strict values of the schematic letters in (13A) seem to be aspects or slices, or guises, accessible to Leonore of entities in the world. *Second*, these entities are undoubtedly infinitely propertied, and may perhaps not be capable of serving as strict values of schematic letters representing internal content parts of thinking. *Third*, yet such massive entities do function as *external targets* of our acts of reference. *Fourth*, we certainly need to posit them in order to give unity to our search for convergencies or samenesses like those represented by '*//*'. *Fifth*, nevertheless, as discussed in Chapter 2, proper names do NOT have the semantic function of presenting such infinitely-propertied entities of the world. *Sixth*, the indexical expressions ('I', 'here' 'now') used by the speaker of (13) and (14) do not present in person anything but experiential aspects or guises of those infinitely-propertied. *Seventh*, perhaps our indexical references do harpoon such massive objects beyond, and behind, their harpooning inside experience those presented and experienced aspects or slices of them.

Now, returning to exegesis of (13), it seems possible that a speaker of (13) may very well simply wish to announce the schematic content diagrammed in (13A). But he or she may, on the other had, wish to put forward a truth or falsehood. In this case the Greek schematic words must function as variables of quantification. Then the *preliminary alpha analysis* of the meaning of (13), as so used, is this:

(13B) There is a person alpha, a place beta and a time gamma such that: I // (am the same as) alpha, here // beta, now // gamma, and Leonore believes that alpha is happy at beta at gamma.

I have called the type of analysis illustrated here "alpha" because of the Greek words used as schematic letters or variables, and "preliminary" because a full exegetical analysis must be given within a framework constituted by the answers to questions (Q1)-(Q4).

Suppose now that the speaker of (13), suspecting that Isadora knows (13) to be true, asserts:

(16) Isadora knows that Leonore believes that I am (now) happy here.

Because the indicators 'I', 'now', and 'here' express nothing but speakers' reference, the sense of (16) is depicted schematically in:

(16A) Speaker's own references: I   (now)   here
      Speaker's claim:

                                    || || ||
      Isadora knows that: [alpha1]   [gamma1]   [beta1]
                                    || || ||
      Leonore believes that: [alpha] is- [gamma] happy   [beta]

Again, the speaker of (16), and (13), may wish to relay the schematic content summarized in (16A), yet he may mean to place a truth sailing in his words. Then he means to assert this:

(16B) There is a person alpha1, a place beta1 and a time gamma1 such that: I // (am the same as) alpha1, here // beta1, now // gamma1, and Isadora knows that: There is a person alpha, a place beta, and a time gamma, such that alpha1 // alpha, beta1 // beta, gamma1 // gamma, and Leonore believes that alpha is happy at beta at gamma.

It is of great consequence to observe that because of (IND*) sentence (13) does not maintain its precise meaning under embedding.

This raises no new semantic questions beyond (Q1)-(Q4) but establishes a most important datum for any linguistic theory, namely:

Semantico-syntactic Datum about Indexical Reference:
A sentence $S(i1, . . . , iN)$ containing the N indicators $i1, . . . , iN$ in indirect speech (*oratio obliqua*) is twofold ambiguous: (a) there is the ambiguity between the schematic and quantification interpretations of the Greek letters of the preliminary alpha-analysis, and (b) there is the orthogonal ambiguity of the shifting places of the indicators $i1, . . . , iN$ in the syntax of the embeddings, so as to preserve frontal position.

Because indicators in indirect speech constructions express nothing but speakers' references, they always have external construal and occur propositionally opaquely, except when the subject of attribution of mental states, conceived in the first-person way, is at once the speaker him/herself.

7. Attribution of Indexical Reference: Quasi-Indicators and Some of Their Main Laws, Essential for the Language of Other Minds

To have perceptual and other experiences we need to have mechanisms of indexical reference at our disposal. Thus, to be able to think of others as capable of having experiences that relate to ours, we must be able to attribute to them indexical references. Hence, for a complete psychological language through which we can communicate and share plans and experiences, we need a language with a mechanism that can be used to attribute, not to make, indexical references. This raises a serious problem. Indexical references are so experiential that they are ephemeral and personal. They are tied down to the flow of subjectivity; yet to refer to the experiences of others we must somehow freeze that flow and bestow intersubjectivity on the frozen segments. How can we do that? Here we are not concerned with the epistemological issues that pertain to these operations, but merely with the representational means of performing them and preserving their results.

Let us perform a *Gedankenexperiment*, which amounts to a Kantian transcendental deduction of the nature of such means of attributing indexical references to others. Let us call such means *quasi-indicators*. We are set, thus, to deduce a *universal* minimal canonical grammar for quasi-indicators.

To begin with, since indicators express speaker's reference pure and simple, quasi-indicators are not indicators. Since references are the structurally unifying operation of all mental activities, they exist only in mental acts. Since indexical references are personal, we must represent then the person whose references we are set in capturing as engaged in some mental activity or having a certain mental state. But to attribute references to others we must represent them within our purview of the world. A fortiori, to attribute indexical references to others explicitly is to construct a picture of how others refer indexically to items in the shared world. This sharing enters the picture as a convergency of what the other refers to with what we refer to. But since the other's reference seizes an item internal to his experience, that convergency lies between our for-us transparent reference and his for-us opaque reference: e.g., between his own personal thisness or I-ness at the time of his mental act or state and our own reference to an object O or a person P, in the ways available to us. Thus, our picture of indexical references must divide the convergence between a component internally connected to the attributed mental act or state and a component external to that act or state, because it is ours. The internal component is the one that in the semantico-syntactic structure we are describing is what the *quasi-indicators proper* represent. Thus, perspicuous quasi-indicators must have the Chinese-Box semantic syntax, but with a connecting overhang.

In brief, then, *if* there are any indicators in a natural language, they conform to the following pragmatico-semantico-syntactic rules.

(Q*.1) Quasi-indicators are internal to psychological contexts. A mechanism for the attribution of an actual or potential indexical reference to a person P must be a semantico-syntactic mechanism Q that appears in indirect speech. Q must appear in the scope of a psychological verb and must appear with internal construal, if not in the surface grammar, at least in the deeper semantic grammar of the language—consisting of the rules of interpretation and implication the speakers must master.

(Q*.2) A quasi-indicator has an antecedent, which is logically—if not so in the surface grammar, at least in the deeper hermeneutic grammar of the language—*not* in the scope of the psychological verb, and prefix, in whose scope the quasi-indicator immediately lies.

(Q*.3) Quasi-indicators represent in the whole psychological constructions containing them the indexical references attributed to the persons mentioned in the psychological prefixes which contain their antecedents and in whose scope they lie.

(Q*.4) Quasi-indicators are, therefore, fully propositionally transparent in their contexts, just in case they are separated from their antecedents by just one psychological prefix.

(Q*.4a) In the case of intervening prefixes they fail to reveal how the persons mentioned in such prefixes refer to what is depicted as being indexically referred to by another.

For instance, in (a) "Carl knows that Mary believes that he himself is unhappy" the quasi-indicator 'he himself' is propositionally transparent with respect to how Carl refers to himself: if he were to express what he knows he would say: (b) "Mary believes that I am unhappy"; yet neither (b) nor (a) reveals how Mary refers to Carl: in (a) the position of 'he himself' is internal and reveals that for some *strict value* alpha available to Mary Carl takes it that alpha // he himself.

(Q*.5) Quasi-indicators (because of their dependency on antecedents) cannot be used to make indexical reference. Quasi-indicators are thus *somehow* like relative pronouns. I say 'somehow' because different natural languages may represent the antecedent-dependency of quasi-indicators in grammatically different ways.

(Q*.6) When their antecedents have largest scope in a sentence S, quasi-indicators may be said to be referentially transparent in that they connect directly to the speaker's references and, because of the convergency of speaker's references and subject's references, if the speaker refers to existents, then quasi-indexical references are also to existents.

(Q*7) Quasi-indicators cannot be replaced with their antecedents or any other co-referring expressions *salva veritate*, let alone *salva propositione*. Since the antecedents express speaker's references, such substitutions would replace *in internal construal* the speaker's references for the subject's indexical ones. Because of the personal nature of indexical references, such substitutions would misrepresent most dramatically the fragment of worldview of the subject allegedly being represented within the speaker's own view.

In spite of the above example in English, the preceding laws of quasi-indicators are meant to be general, deduced in an a priori argument based on the mere possibility of there being a language with quasi-indicators. Now, there is the empirical question—corresponding to Kant's so-called metaphysical deduction of the categories—whether there is in fact any language with quasi-indicators.

Evidently, English speakers in fact live interacting with others, attributing to others all sorts of mental states and acts. A simple examination of the language through which those experiences are lived reveals that English has a rather well delineated system of quasi-indexical mechanisms. It is crucial to recall what we discussed in Chapter 1: Syntactical mechanisms themselves are of little conceptual value, but what counts are the systems of contrasting semantico-syntactic mechanisms. A fortiori, lexical representations as such are of little importance: What matters are the semantico-syntactical contrasts surrounding and intersecting at the different lexical units. This is clearly underscored by the phenomenon of quasi-indexicality, as partially described in (Q*.1)-(Q*.7).

8. Taking Stock

In the discussions in chapters 1–5 we have examined the most surface properties of the mechanisms of singular reference and their role in experience. We have gathered a good collection of data, and have glimpsed into deeper issues. Yet we must not only refrain from theorizing on small collections of data, but must try to assemble as large a collection of data as we can. The more and more complex, the better. In the following chapters we discuss *some* additional roles of referential mechanisms in experience, pursuing our phenomenological linguistics. We also look into *some* theoretical ramifications of the phenomena of reference in other disciplines. Later on we formulate Guise Theory, which ties together all the issues and answers the many questions that have sprung forth.

Notes

1. This need for personal experiences to be connected to the outer, public and shared world is one of the main lessons taught by Ludwig Wittgenstein's private language argument in his *Philosophical Investigations* (Oxford: Blackwell, 1952). As he said, they must have *outward criteria*. For my own formulation of that lesson see "Private Language Problem," in Paul Edwards, ed., *The Encyclopedia of Philosophy*, vol. 6 (Glencoe, Ill.: The Free Press, 1967).

2. In Hector-Neri Castañeda, *Thinking and Doing* (Dordrecht: Reidel, 1975), pp. 53–55, there is a "diagonal" argument against equating propositions with classes of sentences. The key premise is that propositions are truths or falsehoods. Let L be a language, perhaps infinite, A be the class of L's sentences, B be a class of equivalent sentences of L. Let C be the power set of B, and $c(X)$ the cardinal of X. Then: $c(B) \leq c(A) < c(C)$. Consider now the class T of true propositions of the form: *member of A is a member of a member of C*. Then $c(T) \geq c(A) \times c(C) > c(B)$. L, therefore, does not have enough resources to equate classes of sentences with the above propositions—barring ambiguity. I am still persuaded by these facts—more so in fact after reading Patrick Grim, "Logic and Limits of Knowledge and Truth," *Noûs* 22 (1988): 341–67, an illuminating discussion of a battery of issues pertaining to truth and the infinity of propositions.

3. This point was very clear very early to Jaakko Hintikka, in his *Knowledge and Belief: An Introduction to the Logic of the Two Notions* (Ithaca, N.Y.: Cornell University Press, 1962), a book I praised (and still praise) in my review in *The Journal of Symbolic Logic* 29 (1964):132–34. In that book Hintikka also shows awareness of the problems of self-reference. To deal with the personal point of view of believing and knowing, he interprets the free variables in the scope of epistemic operators as ranging over persons known to the agent, or about whom the agent has an opinion. This restriction is, however, serious, for we want sometimes to say that there is someone, call him x, who is not known to Jones and is F, that is, Jones does not know (believe) that x is F. This becomes inconsistent. The problem of self-knowledge and self-belief was also serious. Quasi-indicators were missing. See Robert C. Sleigh, Jr., "Restricted Range in Epistemology," *The Journal of Philosophy* 69 (1972): 67–77, and "On Quantifying into Epistemic Contexts," *Noûs* 1 (1967): 19–21; and Hector-Neri Castañeda, "On the Logic of Self-knowledge," *Noûs* 1 (1967): 9–21.

4. The discovery of this problem is one of Plato's minor epistemological achievements. See his *Meno*.

5. A language with indicators must have expressions (indicators) connected to semantic functions that assign to indicators semantico-pragmatic functions that map contexts of speech into sets of individuals that are the possible denotata of indicators. But the crucial point is that such semantico-pragmatic functions are not thinkable contents. They must be *psychologically*, causally realized as follows: The thinker-speaker is in a speech situation that is an argument of one such function, and he/she thinks the corresponding value of that function. The values of such functions are thinkable contents. See the Appendix to "Direct Reference, Realism, and Guise Theory (Constructive Reflections on David Kaplan's Theory of Indexical Reference)."

Part II
Reference and Experience

6

Perception: Its Internal Indexical Accusatives and Their Implicit Quasi-indexical Representation

1. General Issues and Two Classical Views of Perceptual Accusatives

Perception lies at the interface between mind and reality. It is a special interaction between a thinker's environment and the thinker's conceptual equipment, beliefs, and proclivities to believe. Through that interaction the perceiver gains the materials for building up a view of a world in which to find herself, and if she is sufficiently developed and lucky, she does indeed find herself in the world she creates.[1] Thus, in every perception there are three crucial elements: (a) the impingement of reality on, and the reaction to such impingement on the part of, the thinker's perceptual mechanisms; (b) the beliefs and proclivities to believe that the thinker already has prior to the perception, and those he acquires through that impingement; (c) the reality content of such beliefs. Here we focus on (a). For expediency we shall concentrate on visual perception, and *visual demonstratives*. But the theses to be encountered must be valid, *mutatis mutandis*, for all types of perception.

The visual impingement of reality on a thinker results in the thinker confronting a visual field, a subset of his beliefs being placed in a hierarchy of readiness for his thinking rehearsal, a network of his presuppositions and beliefs being activated either as available implicit premises or nonlogical principles of inference, and the thinker's acquiring certain new beliefs. Our main concern here lies on the contents and composition of visual fields. Succinctly put, a visual field is a hierarchical structure whose apex is constituted by *what* is most distinctly and clearly seen, around which there is a gradual, or sharp, decrease in distinctness and clarity until nothing is seen. But what are those items that are distinctly seen?

From time to time the merits of two views about the *accusatives of perceiving* have been debated. These views may be called *Perceptual Objectism* and *Percep-*

tual Propositionism. They characteristically share an *atomistic assumption*, namely, that each perception deals autonomously with its own accusative in its own immediate terms. The views differ in both an ontological and a linguistic thesis.

The theses of Perceptual Objectism applied to seeing are:

(a) Ontological thesis: Seeing is in its primary reality a relation between a perceiver and an object, or particular; on some versions:

(a.phy) the accusative of seeing is a physical object;

(a.s-d) the accusative of seeing is a sense-datum.

(b) Linguistic thesis: The fundamental type of English sentence about perception is of the type exhibited by:

(1) Abel saw Betty (the book, a river, all the cows in the field).

The corresponding theses of Perceptual Propositionism are:

(a′) Ontological thesis: Seeing is primarily a relation between a perceiver and a proposition (or a state of affairs—and for convenience we shall not distinguish here between propositions and states of affairs); in some versions of Perceptual Propositionism,

(a′.mod) Seeing is a modality of a proposition, indexed by a perceiver.

(b′) Linguistic thesis: The fundamental type of English sentence about perception is for both versions of Perceptual Propositionism the one illustrated by:

(2) Abel saw that Betty voted for Smith,

which involves the proposition or state of affairs *Betty voted for Smith.*

We cannot enter here into all these issues. But it is worthwhile to see what seeing looks like when one examines it from its central axis—perceptual reference— and then glances at the issues debated in those views. Strikingly, those views, as emphasized by their corresponding linguistic theses (b)-(b′), consider their primary topic to be not so much perception, but the *attributions* of perception. We must reverse this project.

2. Perceptual Reference: Indexical Individuals, and the Primacy of Perceptual Fields

Let us start with some data about perceptual situations.

The Drowning-Man Adventure. One day I am hiking near some quarries, when I hear repeatedly the noises "I am here drowning." The hearer's point of view of language seems applicable. The hearer's-interpretation semantic rule of 'I' tells me that each use of 'I' denotes its user. On hearing the quoted sentence I proceed to search for the source of the noise. Guided by the noises I come to a large hole in the ground full of water, surrounded by a thick mist; I see something like a man that looks to me as if he were drowning. Within this background we must distinguish several cases of perceptual situation:

(A) I exclaim, thinking out loud, pointing to a vague silhouette behind the mist, expressing my perceptual judgment:
   (1) *That* IS a man drowning!
   There is in fact a man drowning and I am pointing to him.

(B) I have exactly the same perceptual experience as in case (A), and declare out loud the self-identical perceptual judgment:
   (1) *That* IS a man drowning!
   But this time there is no drowning man; I am hallucinating.

(C) I have exactly the same perceptual field as in case (A), but now I am suspicious about the veridicality of my perceptions, thus, my perceptual judgment is a skeptical one:
   (2) *That* APPEARS TO BE [LOOKS LIKE] a drowning man.
   I am indeed pointing to a drowning man.

(D) As in case (C), I judge:
   (2) *That* APPEARS TO BE [LOOKS LIKE] a drowning man.
   This time there is no drowning man around for me to point to.

Exegesis of the data. The ensuing exegetical observations of the situation manifold (A)-(D) constitute binding criteria of adequacy for any comprehensive theory of indexical reference as well as for any theory comprehensive of perception.

(I) The perceiver's perceptual judgment deploys itself in three dimensions: (i) a *referential dimension* — the judged content is composed of individuals and properties pragmatico-semantic denoted by the expressions used by the perceiver and thought of by him; (ii) a *doxastic dimension* — the judged content constitutes the perceiver's belief about the reality connections between those denotata; (iii) a *reality dimension* — the connections the perceiver posits, or refuses to posit, obtain, or do not obtain, in the fundamental cases and typically, with independence of the perceiver beliefs, as nature (or God) determines.

It is of the utmost importance not to flatten the nature of perceptual judgments by ignoring one or another dimension.

(II) The indicator *that* has exactly the same semantic (language-system, dispositional) meaning in all four cases. (III) The thinking referent of *that* is in each assertion the same: an internal perceptual content present to the speaker in his visual field at the time under consideration, which remains a constant denominator underlying the alternatives (A)-(D).

(IV) In cases (A) and (C) there is *a* referent *beyond* the speaking perceiver's ken: the actual drowning man. This is a very massive entity, with infinitely many properties, most of which will always be unknown to the perceiver. It is the sort of thing we may call *the first Fregean referent* of a singular-referring expression. On David Kaplan's Theory of Direct Reference this referent is directly harpooned, not so much by the speaker's tokening of 'that', but rather, by both his uttering any sentence whatever, including sentence (1), in the context of utterance and the mere abstract pairing of his possible use of 'that' with a pointing to that (Fregean) referent over and beyond the misty silhouette he sees.

(V) In cases (B) and (D) there is no first Fregean referent. Therefore, the *strict referent*, the thinking referent, of the uses of 'that' under consideration is not the Fregean (Kaplanian) first referent intended by the perceiver to harpoon in cases (A) and (B).

(VI) In all four cases the speaker expresses a propositional content that commands his assent. It lies *internally* within his perceptual field. He puts it forth noncommittally in sentence (2), but endorsingly, believingly, in sentence (1). The speaker's tokens of the indexical sentences (1) and (2) are meant to put forward truths that are the pragmatico-semantic denotata of such tokens. The indexical sentences themselves are NOT simply schemata to which the perceiver must assign objects *before* he has anything he can evaluate as true or false. For such an assignment we would have to translate or paraphrase the indicators into some other mechanism of reference. Generally, assumed candidates for such paraphrase are proper names. In Chapter 2, we have seen, however, that proper names cannot perform such a function. It is easy to see that any object referred to in some nondemonstrative way, say, as N, will have to be equated with a demonstrative, *this* or *that*, if N is to appear in some perception. Thus, the equation *A is (the same as) that* or *This is (the same as) A* performs an executive role of identifying the object A, so far thought of in absence, with an object presented as a *this*, or a *that*. This truth of experience and thought is what the person who finally sees N apprehends. But N is of course just an object of thought. In short *there is no royal road to an individual outside our ways of thinking of it.*

(VII) The nature of the perceiver's perceptual judgment depends both on what lies in his perceptual field and on the doxastic repertory he marshals. The interaction of these components determines *what* the perceiver finds in perception. This is clearly evidenced in the fourfold contrast (A)-(D). In cases (A) and (B) the perceiver marshals one and the same set of beliefs and mobilizes them in exactly the same way. The difference in veridical perception and hallucination, between (A) and (B), has to do with the existence of the Fregean first referents *beyond* both the perceptual field and the beliefs supporting it. By contrast, in cases (C) and (D) the perceiver marshals a different set of beliefs and withholds judgment about the existence of a first Fregean referent beyond his perceptual field. These different doxastic bases of the perceptual judgments (1) and (2) determine, at least in part, the kind of perceptual experience the perceiver is living through, and the mental state he is in. This is palpably revealed by the perceiver's use of different copulas. The copula 'IS' in utterance (1), in both cases (A) and (B), signals an existential *doxastic* claim about the world beyond perception, positing an object in physical space-time immersed in the causal order of the external world. The copula 'APPEARS', on the other hand, signals both a noncommittal external claim, withholding both the positing of the physical object and the causal network surrounding it in the physical space beyond the perceptual field, and a commitment to describe what the visual field presents. These copulas, or forms of predication, point to the mobilization of different doxastic repertories, and they not only leave intact, but they also presuppose, a common semantic basis for the referring expressions, even a shared pragmatico-semantic network of strict, thought of referents.

(VIII) Thus, neither the meaning of the demonstrative 'that' in the language system of English, its dialects and idiolects, nor the *strict*, thinking, denotatum it picks on each occasion of its use is the full-fledged physical object, which is nevertheless somehow reached in veridical perception. At best in veridical perception it is a *perceptual slice*, a *this-* or *that-*slice of it. In general, however, the denotatum of a perceptual 'this' or 'that' is just an item composing the visual field, which by occupying the focus of the perceiver's attention has been promoted to the status of a *this* or a *that*.

(IX) The Fregean (Kaplanian) first-order referent assigned by reality to my token of 'that' in my utterance of (1) or (2) in cases (A) and (C) is neither semantic nor thinkingly referential; it functions doxastically in cases (A) and (B). It comes in the perceiver's doxastic domain, *beyond* the contents of the thinking episode in question, *alluded* to by the copula *IS* of the internal proposition expressed by sentence (1).

(X) To sum up, returning to the three dimensions introduced in (I), *the referential dimension* of a perceptual judgment pertains to the representational powers of the symbolism used as a means of thinking: By the convergence assumption discussed in chapter 1, it pertains to the relevant complex of semantic rules of the language system (in its dialects and idiolects) and the pragmatic rules (fundamentally, habitually exercised) for the application of symbols of that system in speech situations. These rules, independently of the perceiver-speaker's beliefs, determine the strict, thought of referents of his perceptual demonstratives. The *doxastic dimension* comes in how those referents are related to each other in the perceiver's mind. Thus, we expected, and found it confirmed, that the forms of predication express the perceiver's doxastic attitude. Finally, the *reality dimension* pertains to the external connection to truth of the perceiver's perceptual judgment and of the whole doxastic pedestal on which the judgment rests. Now, since a mature thinker must at least in principle be capable of dealing with the world responsibly in his or her own terms, the reality dimension must receive some internalization. This consists of the *maximal coherence* the thinker wishes all or most of his/her beliefs to attain. This internalization includes, to be sure, the available opinions of others. But the emphasis on availability is a special requirement of internalization.

(XI) One comment on the ontological debate between Perceptual Objectism and Perceptual Propositionism. The pragmatico-semantic byplay between 'this' and 'that' and the hierarchical nature of perceptual fields, in which *this*es and *that*s appear as constitutive parts of their focal apex, clearly recommend shunting the atomistic assumption shared by both views. We do so. Now, in the preceding discussion we have explicitly sided with the ontological thesis of Propositionism. Patently, its linguistic theses are, albeit different, equally irrelevant to the problem tackled above, and both will have to be discarded in order to appreciate the quasi-indexical character of attributions of perception to others.

3. The Albritton Desideratum, and More Ontological Problems

At the discussion that followed the presentation of the above at the 1984 Stanford Conference on Kaplan, Rogers Albritton, correctly, pointed out that in case (A), when my perception is veridical, there is a sense in which I am referring to a real person (which looks like an infinitely propertied first Fregean referent), and, furthermore, such a referent is the same as what I thinkingly refer to as *that*. These two points seem to me to be absolutely crucial data. The added parenthetical point is not so clear: It depends on one's account of the Fregean referents. The sense in which I refer to the external referent is precisely the sense in which I *believe* that there is a physical entity, a person, who is *the same* as what I find in my visual field. This doxastic reference is what I have tried to elucidate above. The sameness in question, which obtains in cases (A) and (C), and is believed to obtain in cases (A), needs a protracted discussion we cannot carry out here. Nevertheless, we must at least record the following Albritonian

> *Perception-theoretical Desideratum.* In the case of veridical perception the perceptual individual apprehended as a *that* or a *this* MUST be the same as the physical entity posited in the perceptual judgment of the IS-type.

This desideratum raises a most important problem: the urgent need to build an account of some form of sameness that is NOT self-identity. Of course, we cannot deal with identity and sameness in a vacuum: We must have an account of their domain. Thus, we also have the urgent problem of accounting for the individuals that are the arguments of the sameness demanded by the Albrittonian desideratum.

Consequently, our delving into the role of indexical reference in perception brings more problems of the kinds we have found, thus making the urgency of a unified pragmatico-semantic ontology more demanding.

One anticipatory glimpse. Naturally, this desideratum allows a constrictive as well as a liberal interpretation. We can interpret the sameness demanded by veridical perception to be strict identity, or, more liberally, we may allow it to be a weaker form of sameness, for example, one analogous to so-called theoretical identity. In fact, in Guise Theory the sameness in question is simply the general predicational sameness called *consubstantiation*.

4. Indexical Individuals and the Substantival Role of Indicators

Obviously, to think something of the form *this [that] is F* is simply to take the *this* in question as being *there* in experience as an individual suitable for predication, and we think of it as being F. Even if one's experience is wholly hallucinatory, one is therein confronting a hallucinatory *this* or *that*. These are substantival uses of the demonstratives 'this' and 'that'.

Suppose now that I make a perceptual judgment of the form *this brown table is F*. Here the demonstrative 'this' is said to be an adjective. There is a long-standing view that construes a syntactic unity as follows:

(DET) Demonstratives and definite articles form a semantico-syntactic family—composing noun phrases with nouns or noun phrases:

(1) *That* house we saw;   (2) *This* house we see.

(1a) The house we saw;   (2a) The house we see.

(A moral general view (G.DET) treats quantifiers ['all', 'some', 'none'] as of the same type.) Undoubtedly, in part the semantic differences between (1) and (1.a) and between (2) and (2.a) "arises from the absence of accessory indications of distance or nearness, which are characteristic of the pronouns *this* and *that*."[2] Furthermore, the demonstrative pronouns and the definite article share a semantico-pragmatic function of expressing singularity. Nevertheless, before we conclude with Bello that the definite article is a demonstrative, we should consider other semantico-syntactic contrasts. Immediately, it would seem that singularity belongs to all of them, so that if to express singularity is the hallmark of the definite article, then there is something of the definite article in demonstratives. Yet the experiential sense of demonstratives is missing in the definite article. So, perhaps, we may think that meanings of demonstratives could be analyzed in terms of the definite article and some peculiar experiential property.

Let us exegesize *this brown table is F*. The surface grammar suggests that to think this is to confront a *this* that is a brown table. Why not, alternatively, perhaps a *this* that is both brown *and* a table? Initially it does seem that the locution 'this brown table' may be syntactically ambiguous between either of the following parsings:

(Syn.a) This brown, table: This brown [and a] table.

(Syn.b) This (brown table):   This brown-table.

This difference in syntax can be connected to an ambiguity in the word 'brown':

(Sem.a) this looking brown here now, regardless of what the table may look elsewhere or under a different light;

(Sem.b) the table looking brown in normal circumstances, even if not perhaps here now.

Since our natural, default attitude is toward thinking and toward acquiring true beliefs about physical objects, rather than about the looks of things, it seems safe to claim that (b) is most likely the normally intended syntax and semantics of 'this brown table'. There is, however, a good reason to hold that, normal use aside, the correct syntactic parsing of 'this brown table' *is* (Syn.a). The crucial thing is the significant syntactico-semantic contrast that sets both (Syn.a) and (Syn.b) together and apart from other constructions, namely: the juxtapositive/predicational contrast illustrated by (A) and (B):

(A) Juxtaposition: This brown table

(B) Property Predications:
    This which IS [LOOKS] brown and IS [LOOKS LIKE] a table.
    This which IS [LOOKS LIKE] a brown table

The (B) type construction is the basic one, and allows for the diversity of interpretations of the predicates and of different connections between the predicates and the *this* under consideration. On the other hand, the (A) construction is more specialized: Its juxtaposition between the demonstrative and the other expressions represents the IS-form of predication. As we saw in the preceding section, the IS-form of predication is *doxastic*. Thus, *this brown table* includes a doxastic predication smoothing over the cleavage between *this* and *brown table*.

Thus the perceptual judgment *This brown table is F* is really of the form *This, which IS a brown table, IS F*. If so, then the perceptual experience involves a belief that transcends what is being confronted twice: patently at the explicit predication *IS F* and at the implicit predication *which IS a brown table*. The demonstrative 'this' is by itself the main noun phrase; the so-called noun phrase 'brown table' is logically merely adjectival. Clearly, the same considerations apply to all indicators: *Logically, indicators are always substantives*.

5. The Ingenious Quasi-indexical Form of Attributions of Perception

We proceed to study the fundamental attributions of perception, namely, the reports of the contents of another person's perceptual awareness. We want to ascertain the degree to which we can attain propositional transparency in such reports. As we have seen, those contents are indexical. Hence, to report perceptual contents we must phrase them in their quasi-indexical counterparts.

We continue to concentrate on visual perception. Let us scrutinize some attributions of visual perception in order to locate the primary quasi-indexical type. Consider the verb '(to) see'. It appears in several different constructions, which are illustrated by:

(1) John saw the youngest girl of the group.

(2) John saw Mary arrive late.

(3) John saw Mary arriving late.

(4) John saw Mary attacked.

(5) John saw that Mary (had) arrived late.

Construction (1) seems to run against the point noted above that the visual field is a system of states of affairs (or propositions). It seems to make seeing a relationship between the perceiver and each of the objects in the field. Undoubtedly there is such a relationship. (But there is also a relationship between the perceiver and a state of affairs.) It is a paradigm example of what Perceptual Objectism considers the basic form of perception (attribution) sentence. For us this cannot be so for the simple reason that sentence (1) does NOT reveal anything about the contents of John's visual field at the time of his reported seeing. The expression 'the youngest girl of the group', the only one apparently in the scope of 'John saw', expresses a reference made by the speaker of the whole sentence (1), not made by John. It occurs, thus, externally to the psychological prefix 'John saw'. Yet sentence (1) expresses an identification of sorts between an item, whatever it may be, in John's past visual field under consideration and an item in the speaker's world. (To elucidate that sort of identification is one task of the philosophical theory of perception and of reference we seek.) That identification is, according to (1), made by the speaker—John not being at all responsible for it. That is why *we*, the speaker and the hearers, can in (1) put 'Mary' or any other coreferring expression instead of 'the youngest girl of the group', without changing the truth value of the statement. That is, (1) and *The youngest girl of the group is Mary* imply together *John saw Mary*.

Sentences (2), (3), and (4) belong together. They contain the singular term 'Mary' propositionally opaquely. This term expresses in each of these sentences the *speaker's* way of referring to a certain person, and its *position* in the sentences expresses the speaker's identification of the person in her world she calls 'Mary' with something in John's visual field. On the other hand, the expressions 'arrive late', 'arriving late', and 'attacked' have typically internal construal in sentences (2)-(4). If so, they occur propositionally transparently, expressing properties, rather, predications that John finds in his visual field. The present participle 'arriving late' in sentence (3) allows two syntactic construals. It may be taken: (i) as cleft-predicate, by itself, as noted, or (ii) as an attributive modifier of 'Mary'. In case (ii) sentence (3) has the singular term 'Mary arriving late' which is tantamount to 'Mary who was arriving late'. On this construction, (3) is of the same form as (1). Many subtleties distinguish the uses of (2) from those of (3). We will, however, ignore them here and assume that (2) and (3) understood in sense (i) represent similar attributions of perception, indeed, the basic ones, as we will discuss in a moment.

Sentence (5) is the paradigm of Perceptual Propositionism. It allows a double interpretation. In it the term 'Mary' may have external construal, signaling exclusively that the speaker calls a certain person 'Mary', but it may occur with internal construal, with cumulation of reference to a Mary and attribution of possession to John of the name 'Mary' as a way of referring to that person. Now the question appears: Is the state of affairs expressed by the subordinate clause of sentence (5), namely, "Mary (had) arrived late," part and parcel of John's visual field? The answer is either "NO" or at least "Perhaps not." The initial difficulty is this: A statement made with sentence (5) may very well fail to imply:

(6) John saw Mary.

If this implications fails, then clearly the state of affairs expressed by *Mary (had) arrived late* is not constitutive of John's visual field. The situation is, then, of the following sort: John SEES all sorts of things that he CONSTRUES as establishing that Mary (had) arrived late. "John saw" on this interpretation of (5) is tantamount to "John realized", or "it dawned on John."

Suppose now that (5) is used so that (6) is implied. This is not sufficient to place the state of affairs *Mary (had) arrived late* in John's visual field. Perhaps he did not see anybody arriving late, but he saw Mary and other things and then, as before, realized that Mary arrived late. We need more in order to locate the state of affairs in John's visual field. What more? What is needed is BOTH that there be a subject of 'arriving late' in John's visual field and that John correctly takes that subject, that is, believes that subject, to be Mary. In other words, the state of affairs *Mary arrived late* can be in John's visual field ONLY IF it slides into the field down a belief anchored to a state of affairs that is inherently visual.

An *inherently visual state of affairs* is, as we have seen above, a singular state of affairs that has as constituents visual properties or visual subjects only. The visual subjects are the particulars in the visual field that are presented to the perceiver as *this* or *that*, that is, visually demonstrative particulars. (At this juncture it is an open question how visual fields relate to physical space in terms of both contents and geometric structure.)

One outcome of the preceding examination of sentences (1)-(5) is this: None of these sentences is *candid* in the sense of having a clause subordinated to the verb 'see' with total propositional transparency. None has a subject with internal construal that expresses exactly how what appears to John as arriving late appears in his visual field. As noted, however, there is really no doubt as to how it appears and how John refers to whom appears arriving late, namely: Demonstratively, for example, *this [which is a] person*, or *that which seems to be a lady, over there*.

The cleft constructions (2)-(4) come close to revealing the proposition (or state of affairs) in John's visual consciousness. Yet they present this proposition, so to speak, in a dislocated way. On the one hand, though they present the *subject position* they also present an external characterization of it by the speaker. Thus, strictly speaking they leave a blank with an *indication* of its filler, in the proposition that is visually present to John. On the other hand, they present the predicate component of such a proposition, so to speak, in person. Thus, sentences (2)-(4) look very much, respectively, like abbreviations of the following sentences:

(2.a) There is an alpha such that:
Mary is the same as alpha and John saw: alpha arrives late.

(3.a) There is an alpha such that:
Mary is the same as alpha and John saw: alpha was arriving late.

(4.a) There is an alpha such that:
Mary is the same as alpha and John saw: alpha was attacked.

Here 'alpha' *must* stand for a demonstrative way of referring to Mary available to John. The point is that in (2)-(4) there is an implicit demonstrative subject that appears propositionally opaquely at the second occurrence of 'alpha'. In this respect those sentences contrast with first-person present-tense corresponding sentences like:

(2.I) I see THAT lady arrive late.

(3.I) I see THAT person over there arriving late.

The first-person present-tense perception sentences can reveal fully and explicitly how the perceiver refers to, or is aware of, the items in his/her visual field. They accomplish that because in first-person speech a speaker attributes indexical references to him/herself by exhibiting them.

In the attribution of indexical reference to what we take (perhaps mistakenly) to be others, we must resort to quasi-indexical depiction. But now we face a problem. We saw in Chapter 5 that quasi-indicators have indirect speech (*oratio obliqua*) as their natural habitat. Hence, the first occurrence of 'alpha' in (2.a)-(4.a) is out of order. What we need is a quasi-indicator that has 'Mary' as its direct-speech antecedent but it itself is limited to indirect speech. Thus, sentence

(3) John saw Mary arriving late

has a surface logical form that can be depicted as follows:

(3.a*) At time t John saw that alpha* was arriving late then*.

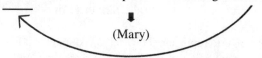

(Mary)

Here, as before, the star attached to 'alpha' and to 'then' signals that these stand for some sort of proxy for John's indexical references to time *t* as *now* and to Mary as a *this* or *that*.

In summary, the perceptual verb 'see' has a basic complex grammar. The sentence 'At time *t* John saw Mary arriving [arrive] late' is superficially misleading, but at bottom clear and clever. It is superficially misleading to the extent that the term 'Mary', the subject of the subordinate clause, is itself referentially transparent, that is, it expresses a transparent reference by the speaker, not by John. Yet 'Mary' appears in the surface grammar in the scope of 'John sees'—even though it has nothing internally to do with John's seeing! The construction as a WHOLE is propositionally transparent since, given that the particulars in John's visual field can only be demonstrative ones, the construction does *not* conceal the nature of the subjects of the propositions (or states of affairs) in John's visual field. It is clever because it takes advantage of the nature of perception to build in a compact formula both referential transparency and propositional transparency—and it attains this with the greatest economy of means: a *tacit* quasi-indicator representing demonstrative reference!

6. The Informational Package of Terms in Quasi-indexical Positions

English does not have a quasi-indicator for third-person demonstrative reference to objects or persons. Thus, there is no analogue to 'then', 'there', and 'he himself' that we can use instead of 'alpha*'. Since indexical reference is irreducible to nonindexical reference, the fact that there is no natural quasi-indicator for third-person demonstrative reference to objects indicates that in the study of the logic of a perception proposition we must deal with an always implicit quasi-indexical operation. This operation produces a quasi-indicator that *anybody* can use in the appropriate linguistic context. Thus, the operation maps certain parameters into an attributed demonstrative reference. This mapping, of course, cannot produce a conceptual reduction. The parameters in question must include the perceiver, the place of perception, the time of perception, and the perceived object. But the mapping must somehow distinguish between any two different modalities in the properties, whether of physical things in physical space or not, that appear in perceptual fields. This generic difference is better construed at the quasi-indexical function. Thus, we must have a SPECIAL QUASI-INDEXICAL FUNCTION FOR EACH TYPE OF PERCEPTUAL MODALITY. In ordinary English sentences about perception, this feature of the quasi-indicators hidden behind expressions like 'Mary' in (3) above is denoted by the context: The verbs 'see', 'touch', 'hear', and so on, signal that the demonstrative reference being attributed to the perceiver is of the appropriate kind, that is, a reference to items in the appropriate perceptual field. It is crucial to fasten to the fact that 'Mary' is NOT a quasi-indicator.

Let us use the symbol 'v' to represent the visual quasi-indexical function as described above. Thus, we can initially represent the expression 'alpha*' in (3.a*) as the formal visual quasi-indicator:

v [John, p, t: Mary]

where p is the place of perception and t is the time. Now we can concentrate on the fact that ordinary language has definite quasi-indicators for self, presented time, and presented place, that is, quasi-indicators of the third-person form for the indicators 'I', 'now', and 'here'. The corresponding quasi-indicators are 'he himself', 'then', and 'there', all appearing in *oratio obliqua* as relative pronouns with an antecedent outside the *oratio obliqua*, as explained in chapter 5. This phenomenon is of the utmost significance. It has to do with the overall unity of experience. The self is no part of any perceptual field, but functions as the common point of origin for ALL perceptual spaces. The time and the place of a multi-perceptual experience are not experienced as parts or elements in just one perceptual field. They are experienced as GENERAL COORDINATES for all perceptual fields of one self. This generality makes the indexical reference to time and space lacking in the local feature of a perceptual modality. Let us for convenience use the sign '*' to represent, in the case of attributions of veridical perception, this interperceptual quasi-indexical function that yields quasi-indicators out of the interperceptual parameters, namely, a physical entity in a physical place at a physical time. Hence, we can represent the temporal multi-perceptual quasi-indicator in (3.a*) as follows:

'then*'   :   *[t, John, p]

We allow that *[a,b,c] is the same as *[a,c,b]. Now we can represent the *surface logical form* of sentence (3), "At place *p* and time *t* John saw Mary arriving late then." Its *initial* analysis is:

(3.a*) At place *p* and time *t* John saw that:
         v [John, *p*, *t*: Mary] was arrving late at *[*t*, John, *p*].

This is only the initial analysis of (3). Account must be taken of the implicit quasi-indicator referring to the place in John's visual field where Mary was arriving late. The complications this brings out exhibit the wisdom of the creators of ordinary language: They, most economically minded, simply left it out in sentences like (3).

7. An Illuminating Proposed Counterexample by William Lycan

The great significance of quasi-indicators even when they are merely implicit in a sentence used to attribute states of mind or episodes of consciousness to others can be seen from a case proposed by William Lycan[3] – as a counterexample against my claim that quasi-indicators are irreducible, but in the end, it turns out, as a highlighting device. Lycan raises the case of John who points to Hud and says:

(9) That man looks disagreeable.

Lycan says that we 'may quite acceptably report John's utterance' by saying:

(10) John said that Hud looks disagreeable.

I have nothing to object to this description. But we must have an exegesis of 'may quite acceptably report'. In the absence of such an exegesis it is premature to conclude with Lycan that (3), namely, 'John saw Mary arriving late', does not have a deep (hidden) quasi-indexical structure. Lycan is at bottom asking for a comparison between (3) and (10), which shows (10) *not* to be quasi-indexical, *in spite of* its background (9), whereas (3) *is* quasi-indexical precisely *because of* its background. And this is a most important challenge. We cannot deal fully with the differences between (3) and (10), but I must at least mention some of them.

   To begin with, given the cleft character of (3) – 'John saw Mary arriving late' – the noun 'Mary' in it MUST be external to the psychological prefix: 'Mary', in terminology I do not like, must occur de re in (3), expressing nothing but speaker's reference. On the other hand, 'Hud' may occur either externally or internally, that is, de re or de dicto, in (10), and this is so given the nature of proper names as we have explained in chapter 2.

Now let 'Hud' occur externally, de re, in (10). Clearly, (10) by itself does not say anything about (9). The attribution of the speech act as reported in (10) leaves it entirely open how the John in question referred to Hud in his speech act. This is the propositional opacity of (10). We cannot retrieve (9) from (10); we cannot derive that John referred to Hud demonstratively. On the other hand, given the fact that perception, especially vision, requires the presentation to consciousness of perceptual fields, one can retrieve from (3) the fact that in his perceptual thinking John referred to Mary demonstratively. This is precisely the whole point of the implicit (deep) quasi-indexical structure of (3). Thus, (3) is propositionally transparent, in that it reveals the primary demonstrative character of the way in which John refers to Mary when he sees her coming late. Here is one reason why the *de re/de dicto* contrast is not exhaustive: It fails to allow for the especial propositional transparency of quasi-indexical constructions.

Notes

1. This "she does find herself in the world" includes Kant's "It must possible for the 'I think' to accompany all my representations" (*Critique of Pure Reason* B 131), which seems to have a strong sense of 'can' characteristic of beings with a high degree of self-consciousness. Our being in the world here, on the other hand, requires a minimal unity of consciousness and allows the being in question never to engage in self-consciousness.

2. Andres Bello, *Gramática de la lengua castellana*, Buenos Aires: Librería Perlado, 1943.

3. William G. Lycan, "Castañeda on the Logical Form of Perception Sentences," in Jody Kreiman and Almerindo E. Ojeda, eds., *Papers from the Parasessions on Pronouns and Anaphora* (Chicago: Chicago Linguistic Society, 1980), pp. 87–93; my response is "The Deep Quasi-indicator in Perception Sentences," ibid. : 94–97.

7

Deliberation, Intentional Action, and Indexical Reference

1. Summary of Main Contentions

For several decades I have been arguing that practical thinking (which manifests the dispositional states of intending, wanting, purposing, and their ilk, and which is exercised in acts of willing, commanding, advising, and their likes) has its own peculiar internal accusatives, and that indexicality is of the essence of such accusatives. I have called such accusatives *practitions*, so that the autonomy of morality, and more generally, the autonomy of practical thinking consists in the autonomy of practitions vis-à-vis propositions, the internal accusatives of believing and contemplative thinking. The unity of reason requires that practical thinking encompass contemplative thinking. Clearly, propositions are conditions for doing, for commanding, for intending, for being obligated. This role, which allows practical reasoning, requires mixed contents of practical thinking, hence such mixed contents are practitions. For instance, the mixed conditional *If it rains, I'm going to stay home* is (in one interpretation) a conditional intention; similarly, the mixed conditional *If Peter comes, please give him this book* is a mixed request. We cannot rehearse here the ENORMOUS COLLECTION of data on which these claims are based.[1] Here we must content ourselves with reflecting on a basic two-pronged hunch. On the one hand, (a) there is a systematic internal connection between the accusatives of practical thinking and the causation of intentional action, and this requires a peculiar formal element that can capture that triggering connection—we need, therefore, practitions. On the other hand, (b) ultimately intentional action is caused in particular situations on particular objects with particular tools, and so on, and this particularity requires the whole panoply of indexical mechanisms to pin down every particular involved in the action.[2]

Let us at least take the briefest glimpse into the wonderful nature of practical thinking.

2. The Fundamental Indexicality of Practical Thinking

Let's continue the examination of the fourfold perceptual situation (A)-(C) discussed in Chapter 6.2. Patently, perceptual situations often lead to action. Which action the agent performs depends on the sort of person she is. She may be generally benevolent, or she may on one occasion, exceptionally, feel benevolent, or she may be a sadist, and so on. Thus, in our quarry adventure, the agent may be deeply concerned with saving the man he believes to be drowning – or he may decide to enjoy the spectacle of a man drowning. In any case, the agent in the story will proceed from his perceptual beliefs to a course of action. He may act quickly in a type of reflex action; but he may perform his action of attempting to save the man intentionally. He may even engage in deliberation, finding himself bound by conflictive obligations: for example, the moral obligation to stop a man's suffering, and, given that he cannot swim, the moral obligation to maintain himself alive for the benefit of his family and of the institutions to which he belongs. Furthermore, he may deliberate about the appropriate means to try to rescue the drowning man he has posited.

Let's extend cases (A) and (B) in chapter 6.2 to include my deliberation. This requires that I take my indexical judgment (1) there – *That IS a drowning man* – as a *true* premise, without engaging in the operations, required by the Theory of Direct Reference, of (i) assigning a referent to my token of 'that' and (ii) testing the resulting Russellian (Kaplanian) proposition for truth. We may accept that my IS-perceptual judgment postulates the existence (or subsistence) of such a proposition as an external target of my thinking, and indeed that my judgment posits this position as true. Yet I do not as agent try to locate it and examine it for truth. We may further agree that this truth somehow guides me from the unknown beyond. But the singular proposition that mobilizes my powers of deliberation and action is the indexical truth within my grasp.

The point deserves dwelling on. When I act intentionally on an object, I care neither about the Russellian (Kaplanian) propositions beyond as such nor about their Fregean (Kaplanian) first referents. These are not crucial. What I need is to bring those doxastic referents somehow *into* my experience through my thinking indexical (that is, experiential) references. Suppose that proper names harpoon Fregean first referents, as the Direct Reference Theory proclaims. Since in the light of chapter 2 this is not quite right, let us say that sentences with proper names express (pseudo-) Russellian-Kaplanian singular [external] propositions. We may start in fact with such singular propositions. Suppose that:

(2) Nelson Goodman OUGHT, by rule 15 of the G.P. Society, to present the Sellars-Chisholm Award to Willard Van Orman Quine at The Ohio State University Sala Magna on June 15, 1990, at 8 p.m.

This is a robust specimen of a (pseudo-) Russellian-Kaplanian singular proposition. Suppose that it is true. Yet that truth, regardless of how much we all rehearse it — and we can all rehearse it in succession or at unison — cannot be involved in the agent's intentional action of doing the action that according to (2) someone ought to perform. Of course, it is possible that someone thinking that (2) may be moved, by that very thought, to do something, for example, to write Quine a letter of congratulations. But for the agent mentioned in (2) to act intentionally there must be an intimate systematic internal connection between what he thinks and what his thinking causes him to do. Doubtless, it is easy to imagine that several may have been kidnapped, and after being drugged deposited in the Sala Magna of The Ohio State University, and that while neither one has any idea of who they are and where they are, it so happens that one of them is named Nelson Goodman, another Willard Van Orman Quine, and the former picks up a parchment from a table and hands it to the latter, thus complying with the obligation mentioned in (2). Clearly, even if Castañeda were caused to pick up the diploma and give it to Quine by his thinking episode that (2), this doesn't count as his intentionally complying with his duty. The *systematicity* of the causal connection between thinking intendingly and acting is missing, and so is the agent's knowing what he* is doing there* then* to whom*. (As before, the asterisk '*' signals quasi-indexicality.)

What is needed is that an agent who believes that (2) also believes a series of indexical equations:

(1.I1) I am (the same as) Nelson Goodman;

(1.I2) This [who is a] man is (the same as) Willard Van Orman Quine;

(1.I3) Today is (the same as) June 15, 1990;

(1.I4) Now is (the same as) 8 pm;

(1.I5) This is (the same as) the Sellars-Chisholm Award;

(1.I6) Here is (the same as) The Ohio State University Sala Magna.

These indexical equations the agent must take to be true, thus equating items in his experience with the Fregean-Kaplanian first referents of the terms. Some morals stand out:

Moral 1. Whatever the role of massive Fregean first referents may be, the indexical half of each equation is crucial. They are the pivots on which turns the agent's intentionally doing what he ought to do.

Moral 2. The problem of interpreting indicators is not one of finding the objects in the world they point to, but at least in the case of intentional action it is the problem of locating objects of the world in experience: by allowing them to acquire an indexical face, or guise.

Moral 3. The equations (1.I1)-(1.I6) must be taken by the agent to be true as they appear to him: They cannot be regarded as schematic equations, in which the indexical components are to be replaced by terms that harpoon massive, Fregean first referents. He needs them as premises in his deliberations.

Persons, objects, places, and times involved in an agent's obligations enter such obligations through specially deontically relevant properties and relations they possess. One ought to pay debts to creditors, return objects to lenders, help people in distress, and so on. In general, the reasons for or grounds of deontic modalities are universalizable. Russellian-Kaplanian propositions are irrelevant for the *creation* of obligations, duties, interdictions, and prohibitions. Good old internal Fregean propositions and internal Fregeanlike practitions (that is, the peculiar internal contents of practical thinking) with full descriptive specification of the relevant properties and relations seem not merely to suffice, but to be required by the universalizability underlying deontic status. Now, for the *execution* of obligations, or the violation of prohibitions, we need indexical truths, which, as illustrated, identify the persons, objects, places, and times, descriptively conceived as noted, with items presented in an appropriate experience. Thus, here again the Russellian-Kaplanian propositions are not merely not needed, but must be shunted by the agent in order for him to act. Russsellian-Kaplanian propositions just do not seem to have a role to play in practical thinking.

To underscore this point, let us observe that an agent who recognizes his conflicts of duties and deliberates to find out what to do may be amnesiac. He may, thus, have only his indexical references and a few beliefs about the corner of the world he is at and about some of his obligations. Yet he has all he needs to act deliberately and intentionally. He does not have to search for the Russellian-Kaplanian propositions having as constituent the unknown Fregean referent his uses of 'I' harpoon. Even if he could think of it, he would still have to equate it with *himself* for him to carry out his plans intentionally.

Nota bene 1. In the oral discussion of an early version of the preceding section, at the 1984 Stanford Conference honoring David Kaplan, John Perry suggested that the agent may act simply because he is so causally wired that his tokening of the sentence '*That* is a drowning man' may cause him to try to help the drowning man—or to refrain from helping and become ready to enjoy the spectacle of a man drowning. We do not have to postulate internal contents that are true or false: The sentence with its mere grammatical meaning may do.

My response to Perry was this. Undoubtedly such a causal situation is feasible in principle. But at most it would explain some extreme form of compulsive action. We must, however, explain intentional action, even action based on a deliberation aimed at finding a solution to a conflict of duties. For these we need premises that are taken by the agent both to be true and to express a truth that is present to the agent from which he may freely act, or refuse to act, not moved by compulsion.

Nota bene 2. Robert Moore suggested that perhaps we can dispense with truth. Perhaps the agent's tokening inferential sequences of sentences, just as we do in logical exercises, may suffice.

My response had two parts. First, in deliberation the agent has to believe his premises and he deliberates in order to elicit a conclusion of the form *I ought, everything relevant being considered, to A*, which he desires to believe. From that conclusion he may go on to infer "Therefore, I shall (will, am going to) A," which he endorses, adopts, as if it were true. (The resolve the agent finally reaches is neither true nor false; it is not really a proposition, but what I have called a *practition*. It has, nevertheless, values analogous to truth-values, which I have called *Legitimacy-values*. See *Thinking and Doing*, Chapters 6 and 10.)

Second, believing is a mental state that involves truth. It is of course an error to say that to believe that *p* is to believe that that *p* is true. This leads to an unwelcome infinity. But to believe that *p* is to place the proposition that *p* on the side of truth. Let me explain the point with a similar case. A child, a machine, lacking the concepts of *apple* and *pear* may yet be able to separate the apples and the pears in a basket and place them in different baskets. But a person who has got the two concepts can sort out apples from pears by classifying them. Likewise, to believe that *p* is not to classify that *p* as true, but it is, so to speak, to place that *p* in the truth bin. To believe that that *p* is true is to classify that *p* as true. For this one needs a (predicative) concept of truth.

Nota bene 3. Paul Benacerraf observed that the special indexical-practitional internal representation, of the *I to do A here now* (with room for many indicators in the action A) of what the agent intends, or is to do, for which I have been arguing, is needed in work in artificial intelligence dealing with the imitation of intentional action. In the formula 'I to do A', the infinitive form of copulation expresses the formal element characteristic of practitions.

Nota bene 4. In the sentence discussed above

(2) Nelson Goodman OUGHT, by rule 15 of the G.P. Society, to present the Sellars-Chisholm Award to Willard Van Orman Quine at The Ohio State University Sala Magna on June 15, 1990, at 8 p.m.

we see the important structural feature of practical thinking: It is a thinking of practitions. This grounds my oldest philosophical thesis:

(D.L) Deontic operators have practitions as arguments and propositions as values.

In (2) the deontic operator *OUGHT, by rule 15 of the G.P Society* applies to the practition *Nelson Goodman to present the Sellars-Chisholm Award to Willard Van Orman Quine at The Ohio State University Sala Magna on June 15, 1990 at 8 p.m.*, also expressed with an infinitive clause. The resulting judgment, (2), is a proposition: True or false, it can be believed, and sometimes even known to be true. But we must stop here.[3]

3. Attributions of Intention: Their Contextually Tacit Quasi-Indicator

Intentions, as this word is ordinarily used, refer not so much to the dispositional mental state of intending, but to the internal accusatives of intending, the intended content. For instance, in *Her intention to donate her services was (will be, is, would be) good*, the past (future, present) tense 'was' ('will be', 'is') expresses the time of the state of intending, yet what is said to be good is the content of that intending, what the agent would express by saying *I'm going (will, shall) donate my services*.

Intentions (internal intended contents) are expressed in direct speech assertions by means of future-tense sentences. Thus, future-tense sentences are ambiguous between (a) expressing a (Moorean, Fregean internal) first-person proposition—a *prediction*—which is true or false, and the proprietary content of believing; and (b) expressing a first-person practition—an *intention* or *resolve*—which is neither true nor false, and is the proprietary internal content of intending, wanting or desiring to do, planning, purposing. This ambiguity is dissolved under embedding in the proper psychological verbs:

PREDICTION:	INTENTION:
I'll go.	*I'll go*
I believe that I will go	*I intend to go.*

Once again we see the allocation to English infinitive clauses of the role (among others) of expressing practitions. We also see that the infinitive subordinate clause 'to go' has an implicit quasi-indicator 'I' as agent-subject. Since the subordinating conjunction 'that' is suitable to announce indicative clauses, which typically express propositions, it is not suitable to announce the infinitive clauses that express intentions. Thus, 'I intend that I to go' is not a sentence. But 'I intend: I [myself] to go' can do, where the colon ':' can be regarded as a generalization of the subordinating 'that' that heralds accusatives of propositional or practitional attitudes.

In any case, the attributions of intention, regardless of grammatical person, have a contextually tacit quasi-indicator. It is quite clear which one it is ('he*/she*', 'I*/myself*'), thus the whole construction is propositionally transparent. The situation is analogous to the attributions of perception, and it can be depicted as follows:

(3) At *t* X intended (will intend): [him/herself*] to A at *t'* .

In light of the discussion of Goodman giving Quine the Sellars-Chisholm Award, the operational states of intending will have as internal content a more indexical intention. To begin with, the time *t'* will be thought indexically by agent X, hence in diagram (3), there will often be an antecedent-quasi-indexical arrow connecting *t**' to *t*, and there will be similar arrows connecting the quasi-indicators in A to their own antecedents.[4]

Notes

1. See Hector-Neri Castañeda, *Thinking and Doing*, (Dordrecht: Reidel, 1975), especially chaps. 2–9, and "Aspectual Actions and Davidsonian Events," in Ernest LePore, ed., *Companion to 'Actions and Events'* (Oxford: Blackwell, 1985).

2. See *Thinking and Doing*, chap. 10.3, and "Conditional Intentions, Intentional Action, and Aristotelian Practical Syllogisms", *Erkenntnis* 18 (1982): 239–60.

3. See especially *Thinking and Doing*, chaps. 7 and 10.

4. The indexicality of contents of intentional thinking and voluntary action is crucially involved in immediate intentional actions, actions to do something right now. But conditional and general intentions need for their causation indexical thinking. This thinking need not itself be a thinking of an intention of the form *I-to-A-here-now*, but may be a contemplative thinking of some indexical minor premise, as we have discussed above with the agent Nelson Goodman. For details see the studies mentioned in note 2. Doubtless, the weakness of the will must be placed within the causation of intentional action. For an account of weakness of will enriched by the proposition/practition distinction, see Hector-Neri Castañeda, "Reply to Michael Bratman: Deontic Truth, Intentions, and Weakness of the Will," in Tomberlin 1, pp. 403–7.

8

Personality, Anaphora, and Verbal Tenses

1. Split Personality and Anaphora: A Letter to Barbara Partee and Emmon Bach

July 25, 1985

Professors Barbara Partee and Emmon Bach
Department of Linguistics
University of Massachusetts
Amherst, Mass.

Dear Emmon and Barbara:

I have finally been able to read your beautiful paper "Anaphora and Semantic Structure".[1] I have enjoyed it very much and have learned a lot from it. You have persuaded me of the general claims of your paper. . . .

I was touched by your reference to my work in your paper and by your use of the war-hero example.[2] Here I would like very much to have your reaction and instruction. I thought that the amnesiac hero could have provided situations for the use of sentences that you regard as improper and mark with '#'. Let me belabor this somewhat. You discuss a series of rules of English syntax that do not permit two pronouns, or a pronoun and a noun, in one simple sentence to be coindexed, or coreferring. For instance, you contrast at

40. I promised *him* to vote for *him*,
     #I persuaded *him* to vote for *him*,

where coreference is fine in the former, but not in the latter. You mark:

42c. #He loves John's mother

thus showing that 'He' and 'John' cannot be coindexed.

Now, it seems to me that the rules you formulate that secure those results are correct under one assumption, namely: *the unity of the personality of the persons talked about*. If this is correct, then perhaps we should distinguish two sets of rules governing anaphora: (A) general rules that maintain the unity of coreference in anaphoric chains regardless of psychological assumptions about the people around us, and (B) special rules that hinge on common assumptions about normal experiences. To develop this let me expand on the hero story.

(C*) MARK, QUINTUS, THE WAR HERO, THE BIOGRAPHER, and MARK.

One day after a bar brawl, Mark was brought unconscious from Los Angeles to Vietnam. There he regains consciousness and becomes a great hero wounded 100 times, celebrated in the newspapers and magazines. At his last battle he is seriously wounded and enters a state of coma. He is returned unconscious to Los Angeles. He develops total amnesia for the whole chapter of his life in Vietnam. During his convalescence he entertains himself by reading magazines. He reads about the hero's exploits and feels some strange fascination for that hero. He studies everything he can about the hero, and ends up writing, under the pen name Quintus, the most authoritative biography of the hero, *knowing who* the hero is better than anybody else, but without knowing that he himself is the hero. His biography turns out to be such a great commercial success that he becomes Quintus. After writing his bestseller, Quintus enjoys some ten years of happy and productive life. Then he falls into a new state of depression and amnesia. He forgets that he is Quintus, yet he maintains a deep interest in this writer. He uses his childhood name, Mark. He lives with his wife, whom he takes to be a nurse at the private infirmary he believes to be his house.

Quintus is being attended by Dr. Hecdnett, who believes in a very methodical third-person causative therapy. He has learned a lot about Quintus and he insists on discussing with his patient the writer and family man Quintus, exclusively in a purely third-personal way, avoiding second-person utterances, deliberately avoiding suggestions or statements that the patient is Quintus, or the war hero. Dr. Hecdnett even refuses to assert premises from which by mere logical means the patient can deduce that he* is Quintus. His program is to CAUSE his patient—*not* to make him deduce—to think of the situation being talked about at some crucial moment in a first person way so that he himself can jump to the hypothesis that he* is Quintus.

One day Dr. Hecdnett is reporting his program and Quintus's progress to Quintus's wife and is urging her to follow a similar approach at home. In the midst of his speech he makes the following statements, where the underscored sentences are the sentences you mark as ruled out under the very same numbers I use, and the '*' is a reminder of the quasi-indexical 'he*':

45*. Quintus is still in need of careful treatment. *Today I talked to him about Quintus* only, exclusively in the third-person way, not about himself.

42c*. He still doesn't recognize his mother as his own, but has accepted that his mother is Quintus's mother, and *he loves Quintus's mother.*

41*. He likes Quintus, and *he said that Quintus is OK.*

50*. Frankly, *I regard him as Quintus's best friend.*

40*. It was easy, *I persuaded him to vote for him* [Quintus], for the membership in the credentials committee. He should have no problem marking the ballot.

79*. *He promised of his own initiative to see (seek) him.*

81*. He is improving so much. *He is so easy to explain to him.*

47*. He is so taken up with Quintus's work, that he wants to expand Quintus's biography of the famous hero wounded 100 times and publish a second edition of Quintus's masterpiece. He wants to call himself 'Quinttus' with double 'tec' to express his admiration for him. *I am relying on him for Quintus's contribution,* for the completion of Quintus's lifetime project.

To conclude, it seems to me that in contexts of use that assume (C*), all those sentences allow a kind of macro-coindexing. On the one hand, there is the whole macro person composed of Mark, Quintus, the war hero, Mark and Quinttus. On the other hand, there is clearly a duality between third-person indexing representing the uses of third-person referring expressions, and second-person quasi-indexical indexing, representing the uses of second-person indicators. Clearly, the speaker, Dr. Hecdnett, refers to Quintus as YOU when he is talking to him AS his interlocutor, and as QUINTUS in the primary therapeutic dialogue. This duality is what led me to speak in the mid-1960s (especially in "Indicators and Quasi-indicators") of perspectival properties, and in 1972 led to guise theory, and in connection with perception and demonstrative reference, to indexical guises and private perceptual fields. I know, this is too much for this. But there are other data being welded together.

H.–N. C.

P.S. Perhaps the discussion of two controverted cases of anaphora may be of some linguistic interest. One is the case like:

(1) Delilah has a cat—in fact she has three cats—; well, THE cat, THAT cat, bit Samson.

There is no need to suppose that the indefinite article of 'a cat' is at bottom definite, nor is it necessary to suppose that the article 'the' is really indefinite. The indefinite article is fine, and it is used for setting the stage where a definite character, THAT cat, will play its role. (See chapter 4, section 6.)

The stage-setting role can occur within indirect speech. Because de dicto expressions represent a cumulation of speaker's reference and attributed references, the speaker can segregate his/her own singular references from a de dicto term. For example:

(2) The King thought that the Queen was having an affair with the White Devil; but as THIS does not exist THE (THAT) affair was impossible, SHE was actually having an affair with each of the Blue Knights.

Here 'SHE' disentangles the speaker's reference, blended with the reference attributed to the King, in 'the Queen'; likewise, the demonstrative 'this' segregates the speaker's reference tangled in 'the White Devil'; the (imaginary) affair is placed on the stage through the cumulative indefinite reference made with 'an affair with the White Devil'. The speaker both disentangles his/her own reference and presents it as the individual of the next piece of the narrative. (See chapter 5, section 1.)

2. Indexicality and Quasi-Indexicality in Verbal Tenses

Verbal tenses contain complex patterns of indexicality and quasi-indexicality. In general, tenses in direct speech clauses are indexical, expressing the speaker's indexical references to time. Tenses in indirect speech clauses may be indexical or quasi-indexical. The old grammatical principle of agreement or concordance between direct and indirect speech verbs in the same sentence is really a principle of agreement between the speaker's indexical tenses and the quasi-indexical tenses of her represented attributions of indexical references to time. The violation of the principle substitutes the speaker's indexical tenses for her quasi-indexical depictions of others' indexical tenses.

Compare:

(1) Yesterday Susan realized that Hal was dying (then*).
(2) Yesterday Susan realized that Hal is dying.

The past tense of *realized* is an indicator in both (1) and (2). The concordance of the past tenses in (1) has the effect of making the past tense of *was dying* a quasi-indicator: It depicts Susan's past thought of the form *Hal IS (now) dying*. The concordance is reinforced by the explicit quasi-indicator 'then*'. On the other hand, the present tense of *is* in (2) expresses the speaker's reference to the time of both speech and death as present. There is, thus, propositional opacity at the present tense of *is* in (2). Given that Susan's realization is past and the realized state of affairs is present, perhaps Susan endorsed a future-tense proposition: *Hal will be dying at time t*, and it is the speaker who equates time *t* with the present.

A Tentative Summary

The main indexical and quasi-indexical dimensions of the English tenses embedded in one psychological prefix seem to be:

1. *Present tense*: characteristically indexical within past and present embedding prefixes, but it may be quasi-indexical in conditioning clauses and in future constructions.

2. *Past tense*: typically quasi-indexical, regardless of whether the embedding prefix is present, past or future, depicting attributed present or present perfect.

3. *Future tense*: indexical when embedded in past and present constructions, quasi-indexical depicting attributed references to a present/future when embedded in future constructions.

4. *Conditional*: quasi-indexical, depicting a future relative to the past of the embedding construction.[3]

5. *Conditional perfect*: quasi-indexical depicting reference to a future earlier than another future, when embedded in a past-tense construction.

6. *Present perfect*: generally indexical, but when embedded in future-tense constructions functions quasi-indexically depicting attributed references to a present perfect.

7. *Past perfect*: quasi-indexical, depicting references to a past preceding the past of the embedding construction.

8. *Future perfect*: indexical when embedded in past constructions, quasi-indexical depicting attributed references to a pre-future when embedded in present- or future-tense constructions.

Notes

1. Emmon Bach and Barbara H. Partee, "Anaphora and Semantic Structure," in Jody Kreiman and Almerindo E. Ojeda, eds., *Papers from the Parasession on Pronouns and Anaphora* (Chicago: Chicago Linguistic Society, 1980).

2. The war hero appeared for the second time in Hector-Neri Castañeda, "On the Logic of Attributions of Self-knowledge to Others," *The Journal of Philosophy* 65 (1968): 439–55.

3. Charles Bally, "Le style indirect libre en français moderne," *Germanisch-romanische Monatsschrift* 4 (1912): 449–556, 597–606.

9

God and Knowledge: Omniscience and Indexical Reference

1. The Problem

In a very intriguing and exciting paper[1] Norman Kretzmann has argued for the thesis (A) that God's omniscience is incompatible with his immutability, and, in an appendix (420–421) suggested by certain results of mine,[2] for the thesis (B) that omniscience is incompatible with theism, that is, the doctrine that God is a person distinct from others. Kretzmann's arguments depend on certain features of indexical reference, that is, reference to times, places, events, objects, or persons by means of demonstrative or personal pronouns or adverbs. The argument for (A) relies essentially on the fact that a person's indexical references to time, for example, by means of the word 'now', are ephemeral: At different times of utterance 'now' refers to different times. The argument for (B) depends essentially on the fact that a person's indexical references to himself, for example, by means of the first-person pronoun 'I', are intransferable: Nobody can refer to another man by means of a genuine first-person reference. Thus, Kretzmann's arguments and conclusions suggest parallel arguments and conclusions for the other types of indexical reference. For example, I can imagine, in the spirit of Kretzmann's arguments, a reasoning intended to show that an omniscient being cannot exist at any place in space, and, hence, cannot be ubiquitous, as a Christian tradition conceives God to be, for an omniscient being knows the truth of every proposition expressible with the sentence 'I am here, but not there', regardless of who it is who says 'I'.

But Kretzmann's essay has an even more important value: Through the two special cases, it raises the general question: How can a person, whether omniscient or not, believe, know, consider, or, in general, apprehend and formulate for himself and by himself a proposition or statement (I will use these terms as having the same referent) that contains an indexical reference by another person?

Kretzmann's arguments for (A) and (B) simply assume that the answer to this general question is: "In no way at all." This is the assumption behind his claim that "Every person knows certain propositions that no *other* person *can* know" (p. 421; his italics). But it seems to me that there is a perfectly accessible way of, so to speak, capturing another person's indexical references intact, so that one can formulate another person's indexical statements qua indexical. This way consists in the use of what I have elsewhere called "quasi-indicators."[3]

Here I want: (i) to show how Kretzmann's arguments for (A) and (B) depend essentially on the assumption that a person's indexical statements cannot be known or formulated by another, (ii) to show the impact of quasi-indexical references on those arguments, and (iii) to explore the effect of indexical and quasi-indexical reference on omniscience.

2. Kretzmann's Argument and Quasi-indicators

Kretzmann's argument for (A) has the following relevant premise:

(4) A being that always knows what time it is is subject to change.

He supports (4) both by an argument and by replies to four objections to (4). His argument is worthy of careful examination; it is:

> Adopting 'it is now t_n' as a convenient standard form for propositions as to what time it is, we may say of a being that always knows what time it is that the state of its knowledge changes incessantly with respect to propositions of the form 'it is now t_n'. First such a being knows that it is now t_1 (and that it is not now t_s), and then it knows that it is now t_s (and that it is not now t_1). To say of a being that it knows something different from what it used to know is to say that it has changed; hence (4). [p. 410, fn 4]

Kretzmann does not assign any special meaning to the word 'now'. Presumably his argument can be understood on the assumption that this word is used by him in its ordinary sense. Letting 'X' be the name of the being he is talking about, Kretzmann's crucial premise is:

(4a) First X knows that it is now t_1 and not t_2, and then X knows that it is now t_2, and not t_1.

(From now on I will use expressions like '(4a)' to refer either to the indented sentence they precede or to a given ordinary statement the sentence in question is supposed to express. The context should make clear which is meant. Double quotes around a sentence will name a statement made with it; single quotes will name the sentence.) From (4a) Kretzmann infers that X knows at t_2 something different from what he knew at t_1. The inference is persuasive, and its examination most instructive.

In ordinary usage an indicator like 'now' or 'I' or 'here' is used, even in *oratio obliqua* [as in (4a) above], to make indexical references by the speaker. Thus, in ordinary usage the occurrences of 'now' in (4a) formulate Kretzmann's own indexical references to times t_1 and t_2, respectively. But since the two occurrences of 'now' refer to two different times, the proposition or statement formulated by the occurrence of the clause 'it is not t_1' in sentence (4a) is different from, but not incompatible with, the statement formulated by the occurrence of the clause 'it is not now t_1' in (4a); and similarly for the statements expressed by 'it is not now t_2' and 'it is now t_2'. Hence, according to (4a), X knew at t_1 two propositions about time, and at t_2 he knew two other compatible propositions about time. Thus, if he knew all four propositions at t_1, X may very well have known at t_2 exactly the same propositions he knew at t_1, and Kretzmann would err in inferring from statement (4a) that X's knowledge, and a fortiori X himself, changed from t_1 to t_2. We must then investigate whether or not X can know at t_1 the proposition that Kretzmann expressed by his use of the clause 'it is now t_2' occurring in (4a). Indeed, can Kretzmann himself know at t_1 the very same proposition he expressed at t_2 by using 'it is now t_2' as part of (4a)? The rub lies here in the indexical reference of 'now'. Obviously, if the indexical reference of Kretzmann's statement at t_2 "it is now t_2" cannot be captured intact at time t_1, then at t_1 this statement cannot even be formulated, let alone be known by X or by Kretzmann himself. Hence, if this is the case, it would seem that Kretzmann is after all justified in deriving (4) from (4a). (I will not stop here to consider the very relevant view that X at any time, as well as Kretzmann at t_1, can apprehend and know the latter's indexical statement at t_2, without being able to formulate it.)

There is, however, a serious but subtle difficulty with Kretzmann's argument. As the preceding analysis shows, the argument relies heavily on the fact that the clause 'it is now t_2' in (4a) expresses an indexical proposition. But it is Kretzmann's own indexical proposition, since *indicators in oratio obliqua express indexical references by the speaker, and leave it open whether the person spoken about refers to the same objects indexically or not.*[4] Thus, when I say "Privatus believes that I (you, this) weigh (weighs) 150 pounds," I do not imply that Privatus has made an indexical reference to me (you, or this). Indeed, my sentences of the form 'Privatus believes that I . . . ' have a certain misleadingness, since Privatus cannot refer to me in the first person! More strikingly, when Gaskon says "Yesterday Privatus thought (guessed, predicted, etc.) that it would be raining now (today)," Gaskon's statement both contains his own indexical uses of 'now' ("today") and fails to imply that Privatus referred indexically to the time at which Gaskon makes his statement. Likewise, Kretzmann's statement (4a) above both formulates Kretzmann's *own* indexical references to t_1 and t_2, and does *not* imply that X referred to t_1 or t_2 indexically. Thus my reason above for saying that it would seem that Kretzmann is after all justified in deriving (4) from (4a) is really irrelevant: for (4a) does not preclude the possibility that the four propositions that X is said to know may be nonindexical, that is, contain no indexical references at all, so that he may know all four of them at t_1. We must, then, reformulate Kretzmann's argument without the word 'now'.

Furthermore, Kretzmann means to be making a general point that has nothing to do with him or his indexical references. His point is both that, to know what time it is at a given time, a person has to make some indexical reference of *his own* that will put him into the stream of changes in the world, and that, thus, that person cannot be immutable. Hence, the very effectiveness of Kretzmann's argument requires that we be able to reformulate it without mentioning or alluding to Kretzmann's own indexical references, that is, without using the word 'now'. We must, then, ask whether or not we can formulate a premise about another person's knowing a proposition that contains indexical references by that person. And the answer lies ready at hand. The crucial premise Kretzmann's argument needs can be formulated adequately and in full generality as follows:

(4b) At t_1 X knows [tenselessly] that it is [tenselessly] *then* t_1, but not t_2, and at t_2, later than t_1, X knows that it is *then* t_2, but not t_1.

The crucial difference between (4b) and (4a) is, phonetically, very simple: the word 'then' instead of the word 'now'. But semantically the difference is enormous: (a) 'now' does, while 'then' does not, express an indexical reference by the speaker; (b) 'then' does, while 'now' does not, attribute to X an indexical reference to time t_1 in the first and to time t_2 in the second conjunct; (c) whereas sentence (4a) cannot be used by Kretzmann or anybody else to make exactly the same statement at times other than t_1 and t_2, sentence (4b) can be used repeatedly at any time by anybody to make exactly the same statement on each occasion of its utterance. Thus, 'then' as used in (4b) is not an indicator: It is, in my terminology, a *quasi-indicator*. Among its syntactico-semantical characteristics are: (i) its appearing in *oratio obliqua*, that is, in a clause subordinated to a verb expressing a propositional attitude; (ii) its having an antecedent not in the same oratio obliqua, which in (4b) is 't_1' for the first occurrence of 'then' and 't_2' for the second occurrence; (iii) its not being replaceable by its antecedent with preservation of the proposition or statement formulated with the whole sentence; in our example, sentence (4b) clearly formulates a different statement from that formulated by

(4c) At t_1 X knew that it was t_1 at t_1, but not t_2, and at t_2 he knew that it was t_2 at t_2, but not t_1.

That statement expressed by (4c) is true if X knows that t_1 is different from t_2, even if at t_1 or at t_2 he does not know what time it is then.

Again, according to (4b), X knows four propositions or statements to be true. Again, the issue is whether or not X can know all four statements to be true at t_1 as well as at t_2. If X can, then Kretzmann's argument for his premise (4) is invalid. Interestingly enough, the problem is now *not* that of reformulating a statement containing indexical references, but the different problem of reformulating a statement containing quasi-indexical references. And by characteristic (c) above, a statement containing quasi-indexical references is repeatable by different persons at different times by means of the very same sentence. Thus, there seems in principle to be no difficulty about finding a formulation of the quasi-indexical statement contained in (4b) and expressed by 'it was then t_2' so that at t_1 X could know it or have any other propositional attitude toward it. We need, however, an important, but perfectly trivial principle, to wit:

(P) If a sentence of the form 'X knows that a person Y knows that . . . ' formulates a true statement, then the person X knows the statement formulated by the clause filling the blank ' . . . '.

This principle must be carefully understood: It establishes a sort of transitivity of knowledge, but it does *not* say anything about detaching expressions of the form 'Y knows that'. Undoubtedly, in most cases such detachment is legitimate. For instance, "Jones knows that Smith knows that $2 + 5 = 7$" does entail "Jones knows that $2 + 5 = 7$." But if the very last subordinate clause of a sentence of the form "X knows that Y knows that $- - -$ " contains quasi-indicators, such detachment may lead to absurdity or to a fallacy. For instance "Mary knows that George knows that he (himself) is in pain" does not entail (since there is no such proposition as) "Mary knows that he (himself) is in pain."[5] Yet, the former entails that Mary and George know the very same proposition about George's being in pain. For perspicuity I will write 'then$_A$' to represent an occurrence of the quasi-indicator 'then' having the expression A as antecedent.

Thus (4b) is compatible with

(4d) Time t_2 is later than t_1, and at t_1 X knows both (1) that it is then $_{t1}$ t_1, but not t_2, and (2) that somebody knows (or would know) at t_2 that it is (would be) then $_{t2}$ t_2 but not t_1.

By (P), (4d) entails that at t_1 X knew not only the two propositions that according to (4b) he knew at t_1, but also the other two propositions that by (4b) he knew at t_2. Hence, it does not follow from (4b) and (4d), or from (4b) alone, that at t_2 X underwent a change in knowledge. Therefore, Kretzmann's argument for his premise (4) is really invalid.

3. Knowledge of Change

Kretzmann defends his thesis (4), that a being that always knows what time it is is subject to change, by replying to four objections. Both the objections and his replies raise very interesting issues, which I will simply not consider here, except for the first objection. An anonymous discussant objects to (4) by saying: A change in the object of knowledge does not entail a change in the knower. Kretzmann argues that sometimes a change in the object of knowledge requires a change of knowledge. He illustrates as follows:

If the object of my knowledge is the *height* of the Chrysler Building, then of course a change in the object of my knowledge does necessitate a change in me. If a 40-foot television antenna is extended from the present tip of the tower, either I will cease to know the [present] height of the Chrysler

Building or I will give up believing that its height is 1,046 feet and begin believing that it is 1,086 feet. [p. 411]

Again, the argument is based on indexical references, this time on those made by means of the present tense. And, again, the question the argument raises is whether or not a person can know at time t_1 (prior to the extension of the antenna) a proposition that he would express at t_2 (after the extension) by uttering a sentence containing an indicator, e.g., "Now the Chrysler Building is 1,086 feet tall." Once again, the answer is "yes," and a way of finding one formulation of that proposition is the method illustrated above, in which we employed principle (P). Thus, suppose that

(5) Kretzmann knows at t_1 that: the Chrysler Building is 1,046 feet high at t_1, and at t_2 it will have a 40-foot antenna extended from its tip, and that the man who makes the extension knows at t_2 that the Chrysler Building is 1,086 feet high *then*.

Clearly, if (5) obtains, Kretzmann knows of the change in height without having to change his knowledge. Of course, at t_2 Kretzmann can use the words 'now' and 'present' to refer to the height of the Chrysler Building, words that were not available to him at t_1. But this is an entirely different issue.

4. Self-Knowledge

Kretzmann argues that omniscience and theism are incompatible on the ground that there are certain propositions that only one person can know. His example is

(7) Jones knows that he (himself) is in the hospital

Clearly, (7) is a statement quite different from "Jones knows that Jones is in the hospital." The statement that Jones knows by (7) is one that Jones would express by saying "I am in the hospital." That is, (7) attributes to Jones a first-person indexical reference. In short, the expression 'he (himself)' in sentence (7) is a quasi-indicator. It cannot be eliminated from (7) by any name or description of Jones that includes no first-person quasi-indicator. It is this fact that leads Kretzmann to say that the statement expressed by the occurrence of 'he (himself) is in the hospital' in (7) cannot be known by any other person. But this does not follow. If Kretzmann, or the reader, knows that Jones knows that he (himself) is in the hospital, then, by principle (P) above, Kretzmann or the reader knows the very same proposition that by (7) Jones knows to be true. Hence, theism is not, by the present route, incompatible with omniscience.

At this juncture one can, of course, raise the problem of other minds. If there is a sense of 'know' in which one cannot know facts of the form "X, different from me, knows that — — —," then there is a sense in which one cannot know another person's *oratio recta* indexical statements, *whether they are about himself or not, and whether they are about physical or psychological matters*. But this is another, though related, issue, which undoubtedly takes a different shape for the case of an omniscient God.

5. Omniscience and Omnipotence

The preceding discussion makes it clear, I hope, that neither theism nor immutability is incompatible with God on account of indexical references being personal, intransferable, and ephemeral. We have indicated, via principle (P), a method for capturing indexical references intact, that is, for apprehending another person's indexical statements qua indexical statements, even though these are ephemeral and intransferable. Other methods can be devised by using other principles of epistemic logic. But all such methods are conceived on the principle that an indexical statement for one person cannot be the very same statement, indexical or otherwise, for another person. This principle has some theological consequences, although not so revolutionary as those which Kretzmann derived from the principle that a person's indexical statement cannot be known by another person. I think it is clear that from the preceding discussion it follows that:

First, the existence of an omniscient being is impossible, or an omniscient being does not know every proposition in *oratio recta*: indexical propositions he must know in *oratio obliqua*, in the form of quasi-indexical propositions.

Second, the existence of an omniscient and immutable being is impossible, or an omniscient immutable being knows the contents of other minds on grounds other than behavior and circumstances: for in order to know of changes in behavior or circumstances he must think of them, quasi-indexically, as known by other persons.

Third, an omniscient being cannot be omnipotent, or omnipotence does not include the ability to derive whatever proposition P a finite person X knows from the proposition "X that $- - -$," where the blanks are occupied by a sentence S expressing P and nothing but P: if P is an indexical proposition, S will have quasi-indicators that cannot be used in *oratio recta*.[6]

Fourth, an omniscient being who is also immutable cannot be omnipotent, or omnipotence does not include the ability to formulate indexical propositions.

6. Knowledge and Self: A Correspondence between Robert M. Adams and Hector-Neri Castañeda[7]

February 26, 1979

Professor Hector-Neri Castañeda
Department of Philosophy
Indiana University
Bloomington, IN 47401

Dear Hector,

It was a great pleasure to meet you. The afternoon and evening that you gave us were the most enjoyable and philosophically interesting that our Colloquium has provided in quite some time. So again, our thanks.

Let me put in writing, and perhaps in somewhat better order, the argument I was working on, and relate it to some things that Rogers Albritton was saying. I take it that you were working with a transitivity principle that can be put as follows:

(1) If A knows that B knows that P, then A knows the proposition expressed by $\ulcorner$that p$\urcorner$ in $\ulcorner$B knows that P$\urcorner$.

It seems to me that (1) is no more plausible than

(2) If A knows that B is saying truly that P, then A knows the proposition expressed by $\ulcorner$that P$\urcorner$ in $\ulcorner$B is saying truly that P$\urcorner$.

I assume further that if (1) and (2) are correct, they should still be correct if A and B are coreferential. Now consider your example of the Editor of *Soul* who knows that the Editor of *Soul* is rich but does not know that he himself is rich because he does not yet know that he himself is the Editor of *Soul*. Let us suppose that he has not yet heard the decision of the Board of Directors of the journal, but he knows that one of seven candidates has been selected Editor, that he is one of them, and that all seven are present in the same room. They have just heard the reading of a will bequeathing several million dollars to the Editor of *Soul*, whoever he may be. Having heard this, they are now chanting in unison, "I am rich," each of them hoping, but not exactly believing, and certainly (we would say preanalytically) not knowing, that it is true of himself. In this situation the following seems to be true:

(3) The Editor of *Soul* knows that the Editor of *Soul* is saying truly that he himself is rich.

From (2) and (3) it follows that the Editor of *Soul* knows the proposition expressed by 'that he himself is rich' in (3). But that is a proposition that we were certain preanalytically that the Editor of *Soul* does not know. I am inclined to think the conclusion to be drawn from this example is that you should reject the principle (2). But if (2) is rejected then I think that (1) ought also to be rejected, since they seem equally plausible intuitively, and since what makes (1) plausible is that the notion of truth enters implicitly into (1) in much the same way that it enters explicitly into (2).

Rogers's example was closely related, in my opinion. The example went something like this:

(4) Alfred knows (having heard it from a reliable informant) that the Chair of the UCLA Philosophy Department knows that he himself is a U.S. citizen.

(5) Alfred knows (having heard it from a reliable informant) that the only ordained Minister who is a member of the UCLA Philosophy Department knows that he himself is a U.S. citizen.

According to (1), if (4) and (5) are both true Alfred knows the proposition expressed by 'that he himself is a U.S. citizen' in (4) and the proposition expressed by 'that he himself is a U.S. citizen' in (5). In fact, they are one and the same proposition, but it seems that Alfred might not know that they are, even if (4) and (5) are true, because he might not know that the Chairman of the UCLA Philosophy Department is the only ordained Minister who is a member of the UCLA Philosophy Department.

In both Rogers's example and my example it is clear that the problem arises because the person who knows the complex proposition ascribing an *oratio obliqua* fails in some way or respect to know who the person is to whom the *oratio obliqua* is ascribed—although of course he does know something that he could give as an answer to the question to whom he is ascribing the *oratio obliqua*. Intuitively it seems to me that at the very least this sort of ignorance keeps one from fully grasping the proposition ascribed by the innermost *oratio obliqua*. The person to whom it is ascribed could not fail to grasp it in the same way, however. For there is nothing I need to know about myself in order to know what proposition I am expressing or thinking if I say or think that I myself am a U.S. citizen.

I rather like the image we were tossing around at the end of the evening's discussion, according to which you should say that by the use of quasi-indicators we do not present the very same proposition that would be thought or expressed by someone who appropriately thought or said the corresponding sentence in *oratio recta*, but neither do we merely describe that proposition; rather we present a proposition that, so to speak, impersonates it. That's rather pictorial and I don't know just how to flesh it out, but I will try to think more about the subject.

Thanks again for your paper and discussion.

Sincerely yours,

Robert Merrihew Adams
Professor and Chairman

April 6, 1979

Professor Robert M. Adams
Department of Philosophy
University of California at Los Angeles
Los Angeles, CA 90024

Dear Bob,

Again, please accept both my thanks for your precious letter of February 26 and my apology for not having been able to respond sooner. But better late than never, as somebody said early enough in history.

I have just reread your letter. It is excellent. I admire and like it more now even than when I first read it. But now I can put down some reflections. I will not exhaust its richness, but at least I want to think "finger-out-loud" in writing this letter.

1. My first impulse was to go along with your suggestion that (1) and (2) below are equally plausible:

(1) If A knows that B knows that P, then A knows the proposition expressed by ⌜that P⌝ in ⌜B knows that P⌝ .

(2) If A knows that B is saying truly that P, then A knows the proposition expressed by ⌜that P⌝ in ⌜B is saying truly that P⌝ .

You note on page 2 of your letter " . . . what makes (1) plausible is that the notion of truth enters implicitly into (1) in much the same way it enters explicitly into (2)." This seems to me true, if it is interpreted very narrowly.

1.1 However, (1) is plausible in a way in which (2) is not. Truth enters in both, and, as you correctly indicate, entering implicitly or entering explicitly is not differentiating enough. But there is a very important difference, it seems to me, between (1) and (2); namely, the evidential component of knowledge: It is not present in (2), but it is present in (1). Whether knowledge is just true belief and evidence, or not, is not crucial: We can agree to pack whatever else is required for knowledge into the evidential component.

1.1.1. You deal with part of the evidential component in the penultimate paragraph on page 3 of your letter:

The problem arises because the person who knows the complex proposition ascribing an *oratio obliqua* fails in some way or respect to know who the person is to whom the *oratio obliqua* is ascribed. . . . Intuitively it seems to me that at the very least this sort of *ignorance* [my italics] keeps one from fully grasping the proposition ascribed by the innermost *oratio obliqua*.

Crudely taken, the end of the quotation does suggest that saying is not enough, that a lack of certain ignorance, that is, the possession of certain knowledge, is required. This is what separates (1) from (2).

2. You are right in connecting your point with Rogers Albritton's. This is also clearer to me now than it was before. In fact the connection is there in your quotation very neatly: the ignorance in question can be construed as ignorance of *which* proposition is the one to be believed. In your example the seven candidates say, expressing hope, not belief, "I am rich." The Editor kows, in the sense of being acquainted (*connaître* or *conocer* or the primary sense of GIGNOSKO), each of the seven propositions being proffered, but he does not know which one to believe—because he lacks the appropriate evidence. Thus, he lacks knowledge in the sense of *savoir*, or *saber*, or *wissen*, or OIDA.

3. The situation does make it true, as you say, that

(3) The Editor of *Soul* knows that the Editor of *Soul* is saying (in the sense of uttering) truly that he himself is rich.

I wonder whether my original temptation to agree with you that (1) and (2) are equally possible was not also motivated by the belief element of knowledge, in addition to the truth element you discuss. That would come about by taking 'is saying' in (2), but not in (3), not merely as uttering, but as asserting. In any case, I do think that that was the sense in which I understood 'is saying' when I first read (2). Yet it makes no difference: the evidential component would still be absent.

4. A most important upshot of the preceding discussion, which your example brings out very nicely, is this: A knows, that is, A *sabe* (OIDE) that-P can be true, in the sense of A *conoce* or GIGNOSKEI that-p, without A knowing-that P. The point I am making is this. Within the sense of knowledge corresponding to *connaître*,

We must distinguish between the relation knowing (or *knows*) between a person and a proposition (or a propositional function, etc.), and the personalized modalities of the form *X-knows-that*. The distinction in English can be signaled with hyphens: relational sense: A knows that -P: modality: A-knows-that P.

I claim in "Perception, Belief, and the Structure of Physical Objects and Consciousness" (*Synthese*, 1977), toward the end, in Part II, that the distinction has to be made between relational and modalized propositional attitudes, and that the relational proposition "X believes that -P" implies the modal proposition "X-believes-that P" (this is law (R-M) at the bottom of p. 335). On p. 339 I claimed that the equivalence of pairs of corresponding relational and modal propositions distinguishes non-perceptual states of mind from perceptual ones. (These are put in laws (P*1), and (R-M), and M.R.1.) and M.R.2.), pp. 338–39.)

Now, your example shows that the relation of knowing (*conocer*, GIGNOSKEIN) can hold between a thinker and a proposition without the corresponding modalized psychological proposition with the modality *X-knows-that* being true. Does this refute my claim about the distinction between perceptual and non-perceptual states of mind (including states of consciousness)? My first reaction was to say no, because knowing is not just a psychological state or modality. But that seems to me wrong. I believe that your example refutes the generality of my claim in "Perception, Belief, . . . ". I still think that the special law for believing and believing-that is correct. In any case, your example is strong evidence in favor of making the relation-modality distinction, and it remains open how far the equivalence between the corresponding pairs of relation and modality stretches. Unfortunately, I cannot enter into that investigation here-now.

5. Your formulation of Rogers Albritton's example seems to me to be right, as I remember Rogers's discussion. Let me discuss it somewhat differently. The example is:

(4) Alfred knows that the Chair of the UCLA Philosophy Department knows that he himself is a U.S. citizen.

(5) Alfred knows that the only ordained Minister in the UCLA Philosophy Department knows that he himself is a U.S. citizen.

By principle (1) above Alfred knows the proposition expressed by the occurrence of the clause 'he himself is a U.S. citizen' in (4). Let us call it P. By (1), too, Alfred knows the proposition expressed by the occurrence of that clause in (2). Let us call it Q. It is natural to think that P is the *same* as Q. Call this *thesis 1*. It is further, natural to think that P and Q are *strictly identical*, that is, that the sameness just mentioned is strict (full, conclusive) identity. Call this *thesis 2*. I have committed myself to these two theses. In "Omniscience and Indexical Reference," where I introduced principle (1) under the name "(P)", my argument against Kretzmann depends on the assumption that P=Q.

I have distinguished between propositional identity and propositional sameness. This is a novelty as far as our discussion has reached. But it is a novelty that goes hand-in-glove with my theory of guises. In "Perception, Belief, . . . " I extended the original guise theory, developed for ordinary object, to propositions (which I identify with states of affairs). Thus, I am already committed in this paper to allowing jointly the falsity of something of the form "P=Q" and the truth of something of the form "P s Q," for an appropriate concept of sameness. In that paper a proposition has propositional guises, so that two of these, strictly different, are nevertheless the same in that they belong to one and the self-same proposition.

5.1. In any case, I claimed in "Omniscience and Indexical Reference," as well as during the last round of discussion at dinner with you and your colleagues, that P is strictly identical with Q. Rogers's example (4)-(5) was not meant to refute this, but an additional thesis I endorsed under David Kaplan's and Tyler Burge's questioning. That thesis is not absolutely clear to me now, but I believe it was something like this:

(6) When one thinks propositionally, if one has awareness of so thinking, one knows which proposition one is thinking.

I remember adding the condition of second-order awareness because one can think without being conscious that one is so doing: the sort of thing I described in "On Knowing (Believing) that One Knows (Believes)" (*Synthese*, 1970), in connection with Fichtean consciousness and Hintikka's KK* thesis, and I called an Externus-type of consciousness.

There is the question as to what exactly it is to know what one is thinking. I do not recall that we discussed this in great detail, although I have a vague impression that something was said at some time by somebody, perhaps Tyler, about relations of the proposition one is thinking of to objects one knows nothing about. At any rate, we were for the most part thinking of the internal constituents of a proposition. At that point I should have mentioned my discussion of propositional guises in "Perception, Belief, . . . ". Yet I do not recollect having done so.

5.2. There was, however, an agreed-upon context with respect to which David's question was understood and our discussion was (it seems to me now, at any rate) intelligible. Without making the issue sufficiently sharp, the point of David's question seems to me to have to do with our theoretical differences on propositions. By adopting individual guises I have no individual substrates – and a singular proposition, attributing a property to an individual, of the form "The F is G," is, barring ellipses in the expressions 'The F' and 'G', transparent, onto- logically transparent, we may say: The entity that is the subject is revealed per- spicuously and so is the predicated attribute. On my Guise-Consubstantiation- Consociation-Conflation theory the referents of definite descriptions are guises, something like Fregean senses, and there is no primary referent; physical objects are systems of guises mutually consubstantiated. I have no room for a Russellian analysis of definite descriptions.

David, on the other hand, distinguishes states of affairs (or propositions) from the presentational elements with (through) which we think states of affairs (or propositions); a singular proposition is "composed" of an individual and an attrib- ute. Thus, roughly put, certain sentences may reveal what we think up to the presentational elements, without revealing the proposition which we aim at, or which underlies those presentational elements. For me the presentational ele- ments are part and parcel of the proposition, which is the thought content. Thus, there is a sense – regardless of how hard it may be to make it precise – in which for David one may fail to know the proposition one is thinking, whereas for me this is not so. (We agree, of course, that one may not know what proposition a certain sentence formulates.)

5.3. In that context, Rogers's example (4)-(5) is powerful. Having proposition P and proposition Q before his mind, in an episode of extremely attentive reflec- tion, Alfred should, on my view, "see" the internal components of P and Q, and should "see" that they are strictly identical. (Bringing in my propositional guise theory we must, to underscore the difficulty, have Alfred consider P and Q at the same level of analysis, so that the guise of P being considered by Alfred would reveal itself to Alfred to be identical with the guise of Q that he is considering: He should be considering the same propositional guise twice.)

5.4. Rogers's example seems to me to show *not* that the transitivity of knowl- edge recorded in (1) is false, but that my *underlying assumption*, viz., that P=Q, is false. Let us examine the motivation for that assumption. Its foundation seems to lie on:

(7) The Chair of the UCLA Philosophy Department is the same as the only ordained Minister in the UCLA Philosophy Department.

Given my guise theory, (7) is true only if (aside from special conventions) the locution 'is the same as' does not express strict identity, but consubstantiation. Clearly, the sameness of (7) is not necessary identity, but contingent identity, as the saying goes.

Thus, thanks to Rogers's example I have learned that I have assumed the strict identity of P and Q on the basis of a non-strict identity, but consubstantiational sameness, as formulated in (7). Is this correct? In general the answer should be negative. "The F is G" is not strictly identical with "The H is G"—even though they may be said to be the same, contingently, if the F is contingently the same as the H. Moreover, even if the F is necessarily the same as the H, we must still distinguish the two propositions "The F is G" and "The H is G." In short, the differences in propositions are cut more finely than the differences in objects.

5.5. Rogers's example (4) and (5) deals, however, with very special propositions. The innermost propositions are first-person ones. Thus, the principle that underlies my assumption is actually this:

(8) If C* (the F, the H), then $I_{the\ F} = I_{the\ H}$ where 'C*' is consubstantiation (roughly, ordinary so-called contingent identity), and 'I_x' denotes the first-person individual concept, guise, sense (at this point we need not be more precise) of X.

Obviously, from (8) we obtain:

(9) If C*(the F, the H), then that $I_{the\ F}$ is G = that $I_{the\ H}$ is G.

Principle (8) is the principle that a system of mutually consubstantiated individual guises have just one first-person guise. For instance, the first-person guise of the Editor of NOÛS is (by (8)), one and the self-same as, strictly identical with, that of the author of this letter, and that of the person you wrote to, etc.

5.6. Is (8) correct? Now, thanks to Rogers, I am inclined to think that it is not correct. Thus, I am now inclined to multiply the first-person guises. Since they are derivative on other guises, we can obtain one first-person guise for each third-person guise of the mental type. If we call each first-person guise a self, we have then one self per definite guise (or characterization) of each person (that is, each system of mutually consubstantiated guises that include some personal guises).

This new multiplication of entities bothers me. Is this the epicycle that breaks guise theory?

I forgot the number of epicycles Rogers regards as fatal, and here we have an infinity of first-person guises. But perhaps they all count as one epicycle: they originate in *one* type of problem, namely, the one well illustrated by Rogers's own brilliant example (4)-(5).

6. If the above multiplication of guises does not prevent us from developing the theory further, we have then Rogers's difficulty resolved by the rejection of principle (9), and with it, the rejection of principle (8). Thus, we can continue to hold (6), whatever its precise formulation may ultimately be.

This is interesting. The rejection of (8) and (9) saves (6), and this gives us a firmer hold on the difference between David and me. By defending (6) from Rogers's attack I can illustrate better, and even refine, the sense in which my PROPOSITIONS or STATES OF AFFAIRS, but not David's, are *fat* – as I called them – and have all the essential presentational features through which we think reality (or unreality, for that matter) (see "Perception . . ." p. 329).

7. Your suggestion at the end of your letter, which you also made at dinner, is important independently of the preceding discussion. I have assumed throughout my papers on indicators and quasi-indicators, from the very beginning in 1963, that a quasi-indexical clause of degree one expresses in its *oratio recta* context the identical proposition that a corresponding indexical sentence paired with a certain context of utterance expresses. But consider:

(10) Jones: I am rich.
Alfred: Jones believes that he himself is rich.

There is, I have assumed all along, just one proposition, which is both asserted by Jones and thought by Alfred to be the accusative of Jones's believing. This assumption you construe to be challenged by Rogers's example (4)-(5). I can still defend it. In the light of the previous multiplications of first-person guises, or selves, I have the complication that Jones asserts a whole infinity of first-person propositions. His assertion is one schema or matrix that captures them all. Here we have a new wrinkle, on top of the bothersome infinity discussed above. Perhaps the epicycle, although still one, is becoming unbearable. There is much more to this, it seems to me. But I'll ignore it.

In any case, given the infinity of first-person propositions Jones asserts, there is certainly one which is identical with the one Alfred takes to be the accusative of Jones's believing.

8. Your suggestion about distinguishing indexical from quasi-indexical propositions is not required by Rogers's example. But it is important in its own right. I will not search for reasons supporting it. I want simply to note that it is within the grain of Guise Theory. If we distinguish indexical from quasi-indexical propositions, we must still recognize that they are related by a most *intimate degree of sameness*. This is good. Yet it will destroy my argument against Norman Kretzmann. The matter should be carefully studied. Perhaps Kretzmann was right after all, even though his reasons did not penetrate to the roots of the problem. You may be providing the only line of possible defense for our good mutual friend, Norman.

8.1. Your contrast between thinking a proposition in person, a phrase I have used, and thinking an impersonation of a proposition is good. This can describe that high degree of intimacy between corresponding indexical and quasi-indexical propositions.

Bob, I guess this is all I can do today.

Thank you very, very much for your letter, and, again, for having had me in your midst and having provided me with deep and friendly discussion. My best regards to the philosophical gang at UCLA.

Cordially,

Hector-Neri Castañeda

January 4, 1980

Professor Hector-Neri Castañeda
Department of Philosophy
Indiana University
Bloomington, IN 47401

Dear Hector,

I must apologize first for not having replied much sooner to your letter of April 6. 1979 was complicated for me personally in various ways, and I have wanted to do justice to your letter, which broadens and deepens the discussion in many respects. There is so much in it that I don't know whether I shall succeed in doing it justice, though I have read it several times and it has sent me to some of your other papers.

I am not convinced by your defense of the transitivity principle

(1) If A knows that B knows that P, then A knows the proposition expressed by ⌜that P⌝ in ⌜B knows that P⌝ .

I still think (1) is no more plausible than

(2) If A knows that B is saying truly that P, then A knows the proposition expressed by ⌜that P⌝ in ⌜B is saying truly that P⌝ ,

which I argued that you should reject. You point out correctly that there is an evidential component that is present in (1) but not in (2), and also that there is a belief component that is present in (1) but not in (2) on the interpretation of (2) that I in fact intended. But the evidence and the belief that are allowed to be missing in (2) are *B*'s evidence and belief — not A's. And I do not see how their absence affects what A knows. In both (1) and (2) we are concerned with a situation in which A knows, and therefore believes on good enough evidence, that the proposition to which B is related (by knowing in (1), by uttering in (2)) is true. What concerns us is whether *in* knowing that the proposition to which B is related is true, that proposition is presented to A in such a way that A knows *it* (not just is acquainted with it, but knows it as true). Your argument for holding that (1) is more plausible than (2) would work, it seems to me, only if B's believing and/or having evidence were responsible for the proposition's being presented to A in the required way. But if I understand your theory, it is not B's believing and/or having evidence, but A's using or being able to use a quasi-indicator, that is supposed to be responsible for the proposition's being presented to A in the required way in the relevant cases.

Reflection on things you say in your letter, however, has led me to think that the best way for you to deal with these problems may not involve rejection of (1) and (2) after all. In arguing that you ought to reject them I was assuming that it is part of your position that, as you put it,

(11) A quasi-indexical clause of degree one expresses in its *oratio recta* context the identical proposition that a corresponding indexical sentence paired with a certain context of utterance expresses.

And I took it that you understand (11) to imply that

(P*) the proposition expressed by 'he himself is rich' in 'The Editor of *Soul* is saying truly that he himself is rich'

is identically the same as

(Q*) the proposition the Editor of *Soul* would express by saying, 'I am rich.'

Apart from this assumption my example does not prove that you ought to reject (2). It might be taken as showing rather that the Editor of *Soul* can know P* without knowing Q*.

Of course my assumption was correct. You explain that you have assumed (11) from the beginning. But you articulate, more clearly than I had seen, the point that Rogers's argument can be understood as an attack on (11). The problem for you, in Rogers's example, is to reconcile (11) with

(6) When one thinks propositionally, if one has awareness of so thinking, one knows which proposition one is thinking.

In order to accomplish this reconciliation you are on the verge of abandoning the principle that

(8') A system of mutually consubstantiated individual guises have just one first-person guise.

But I think even this desperate measure is not enough to reconcile (11) with (6) in every case—and specifically not in my example in which

(3) The Editor of *Soul* knows that the Editor of *Soul* is saying truly that he himself is rich

is true although the Editor of *Soul* does not know that he himself is rich. According to (6), if the Editor of *Soul* in this case is aware of what he knows, he must know which proposition he knows the Editor of *Soul* is saying truly—namely P*.

And if he is thinking about what he is saying, he must know which proposition he is expressing by saying, "I am rich"—namely, Q*. But according to (11), as I have noted, P* = Q*. And I take it to be your view (expressed in section 5.3 of your letter) that if the Editor is reflecting attentively (as we may suppose him to be) and knows which proposition P* is and which proposition Q* is, he will see that they are strictly identical, given that they *are* strictly identical. So the Editor must know that Q*, the proposition that he (himself) is rich, is a proposition that the Editor of *Soul* is saying *truly*. But that is precisely something that he does *not* know.

This difficulty cannot be escaped by having a different first-person guise to go with each third-person guise. For only one third-person guise is involved here—the one the Editor associates with 'the Editor of *Soul*.' It is not, in this case, that the Editor does not know that the first-person guise associated with this third-person guise is consubstantiated with the first-person guise associated with some other third-person guise; the problem is rather that he does not realize that it is *his own* first-person guise.

Perhaps I can press this argument a little harder. If the problem is to be dealt with by abandoning (8′), then the proposition which the Editor of *Soul* is supposed to know is expressed by 'he himself is rich' in 'The Editor of *Soul* is saying truly that he himself is rich' is presumably one that he could express indexically in *oratio recta* as 'I$_{the Editor of Soul}$ am rich.' By (11) that should be the proposition he is expressing by saying, "I am Rich"; and then by (6) he should know that he is expressing it. But he does not know that he is expressing it, or indeed that he has the first-person guise expressed by 'I$_{the Editor of Soul}$', because he does not know that he is the Editor of *Soul*. So the combination of (11) and (6) still leads to an unacceptable result in this case.

I am pleased that abandoning (8′) does not help here, because it seems to me to be something that you should not abandon. It is not just that the multiplication of first-person guises would be one epicycle too many. Wouldn't it be incongruous with the role that first-person guises are supposed to play? Aren't they supposed to form propositions that the speaker can frame, and know he is framing, no matter what third-person guises he knows he has? I put this in interrogative form, because I obviously understand the theory of guises far less well than you do, and it may be that I am missing something.

On the whole I think you would do best to abandon (11). In the terms you use in section 8 of your letter, you should distinguish indexical from quasi-indexical propositions. A quasi-indexical proposition "impersonates," but is not identical with, the corresponding indexical proposition. I guess I was suggesting that before, but I did not see the point of it so clearly. If you make this distinction, then my argument does not compel you to give up the transitivity principles (1) and (2).

But as you also point out in section 8 of your letter, this distinction destroys your argument against Kretzmann. What should we say then about omniscience? The particular difficulty raised by Kretzmann, if I recall, involves issues about time that do not fit very well into our present discussion. But there is a more general problem if we distinguish indexical from quasi-indexical propositions and take propositions to be the objects of knowledge. If there are indexical propositions that are not identical with any propositions that can be presented quasi-indexically or non-indexically, they cannot be known as true except by the right people and/or in the right contexts. And since God can't be all the right people, and perhaps can't be in all the right contexts, he can't know all of them. In particular, if there are thinking beings distinct from God, he can't know their first-person propositions – for example, he can't know precisely the same thing I know when I know that I (myself) am the only son of Arthur and Margaret Adams. Frankly, this is not a problem about omniscience that greatly disturbs me, as a philosophical theologian. We can still say that God knows all the quasi-indexical propositions. In an important sense he knows all the facts. Since he is not me, it is no limitation on his cognitive powers that he cannot know that he is me. If exclusively indexical propositions are among the objects of knowledge, nothing that it makes sense to think of someone distinct from me as possibly knowing could be precisely the same thing that I know in knowing who I am. But it is no more reasonable to insist that an omniscient being must know all such indexical truths than to insist that an omnipotent being must be able to do the logically impossible. Kretzmann's original problem, if conjoined with certain views about time, may pose a more difficult problem for those who believe that God is strictly immutable; but this is not the place to go into that.

One more comment: In section 4 of your letter you suggest that my example refutes the general principle

(R-M) For any propositional attitude or state of consciousness E'ing, for any propositional guise that-$\phi(p)$, and for any person X: if X E's that-$\phi(p)$, then X-E's-that p,

which is asserted on p. 339 of your "Perception, Belief, and the Structure of Physical Objects and Consciousness." It seems to me that my example does *not* refute (R-M). The reason for thinking it does refute (R-M) is that it "shows that the relation of knowing (*conocer*, GIGNOSKEIN) can hold between a thinker and a proposition without the corresponding modalized psychological proposition with the modality *X-knows that* being true." For in my example the Editor "knows in the sense of *connaître* or *conocer* . . . each of the seven propositions being" uttered by the seven people in the room, but "he does not know which one to believe" and therefore "lacks knowledge in the sense of *savoir* or *saber* . . . " (section 2 of your letter). I think we are in danger of being misled here by the "surface grammar" of *connaître* and *savoir*. It is true that *savoir* most naturally takes its place in an epistemic modal operator, and that *connaître* most naturally takes a nominal object. And it is true that both these verbs get translated in English (which on this point is imprecise) as 'know'. But 'X-sait-que p' does not "correspond" to 'X connait la proposition que-p' in the same way that 'X-believes-that p' corresponds to 'X believes the proposition that-p'. *Connaître* and *savoir* do not constitute a single propositional attitude which can take both relational and modal forms; therefore I think you are unfair to yourself in fusing them to form a single instance of E-ing that would be a counterinstance to (R-M). To know (*savoir*) a proposition involves believing it; to be acquainted with (*connaître*) it does not.

Once again, my thanks for the rich and interesting thoughts that provided the occasion for this discussion. With my best wishes for you in 1980.

Sincerely,

Robert Merrihew Adams

March 16, 1982

Professor Robert Merrihew Adams
Department of Philosophy
University of California
Los Angeles, CA 90024

Dear Bob:

At long last I am able to respond to your letter of January 4, 1980. It is an extraordinary document in eliciting so much concordance. Please forgive this tardy reply.

1. Our *only* difference is the minor one concerning:

(1) If A knows that B knows that P, then A knows-that [not just knows *it*] the proposition expressed by ⌜that p⌝ in ⌜B knows that P⌝.

It still seems to me that (1) has better credentials than:

(2) If A knows that B is saying truly that P, then A knows-that [not just knows *it*] the proposition expressed by ⌜that P⌝ in ⌜B is saying truly that P⌝.

My reason continues to be that in (1) there is an epistemic element not present in (2). In the two cases we have been considering so-called *de dicto* knowledge. Thus, since according to (1) A knows that B knows, she is privy to B's reasons for what he knows. On the other hand, according to (2) what A knows is that B is performing a speech act the content of which is a truth, but nothing is said about either B's or A's reasons for believing the truth in question. For instance, I may have good reasons for believing, and, hence, I may know, that Solomon Feferman is speaking veridically when he presents a theorem about inaccessible cardinals. Since we are discussing *de dicto* beliefs, by hypothesis, I understand the theorem; yet I may not be able to understand Feferman's or any other reasons for it.

You may want to argue that principle (2) is one of those that justify knowledge by testimony. This I can accept. Because we can go on to insist that testimony-based knowledge is inferior to knowledge based on reasons directly connecting the knower with what he/she believes. This certainly suits both the claim that (1) has stronger credentials than (2) and my view that knowledge is a genus (or determinable) with many subordinate species (or determinates), most of which are indexically individuated. (For discussion of the latter see Castañeda 1979.)

2. Almost immediately after my response to your first letter, prodded by discussions with Michael Pendlebury, I renounced the tenet that:

(11) A quasi-indexical clause of degree one expresses in its *oratio recta* context the identical proposition that a corresponding indexical sentence paired with a certain context of utterance expresses.

In consonance with the theory of both individual and propositional guises developed in "Perception, Belief" I opted for the manifold view that: (i) there are quasi-indexical guises corresponding to personal I-guises; (ii) the quasi-indexical sentences corresponding to the first-person pronoun express *quasi-indexical propositional guises*; (iii) these quasi-indexical propositional guises are *intimately equivalent* (a phrase I recall having used at our discussion in your February 1979 colloquium) to their corresponding first-person propositional guises; (iv) intimate equivalence is a special case of logical equivalence (in the logic of the self) that puts together I-guises in the same *conflational* packages; (v) this conflational view of such guises suits the intimacy of the equivalence in question, which should hold independently of the existence of the guises under consideration; (vi) if one of them exists, however, as always, the conflated guises are mutually consubstantiated.

That there are quasi-indexical guises that go with a given I-guise is clear once one reflects on the fact that a quasi-indicator *has to have* an antecedent. Hence, a third-person antecedent brings in a third-person element in the reference expressed by the quasi-indicator. This point was lurking behind the discussion of the irreducibility of the quasi-indicator 'he*' corresponding to the first-person as early as "He" (see especially, pp. 151–57). Yet at that time I had no Guise Theory with which to deploy the results of the exegesis of 'he*'. Your first letter helped me become clearer about the phenomenon.

3. Your discussion in your second letter of the tension between (11) and (3) is brilliant. I welcome your forceful attack on (11). I certainly want to maintain the uniqueness of each self at a given time. Thus, I am delighted to have both your recommendation and your description of quasi-indexicality:

On the whole I think that you would do best to abandon (11). In the terms you use in section 8 of your letter, you should distinguish indexical from quasi-indexical propositions. A quasi-indexical proposition "impersonates," but is not identical with, the corresponding proposition. I guess I was suggesting that before . . .

4. Your discussion of the impact of my giving up (11) on my disagreement with Norman Kretzmann is very reassuring. I concur with you that:

We can still say that God knows all the quasi-indexical propositions [i.e., propositional guises—H-N.C.]. In an important sense he knows all the facts. Since he is not me, it is no limitation on his cognitive powers that he cannot know that he is me. If exclusively indexical propositions [i.e., strictly indexical propositional guises] are among the objects of knowledge, nothing that it makes sense to think of someone distinct from me as possibly knowing could be precisely the same thing I know in knowing who I am.

5. Your last point is excellent. It captures very well a central commitment of perceptual Guise Theory to the strict privacy of all indexical references, even to the point of postulating (as others, e.g., Bertrand Russell, have done before) private perceptual fields. I have also insisted that there is a *creative* aspect to indexical reference, which makes it not merely contemplative or descriptive. To refer indexically is to *constitute* the items of experience. This is—I believe—clear in the discussion, in "Perception, Belief," Part II, of the move from propositional zero-guises to logically structured guises that compose a perceptual field. Clearly, this idea is at bottom the idea that full knowledge on the part of a person S of what another person S′ refers to indexically would be feasible only if S is the same, consubstantiationally the same, as S′.

Given the intimacy of the equivalence between indexical and their corresponding quasi-indexical propositional guises, there is a strong sense in which God's knowledge of all the true quasi-indexical guises of a true indexical proposition puts him in knowledge of *the* fact, corresponding to them all. Indeed, that fact is nothing more than the true proposition of which all of them are intimately equivalent guises. God certainly knows all the FACTS (in the capitalized sense of "Perception, Belief").

6. Your defense of principle (R-M) is convincing. I like (R-M) very much, and I delighted to see my misgivings about it were unjustifiedly rash. Thank you very much.

In conclusion, Bob, your clarifications have been most rewarding. I suspect that you know Guise Theory better than I—at least as well as William Richards and Tomis Kapitan.

Hoping to receive further enlightenment from you both in metaphysics and on Leibniz,

With cordial best wishes,

Hector-Neri Castañeda

Notes

1. In "Omniscience and Immutability," *The Journal of Philosophy* 63 (1966): 409–21.
2. In " 'He': A Study in the Logic of Self-consciousness," *Ratio* 8 (February 1967); this article will be cited as *He*. See also my "On the Logic of Self-Knowledge," *Noûs* 1 (March 1967).
3. In "Indicators and Quasi-indicators," *The American Philosophical Quarterly* 4 (April 1967): 85–100 [chap. 12 of this volume].

4. For some problems about indicators in *oratio obliqua*, see "Indicators and Quasi-indicators," sec. 4.

5. For a discussion of the irreducibility of the quasi-indicator 'he (himself)' see *He*, sec. 2; see "Indicators and Quasi-indicators," for a total defense of the irreducibility of quasi-indexical reference.

6. For a detailed discussion of this type of inference, see *He*, sec. 4, and "Indicators and Quasi-indicators," sec. 5 [this volume pp. 218–23]. For a recent discussion see William J. Rapaport and Stuart C. Shapiro, and Janice M. Wiebe, "Quasi-Indicators, Knowledge Reports, and Discourse," *Technical Report* £86–15, SUNY Buffalo, Department of Computer Science, 1986.

7. These letters have been edited by James E. Tomberlin.

References

Castañeda, Hector-Neri. 1966. "He: The Logic of Self-Consciousness," *Ratio* 8 (1966): 130–57.

Castañeda, Hector-Neri. 1967. "Omniscience and Indexical Reference," *The Journal of Philosophy* 64 (1967): 203–10. [This chapter, sections 1-5.]

Castañeda, Hector-Neri. 1970. "On Knowing (or Believing) that One Knows (or Believes)," *Synthèse* 21 (1970): 187–203.

Castañeda, Hector-Neri. 1977. "Perception, Belief, and the Structure of Physical Objects and Consciousness," *Synthèse* 35 (1977): 285–351.

Castañeda, Hector-Neri. 1979. "The Theory of Questions, Epistemic Powers, and the Indexical Theory of Knowledge," *Midwest Studies in Philosophy* 5 (1979): 193–238.

Kretzmann, Norman. 1966. "Omniscience and Immutability," *The Journal of Philosophy* 63 (1966): 409–21.

10

Self and Reality: Metaphysical Internalism, Selves, and the Holistic Indivisible Noumenon

1. Modest Transcendental Realism: The Cogito, The Balloon, and The True

The most radical forms of skepticism force us into Metaphysical Internalism. This is, very roughly, the view that all thought and talk about the world and the reality underlying it are internal to experience, whatever reality may be in itself beyond experience, indeed, even if there is no reality beyond experience.

The world we encounter might certainly be all illusory, exhausted in its own appearance. Our lives could be coherent hallucinations created by an Evil Demon. Each of us could be a brain in a cask, perversely, or happily, manipulated by a clever experimenting scientist. I might have always been just an immobile, computerlike artifact at the center of a huge spaceship the likes of which will not yet be dreamed of on earth for centuries, and my experiences and beliefs, piecemeal hallucinatory, could be caused by the interaction of cosmic rays and waves impinging on my electronic parts made of some unfathomable materials.

These are, of course, mere philosophical fantasies. Nevertheless, they are philosophically salutary – if we do not, depressed, stay with them. They can be neither proved nor disproved. Obviously, any argument offered, whether pro or con, if its premises are not inconsistent, can always be rejected by an opponent. The rejection recipe is simple: Choose one premise, claim that *at it* the argument begs the question, and demand a proof of that premise; repeat the procedure for the new argument, and for each of its successors; if, at some round of argumentation you are tempted by the premises, complement the argument with a modus tollens, and take it as a proof that the least attractive premise is false.[1]

My purpose here is neither argumentative nor dialectical. I am not concerned with building an argument that finally, and conclusively, establishes radical skepticism. I immediately surrender to Descartes's nondemonstrative hyperbolic techniques of doubt. Thus, obversely, I desire NOT to engage in a refutation of radical skepticism to secure the metaphysical basis for our daily living. Radical skepticism is cathartic; it *can* be treated optimistically: In the final analysis, it must be swallowed whole in one gulp and then allowed to do its job in oblivion. (But I understand the manifold passions for professional skepticism.) My aim here is hermeneutical and constructive, namely, to subject the phenomenon of radical skepticism to exegesis in order to distill the deep reality-content of the world in which we find ourselves.

Most of us do not believe the skeptical arguments. But are we justified in supposing that there is a reality beyond, and underlying, experience?

The mere affirmative answer to this question is *Minimal Transcendental Realism*. It is compatible with Metaphysical Internalism. As I interpret Kant, his Copernican Revolution is his adoption of Metaphysical Internalism. Some philosophers would say "antirealism"; this expression is, however, not adequately descriptive. Kantian terminology, albeit archaic and tainted with the suggestions and images of Kant's own views, is more apt: Radical skepticisms strangle our complacency with transcendent metaphysics and thrust us into transcendental idealism. The outcome is that, with the exception of the account of what he calls the problematic noumenon, we are limited to do, as I have sometimes called it, phenomenological ontology.[2] His claim that, properly speaking, we have only a *negative* concept of the noumenon is his endorsement of Minimal Transcendental Realism.[3]

According to Metaphysical Internalism I must not try to break my possibly nonexisting head attempting to beat the skeptical arguments: I must yield to the deepest skeptical doubts and concede that all my experiences could, in principle and in fact, be illusory. I must, then, turn to inside experience and follow Leibniz's internalist advice,[4] making my problem that of understanding the contents and the structure of the experienced world, however illusory these may be. I must understand them from *inside*, not from without as God may see them; even the skepticism of the past, whether composed of events in the external world or of speech acts that have a semantic unit across time, should be granted, and acknowledge that the past is posited within the bounds of present experience.

Enter Minimal Realism. We fasten to a minimal transcendent-pointing framework—we may call it *transcendental*—, within which we must vicariously and holistically connect our experiences from within to a reality beyond merely pointed to. Within the structures of that framework we can posit a hierarchical quilted world with varying degrees of uncertainty. By fastening to those posits, we can live our autobiographies with variegated degrees of limited certainty. Happiness? It must lie somewhere in the interaction of those posits and the succession of our experiences.

Minimal Realism is indispensible if the whole of experience is not to become lost in a total circle of fiction. Clearly, a character in a fictional story may be said to engage in, say, skeptical doubts concerning the possibility of an Evil Demon who deceives him at every thought. But the character is *said* to do that, he does not *actually* do anything. This difference spans the difference between literature, or science fiction, and artificial intelligence. Thus, when I (whatever I may really be) engage in that reflection, I indeed *engage* in it. More generally, as Descartes pointed out (at the beginning of his second *Meditation*), regardless of how much the Evil Demon may deceive me, he cannot deceive me about two things: (i) that I think, and (ii) that I am having such and such thoughts. These are for real.

(D.2) But I am persuaded that there is nothing in the world. . . . But [I have supposed] there is an I don't know what that deceives, too powerful and too cunning, who uses all his skills to deceive me always. Then there is no doubt that I exist, if he deceives me, and that regardless of how much he deceives me to the full extent of his wish, he will never be able to make me nothing, as long as I *think* that I am something [whatsoever mistaken this thought may be]. This way then after thinking attentively, having examined all these matters carefully, it is necessary to end [conclude], and to record as a constant [i.e., as an unchangeable truth] this proposition *I am, I exist*, which is necessarily true whenever I assert it, or I conceive it in my mind.

This is the end of Descartes's methodological, nondemonstrative doubt. He was making several connected points.

First, in (D.2) Descartes is remarking that we can conceive all alleged truths about the external world to form an exhaustive set or whole, which I will hereafter call *The Balloon*, and, further, that the arguments for radical skepticism put the doubter in a position of transgressing all particular experiences in which she deals with parts of the world, in order to transact with the world as a whole, thinking The Balloon, so that the situation can be depicted thus:

(1) I think that (The Balloon).

In other words, Descartes was making a wholesale application – of the sort Kant would have called "transcendental" – of Kant's general *I-think* principle: "It must be possible for the 'I think' to accompany all my representations" (Kant 1781, B131).

Second, Descartes in (D.2) observes that the Evil Demon can make me doubt The Balloon in its entirety, the whole of it, and, distributively, each part of it. But the prefix *I think that*, hereafter called (in Kantian style) the *transcendental prefix*, is beyond doubt. Therefore, its components, which we shall henceforth call the transcendental *Thinking I* and the transcendental *Think*, reach metaphysical rock bottom. Of course, it is part of that rock bottom that the *Think* has The Balloon as its total tail, whether this is wholly illusory or not, and that on particular occasions of customary thinking certain parts of The Balloon will function as partial tails of my thinking. The Balloon may be a fiction, but that I exist thinking The Balloon or parts thereof is NOT a fiction. Hence, (mTR*) There is a minimal transcendent dimension of experience underlying what is thought through the transcendental Thinking I.

Third, a crucial point Descartes makes in (D.2) is that the certainty of *cogito* (I think-I exist) is NOT the certainty of a deduction. As he well knew and insisted all along, his search for a fundamental certainty cannot be derived from anything else. The certainty of the *cogito* is fundamental because it is the terminal certainty of his quest. He makes deductions: His skeptical arguments are deductions and generalizations; but the proceedings culminate with reflections on the role of the Evil Demon's deception or the wholesale illusion of experience for whatever causes. These reflections are doings and they conclude, that is, end up, with the doubter's *metaphysical-phenomenological grasping* of an ultimate reality—this is the metaphysical aspect of the grasping—that appears—this is the phenomenological aspect—as a thinking I confronting a whole but perhaps wholly empty world, including the I's own embodiments in that world.

Fourth, the transcendental I of the methodological doubt exists with certainty only *during* the skeptical experience. Descartes says "with necessity," but it is not clear that by 'necessary' he means, etymologically, nonceasing, that is, constant, which is another word he uses. The doubter's existence as well as his or her thinking are constant parameters during the whole skeptical proceedings. In any case, Descartes leaves it, in (D.2), quite open that the transcendental I of a particular skeptical experience may vanish when the experience ends, that if the experience is repeated, the transcendental I's involved may be entirely different.

This brings us to a *fifth* crucial point that pervades (D.2), which Descartes did not appreciate fully—at least he did not dwell upon it as fully as he should have done. The point is that the I on which the hyperbolic doubt concludes is not internal to The Balloon. That is why Kant called it *transcendental*, transcending The Balloon without being transcendent in the sense of being beyond experience, that is, the experience of the methodological hyperbolic doubt. That I is beyond the world in The Balloon, and it is all of reality as this can be grasped in that encompassing doubt. Hence, the empirical I's within The Balloon may be different from the transcendental I thinking of them as the same as itself inside The Balloon.

Descartes did not savor fully the nonworldliness of the transcendental I of his *cogito*. Having realized that the *cogito* ended with an existent, but with no content, aside from facing a whole world of experience, he hastened to ask *what am I?* But this question involved a tremendously important though apparently insignificant shift of sense and referent in his new use of the little word 'I' (or 'je' and 'ego'). This question is NOT the question about the transcendental I that thinks The Balloon. This latter question would ask about the structures connecting the transcendental I without and The Balloon within or as the accusative of the transcendental Think. Descartes's question, on the other hand, is about *an I within The Balloon*.

We must ask the unasked question and then try to fill in an account of the connection between the non-worldly transcendental I and the many I's within The Balloon.[5]

Now, the *cogito* possesses a second dimension of transcendental realism. It has to do with the transcendental *Thinking* of The Balloon. The thinking of The Balloon is also externally real, as real can be, indeed *thinking* as such is the internal, experienced manifestation of whatever it may be in the reality beyond, which underlies experience. Thinking *is* itself a real representing—whatever this may ultimately really be—of a perhaps empty representation of a hallucinatory world.

Moreover, in the reality beyond experience lies the source, the *transcendent source*, of the thinking of what is thought in The Balloon. The nature of that source is, of course, at the level of the radical skepticism of the Evil Demon, as unknowable as the transcendent self underlying the transcendental I. For instance, according to the Evil Demon "hypothesis," the transcendent source is the Demon's network of deceptive operations; according to the Clever Scientist "hypothesis," the Scientist's manipulations; in the case of the self-propelled isolated computer or brain, it is the electric or physicochemical activity inside the computer or brain. To be sure, wilder hypotheses come forth with their own unknown transcendent sources. In particular, the self-propelled computer shows that the transcendent self may be at the core of the transcendent source. We include both dimensions of transcendence under the heading of Minimal Transcendental Realism. Of course, none of these so-called hypotheses is a genuine hypothesis. They are nothing but suggestive analogies of how noumenal reality could be conceptualized within our experiential resources; there is absolutely nothing to elicit a preference for one over the others. This total parity concerning their validity shows (as Kant well knew) that once we recognize the force of radical skepticism, we must simply aquiesce in the ineffability of the underlying reality.

Two additional aspects of transcendence must yet be latched on to Minimal Transcendental Realism.

To begin with, The Balloon is precisely what may be wholly illusory. Yet it also has a two-directional dimension of transcendence. On one direction, it has a transcendent source. At worst exactly the same transcendent source of my *thinking* The Balloon is also the very same source of my thinking *the contents* of The Balloon. On the other direction, there is an internal pointing to transcendent reality within the experiences inside, composing The Balloon. The fundamental *attitude* we must take toward the world is that of transcendent realism. We must live our ordinary experiences as if normally what we experience is real beyond them. Any questioning stops the natural flow of one's autobiographical living; it may, of course, start a stream of philosophizing. After all, the metaphysical possibility of error does not affect the order of experiences. We simply take—and must take—it for granted in our basic daily experiences that we are not the toys of an Evil Demon or the thinking gadgets of a clever scientist, or the accidental connivance of we do not know what that causes us to have wholly illusory experiences.

Second, experience is hierarchical. We ascertain within it different layers of *irreality*. We have within our experiences of The Balloon what we call simply illusions, misperceptions, delusions; we distinguish within experience tiers of fiction: original fiction, and fiction created within fiction, and so on, and variegated mixtures of so-called reality and fiction. These hierarchies of internal nonreality presuppose a *ground floor* of The Balloon on which we set them up.

The metaphysical doubt is, in effect, the overall doubt about the ground floor we need. This is the realm of physical objects orderly interacting in spacetime. It is this ground floor of The Balloon that we take in our naive attitude to be real in the strongest metaphysical sense. Thus, our transcendental pointings of our naive attitude are pointings to the reality beyond experience of the ground floor. The metaphysical doubt is, in effect and essence, a sweeping doubt about the physical ground floor of The Balloon. It succeeds, its polemical tone aside, in establishing that the customarily unquestioned ground floor taken for granted in daily living is not logically or mathematically secure.

Notwithstanding, still within the morals of what Descartes taught us, each of us can affirm a transcendental experience of radical skepticism:

(Di*) Regardless of how much the Evil Demon, the Mad Scientist, or the Reality Beyond may deceive me, it cannot make me doubt that I need a ground floor of believed content of experience at the basis of, and inside, The Balloon, through which I point in every act of thinking the contents of that ground floor to the transcendent reality underlying experience holistically.

Doubtlessly, here we still lack metaphysical certainty about transcendent reality. We merely acquire an *ontologico-epistemological* dimension of realism: Experience rests on a fundamental transcendental taking for granted both that it has a ground floor and that, so to speak, each placing of a tile on that ground floor, through the rehearsal of a belief about physical reality, is a pointing to the reality beyond experience.

The transcendental *Thinking I* and the transcendental *Think* deliver poitings to transcendent reality. They deliver transcendent reality as target, so to speak, as blindly and merely hooked at the ends of their long harpoons. The Balloon delivers a network of pointings. For instance, each perception we take to be veridical, each belief we come to adopt considering it to be true, is a pointing in the direction of transcendent reality. The pointing is, continuing to use Kant's jargon, transcendental: It reveals that something lies beyond, but it does not reveal *what* it intrinsically is.

What the transcendental *Thinking I* and what the transcendental *Think* harpoon may BE, for all we can ever *really* know, one and the very *same* thing. That same thing is precisely what in constructing The Balloon, we may be pointing to. Indeed, we can say very little more than this about transcendent reality. It is of the utmost importance to appreciate that as far as we can consider it, it is an INDIVISIBLE WHOLE. As Kant remarked about his negative problematic concept of the noumenon, it is so far beyond our experience that even calling *it* "it" is already too presumptuous, if we do not dissociate from this use of 'it' semantic contrasts that give it is meaning—for example, its being a singular pronoun; of course, the plural 'they' is by far much more misleading.

Frege appreciated well Kant's insight into the noumenon. He understood deeply both the holistic role of the noumenon in the total unified experience of the world at large and its iterative role in the piecemeal transcendental pointings to it in each of our believings. In each claim of truth we make we point holistically to the problematic noumenon, and for us then the only-blindly pointable transcendent reality is what underlies and undergirds the undifferentiated *The True*, which Frege postulated as the ultimate indivisible convergent referent of all true propositions. Propositions, or Thoughts, are internally to experience what they really are, and when we take them to be true, we represent to ourselves a GUISE of a small part of The True. But there is no reason to suppose that that part is a transcendent part of The True. *Frege's The True is inside experience the fundamental internal guise of the Kantian noumenon.*[6]

We have discussed three several-pronged transcendental dimensions of the transcendental prefix. Together we shall call these *Modest Transcendental Realism*. Patently:

(MI.Mr*) Modest Transcendental Realism is compatible with Metaphysical Internalism and anchors it to transcendent reality (The True, the Whole Indivisible Problematic Noumenon).

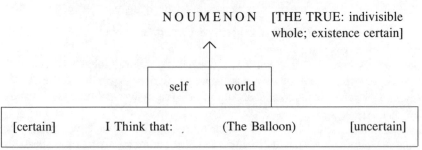

2. The Ontological Semantic Dimension of Ordinary Words

The three aspects of the noumenon, subsumed under Modest Transcendental Realism, are just about all we can say concerning transcendent reality. From there on, everything we can say will have to be *internal* to the complex:

(1) I Think (The Balloon).

In particular, the vocabulary for making reality claims—for example, first-order mechanisms like existentially meant verbal inflections and words like 'exists' and 'really', as well as second-order mechanisms like 'true'—have full-fledged metaphysical applications only as allowed by Modest Transcendental Realism. That is, these words serve their speakers to *perform* metaphysical pointings to

The True, but their meaning consists of their essentially internalistic, or phenomenological use.

In the most common, internalistic, use of the word, reality is the ground floor of The Balloon, in particular, the physical world. The Balloon, of course, includes much more. As we observed, it has a hierarchical structure: reality or brute facts at the bottom, our experiences thereof, and the diverse tiers of nonfacts or nonreality above — illusions, hallucinations, dreams, conjectures, unverified hypotheses, intentions, unrealized plans, obligations, unfulfilled duties, fiction, and so on.

The ordinary vocabulary of natural languages for claims about reality has an *ontological semantic dimension*. Ordinary reality claims are about the *ground floor* of the world we confront in experience. Each making of a reality claim includes a pointing in the direction of transcendent reality as well as a positing of a part of the ground floor, and carries with it the suggestion that what is so posited may, in fact, be itself in, or have a counterpart in, The True beyond. To illustrate, while being deceived by the Mad Scientist, I distinguish between my veridical perceptions and my dreams, and from both my imagined situations and my creation of pieces of fiction. By claiming that my perceptions are *veri*dical, I am claiming, *internalistically*, that the acquired perceptual content belongs to the ground floor of the totality of my experienced contents, to the (internalistically) real world, namely, the ground floor of The Balloon. Underlying this internalistic claim of reality is the deeply seated *taking it for granted* that there is *beyond* a noumenon, which is somehow responsible both for my having the perceptions in question and for these possessing the content they have.

3. The Fivefold Ontological Dimensions of Certainty

Reflection on the Evil Demon challenge, or on its alternatives, has unveiled two dimensions of *cogito* certainty:

(a) The *metaphysical* certainty of the three aspects of Modest Transcendental Realism: This is a wholly existential and contentually unspecific knowledge that there is simply a reality, to which we can point as a whole in every experience, which underwrites the metaphysical fact that there is experience of a (perhaps wholly illusory) world, and which is directly but blindly harpooned by the Thinking I (whatever and however this may in itself be).

(b) The *ontological* or *semi-internalistic* certainty that the transcendental Thinking I of the radical doubt exists confronting, even surrounding, the world, indeed The whole Balloon, with its Thinking.

A quick reminiscence suffices to remind us that The Balloon may very well contain, so to say, its local I's. There are inside The Balloon many first-person propositions (possible states of affairs, thought contents) like the following:

(B1) I am shorter than Robert Sleigh, Jr.

(B2) I feel a pain on my neck.

(B3) I read Sellars's *Science and Metaphysics* many years ago.

The Evil Demon may definitely sweep away (B1)-(B3) with its tornado of doubt. My height and my eyes, Sleigh and Sellars, my neck and Sellars's book, all might be mere figments of my imaginings forced by the Evil Demon. Can He make me believe that I have a pain that does not exist? Here I want to set this question aside. Here is something of much greater importance. This is I. Can the Evil Demon mislead me about me, that is, I as I appear in (B1)-(B3), *inside* The Balloon? We have grasped the indubitability of the I without The Balloon, which doubts (B1)-(B3) and the rest of The Balloon. But here we have local, internal (empirical) I's. *If* these I's are the SAME in some strong sense of 'sameness' as the Thinking I of the transcendental prefix of (1), then the certainty of the Thinking I spills over into The Balloon over the local I's. Hence, if so, two further dimensions of certainty surface:

(c) The *metaphysico-ontological* or *trans-internalistic* certainty that the local I's in The Balloon are also anchored to transcendent reality.

(d) The *phenomenological* or *internalistic* certainty that within the domain of the appearances constitutive of The Balloon the local I's in The Balloon are on the ontological ground floor of The Balloon: The ultimacy of the reality of the transcendental I supports The Balloon, and this support also spills over the local I's and disperses throughout them. The force of this internalistic certainty is epitomized in the following implication (signaled by the double arrow):

(C*.Ex) *Internal Cogito Axiom*:
S(I) $\Longrightarrow$ I exist
where 'S(I)' is any sentence in direct speech, containing uses of the indexical first-person pronoun signaled by 'I'.[7]

This ground floor, dispersed existential certainty of the transcendental I requires the certainty of the embodiment of those local I's, that is:

(e) The *phenomenological* or *internalistic* certainty that every local I in The Balloon must be tied down to, that is, must be the *same* as, a ground floor resident of the world, that is, a resident so chained by the structure of the world that it cannot leave The Balloon. Such a native resident of the world is, of course, a natural victim of the radical skepticism of the Evil Demon. Thus, here again, we find the certainty of the phenomenological necessity of *there being* something in the ground floor, but not the certainty or necessity of anything in the ground floor that realizes or embodies any local I.

4. Selves, I-Guises, and the Multifarious Semiotics of First-Person Reference

According to (c) the I's in The Balloon have a full-fledged transcendent existence, (but, to be sure, unspecifiable in transcendent content) — provided that, and to the extent that, they are the *same* as the Thinking I of the transcendental prefix. This proviso needs attentive examination. Undoubtedly, from the mere linguistic fact that we have the same mark 'I' in (B1)-(B3), it follows neither that the three occurrences of 'I' are used to think the very same entity, nor that what they denote is exactly the same as what the word 'I' denotes in the transcendental prefix of (1). The issue is *not* that different persons may be uttering (B11)-(B13). We are assuming that there is a personal unity of reflection, experience, and world throughout this meditation. In a *general* sense all the uses of 'I' that we are considering are uses of the first-person pronoun by the same ordinary person. In that sense, we assume that they all are uses by that speaker to refer to the same entity. But obviously, there is more to the thinking reference of the speaker than that general sameness. The meditation occurs in the first person, for the first person, and all the samenesses that the thinker-speaker does not know are unavailable to her. Yet her thoughts have a definite content. Thus, by using the first-person pronoun, the speaker is somehow referring to an entity – which in *some* sense, loudly crying out for analysis, is, of course, the *same* as the speaker. Besides all that, which may be inaccessible to her, she is thinking of an entity *as* a thinker of such thoughts in such and such circumstances. And this makes an enormous difference. For instance, the thinker engaged in the transcendental meditation responds to the brain-in-the-cask "hypothesis" without any assumption of her being embodied; the thinker that thinks (B11) to be probably true must perforce be embodied; the thinker thinking (B3) must think of himself as having a history. This raises a serious question about the sense of diachronic identity between I's.

Let us say that an entity conceived *as* in some way or other is a *gross individual guise*. We may say that a gross individual guise is an ordered pair (x, G), where x is conceived as, *qua*, the G. Applying this idea to the I's, we have been considering, let us introduce some terminological order. We call each I thought of in a given unitary propositional text pertaining to the ground floor of The Balloon an *empirical gross I-guise*. Temporarily, let us conceive the unitary manifolds of such gross I-guises as somehow constituting entities to be called *empirical selves*.

The metaphysical certainty of one's own existence is the assurance that there *exists* something problematic, unspecifiable, beyond experience, which underlies one's own uses of the first-person pronoun. These uses are semiotically complex. The uses of 'I' in the transcendental prefix *I Think* in (1) have at least the five crucial roles we pass on to discuss.

First, 'I' in (1) represents a successful gesture of *pointing to* the transcendent self.

Second, 'I' *depicts* in the context of sentence (1) the semi-internalistic role of the Thinking I vis-à-vis The Balloon. To think proposition (1) is to think of oneself as without The Balloon; yet this *without* is not a transcendent 'without'. The I-Thinking-that in (1) is apprehended in (1) as at the boundary of The Balloon, and it is *internalizable* by its being thought of within a larger Balloon:

(2) I Think that {I think that (The Balloon)}.

In proposition (2), we have the Extended Balloon: {*I think that (The Balloon)*}. This process is iterative with no end. This iterativitity makes it clear that the Thinking I is already in (1) a Thought-of I. In a sense, then, the true Thinking

I is the *unthought of* I, which thinks (1), or (2), or any other more encompassing proposition of this sort. The iterative embedding of (1) or its successors in a more encompassing Extended Balloon merely introduces *another* thought-of I, thus, revealing by adumbration a semi-internalistic, inexhaustible reservoir of Thinking I's from which Thinking-Thought-of I's can be extracted. Let us call that inexhaustible reservoir the *transcendental I*.

This brings in a *third* role of the first-person pronoun 'I' in(1) and (2): Also semi-internalistically, each use of 'I' points to the internalizability of the transcendental I, or rather, to its sliceability in Thinking-Thought-of slices (hereafter called *transcendental gross I-guises*) that can be internalized in Extended Balloons.

A fourth role of depiction by the first-person pronoun in (1) is this: The internal inexhaustibility of the transcendent I is an internal representation within (extended) experience of the inaccessibility of the transcendent self.

Fifth, as already noted, the 'I' in the transcendental prefix of (1) anchors the uses of 'I' to denote an empirical self within The Balloon.

The structure of the internalistic certainty of the empirical I's includes the substructures of indexical reference in general. Referring to oneself *qua* oneself as in the midst of the world is to refer as such to a thinker as *presently* involved in the very experience of making the referring in question.

The nonworldliness of the transcendental I infects the empirical I's. But we cannot go into this here. Furthermore, first-person reference is just one case of demonstrative or indexical reference to items that are presented or present in an experience, which is lived through the very structure of the references in question. Therefore, to understand fully the structure of the internalistic certainty of one's existence, it is necessary to place the psycholinguistic phenomenon of first-person reference within the context of its general type of *indexical reference*. Additional aspects of the semantics of the first-person pronoun become crucial. The nonworldliness of the I's turn out to be hand in hand with the nonworldliness of the strict denotata of all other indexical references.[8]

5. The I-Manifold: Strict Semantic Denotation versus Doxastic Denotation

We have encountered a somewhat bewildering multiplicity of entities at the end of the semantics of the first-person pronoun. We have also felt pressure for some sort of identification among them. Here we cannot tackle the problem in full. If we yield to the pressure for identification, we find a long, impressive array of equations. We deliberately formulate them by means of the problematic word 'same', intending to pose a problem at it. To begin with, where for convenience the adjective 'gross' is left tacit we have:

Ontological Unity of the World of a Given Subject:

(TI.TI*)   Each transcendental I-guise, that is, each Thinking-Though-of I, is *the same as* its corresponding transcendental I.

(TI.TI*.1) I [Thinking an Extended Balloon] am *the same as* my (semi-internalistically) underlying transcendental I.

Metaphysical Anchoring of Experience:

(MA*)   The transcendental I is *the same as* its transcendent self [which underlies from beyond experience its thinking a Balloon].

By equation (TI.TI*) all the members of the iterative infinite sequence of Extended Balloons have the unity of one and the same underlying unthought-of transcendental self. Since each Extended Balloon thought of is explicitly encompassed by a transcendental I-guise, (TI.TI*) derivatively unifies both the Balloons and the possible experiences of a given subject. Equation (MA*) is, by contrast, a *metaphysical*, trans-semi-internalistic principle tying the knowable world of experience to the (problematic, indivisible) noumenon.

Moving into The Balloon we find the *empirical I-guises*. Here, again, positing a unity of reference is the simplest and most straightforward justification of the use of the first-person pronoun. We postulate:

Internalistically, within The Balloon:

(Ei.ES*)   Each empirical I-guise is *the same as* the empirical self.

Semi-internalistically, a Bridge between the Prefix and The Balloon:

(Ti.Ei*)   Each transcendental I-guise [of the prefix], is *the same as* each of the empirical I-guises [in its corresponding Balloon].

(TI.ES*)   Each transcendental I *is the same as* the empirical self it encompasses.

Some of these equations can be derived from others by the transitivity of sameness, but this is part of the problem. Also by transitivity, (Ei.ES*) identifies all the empirical I-guises. This requires investigation concerning the unity and identity of empirical selves across time. Equations (Ei.ES*) and (TI.ES*) raise, and are contributions to, the fundamental problem of the synchronic unity of an I.

By the above equations, all the uses of the first-person pronoun captured in (1), (2), and (B1)-(B3), from the perspective of one person, denote the same everywhere. This cries out for elucidation.

As we have pointed out, we are considering entities as they are thought of and referred to by a thinker putting her world together after the skeptical devastation brought about by the Mad Scientist, or the Evil Demon. Thus, we found the thinker thinkingly referring to individual guises. If that thinker's thinking is deployed or embodied in language, then there is a *fundamental semantic dimension* in which the *strict semantico-pragmatic denotations* of the thinker's terms are precisely what the thinker refers to, namely, individual guises. Otherwise, the terms are not capable of carrying the thinker's thoughts. If the terms in question gain their denotation in the pragmatic context of use, then these, as they exist in the thinker's psycholinguistic speech habits, do not have a denotation. Their general meaning is, then, a schema to be filled in by the pragmatics of the context of use. (In more fashionable jargon: The general meaning of a term is only a function that assigns a function of the context which assigns a denotation to the term.)

We must, therefore, distinguish different ways in which a proffered singular term, or the corresponding mental content it overtly represents, can be said to refer to, or aim at, its denotata. Here we are concerned with the referential uses of the first-person pronoun. Clearly, then, each token of 'I' *strictly (semantico-pragmatically) denotes* an I-guise being thought of; it *mediately denotes doxastically* the transcendental I, by virtue of being part of an expression of thought that *occurs* within a network of beliefs, which includes the assumption of a unity of the thinker's experience; and it *points to*, or *most mediately denotes doxastically*, the transcendent self—which in the naive attitude of daily living is not even conceived, but underwrites the naive realism of the daily attitude.

6. The Variegated Sameness in the I-Network

The above principles establish, but only programmatically, subject to an acoming theory, the unity across the I-manifold. That theory has to deal with the problems mentioned, as well as with others. For instance, by the transitivity of sameness, the preceding equations also imply:

(TS.Ei) The transcendent self [BEYOND the inexhaustive transcendental prefix] is *the same as* any empirical I-guise [IN The Balloon].

This contains an important grain of truth, namely, the one that underlies the dimension of certainty (c) described earlier. But (TS.Ti) must not be understood as transferring the properties of an empirical I-guise to the transcendent self—the noumenon. This is precisely Descartes's error in his *Second Meditation* when he derives from the certainty of the *cogito* that he is a transcendent mental substance. Pointing out this error is the main task of Kant's "Paralogisms."

We must, consequently, interpret (TS.Ei) in such a way that the sameness it proclaims is *not* strict identity. Since (TS.Ei) is a consequence of the previous equations, there is at least one sameness in the latter that is not strict identity.

Having differentiated sameness from strict identity, we need a general account of identity, sameness, predication, and guises. *One* such account, built on the distinctions drawn between strict semantico-pragmatic reference and doxastic reference and pointings-to, can be found in Guise Theory.[9] Since we are now dealing with the structures inside The Balloon we may stop this round of investigation. Perhaps one small appendix may not be amiss to round out our discussion.

7. The Transcendental Prefix and Experience

Our reaction to the Evil Demon hypothesis followed Descartes in considering the whole world and experience, The Balloon, encompassed by Kant's transcendental prefix *I think*. This is, however, a serious error, for as Descartes himself had casually shown, the Kantian prefix is only a fragment of the relevant prefix, to wit: *I think now*. This is, to be sure, at the heart of Descartes's claim that thinking and extension are two distinct attributes characteristic, respectively, of the mental and material substances. A comprehensive study of indexical reference suggests that the true transcendental prefix is, therefore, the extended one: *I think here now*. By the same Cartesian considerations that led Descartes to the indubitability of the doubting I, we reach the indubitability of both the *now* and the *here* of the doubting. Those considerations are simply that all doubts, regardless of how radical they may be, can always be imprisoned in the subordinated Balloon, and in so doing, a new transcendental prefix *I think here now* springs forth at every turn:

I think here now that (I think here now that [. . . The Balloon] . . .).

We may speak here of the extended *cogito* and of the indubitability of the transcendental *I-Here-Now*'s.

This extended *cogito* is Cartesian only in structure. Its contents are anti-Cartesian. For one thing it provides only an I that exists in time and in space. For another, there is the problem of transferring the transcendental *I-Here-Now*'s into The Balloon and determining the sense, scope and laws of the different sameness relations connecting the transcendental times and places with their empirical counterparts, and those between the empirical counterparts themselves. Patently, we need the Guise Theory of times and places to go hand in hand with that of the I-guises and selves, and of physical objects.

Kant would have insisted against Descartes that the extended transcendental prefix delivers only an *I*, and that we must add a *here* and a *now* from inside experience. The question arises in relation to Kant: Does the fact that a transcendent reality underwrites the transcendental I-Now guises also extend, first, to there being in the noumenon something like time (duration, or becoming, as Bergson suggested)? If so, is there in the noumenon something like space that underlies the Here-component of the extended transcendental I-Here-Now guises? Of course, Kant might have, on the one hand, resisted recognition of the extended transcendental I-Here-Now guises. On the other hand, he would have insisted that, although his official theory about the limits of knowledge precluded knowledge claims about the noumenon beyond its negative concept, his official epistemology and philosophy of mind made ample room for *metaphysical faith*—just as they did for theologico-religious faith. Thus, *unofficially*, one can believe—without knowledge—that the noumenon is this or that, indeed, that it is exactly as science and intersubjective experience tell us the phenomenal world is.

Notes

1. For details see Castañeda 1984.
2. In the context of developing a material and experiential semantics for ordinary language I contrasted transcendent metaphysics with phenomenological ontology in Castañeda 1974. The proposed phenomenological ontology-semantics was later on called Guise Theory.
3. See Kant 1963, Preface to the Second Edition, A286ff, B287ff.
4. Leibniz 1690. He formulated his Internalism as follows: "Indeed, even if this whole life were said to be only a dream, and the visible world only a phantasm, I should call this dream or this phantasm real enough if we were never [internally] deceived by it when we make good use of reason." (Loemker 1976, p. 364.)
5. Descartes should have moved the rest of *Meditation* II beginning with its fourth paragraph to *Meditation* IIbis. What follows above in the main body of the essay is one (anachronistic) way of furnishing the "missing" part of what "should" have been *Meditation* II.
6. See Frege 1892.
7. Descartes is not denying (C*.Ex) when he replies to Gassendi:

> for when you say that I could have indifferently concluded the same thing [that I exist] from each one of my other actions, you seriously misinterpret me, for there is nothing in them of which I can be entirely certain, that is the metaphysical certainty which is the only one at issue here, except thinking. For, for example, THIS INFERENCE WOULD NOT BE SOUND: *I walk, therefore, I exist*, if only the interior knowledge that I have is of a thinking episode, from which alone the conclusion follows. [at the end of section I of the third response to the Fifth Objections to the *Meditations*; my capitals]

Descartes is merely pointing out that at the transcendental level of the methodological hyperbolic doubt, the premise of the quoted inference is false, hence, an unsound transcendental argument. The inference is, of course, valid, and internalistically sound if the premise is true.
8. For a preliminary treatment of these matters see Castañeda 1981. For a sustained discussion of the self see Castañeda 1987, and for a most comprehensive study of indexical reference see Castañeda 1982 and chaps. 4–7 of this volume. 1987. See also the studies by Robert M. Adams, John Perry, and the replies to them in Tomberlin 1983, and the studies by Esa Saarinen and by David W. Smith in Tomberlin 1986.
9. For an account of Guise Theory, see chap. 13 of this volume (pp. 235–61); and for criticisms of it and responses, see the essays by Alvin Plantinga, Romane Clark, and replies to them in Tomberlin 1983; the studies by Jay Rosenberg, David W. Smith, Jeffrey Sicha, and replies to them in Tomberlin 1986; see also Tomberlin 1984 and subsequent reply. Reply to Plantinga appears in chap. 14 of this volume. See also the papers by Friedrich Rapp, Klaus Jacobi, Guido Küng, Paolo Leonardi, Wolfgang Künne, Tomis Kapitan, and Hans-Dieter Heckmann, and Castañeda's replies in Jacobi/Pape 1989.

References

Castañeda, Hector-Neri. 1974. "Thinking and the Structure of the World." *Philosophia* 4 (1974): 4–40. Also in *Critica* 6–18 (1972): 43–81.
——. 1981. "The Semiotic Profile of Indexical (Experiential) Reference." *Synthese* 49 (1981): 275–316.
——. 1982. *Sprache und Erfahrung: Texte zu einer neuen Ontologie*, transl. by Helmut Pape. Frankfurt.
——. 1984. "Philosophical Refutations," in Fetzer 1984.
Castañeda, Hector-Neri. 1987. "The Self and the I-Guises, Empirical and Transcendental." In *Theorie der Subjektivität*, edited by Konrad Cramer, Hans Friedrich Fulda, Rolf-Peter Horstmann, and Ulrich Pothast. Frankfurt.
Descartes, René. 1641. *Meditations*.

Fetzer, James, ed. 1984. *Principles of Philosophical Reasoning.* New Jersey.
Frege, Gottlob. 1892. "Sense and Reference." E.g., in Geach and Black 1980.
Geach, Peter, and Max Black, eds. and transls. 1980. *Translations from the Philosophical Writings of Gottleb Frege.* Oxford.
Jacobi, Klaus, and Helmet Pape, eds., 1989, *Das Denken und die Struktur der Welt,* Berlin.
Kant, Immanuel. 1781. *Critique of Pure Reason.* 1st ed. (2d ed. 1787). Translated by Norman Kemp Smith. London and New York (1969).
Leibniz, Gottfried Wilhelm. 1690. "On the Method of Distinguishing Real from Imaginary Phenomena." in Leomker 1976.
Loemker, Leroy E., ed. and transl. 1976. *Leibniz's Philosophical Papers and Letters.* Dordrecht.
Tomberlin, James Ed., ed. 1983. *Agent, Language, and the Structure of World.* Indianapolis.
Tomberlin, James E. 1984. "Identity, Intensionality, and Intentionality." *Synthese* 61 (1984): 111–31.
Tomberlin, James E., ed. 1986. *Hector-Neri Castañeda.* Dordrecht.

11

Fiction and Reality: Ontological Questions about Literary Experience

A main cause of philosophical illness—one-sided diet: one nourishes one's thinking with only one kind of example.

Ludwig Wittgenstein, *Philosophical Investigations*, 593

. . . it is not the real beings, but rather the imaginary ones that exercise the most profound and the most durable influence . . .

Anatole France, 'Putois', II

1. A Startling Case

Hans Kraut, the distinguished but not very famous novelist, wrote *There Is a Future* five years ago. On page 2 we read this passage:

(N*) Pamela had rented again the old bungalow at 123 Oak Street. She had it decorated and furnished exactly as she had done 20 years before. Her bed has the same pale blue sheets and pillowcases it had that afternoon when she strangled Randolph. She still loves him. She still hates him. She still lusts for his kisses and his embraces. She is still angry with him. But now she . . .

Kraut tells us that 123 Oak Street is not far from downtown Martinsville, and it is only half a block from 11th street.

A year after Kraut's novel was published, Philip McJohn, a journalist working at the *Martinsville News* in a certain city called Martinsville, was covering a fire at 123 Oak Street, which is not far from downtown Martinsville, only half a block from the intersection of Oak Street and 11th Street. He wrote a report that said in part:

(R*) Pamela, now 45 years old, had rented again the old bungalow at 123 Oak Street. She had it decorated and furnished exactly as she had done 20 years before. Her bed had the same pale blue sheets and pillowcases it had that afternoon when she strangled her companion Randolph Reilly. She still loved and hated him both with equal passion. . . .

Since Pamela died in the fire and she had no relations of any sort there was nobody interested in suing Hans Kraut for having defamed Pamela. The fact, however, is that Kraut had no idea at all about the incidents reported in the *Martinsville News*. He had simply conceived a story that matches reality even to the point of having occurred in cities with the same name and in houses located at the same addresses! But this is not right, is it? Surely, there are no two cities and there are no two houses located at the same address, in the proper sense of 'there are'. It is a sort of category mistake to say that we are dealing here with *two* cities, *two* houses, *two* Pamelas, *two* Randolphs, and so on. There is just *one* city, *one* Pamela, *one* Randolph, *one* house, etc., if we want to speak correctly and truly, namely, the Pamela, the Randolph, the house, the bed, which Philip McJohn mentions in his newspaper report. When we count houses and people, we do not count fictional houses or fictional people. Reality is one and indivisible and cannot be mixed up with fiction, especially when we count entities. Fictional entities are not entities. Or are they? Well, isn't it part of the situation that Kraut describes a person, and a house, which are involved in certain adventures? Isn't it true that the house he describes was peopled and located exactly as McJohn reports? If this weren't so, what sense can one make of the fact that Kraut could have been sued? Can we say that Kraut had a premonition of the events that happened a year later in Martinsville? Kraut's ficiton is fictional because he wrote about the house and about the Pamela McJohn reported about later, only because he had no perceptions or basis for believing what he described, isn't it? It would seem, then, that the fictional entities are entities alright, but they are the very same actual entities McJohn described. Thus, on this view we have just one Pamela, one house, one city, and so on, the same ones described both by Kraut and by McJohn. But this seems wrong. In the present case, because of the tremendous coincidence, it appears that both the novel and the newspaper report are about the same persons and objects. But this is only an extreme case. We must complicate the data. That unifying view of fiction and reality won't do in the most common cases of novels that do not correspond except in a small degree with the biographies of real persons. No, we must return to the view that Kraut's Pamela is a fictional person, whereas McJohn's Pamela is a real one. There is in reality one Pamela; but there are altogether, in the *total* experience we have of both the novel and the newspaper report, two Pamelas, two houses, two Oak Streets, two Randolphs, and so on. And we must sort out their relationships.

The preceding reflections run quickly over the main tensions in the connections between fiction and reality. Our experience includes both, not only separately as in the preceding cases, but also together in intimate mixture as in historical novel, satire, and *roman à clef*. We must, therefore understand the patterns of the relationships between reality and fiction.

2. The Fundamental Ontology of Fiction

Philosophy is the search for the largest and most pervasive patterns of the world and of our experience—the patterns that, regardless of specific contents, characterize the main types of experience. Among such types of experience we have our rich literary experience in which we confront fictional entities. Thus, a philosophical understanding of our experience of fictions requires an understanding of the general structure of fiction as a genre, independently of the particular structures of each novel or story. That understanding includes, of course, an understanding of the general connections between fiction and reality. Again, the specific and particular connections are philosophically important primarily as illustrations of the general structure. Naturally, there are multiple connections, and we cannot consider them all in a short essay. Here we only consider the most fundamental philosophical questions pertaining to those multifarious connections. These are:

(a) What sort of entities are fictional entities? What systematic relationships do they have to real entities? Can we consider fictional entities and real entities to be composed of the same basic elements? If so what are these?

(b) What are the special, peculiar categories that characterize the realm of the fictional?

(c) Since our experience has a total unity, the fictional and the real are simply special contents of our total experience related by certain bridging principles. What are the chief bridging principles? In what way are the special categories of the fictional involved in such bridging principles?

A general theory that furnishes answers to questions (a)–(c) is an ontological theory that deals with the ontological foundations of literature. Obviously, only a general theory can provide a satisfactory and adequate answer to those questions. Of course, the general theory has to be built piecemeal, but no single piece can provide the sense of the whole structure. And it is the whole structure what we want to understand as philosophers. (This is why philosophy can only be analytic in the examination of data, but must be synthetic, constructive, systematic in order to produce what it is meant to do.) Hence, two important methodological precepts must guide us: (i) we must gather a large collection of complex and diversified data, so that we can see more 'points' of the pattern we aim to hypothesize, and (ii) our theory can only be tentative, subject to the corrections that its necessary embedment in more comprehensive theories requires.

3. Some Criteria of Adequacy for any Ontological Theory of Fiction

A review of the above data and reflections in section 1 reveals some crucial points that must be conformed with and also illuminated, by any theory of the structure of our experience of fiction. These are points through which the ontological pattern we are to hypothesize must pass. They yield, in that sense, criteria of adequacy for any theory of the ontology of fiction and reality, namely.

(C1) *Thinking is impervious to existence*: We think of the existing as well as of the nonexisting, not only when we err (as when one thinks that there exists a King in Canada), but even when we know that we are thinking of the nonexisting (as when one deliberately creates fiction or discusses mythical entities).

(C2) *Thinking is primarily thinking of what is taken to be real*: Since thinking is a powerful means of conquering one's environment in order to survive and to increase the quality of one's life, the primary type of thinking is that which takes what is thought of as part of the real world, that is, as governed by the laws of nature. As Kant put it, "nothing is an [actual or real] object *for us*, unless it presupposes the sum of all empirical reality as the condition of its possibility" (*Critique of Pure Reason* A582 = 610).

(C3) *Thinking of a fictional character, state of affairs, or course of events as such is thinking of something as not real, as not governed by the laws of nature in the same reality*: This is fully illustrated by the contrast between Kraut's (N*) and McJohn's (R*): To think of a piece of fiction *qua* fiction is to think of contents (objects, properties, states of affairs) as segregated from reality, even if the same laws govern the fiction and reality.

(C4) *The adventures of fictional entities are created*: They do not have an ontological status independently of the invention of the stories in which the fictional entities function. There is no strangling of the fictional Randolph by the fictional Pamela until Kraut invents it in *There is a Future*.

(C5) *A fictional object is not a real object*, in spite of how detailed and complete its description may be, and regardless of how much its descriptions coincide with historical accounts. This is what (R*) and (N*) bring out very sharply.

(C6) *Some fictional entities are not even possible objects*: Some stories deal with contradictory objects, and in some cases the contradictions have been deliberately introduced.

(C7) *Real objects are complete in that "one of every [pair of contradiction] possible predicates [i.e., properties] must always belong to them"* (Kant, ibid., A573 = B601). Fictional objects, on the other hand, are incomplete. A fictional object is what it is created as, and it cannot have other properties than the ones it is created, or re-created, with. Now in most stories there is an implicit assumption that the human beings which the story deals with are fully human. Hence, there is a general assumption that such fictional humans are in possession of all the standard properties humans have. Yet there is an indetermination of properties: no particular shade of color, for instance, is given; no exact weights and heights, no precise lengths of toes, thumbs, or intestines are assigned. Yet, by virtue of (C5) and (C6) we must understand that a fictional hero is not merely, even in the most coincidental of the cases, a real hero deprived of specific and particularized properties or features. Fictional objects remain wholly unreal, in a segregated realm of their own. The difference between the real and the fictional realms is abysmal.

(C8) *The possession of properties by fictional objects is, thus, very different from the possession of properties by real objects.* There is a sense in which real objects have properties and unreal ones do not have properties. There is, of course, a generic sense in which both real and unreal objects have properties. This distinction in predication or having properties must be clarified by an illuminating theory of fiction and of predication.

(C9) *Many stories are about real objects*: There are tales about national heroes that few people take for actual truths, yet they are propagated because they reveal the heroes' personalities. There are pseudo-historical novels; there are satires and ironic fables. They all depend crucially on an identification of persons, objects, and events of the real world with persons, objects, and events, respectively, of the satire or fable in question. This widespread phenomenon seems to collide with (C5)-(C7).

(C10) *Fictions about real objects or persons are only externally so*: The identifications of objects and persons that take place within a piece of fiction involve the type of predication, or of having properties, mentioned in (C8), but the identification of a fictional entity with a real entity is, although external to the core of the story, also a fictional identification. An elegant theory would treat both types of identification as involving the same type of predication.

(C11) *The unity of total experience, of fiction and reality, is manifested in those external identifications*: It would seem that the very same entity can appear in reality and in fiction, provided it is self-consistent, and the very same properties that appear in fiction appear in reality.

(C12) *Fictional objects undergo changes in the pieces of fiction in which they have been created*: The unity and self-identity of the subject of changes of fictional entities in fiction seems to be of the same sort as the unity and self-identity of the subject of real change in the case of real objects.

(C13) *Fictional objects undergo changes from story to story*: Don Juan changes a good deal from Moratin's story to Zorrilla's play, and he undergoes further changes in the German writers and in Bernard Shaw's. The unitary subject of those changes must be clarified.

4. The Fictional/Actual Ambiguity

Let us consider a fragment of Kraut's (N*) from his novel *There is a Future*:

(1) Pamela had rented again the old Bungalow at 123 Oak Street.

This sentence also appears in McJohn's report that includes (R*). And we saw that the sentence makes two different statements, and that each statement is true. But we must be sure not to confuse the two statements: Kraut's statement is a fictional truth, whereas McJohn's is a factual truth. Are we to say, then, that sentence (1) is ambiguous? This seems strong, yet that is precisely what we should say. It is ambiguous precisely in the sense just explained: It has been used to formulate two different truths. The recognition of this ambiguity is crucial.

Sentence (1) is used to make two different statements in another respect: different persons can be, are in fact, named 'Pamela' and it can be said that each token of (1) makes a different statement for each Pamela that the speaker, whoever he/she may be, has in mind. Yet that variety of statements does not seem well described by saying that sentence (1) is ambiguous depending on which Pamela the sentence is used to refer. (It seems all right to say that the sentence, because of the proper name it contains, is referentially ambiguous. But one knows that referential ambiguity is not ambiguity which has to do, not so much with reference, but with sense.) There is a fundamental *unity of sense* in the sentence 'Pamela had rented again the old bungalow at 123 Oak Street', regardless of which Pamela a person may use it to talk about. One apprehends, or comes to know, that *one* meaning of the sentence, when one comes to know, for example, that the sentence is a translation of the Spanish sentence *Pamela ha alquilado de nuevo la vieja casita en al número 123 de la calle Oak*. One does not apprehend any particular truth that the sentence can be used to express or communicate, but one, nevertheless, apprehends its meaning. Here we will have to enter into the problem of the semantics of proper names. The proper account has to illuminate and relate that diversity of reference of proper names with the unity of the meaning of the sentences containing proper names. I have provided such an account elsewhere (see chapter 2).

The main crux of the account is that proper names do not have a semantic role of referring, but only a semantical role of functioning as free variables of quantification; they have an important causal and epistemic role. Thus, the unity of the meaning of sentence (1) is the unity of the propositional function

(2) x has rented again the old bungalow at y.

Each of the names that occupy the places of the variables x and y have causal roles of being such that he who perceives them in a sentence is caused by his perception to think of the appropriate referents, in whatever form he can think of them. Needless to say, a hearer may think of those referents in ways different from the ways in which the speaker is thinking of them when he speaks, and different hearers may be caused to think of the same referents in different ways – this happens of course, when the speaker succeeds in communicating his message: The success of standard communication is determined by the communicator's and the audience's thinking of objects that are contingently the same: communication of the sense, which the speaker associates with the name on the given occasion of utterance, is not required. This is, obviously, as it should be. The role of communication in normal living is to coordinate actions for the fulfilment of plans and projects. For that, coreference suffices, although identity of sense, if it obtains, is not in the least harmful.

Can we treat sentence (1), 'Pamela had rented again the old bungalow at 123 Oak Street', as having a unity of sense, within which the diversity of Kraut's fictional statement and McJohn's actual truth can be understood as specifications? Undoubtedly there is a common structure to the two statements that sentence (1) formulates here. That unity has to be brought forth by any adequate account of fiction. Yet it is not clear that underlying unity of sense excludes an important difference of sense that lies on the surface. To appreciate this alternative consider

(3) This is red.

The sentence 'This is red' has the referential diversity that sentence (1) has: The demonstrative 'this' can be used to refer to different objects. Yet, as in the case of (1), there is a unity of sense in (3), which one knows, for example, that it means the same as the French sentence 'C'est rouge'. There are differences between demonstratives and proper names that must be understood (see chapter 2, section 15, and chapter 5). But, in another dimension, sentence (3) allows of an important diversity of truths. Whenever a person uses (3) with the intention of stating a truth in an actual context of experience, 'this' being used as a genuine demonstrative, that person is thinking of a specific shade of red. He is attributing in his thoughts at least that specific color to the object he calls 'this'. Since properties are precisely what function as sense of predicates, or determine the differences in senses or meanings, it is clear that we could understand the full meaning of 'red' to vary when it is used in sentence (3) to attribute to an object a different shade of red. Thus, sentence (3) can be used in the following ways to make statements about reality:

(3.1) This is red_g — that is, this is generic-red.

(3.2) There is a shade f-ness of red_g such that this is f.

(3.3) This is red_1 — that is, this specific red_1.

(3.4) This is red_2.

The senses (3.1) and (3.2) are on certain views the same. But we are not interested here in ontological reductions. The important fact is that sentence (3) has the unity of sense, that (3.1) and (3.2) represent, in that whatever statement S it is used to make, S is either (3.1) or (3.2) or a statement like (3.3) or (3.4) which not only implies (3.1) and (3.2), but the speaker knows that this implication holds. To be sure, there is also the underlying structure.

(4) This is − −, where the blank represents a property of the redness family, whether generic or specific.

Here I need not commit myself to an account of the meaning of color words. All I need here is the model I have described in order to try it out in fictional sentences.

Now, is the diversity of statements that Kraut and McJohn made with sentence (1), 'Pamela had rented again the old bungalow at 123 Oak Street' analogous to the diversity of specific perceptual statements a person can make with sentence (3), 'This is red'? The point of the analogy is to maintain a general unity of meaning underlying a diversity of specific or particular meanings for sentence (1). The analogy is certainly strong in one other respect: Just as there is an indefinitely large, and perhaps infinite, number of determinate shades of red that one can think and point to, there is an indefinitely large, and surely infinite, number of stories to which sentence (1) can belong. Obviously, given the diversity of entities to which proper names can refer to, there may be (in fact there are) many different stories in which characters named 'Pamela' appear. Such characters may be as different from each other and as numerically diverse from each other, as they seem to be from the real persons named 'Pamela'. It is in principle feasible that in different stories wholly different characters satisfy sentence (1).

The segregation of fiction from reality that Kraut's (N*) and McJohn's (R*) have urged upon us does make the fictional/actual ambiguity of 'Pamela had rented again the old bungalow at 123 Oak Street' understandable along the lines of the ambiguity of 'This is red'. But we must press further. The ambiguity of 'This is red' has been located on the ambiguity of 'red', except for the case of (3.2), which introduces a quantificational structure. Can we place the actual/fictional ambiguity in some predicative element of (1), 'Pamela had rented again the old bungalow at 123 Oak Street'? We shall see.

5. Basic Ontological Theories of Fictional Truths

If we pursue the ambiguity approach advanced above, we have in principle the following options:

(T1) The sentence 'Pamela had rented again the old bungalow at 123 Oak Street' has the fictional/actual ambiguity, because the predicate exemplifies the fictional/actual ambiguity.

(T2) The sentence is ambiguous, because the subject terms are ambiguous.

(T3) The sentence is ambiguous, because the copula is ambiguous.

Naturally, the actuality/fictional ambiguity approach can be set aside. Then the fact that the sentence 'Pamela had rented again the old bungalow at 123 Oak Street' expresses one truth in Kraut's novel and another in McJohn's newspaper report must be accounted for in some other way. Before going any further, it may be worthwhile to note a view that looks very unpromising, namely:

(T0) The whole sentence 'Pamela had rented the old bungalow at 123 Oak Street' is ambiguous; in one case it has the fictional meaning Kraut gave it, in the other case it has the actuality meaning, the standard one in which McJohn used it, but it is the sentence *as a whole* that has the ambiguity, without any of its component parts being ambiguous.

This wholistic thesis has little to recommend it. Undoubtedly, there are sentences that have no ambiguous components, and are yet ambiguous as wholes. But in such cases there is a syntactic ambiguity. For instance,

(5) John ought not to go

is as a whole ambiguous, depending on how one construes the scope of the negation 'not'. One can take (5) as meaning the same as 'The following is not the case:

John ought to go'; and one can, alternatively, regard (5) as meaning the same as 'John ought to do the following: not go'. If the difference in scope does not change the meaning of 'not', then there is no ambiguous term in (5). There are also the exciting cases that led Chomsky to great linguistic theories, like 'They are flying airplanes'. Here, of course, we have an in-between case, given that the referent of 'they' changes.

There is, however, no syntactical feature in 'Pamela had rented again the old bungalow at 123 Oak Street' that justifies claiming that it is syntactically ambiguous. Even if there were some syntactical ambiguity in that sentence, the main point is that we *cannot* construe the difference between fictional sentences and actuality sentences as one of systematic syntactic ambiguity involving scope distinctions.

There are other *wholistic views*, besides (T0). One that has often been defended is this:

(T4) The sentence 'Pamela had rented again the old bungalow at 123 Oak Street' has the same meaning whether one uses it in fiction, as Kraut did, or one uses it to describe a real person, as McJohn did. The difference in the statements made by Kraut and McJohn lies in the fact that Kraut's utterance is in the scope of an operator, explicitly formulated by the title of his novel and by his note to the effect that all the characters in the novel were fictive and had no basis on reality. That story operator can be represented by the locution 'In *There is a Future* (by Hans Kraut)'.

According to view (T4) the contrast between Kraut's statement in (N*) and McJohn's in (R*) can be more perspicuously put as follows:

(1.K) In *There is a Future*: Pamela had rented again the old bungalow at 123 Oak Street.

(1.MJ) Pamela had rented again the old bungalow at 123 Oak Street.

Naturally, both (1.K) and (1.MJ) are true, but neither one implies the other. It is this non-implication that in (T4) accounts for the segregation of fiction from reality. And that segregation is nicely represented by the story operator. Each story corresponds to one story operator, which segregates the story in question from all other stories and from reality.

A novel theory, (T5), holds that two senses of 'truth' are involved. This theory must be distinguished from the claim, undoubtedly correct, that there are different *criteria* of truth. I do not like this theory because I want to keep my meta-language univocal.

Let us look into the above theories. I do not propose to engage in a sustained refutation of the views that I do not hold. There is not enough space to do so, for one thing. But, more importantly, there is no easy way of refuting a plausible theory. The plausibility of a theory is just its being satisfactory for certain *desiderata* in its conforming with an illuminating collection of relevant data. Thus, a refutation of a plausible theory requires developing the theory to the breaking point. In general, the best policy is to examine complex data and let the data suggest the simplest theory.

6. Theory (T1): Predicate Ambiguity

Theory (T1) has sometimes been held. It can gain strength by being embedded in a larger theory that allows predicates a systematic ambiguity depending on whether they apply to real entities governed by the laws of physics, or whether they apply to nonphysical entities. I have in mind views like Sellars', which include the thesis that predicates attributing properties to sense impressions do not mean exactly the same as when they are used to attribute corresponding properties to physical objects. In brief, the predicate fictional/actual ambiguity can be a powerful view if joined to a larger predicate ambiguity theory (see appendix to this chapter).

To the extent that fictional truths are wholly segregated from actual truths, it seems plausible to say that the colors of fictional objects, for instance, are not quite the same properties as the colors of physical objects. The colors of physical objects, and the colors of visual patches, whether physical or not, are visible. The colors of purely fictional entities are not visible. Even if one were to hallucinate and had perceptual experiences of fictional objects, for example, see Don Quixote charging against the local television tower, it is clear that the Don Quixote in the hallucination differs from the Don Quixote of Cervantes' *Don Quixote* in very much the same way in which McJohn's Pamela differs from Kraut's Pamela. The fact then is that our total experience includes: (a) the fundamental actual world; (b) the multifarious half-worlds of fiction; (c) the multifarious fragments of worlds of hallucination; and (d) others besides, which are properly left out of consideration here.

The segregation of fiction from reality can bestow plausibility on the thesis that different predicates and properties are involved in each. That segregation also makes clear the point in the transpreceding paragraph, namely, that the thesis of predicate the fictional/actual ambiguity is even more plausible if it is part of a large similar theory. The segregation of hallucinations and illusions from reality construed along the lines of a predicate hallucinatory/actual ambiguity goes hand in hand with the predicate fictional/actual ambiguity. We would have, then, a unified view of total experience and of our total language.

There are trivial and natural objections to the predicate ambiguity view. It may be adduced that empirical properties, like colors and shapes, smells and sounds, appear both in fiction and in reality. There is no learning one set of predicates and then learning the other. (I won't stoop to consider the silly argument that dictionaries do not give both a fictional and a real meaning for color words.) Indeed, the very fact that we use the same words suggests that we are dealing with the same properties.

I think that there are powerful reasons for not adopting view (T1). But these reasons do not prove (T1) to be erroneous, or prove (T2) or (T3) to be correct. Here I am making the general point, which we all know in theory but which many forget in practice, to wit: No theory is a deductive conclusion from its data. The relationship between theory and data is a dialectical one. The theory illuminates the data by organizing them in exciting (and satisfying) ways, and by unifying them in fruitful and economical ways. There is no clearcut criterion of excitingness and satisfyingness: here is room for personal choice. But fruitfulness is something else. A theory is always ad hoc insofar as it is conceived to illuminate a previously collected set of data. If the theory is fruitful it will either illuminate additional data automatically or it will illuminate them with minor changes. The number of changes and the quality of those changes should involve exciting economies and greater or lesser degrees of satisfyingness. But I am also making a special point that illustrates this general point. The fact that we use the same predicates in fiction as in descriptions of the actual world indicates a very intimate unity among the properties those predicates express in the two types of discourse. How intimate that unity is, is a matter of theory. The predicate ambiguity theory (T1) is not an economical theory, but it can provide an account of that intimacy of the two sets of properties. Theory (T1) will have to be supplemented with a system of principles relating the fictional property expressed by a predicate P to the actuality property expressed by P. The theory will have to be extended with an account of how, when one learns that P expresses a certain actuality property f-ness, one also learns, or acquires, the mechanism for learning by oneself, or for learning on some simple additional experiences, perhaps of some literary content, that P can also be used to express fictional properties $*f^i$-ness corresponding to f-ness.

No, theory (T1) *cannot* be easily refuted. But I do not like its complexities. I prefer to believe that the same properties are involved both in truths in fiction and in truths about reality. Thus, there is no need to explain what sort of function the asterisk in $*f^i$-ness represents, and there is no need to introduce a multiple-tiered account of concept-acquisition.

Furthermore, the impressive unity and homogeneity of consciousness in our total experience, whether we experience fictions or hallucinations or realities, can be better understood if we suppose that the same properties are involved in hallucinations, in veridical perceptions, and in fiction. Since the contents of consciousness are qualities and properties, nothing can illuminate that unity and homogeneity better than the thesis that exactly the same qualities and properties are the contents of consciousness, whatsoever the type of experience one has. Hence, thesis (T1) is diametrically opposed to my Leibnizian-Kantian conception of the unity of experience, not to mention the homogeneity of consciousness.

7. Theory (T2): Subject Ambiguity

We have already noted in section 4 that, on what I take to be the best view of the roles of proper names, within the realm of reality the sentence 'Pamela had rented again the old bungalow at 123 Oak Street' is referentially ambiguous. But we are not interested in that kind of ambiguity. It may be held, however, that that is precisely what is at stake in the contrast between Kraut's and McJohn's statements. Perhaps, it may be said, those two statements are different in the way in which two statements made by the sentence are different when one speaker refers to Pamela Smith, her neighbor, and the other refers to Pamela Jones, his girl friend. This referential ambiguity of the subject expressions will ultimately yield the view that, ontologically speaking, *the domain of fictional entities is entirely different from the domain of actual entities*. Let us call this view (T2.R).

View (T2.R) is very nice. It allows that all predicates, connectives, and other abstract expressions have exactly the same meaning both in fiction and in nonfiction, in true utterances and in false ones. This conforms to my strong Leibnizian conception of the *qualitative unity* of experience.

The main difficulty for view (T2.R) lies in characterizing fictional entities and in explaining how they can be the same entities about which we can both invent tales and fables and narrate true adventures. Thus, the *structural unity* of fiction and reality, which, for instance, allows the real Washington to be the hero of the apocryphal story involving his father's cherry tree, is a serious problem. But it must not be misunderstood. We have already noted that some entities are purely fictional, like Pegasus, Kraut's Pamela, and Don Quixote. Hence, the problem is not to be solved by picking out some real objects and placing them in fictional worlds. The problem has to be solved by allowing some fictional entities, the majority of them, in fact, to remain purely fictional, in spite of how closely similar they are to real entities, and yet allowing some real entities to appear in fiction both with their real identity and with drastic changes which are strictly fictional. The problem is accentuated by the fact, noted in section 3, that fictional entities are necessarily incomplete, whereas real entities are complete in the strong sense Kant indicated.

Again, as in the case of theory (T1), there is no refutation of theory (T2.R). There are problems that (T2.R), like all other plausible theories, must face. In particular, the problem of the individuation of fictional entities is a serious one; yet it is often discussed very cavalierly. Given the incompleteness of fictional entities, there is a clear sense in which they are not fully individuated as real objects are. But this is a problem for all theories. I am not, however, interested in developing here view (T2.R). But it should be developed in detail. My reason is that the progression of criteria (C1)-(C13) in section 3, suggested by the data collected in section 2, emphatically points to theory (T3) as the most illuminating one.

Obviously, a strict theory (T2) that assigns different meanings to the subject expressions, whether these are proper names or not, is very precarious. For one thing, to assign different meanings to definite descriptions is to endorse theory (T1): It is to take the predicates in a definite description that appears in a piece of fiction as expressing different properties from the ones it expresses when it appears in a true historical narrative. But it is more than that. It also involves the thesis that the fictional entities belong to a different domain from that of the actual entities. We still have to face the problems of the individuation and incompleteness of fictional entities.

8. Theory (T4): Story Operators

Before developing theory (T3) let us make some comments on (T4). This theory is absolutely correct concerning the thesis: There are story operators. There is no denying that all the sentences in a typical novel are prefaced by the title, so that they are all in the scope of an operator of the form 'In . . . (by . . .)' or simply 'In . . . ', and even more complex operators of the form 'In . . . , by . . . , published by . . . in such and such a place in such and such a year'; and so on. The issue cannot be about there being story operators. The issue is whether sentences like those in passage (N*) from Kraut's novel *There is a Future* must be understood *only* as embedded in constructions prefaced by one or another of the appropriate story operators. In other words, the issue is whether it is correct to detach fictional sentences and consider them as fictional, alright, but outside the scope of all story operators.

Is it ever legitimate to deal with fictional sentences outside the scope of all story operators? It seems to me that it is legitimate. I am prepared to insist that this legitimacy is a matter of degrees. That it depends in part on how widespread the knowledge of the relevant pieces of fiction is, and in part on how much the relevant story operators are remembered by the speakers of the language. There is, in my opinion, a *culturalization of fiction* as a crucial datum that must be taken into account. Most of us know that Santa Claus is a fictional character. But we do not have a clear idea of how the fiction started, nor do we know how to subordinate sentences about Santa Claus to the appropriate story operators. Santa Claus is a piece of common property. It belongs to our culture, under no story operators. We refer to him in the same casual way we refer to neighbors and colleagues – but we know that everything we say and think about him is fictional. Yet we attribute to him some of the very same properties we attribute to our neighbors and colleagues, for example, that he wears clothes, has a beard, two eyes, is old, travels South, loves children and reindeers. He is segregated as a fictional person, but he is not incarcerated in the scope of any story operator.[1]

The Devil was a quasi-real character for many people for centuries. The fictional, as Anatole France said, can be most influential. His hero Putois is a fictional character within the main fiction of the story. It was invented by a (first-order fictional) character in order to refuse a boring dinner invitation: she had to await the gardener Putois. Then everybody in the story acquired the habit of blaming unexplainable events, or events not to be explained, on Putois. The situation developed in such a way that Putois was just an invisible member of the community, even more real than other members of it. Yet some people knew that he was a fiction. In the experience of those persons Putois, although fictional, played a very important role. It was utterly impossible to place sentences about him under any story operator.

No doubt, we can always invent a story operator for those fictional characters that have been an integral part of our lives. There is the neutral 'It is said that', for instance. Perhaps one can and should distinguish an infinite family of particular operators of the *it is said that* family, one for each character one no longer knows its original habitat. Notice once again how hard it is to refute a plausible view. This multiplication of neutral operators may seem bothersome; yet it is in principle unobjectionable. It certainly does the job of segregating fiction from reality. The problem then becomes that of accounting for the connections between fiction and reality, connections we rely upon in order to understand satires, pedagogical tales, etc.

The mixture of reality and fiction which constitutes satires, historical novels, and so on, is really a serious problem. It is structurally parallel to the problem of connecting our beliefs about the real with the real itself. Thus, a powerful theory is one that treats both as species of the same problem and gives them both the same solution.

There is another mixture problem. In criterion (C13) in section 3 we already noted how fictional characters leave their original stories and migrate into other stories, often undergoing important evolutions. This phenomenon is the basis of many a profession in comparative literature. The great literary writers are precisely those who can manage to create fictional heroes that take on an independent 'life' of their own and develop in the works of other great writers. Those great fictional heroes belong in the end to no particular story: no story operator can capture the whole of the hero's 'vitality'. Such heroes, like Hamlet, Faust, Don Juan, Don Quixote, Anna Karenina, Nora, Oedipus, and their majestic colleagues, are part of our living cultural heritage just as crucial and solid as was Putois for his community.

In terminology I disapprove of, I am here making the point that, in the reference to fictional persons across difference stories, one is making a *de re* reference. I do not like the terminology that contrasts *de re* with *de dicto* occurrences of expressions in psychological, modal, or fictional sentences, because the phenomenon I have called *quasi-indexical reference* is neither *de re* nor *de dicto* in the standard ways of making this distinction (see chapters 5 and 12). The following sentences illustrate the contrast:

(6.*d*) Anthony believes the following: that the President is married.

(6.*r*) Anthony believes of the President that he is married.

(7.*d*) Columbus believed that Castro's island was China.[2] (Attributing to Columbus, the belief that he would have formulated, by referring to Castro, by saying, for example, "Castro's island is China".

(7.*r*) Columbus believed that Castro's island was China. (Here the expression 'Castro's island' is the speaker's own, so that what is said is this: Such-and-such is Castro's island and Columbus believed the following: that such-and-such was China.)

The force of the so-called *de re* constructions, like (6.*r*) and (7.*r*), is that the reference to the entity referred to by the expression occurring *de re* is made (in the simple cases like the ones above) by the speaker of the whole sentence, not by the person mentioned as the one who believes (thinks, says, and so on). That is to say, when the expression occurs *de re* its referent is treated by the speaker of the whole sentence as *on a par* with the person who is said to believe (think, say, and so on). Note, for instance, now (6.*r*) treats the President and Anthony on a par, and (7.*r*) treats Columbus and Castro's island (and Castro, too) on a par. In contrast, the *de dicto* sentence (6.*d*) leaves the expression 'the President' in the scope of 'Anthony believes', so that the speaker himself is not committed to the President as he claims that Anthony is. In normal interpretations of (6.*d*) there would be an attribution to Anthony of the belief that there is a President, whereas the speaker of (6.*d*) is not so committed: he can conjoin (6.*d*) consistently with "But the President doesn't exist!" The same is true of the false (7.*d*).

The point of the mixture of fiction and reality, on the one hand, and of the references to fictional entities across different stories, on the other hand, is simply that fictional entities so involved must be treated as having a status *outside* the stories they inhabit — *somehow* on a par with the persons who deal with them. This 'somehow' is a serious problem. But theory (T4) has the defect of not even allowing this problem to be raised.

9. Theory (T3): The Fictional/Actual Ambiguity As a Copula Ambiguity

Criteria (C8)-(C10) in section 3 strongly suggest that the fictional/actual ambiguity we found in sentence (1) 'Pamela had rented again the old bungalow at 123 Oak Street' as used by Kraut and McJohn must be construed structurally, and neither wholistically nor contentually. If the sentence is not wholistically ambiguous, then it has an ambiguous component; if it is not contentually ambiguous, then the ambiguity cannot lie in one of the components that express content, either the subject or the predicate, or in predicates or individual terms that may be components of these. The ambiguity *must* be placed, then, on a component of the sentence that expresses the structure of the relevant truth; that component can only be the copula. Thus, on view (T3), suggested by criteria (C8)-(C10), we must construe the copula represented in the inflection of the verb 'had rented' as ambiguous. We have, on this view, therefore, two interpretations of (1). For convenience we can signal them by using the subscripts 'A', to indicate the actuality copula, and 'F', to indicate the fictional copula, as follows:

(1.F) Pamela had$_F$ rented again the old bungalow at 123 Oak Street,

and

(1.A) Pamela had$_A$ rented again the old bungalow at 123 Oak Street.

Kraut made the statement represented by sentence (1.F), whereas McJohn made the statement represented by sentence (1.A).

This Predicational View of the contrast between fiction and reality gains body by virtue of the following central tenets:

FC**.1. Every real object can appear in a piece of fiction.

FC**.2. Every property, whether instantiated in the real world or not, can appear in a piece of fiction.

FC**.3. Every state of affairs, or proposition about reality can appear in a piece of fiction, in person, so to speak, or vicariously through a counterpart fictional state of affairs, or proposition in which fictional predication occurs instead of actuality predication.

FC**.4. No fictional state of affairs can occur in reality, but some fictional properties and some individual guises do occur both in reality and in fiction.

FC**.5. A piece of fiction is an ordered pair (S, λ), where S is a story operator and λ is a class of states of affairs, or propositions, some of which are fictional in that they have fictional predication.

FC**.6. The creation of a story, or a piece of fiction, is precisely the contingent and empirical episode of thinking a class λ of states of affairs, or propositions, some of which are fictional, as forming a unified class, and that episode of thinking is precisely what empirically subordinates the members of λ to one or more story operators.

FC**.7. Once a fictional proposition or state of affairs has been thought of, or created, by a fiction-maker, it is public property to the extent that it is publicized and can be considered by others outside the scope of the original story operators involved in its creation.

Perhaps some comments on the preceding tenets may not be amiss. *First*, what exactly it is for an object to appear in a piece of fiction has to be clarified, and this holds both for purely fictional, incomplete objects, and for real objects. We must tackle the problem of individuation, and we must handle the problem of fictional individuation as a special case of the general problem of individuation. *Second*, the overall unity of experience and the general homogeneity of consciousness are beautifully accounted for by FC**.1–FC**.3. In the sense that what is real can appear in fiction, but not vice versa, fictional consciousness is a generalization of ordinary consciousness of actuality. *Third*, fictional truths proper, that is, the truths that include nothing but fictional predication, are maximally segregated from reality: Each one is segregated by itself thanks to fictional predication. Yet, *fourth*, each fictional truth can mix with any actual falsehood and with any actual truth without any risk of confusion. This particularly accounts well for the strong similarity between Kraut's (N*) and McJohn's (R*), even though neither one was making the other's statements. Of course, we still have the problem of whether the Pamelas they were describing are in some sense one and the same, or simply similar persons. We shall deal with this problem below when we deal with the problem of individuation.

Fifth, the act of fiction or myth creation is an empirical matter analogous to the coming into (or the causation of the) existence of actual objects. FC**.6. gives theoretical character to this intuition. Yet there is a sense in which a literary creator does not create *ex nihilo*: He arranges materials, conceptual materials if you wish, in certain patterns. This is the sense in which not only the properties a literary creator attributes to his/her characters are the same properties the universe as a whole has, but also in that the created characters are conceptions that have some prior status. Let me explain this. Consider once again Kraut's *There is a Future*. He has created a character that he calls 'Pamela'. He utilizes the pre-given properties *being named 'Pamela', living in a bungalow, having rented a bungalow, living at a house on a street named 'Oak Street', having strangled someone, loving a man, lusting for a certain man*, and so on. But Kraut also uses the individuals: *the* house at 123 Oak Street, *the* woman named 'Pamela', *the* bungalow Pamela rented again, *the* man Pamela strangled, etc. These individuals were created by Kraut only in the sense that he put some of them together, on the one hand, and attributed properties to them, on the other. But the mere individuals listed as essentially characterized by the properties mentioned in their listing have a *status* that is prior to, and independent of, Kraut's literary creation. The status here at issue is not, of course, existence, or reality, or actuality. It is a status as a *possible object of thought*, and we need not hypostatize it in a Platonic realm. We can even adopt a reductionistic view and consider such a status as ultimately built into our linguistic habits in that those possible objects of thoughts are equated with possible definite descriptions we can frame given the language we possess, but need not ever frame. But I am not interested in these deeper *metaphysical* issues pertaining to the connection between language, thinking, and what we think. Our discussion here pertains, rather, to phenomenological ontology. Here it suffices to note that what we think and express by means of definite descriptions is logically, and ontologically, prior to artistic creation. But artistic creation is creation, so that it bestows on those possible contents of thinking a contingent and empirical status akin to reality, but very short of reality. This contingent and empirical status is what the fictional copula signals. In short, then, there are two statuses we must consider when we consider the ontological structure of fictional entities:

FC**.8.   Fictional entities are a special subdomain of thinkable entities. If we use logical quantifiers only for individuals, then the most comprehensive and most fundamental quantifiers are those that range over all *thinkable* individuals, whether they exist or not, whether they are fictional (that is, occur in an actually conceived piece of fiction) or not, whether they have ever been thought of or not.

FC**.9.   Fictional entities are a special subdomain of thinkable entities that have been *actually* thought of. Thus, fictional entities are in an empirical class and have a shadow of reality, so to speak, but a shadow that springs forth from the full reality of episodes of the thinking that creates pieces of fiction. The empirical fictional status of fictional entities is expressed by the fictional copula.

Sixth, although on the predicational view of fiction propounded here the empirical fictional status is a form of predication, one can, of course, introduce special quantifiers to represent that status. These fictional quantifiers will be introduced so that the most general thinkability quantifiers have a domain that includes that of fictional entities.

10. Ontological Atoms of Individuation: Individual Guises

The individuals mentioned in the preceding paragraphs are very thin. They are what definite descriptions present to consciousness. Thus, the individual *the woman named 'Pamela' living on Oak Street* is different from the individual *the woman who rented again the old bungalow at 123 Oak Street*. These are the individuals that have as thinkables an ontological status logically prior to their fictional status in Kraut's novel *There is a Future*. That status involves a certain ontological isolation, so to say. Kraut's creation consisted of tearing that isolation apart and putting those thin individuals together into one fictional character. Thus,

FC**.10.A fictional character is a system of thin thinkable individuals put together by a fiction maker.

FC**.11.An action of fiction making is an episode or process of thinking through which a system of thin thinkable individuals is built up.

Now, real objects as we ordinarily conceive of them are objects that, as we say, satisfy an infinite number of definite descriptions. Some definite descriptions may appear in pieces of fiction, with the implication or suggestion that they are satisfied by real objects or not. Thus, we can at least for the sake of unity consider that ordinary objects are also systems of thin thinkable objects, one such thin object for each description that the object satisfies. For example, we can consider the ordinary object with its infinite properties that is a man, as an infinite system of thinkable objects. For specificity, consider the system of thin thinkable objects that includes the following: *the* person who is writing this paper, *the* person who wrote the previous page, *the* person who wrote 'Thinking and the Structure of the World', *the* editor of NOÛS, *the* man named 'Hector-Neri Castañeda', my present temporary self. Each of these thinkable individuals is an atom of individuation. They go together in reality, and this going together in reality is formulated by saying that they are all the *same* person. Thus, this word 'same' in the sense of *contingent* identity or sameness is simply the expression of that relationship of togetherness in actuality that those individuals possess. That togetherness is not a creation by anyone – assuming a non-theistic metaphysics for the time being. And that is the rock bottom difference between the togetherness of the thin thinkable individuals that Kraut put together to compose each character of his *There is a Future*, and the togetherness in actuality that maintains each ordinary object as a multiple-faceted and multiple-propertied entity. Both togethernesses are contingent, empirical. One is created by man; the other is not created (or created by God, if you wish). One is governed by the laws the fiction maker decides upon; the other is governed by all the laws of nature, without exception (because God so decided?).

The preceding paragraph contains a radical move. Therefore it should be gone over in slow motion. In the case of fiction it seems natural to take each definite description as denoting a thinkable entity, and to make each of these thinkable entities as thin, as having no more to it than what the definite description denoting it says or reveals. Naturally, this leaves us with several problems: (*a*) how are the properties expressed by the predicates in the definite description involved in the thinkable denoted by the definite description? (*b*) how is it that there is no more to that thinkable, how is it that those properties exhaust it? (*c*) what is it to predicate properties of such thinkables? and so on. But we cannot worry about these problems right at this moment. Since they cannot be brushed aside, we will consider them subsequently.

There is no difficulty in introducing such thin thinkable entities when we are dealing with fiction. After all, each fictional entity is given in a piece of fiction, so that we have nothing but words, definite descriptions, to introduce us to fictional entities. The whole procedure seems nothing but a hypostatization of the senses (or meanings) of the definite descriptions that appear in pieces of fiction. (In fact this is all it is, together with the remark that phenomenologically we find in our experience those hypostatizations: we need a deeper metaphysics to reduce them.) Yet I have done something else, which is radical. I have proposed that we apply to ordinary objects and our descriptions of them, not only the ones that have been proffered by some person or other, but all the possible definite descriptions that apply to ordinary objects, precisely the same analysis that I applied above to fictional entities and our definite descriptions introducing them in pieces of fiction. The problems noted above, (*a*)–(*c*), and others become, naturally, more pressing. Perhaps they will be unsurmountable. But just for ontological enlightenment let us consider as a philosophical adventure, the ontological picture I have suggested: that *ordinary real objects are, like fictional characters, systems of thin thinkable objects denoted by those definite descriptions that we normally say corefer contingently.* Consider this fully, with tolerance, as a metaphysical experiment.

We are considering each definite description as denoting a unique thinkable object. Thus, we have the following distinct thinkable objects:

(6)   *The* author of *Science, Perception, and Reality*, London, Routledge and Kegan Paul, 1963;

(7)   *The* author of 'Empiricism and the Philosophy of Mind';

(8) *The* coeditor with John Hospers of *Readings in Ethical Theory*, New York, Appleton-Century-Crofts, 1952;

(9) *The* chairman of the department of philosophy of the University of Minnesota in 1954;

(10) *The* philosopher discussed in *Action, Knowledge, and Reality*, Indianapolis, Bobbs-Merrill, 1975;

(11) *The* person born in Ann Arbor, Michigan, on May 20, 1912, who served as a caddie to R. W. Sellars, when he played golf with DeWitt Parker.

I have italicized the definite 'article' in order to underscore that each description is to be conceived as denoting an object, a thin object, exhausted by the properties contained in the description. The point of view, which seems proper for fiction, that I am pressing is the naive point of view before Russell's 'On Denoting' introduced the view that a definite description is to be analyzed as a complex of quantifiers and identity. In the case of a nonexisting entity like *the* present president of Canada it is clear that the entity in question (even if in the end we consider it to be a mere *façon de parler*) cannot have other properties than the ones just mentioned in characterizing it. Palpably, *the* present president of Canada, by not existing, cannot be said to be tall or to be short, or to be young, or married, or a father, or anything else except that he is a president, a present president, a president of Canada, and a present president of Canada. We may, perhaps, attribute to him tautological properties like being tall or not tall.

Now think of the individuals (6)–(11) in exactly the same way. Each one of them has just the properties revealed in characterizing them.

A bit of historical research establishes two important facts about those individuals (6)–(11):

Fact 1. Each of the individuals (6)–(11) exists.

Fact 2. The individuals (6)–(11) are *contingently the same* (person, individual).

These two facts go hand in hand. The completeness of real objects, registered in criterion (C7) in section III, which differentiates them from fictional and other nonexisting objects, enters here. Because (6) exists, for any property F-ness, either

(6′.a) *The* F author of *Science, Perception, and Reality*, London, Routledge and Kegan Paul, 1963, exists

or

(6′.b) The non-F author of *Science, Perception, and Reality*, London, Routledge and Kegan Paul, 1963 exists.

This is the completeness of the reality of (6). But then there would also be other individuals uniquely characterized by some property F-ness per individual which also exist. And these individuals are contingently the same. This is precisely what is involved in the contingent sameness between (6) and each of the others (7)–(11).

In short, reality or existence is *limited communion*, as Plato explained at *Sophist* 252–53, not, however, only a communion of Forms, as he thought, but also a community of thinkable individuals. The ordinary expressions 'contingently the same', 'contingently identical', and their like are all expressions of that communion involved in reality. These expressions describe a structural feature we find in experience, and it corresponds to what, in the theory I am sketching, is the account of actuality predication.

The contingent sameness that connects any two individuals of (6)–(11) is what gives unity to the system of individuals who is the ordinary person we think of as an infinitely propertied object that satisfies the descriptions characterizing the individuals (6)–(11). That contingent sameness of actuality is different from the fictional sameness that links thinkable individuals and, thus, builds fictional characters. The thinkable, atomic individuals are the selfsame, whether they are put together into fictional characters by fictional sameness, or whether they are put together into real objects by the contingent sameness of actuality. Here again we find another crucial element that accounts for the unity of experience and for the homogeneity of consciousness: In all types of consciousness and of experience we deal with the same properties, whether qualities or relations, the same atomic individuals, hereafter called *individual guises*, the same logical forms of composition, and the same truth values.

The difference between fictional characters and ordinary objects does not, therefore, lie in their building blocks, or in their properties, but in the way those building blocks are put together, or, if you wish, in the kind of glue that holds them together. Real, actual, or existential contingent sameness holds an infinite set of individual guises together in one ordinary infinitely propertied object. Fictional contingent sameness holds a finite set of individual guises, grouped differently, of course, together in one fictional character.

Because of the completeness of real objects, when one thinks of an individual guise as real one believes it to be connected by existential contingent sameness to an infinity of other guises, some of which one can construct in the pattern of (6′.*a*) or (6′.*b*) above. This is important and one example may be helpful. Consider

(12)   John believes that the author of *Science, Perception, and Reality*, London, Routledge and Kegan Paul, 1963, is the same as the person who coedited *Readings in Ethical Theory* with John Hospers.

Clearly, in the normal sense of sentence (12), John believes that a certain contingent identity (as we say) holds in the real or actual world. He is indeed correct. By believing that identity to hold in the *real* world, John believes that an infinity of such contingent identities also hold. This belief is not necessarily rehearsed, or actualized, when John actualizes the belief attributed to him by (12). That is, it may very well be the case that:

(13) John is thinking at time *t* that the author of *Science, Perception, and Reality* (London, Routledge and Kegan Paul, 1963) is the same as the person who coedited *Readings in Ethical Theory* with John Hospers.

without it being the case that

(14) John is thinking at time *t* that there is an infinity of guises related by existential contingent sameness to the author of *Science, Perception, and Reality* (London, Routledge and Kegan Paul, 1963).

But the belief that would be rehearsed if (14) were true is part and parcel of John's believing what according to (12) he believes. This contrasts sharply with the following:

(15) John believes both that there is no president of Canada and that, tautologically, the present president of Canada is a president.

In this case by believing that the present president of Canada is not real, John has no further beliefs about that nonexisting individual (guise) being the same contingently as any other individual. John correctly seizes the incompleteness and the ontological isolation of the nonexisting (whether in reality or in fiction).

11. A Metaphysical Note

The individual guises (6)–(11), which can be indistinctly referred to with the name 'Wilfrid Sellars', are part and parcel of a system that is an infinitely propertied real object (see chapter 2 for the semantics of proper names). Naturally, those individual guises are in no way mental entities. Even if we were no longer capable of thinking or of consciousness, the fact is that each of the guises (6)–(11) is contingently the same as any other guise of that set, and each of them exists. Hence, the division of that infinitely propertied object in the world into those and other guises is not a merely mental operation. All those guises do combine into one person in the real world. But perhaps a deep metaphysical analysis can show that, since our individual guises are denoted by definite descriptions, those guises are somehow dependent on language, especially if it is established that all discriminations that one thinks of must be made through a language one can use to formulate them. In short, if thinking depends on language, and those distinctions that are thinkable cannot have a status in the external world without a language that formulates them, then perhaps we should adopt a Kantian view of the matter. Perhaps what the universe is, independently of a consciousness that thinks of it, is one noumenon or more noumena, without distinctions, and then when consciousness appears it forces distinctions through its linguistic structure. Then we can speak, as Kant did, of the *transcendental object* that underlies a family of guises connected by existential contingent sameness. We point in our thinking (and speaking) to such a transcendental object. And we must hasten to add, with Kant, that nothing further can be said about that transcendental object; that, for all we know, all systems of guises that belong together may point to the same transcendental object, the one indeterminate noumenon. If this is the case, then there is just one absolute object that is the subject of all predications, but those predications belong to it only to the extent that that absolute or noumenon is categorized by a language a thinker could use to think of it. But we must, further, hasten to explain that this preceding remark itself is misleading! Those words 'it', 'noumenon', 'absolute', 'subject of all predication' all appear in sentences and have meanings that presuppose a linguistic framework—hence, they already place the underlying reality pointed to through our thoughts of guises and properties *within* the context of a phenomenological ontology, namely, the one that goes with the linguistic framework we are using. What we need here is to go beyond Kant's negative concept of noumenon to Wittgenstein's concept of what is shown but not said.

We can postulate a metaphysical, utterly transcendent unity corresponding to each system of individual guises that belong together by virtue of existential contingent sameness linking any two of them. And we can attribute the partition of that unity into guises to the mind, or the language through which the mind thinks, but then, as in Kant's noumenal unity, that unity remains ineffable. Alternatively, we can simply consider that unity to be simply the unity of the systems of individual guises that go together: Why postulate an unthinkable or mysterious substrate beyond the guises? On this alternative view, the metaphysical ontology and the phenomenological one coincide.

In any case, the profound issues pertaining to the connections among language, thinking, and ultimate reality lie beyond the scope of our present project. But those issues must be considered too.

12. Theory of Predication

Let us tackle questions (*a*)–(*b*) formulated in section 10. They are:

(*a*) How are the properties expressed by the predicates in a definite description involved in the individual guise denoted by D?

(*b*) How is it that those properties mentioned in (a) exhaust the guise in question?

(*c*) What is it to predicate properties of individual guises?

The answers to these questions are crucial tenets of the theory I am outlining here. This theory has been formulated more fully elsewhere. It can be called the *Guise-Consubstantiation-Consociation-Conflation Theory*, and, for convenience, the G-CCC theory. More details and more evidence, especially evidence arising from the problems of referential opacity of psychological contexts and from perceptual facts (see chaps. 5, 6, and 13).

The answer to question (*b*) conforms to criterion (C7) in section 3 regarding the incompleteness of fictional objects. It is clear, too, that perceptual objects are incomplete. We never see the infinite manifold of properties that ordinary real objects have. I mention this to reinforce the tenet discussed above that we deal characteristically, in person, only with finite objects, the individual guises for which we can frame definite descriptions, each description containing, of course, only a finite number of predicates. We have then linguistic finitude and mental finitude.

Now, the first part of the answer to question (b) is furnished by these theses:

(G.1) Each individual guise is an entity composed of a set of properties and an individuating operator.

(G.2) The canonical representation in English of an individual guise is a generalized version of the standard definite description, namely:

(g) *the individual which alone is the following*: F_1, F_2, . . . , F_n, where F_1-ness, F_2-ness, . . . , F_n-ness are monadic properties.

(G.3) The definite article 'the' signals the individuating operator. Here the result of the operation of the operator *the* on an operand is conceived on the model of the part-whole relationship. Thus, an individual guise is conceived of as a complex having both the set of properties [F_1-ness, . . . , F_n-ness] and the operator *the* as components.

An alternative view can take the operator *the* as a mathematical function mapping a set of properties into an individual guise. But this view, although clearer, has the ontological disadvantage of delaying the answer to the question about the *nature* of individual guises. A function only informs us that there is a correspondence between the operand (or argument) and the value of the operation, but it does not tell us anything about the internal composition of that value. At sometime or other we must pursue the question about what exactly the values of the individuator *the* are. The composition, rather than function, view we are deploying here emphatically says that the core or content of an individual guise is a set of properties. On this view the individuator *the* is the same for all individual guises.[3] This is as it should be since the individuator is that which establishes the category to which guises belong.

The preceding theses (G.1)–(G.3) also provide a partial answer to question (a). The remaining part of the answer can only be given after we secure an answer to question (c).

The fundamental move in our answer to question (c) is to reduce the predication of contingent properties (to individuals) to the attribution (to individual guises) of one or the other of the two relations of contingent sameness we have discussed in section X. This provides a simpler and unified view. Consider one example, to wit:

(16) The author of *Science, Perception, and Reality* is brilliant.

The sense of 'is' must be determined. Let us suppose that 'is' expresses in (16) the existential copula. Hence, (16) must be analyzed as:

(16*a*) The author of *Science, Perception, and Reality* is-existentially-contingently-the-same-as the brilliant author of *Science, Perception, and Reality*.

In general, the mechanisms of predication reduction are as follows:

(P*.1)   A sentence of the form 'The F one is G', where the sentence expresses a proposition about reality, not about fiction, is of the logico-ontological form 'The F one is-existentially-contingently-the-same-as the GF one'.

(P**.1) A sentence of the form 'The F one is G', which expresses a proposition about the fictional entity 'The F one', is of the logico-ontological form 'The F one is-fictionally-contingently-the-same-as the GF one'.

These two principles of predication place the remaining theoretical task on the problem of elucidating the two sameness relations we have been discussing (see chapters 13 and 14). I merely add that the sameness relation mentioned in (P*.1) is called *consubstantiation*, and it is governed by laws of consistency (only self-consistent guises can be consubstantiated with anything), completeness (or logical closure of consubstantiation), and others. Self-consubstantiation is tantamount to existence. Consubstantiation is an equivalence relation within the realm of existents. On the other hand, the sameness relation involved in (P**.1) is called *consociation*. This is not governed by the laws of consistency (self-contradictory guises can be parts of characters of pieces of fiction), or completeness (this is criterion (C7) of section 3).

Consubstantiation and consociation are both contingent forms of external predication. They contrast with two other forms of predication. On the one hand, there is the *internal predication* in which propositions expressed with sentences of the form 'The FG one is F' (like 'the present president of Canada is a president').

There is, on the other hand, the external predication of the non-contingent type in which two sets A and B of properties can be equivalent, so that the guise having A as its core is the same, non-contingently, as the guise having B as its core. This external form of predication I call *conflation*.

To conclude this brief outline of the G-CCC theory let us say something about the principles of truth for the subject-predicate propositions that the theory recognizes. For convenience let us represent the core set of a guise a as $/a/$, and let us represent an individual guise whose core is the union of a core $/a/$ and a unit set {F-ness} as $a[F]$. We call the guise $a[F]$, corresponding to a guise a, *the F-protraction of a*. The following are rules of truth of the G-CCC theory, where C* is consubstantiation, C** consociation, and *C conflation, and $a(F)$ represents the internal predication of F-ness to a, that is, sentences of the form 'a is-internally F':

(1P.T1) '$a(F)$' is true, if and only if F-ness ϵ $/a/$.

(*C.T1) '*C(a, b)' is true, if and only if $/a/$ is logically equivalent to $/b/$.

(C*.T1) 'C*(a, b)' is true, if and only if a exists and is, in the ordinary sense of these words, actually contingently identical with or the same as b.

(C**.T1) 'C**(a, b)' is true, if and only if either (i) the guises a and b are thought
to be the same object, whether a fictional object or a real one; or (ii)
b is a protraction of the form a[x believes (thinks, supposes, im-
agines. . . .) that u is F], where 'x' is an expression referring to a
person 'F' stands for an adjectival expression, and 'u' is a schematic letter representing a subject position; etc.

Clearly, (C**.T1) must be continued, so that other expressions not of the subject-
predicate form with a schematic letter 'u' appear in the scope of a psychological
verb.

Perhaps it should be noted that it is built into (C**.T1) that thinking of two
individual guises as fictionally the same, for example, as when one composes a
short story in which one writes, say, 'a is F', is to think of the guises a and a[F]
as related by thinking. Fictional sameness is a special case of sameness wrought
by thinking. Once created it is part of the common world of culture.

There are some special features of the G-CCC theory, which add depth to our
treatment of fiction and its connections with reality. Among them is this: the G-
CCC theory is a two-tiered edifice: The lower tier contains the general theory of
properties and guise composition; the higher tier contains the theory of predication and states of affairs (or propositions) and facts. One consequence of this two-
tiered character is the distinction between negation, conjunction, disjunction and
other so-called connectives as property structures, on the one hand, and, on the
other, negation, conjunction, disjunction, and so on, as propositional structures
(see chapter 13).

Let us return to questions (a)-(c). Clearly, the answer to question (a) is this:
the properties mentioned in a definite description D which denotes an individual
guise a are involved in a in two ways: (i) they enter into the core set of a: They
belong to /a/; (ii) they are involved predicatively in those propositions or states
of affairs that are true by principle (1P.T1).

The answer to question (b) is also clear. The properties mentioned in a definite
description D that denotes guise a exhaust a in precisely the sense in which they
are involved in a. This is the finitude or incompleteness of a.

The answer to question (c) is also obvious. To predicate a property F-ness of
a guise a is, in accordance with the G-CCC theory, to formulate one of the four
singular propositions: a(F): C*(a, b); C**(a, b); *(a, b). We also recognize
genuine-identity propositions of the form a = b. On the G-CCC theory genuine-
identity propositions are necessarily true or necessarily false, and for the most
part trivial, if they are true.

13. Possible Worlds

Nowadays it is customary to formulate practically everything in terms of possible
worlds. The terminology is very fashionable, it has its value, but it does not do
as much as some philosophers seem to believe it does. Undoubtedly, those philos-

ophers who have reacted against possible world semantics have a point; but it can also be misplaced. There is no doubt that whenever we distinguish alternatives we can speak of possible worlds, using the expression 'possible world' to refer to any alternative. Thus, in the case at hand, those propositions that constitute a story or some other piece of fiction can be said to constitute a possible world, or a fragment thereof. Naturally, these worlds must be conceived not so much as alternatives to the real world but as worlds connected with it. Here possible world semantics can be useful: it can provide a clear set-theoretical model for the structure of the relation connecting a piece of fiction with the real world. That would be called the accessibility relation. To the extent that there are sub-fictions within pieces of fiction as, for instance, Cervantes' *Don Quixote* and Shakespeare's *Hamlet* are famous for, there is an, in principle, infinite chain of elements in a line of accessibility. The problem is the structure of that relation. Is it symmetric? transitive? and so on.

I do not propose to construct a so-called formal semantical system for fictional entities. They must, to be sure, be constructed. But they must be constructed after we have decided what sort of structure fictional possible worlds have. It is evident both from the preceding discussion pertaining to the examination of data and the formulation of criteria of adequacy and from the outline of the G-CCC theory, that fictional possible worlds are *not* to be constructed from actuality propositions about real objects. Fictional possible worlds *can* have reality propositions, whether true or false; but what really characterizes a fictional possible world is its containing some fictional propositions, that is, some consociational ones. This has one important consequence: We must distinguish several structures of fictional possible worlds. There is, *first* the structure which takes as its designated world the union of the real world (that is, the set of actuality propositions that are true) and all true fictional propositions, regardless of which story or myth makes them true. Then we can construct accessibility relations that take different types of alternatives. *Second*, we can take the real world as designated and take in it as true those modalized propositions Sp. where S is some story operator and p belongs to the story s corresponding to S. Naturally, the S-worlds accessible to the real world will have those propositions belonging to s. What else besides? It seems to me that there is *no general answer* to this question. In part the answer depends on s and in part it depends on the purpose of the whole construction. The story s assumes a network of laws governing the events composing s, and those laws determine a good deal of what variations s can have and yield a useful alternative to s. The purpose for the whole exercise is also crucial. We may be interested, for example, in determining how far the S-worlds depart from the real world, or how much they depart from the S'-worlds of another story operator S' for another story s', which takes certain characters from s, but not all. Naturally, there are family trees of stories, which consist of stories that were inspired by previous stories and have different degrees of overlapping. Further, different criteria of character individuation in a story also vary with the genre of the story in question.

There are, besides, the accessibility lines mentioned above that connect stories within stories, and the laws of nature may be different at different levels.

In sum, what is needed is a careful examination of cases with different purposes, and the building of set-theoretical models that stay close to the main features of those cases. Here again it is important to keep in mind both that theories must be based on large collections of carefully examined data, and that mathematical structures must be developed sometimes with little connection to data, so that the mathematical formalisms can be created in a large variety of types. The error one must guard against is to suppose that because one has devised a mathematical formalism with an eye on some datum one has thereby provided an illuminating interpreted theory for that datum and its family of data.

14. Conclusion

To conclude these reflections and theoretical constructions let us return to the initial questions that provoked these lucubrations. Let us take them in order.

First we asked: (a) What sort of entities are fictional entities? What systematic relationships do they have to real entities? Can we consider fictional entities and real entities to be composed of the same basic elements? If so what are these? Palpably, we have answered (a). We have shown that indeed ordinary real and fictional entities are differently constructed systems of individual guises, all belonging to the same pool of guises. We have revealed that the most fundamental systematic connection between fictional and real entities is precisely their having the same pool of buiding blocks. Naturally, the contingency of fiction can make use of all the guises in the pool of thinkables, whereas the contingency of reality can only make use of the self-consistent guises. There is no point in repeating all the details given above or in the additional essays referred to for further clarifications and developments.

Our second initial question was: (b) What are the special, peculiar categories that characterize the realm of the fictional? This we answered in full. The most fundamental categories governing the realm of the fictional are *consociation* and the story operators of the form '*In such-and-such a story by so-and-so it is the case that*'. Other operators can be derived. Consociation should also be indexed relativizing it, as well, to sets of persons, times and places.

Our third question was: (c) Since our experience has a total unity, the fictional and the real are simply special contents of our total experience related by certain bridging principles. What are the fundamental principles of that sort? In what way are the special categories of the fictional involved in such bridging principles? This question covers a good deal of territory. Perhaps the principles we have formulated here cannot constitute a sufficient answer to (c). However, we have formulated above some fundamental bridging principles: FC**.1–FC**.11. and the remarks about the accessibility relation in section 13 do constitute at least the main body of the answer to question (c). It is obvious from those principles how the special categories of the fictional enter in the bridging principles connecting the fictional to the real.

We have, therefore, in the G-CCC theory, especially as developed here, a systematic account of the ontological structure of fiction. It is a trivial exercise to see that the G-CCC theory satisfies the criteria of adequacy formulated in section 3, together with the additional criteria introduced in the ensuing discussion. It is, thus, a good basis for the development of the more specific accounts suggested in section 13 concerning the different structures of possible fictional worlds. There are crucial problems that we have not been able to discuss here. They must be approached after the foundations laid down here have been solidified. Among such problems are: the problem of the *ontic unity* of a story, as contrasted with its aesthetic unity; the problem of the criteria for the *identity* of fictional characters across different stories; the problems pertaining to the *unity* of real or fictional characters in other artistic media.[4]

Appendix

An excellent example of a theory of type (T1) and of type (T4) both together is the following Fregean theory suggested by Cocchiarella upon reading this paper: (i) the predicates in fictional sentences denote not the properties they refer to in direct speech, but their senses, (ii) understanding that fictional predicates lie within the scope of story operators. This is a very systematic view. It has its attractions. But it will have to be complicated in the case of sentences which, within pieces of fiction, lie in the scope of modalities, psychological verbs, and substory operators. We will need resort to higher referents and senses. Furthermore, it must assign to singular terms in fictional sentences their senses as referents. Moreover, the copulae linking a subject term and a predicate in a fictional sentence, like Kraut's 'Pamela had rented again the old bungalow at 123 Oak Street', must, too, be assigned a different role or meaning. Hence, this Fregean theory is also of types (T2) and (T3). It is too complicated for my philosophical taste. I do not like it, further, because I find that the referent and the sense of a predicate or a singular term are the same whether they appear in *oratio obliqua* or in *oratio recta*. See my "Identity and Sameness," *Philosophia* 5 (1975): 121–50.

Notes

1. This is a very important datum that has often been neglected. I suppose Hegel knew it well, and, of course, it was stressed by Meinong and his students. A brilliant formulation of it appears in a passage from Theodor Lipps's "Weiteres zur 'Einfühlung'," *Archiv für gesamte Psychologie* 4 (1903): "I do indeed not talk of the historical Mephisto, but of Goethe's or, more accurately, of the Mephisto of fiction. But the latter has a peculiar kind of being. No doubt, he has been *called into being* some time ago by Goethe. But after he has been called into being and has achieved artistic representation in fiction, he has *a kind of reality*" (My italics. The two points they make will be clarified below, where I will distinguish two statuses of fictional entities.) This translation is Reinhardt Grossmann's, who quotes the passage secondhand from Alexius Meinong's quotation of it in his *Gesammelte Abhandlungen*, vol. 1, p. 599. Grossmann's translation appears on p. 165 of his *Meinong* (London and

Boston: Routledge and Kegan Paul, 1974). For a more comprehensive discussion of the relationships between literary and factual languages, see Hector-Neri Castañeda, "Objects, Existence, and Reference," *Grazer Philosophische Studien* 25/26 (1985/1986): 3–59. For complementary discussion of the story operators and the contrast between fictional and existential predication, see Wolfgang Künne, "Perception, Fiction, and Elliptical Speech" and Hector-Neri Castañeda, "Fiction, Perception, and Forms of Predication" in Klaus Jacobi and Helmut Pape, eds., *Das Denken und die Struktur der Welt: Castañedas epistesmologische Ontologie in Darstellung und Kritik* (Berlin: De Gruyter, 1989).

2. This example was put to me by Ernest Sosa, who heard it from Roderick M. Chisholm.

3. For a discussion of the problem of individuation, a formulation of seven criteria of adequacy for its solution, and further data for individual guises, see my "Individuation and Non-Identity: A New Look," *American Philosophical Quarterly* 12 (1975): 131–40.

4. I am grateful to Michael Pendlebury and Nino Cocchiarella for having criticized my grammar and my style, and for having suggested some conceptual clarifications. Pendlebury suggested that I should at least mention Theory (T5). Cocchiarella suggested the Fregean theory discussed in the appendix.

12

The Language of Other Minds: Indicators and Quasi-Indicators

1. Purpose, Problem, and Conventions

Crucial to many problems in the philosophy of mind, epistemology, and metaphysics are: (A) a clear understanding of the roles and interrelations of the types of words we employ to refer to the entities we encounter, and (B) a clear understanding of the logic of cognitive and linguistic verbs (like 'think,' 'suppose,' and 'infer,' on the one hand, and 'say,' 'inform,' 'argue,' and 'show,' on the other). My ultimate purpose here is to make a contribution toward both (A) and (B).[1,2]

My contribution toward (A) consists mainly in showing, via principles (Q.7)–(Q.10) below, that a certain mechanism of reference to particulars, which is indispensable to a conceptual scheme that allows for the possibility of other persons or selves, is a unique logical category of reference not reducible to the better-studied mechanisms of reference, namely, demonstrative pronouns or adverbs, proper names, singular descriptions, and ordinary variables of quantification. This irreducible mechanism is constituted by what I call quasi-indicators. Following Goodman,[3] I call *indicators* the personal and demonstrative pronouns and adverbs like 'this,' 'that,' 'I,' 'you,' 'here,' 'there,' and 'now,' when they are used to make a strictly demonstrative reference, i.e., when they are used purely referentially either to single out an item present in the speaker's current experience or to pinpoint a self that is a relatum in the cognitive relation evinced by the speaker. I call *quasi-indicators* the expressions which in *oratio obliqua* represent uses, perhaps only implicit, of indicators, that is, uses that are ascribed to some person or persons by means of a cognitive or linguistic verb. For example, suppose that at a certain place p and time t, A says to B: (1) "I am going to kill you here now." Suppose that C reports this by asserting: (2) "A said to B at p at t that he was going to kill him there then." Sentence (2) contains the quasi-indicators 'he,' 'him,' 'there,' and 'then,' which represent uses, ascribed to A, of the indicators 'I,' 'you,' 'here,' and 'now,' respectively. We shall see that the very same marks or noises 'I,' 'you,' 'here,' 'there,' 'he,' 'this,' function as either indicators, quasi-indicators, or something else. It is a mere accident of grammar that the same physical objects are used in different logical roles. The underlying rationale is this: Indicators are a primary means of referring to particulars, but the references made with them are personal and ephemeral; quasi-indicators are the derivative means of making an indexical reference both interpersonal and enduring, yet preserving it intact.

My contribution toward both (A) and (B) together consists of the formulation, with as much precision as I can here, of the fundamental principles of the logic of both indicators and quasi-indicators in *oratio obliqua*. In this regard principles (I.5), (I.12)–(I.14), (Q.2), (Q.11), and (Q.12) are the most important of the lot.

I have aimed at an exhaustive treatment of the basic logic of singular indicators and quasi-indicators in *oratio obliqua*, except for the treatment of the obvious indicators and quasi-indicators included in verbal tenses (see chap. 8, sect. 2).[4]

To simplify the discussion I shall abide by the following conventions: (1) single quotes will be used to form names of sentences or expressions; (2) double quotes will be used to form names of statements made or that can be made by uttering the quoted sentences on given occasions; (3) numerals within parentheses will be used as either names of sentences or names of statements, the context indicating which one is meant; (4) the phrase 'statement of the form " . . . " ' will be short for 'statement made by the sentence of the form " . . . " (if assertively used by a certain person on a certain occasion)'; (5) an asterisk '*' after a word or phrase indicates that the word or phrase functions in a given sentence as a quasi-indicator; (6) 'statement' and 'proposition' will be used interchangeably in the sense these words have been used by Strawson and others.[5]

2. Indicators

Let us start our investigation by listing some well-known properties of indicators. These properties determine the special roles of indicators in *oratio obliqua*.

(I.1) Indicators formulate a personal reference to a single entity made primarily by the speaker, made derivatively by the hearers, and not made at all by other persons. Here we shall be concerned with primary reference only.

(I.2) Reference to an entity by means of an indicator is purely referential, that is, it is a reference that attributes no property to the entity in question. Since an indicator expresses an act of placing an item in a person's experience or expresses an act of pinpointing the person who enters in a current cognitive relation, it can at most be said that the use of an indicator indirectly, or implicitly, attributes to an entity the property of being a thinker or the property of being placed in a thinker's (or speaker's) experience at the time of thinking or speaking.

(I.3) Reference by means of an indicator is neither identical with, nor equivalent to, reference by means of descriptions that contain no indicators. By (1.2) reference by means of an indicator could at most be equivalent to reference by means of a description that has no indicators but attributes to the referred entity just the property of being a thinker or of being placed in a thinker's (or speaker's) experience at the time of thinking (or speaking). But this is, of course, false. On the one hand, this attribution by being direct goes beyond what a mere indicator can accomplish. On the other hand, such a description would have to have a word that refers to the thinker (or speaker) in question without in the least attributing to him any property at all, and similarly for the time of thinking. But since the description under consideration has no indicators, there is no way for it merely to refer to the thinker or to the time of his thinking. Thus, at least one sentence *S* containing an indicator *I* formulates or can formulate, as uttered on a certain occasion, a statement not equivalent to the statement formulated by any other sentence that differs from *S* by having descriptions with no indicators instead of *I*.

(I.4) Indicators have a *referential priority* over all names and descriptions. A person may use a name or description correctly, and yet fail to refer to the object to which he purports to refer because there may be not one, but many objects which have the name in question, or the properties mentioned in the description. However, a man who uses an indicator correctly cannot, because of a multiplicity of candidates for reference, fail to refer to the object he purports to refer to.

(I.5) The first-person pronoun has a strong *ontological priority* over all names, contingent descriptions, and other indicators. A correct use of 'I' cannot fail to refer to the entity it purports to refer; moreover, a correct use of 'I' cannot fail to pick up the category of the entity to which it is meant to refer. The first-person pronoun, without predicating selfhood, purports to pick out a self *qua* self, and when it is correctly tendered it invariably succeeds. On the other hand, correctly used names, contingent descriptions, and non-first-person indicators may fail either to even pick out a referent or to pick out the intended category. The time- and space-indicators, for example, 'now' and 'here,' have a weak ontological priority over names, descriptions, and other categories of third-person indicator. They succeed in always picking out a time or a place, although they may in principle fail to pick out the category of physical or external time and space as in a dream. (These ontological priorities are one of the fundamental facts underlying Descartes's *Cogito* and Kant's theses on the transcendental self and on space and time as forms of perception.)

It might be induced that this contrast between 'I' and the other indicators is misguided, on the ground that 'I' is analyzable in terms of 'this' or 'here now.' Reichenbach, for instance, claims that "the word 'I' means the same as 'the person who utters this token'."[6] This claim is, however, false. A statement formulated through a normal use of the sentence 'I am uttering nothing' is contingent: If a person utters this sentence he falsifies the corresponding statement, but surely the statement *might*, even in such a case, have been true. On the other hand, the statements formulated by 'The person uttering this token is uttering nothing' are self-contradictory: even if no one asserts them, they simply cannot be true.

The first-person indicator is unanalyzable. On the one hand, if 'ϕ' stands for an analytic predicate, i.e., a predicate such that the statement of the form "Everything is ϕ" is analytic or necessarily true, then, obviously, the first-person indicator 'I' cannot be defined as 'the only person who is ϕ.' On the other hand, if 'ϕ' stands for a contingent predicate, then the normal singular statements of the form "I am ϕ" assertable by human beings are contingent. This is so, because all such statements entail the corresponding singular statements of the form "I exist," which are contingent, since they can be false, i.e., since the corresponding singular statements of the form "I might have not existed" are true. The corresponding singular statements of the form "I am not-ϕ" are also contingent. Yet the corresponding statements of the form "The only person who is ϕ is not-ϕ" are self-contradictory. Hence, the first-person indicator cannot be analyzed in terms of any other expressions whatever; *a fortiori*, it cannot be analyzed in terms of the other indicators. In particular, 'I' cannot be analyzed as 'this self' or 'the self here now': A person's statements of the form "I am not-a-self" are contingent, while his statements of the form "This self (or the self here now) is not-a-self" are self-contradictory. (The unanalyzability of 'I', especially its unanalyzability in terms of [third-person] demonstratives, is another fundamental fact underlying the idea of the transcendental self.)

Evidently, parallel arguments hold for the second-person indicators, the third-person indicators referring to persons or objects, and the time- and space-indicators. For instance, the object-indicator 'this' cannot be defined in terms of any description, since the indicator attributes no property at all to the object it refers to; and it cannot be defined merely indexically as 'here now,' for statements of the form "This [meaning an object] is not here now" are contingent, while statements of the form "What is here now is not here now" are self-contradictory, if the two occurrences of 'here now' have the same reference.

It must be noted that the words 'now' and 'here' are sometimes replaced by 'this,' as, for example, in "Here (this) is a good place to park." But this in no way argues against the unanalyzability of the time- and space-indicators. What we have here are two interesting features of ordinary language: (i) the grammatical fact that 'here,' 'there,' and 'now' are primarily adverbs, and lack, therefore, the syntactical flexibility of substantival pronouns, so that in certain constructions they are replaceable by some other expression; (ii) the words 'this' and 'that' have two indexical uses: (a) as general signs of third-person indexical reference, and (b) as categorical indicators of third-person indexical reference to objects. It is in their use (a) that 'this' can replace 'now' and 'here,' and 'that' can replace 'there.' Obviously, 'here,' 'there,' and 'now' are not definable in terms of use (b) of 'this' or 'that.' For instance, 'here' is not analyzable as '(at) the place occupied by this object,' since "Nothing is here" is contingent, while "Nothing is at the place occupied by this object" is self-contradictory.

In sum,

(I.6) There are five irreducible indexical roles, whatever noises or marks we may employ to discharge them: first-person, second-person, third-person (specious) present-time, and (speciously) presented place. [(I.6) is supplemented by (I.15) below, after (Q.5).]

(I.7) The pronoun 'I' and all descriptions primarily, and all names derivatively, have an *epistemological priority* over all other indicators. A person's own uses of the first-person pronoun differ radically from his uses of the other indicators. One's knowledge or belief about oneself must be in the first-person form for it to be really self-knowledge or self-belief. On the other hand, to retain knowledge or belief, or merely to re-think, of the objects or persons originally apprehended by means of indicators, one must reformulate one's knowledge or belief, or thought, of those objects in terms of names or descriptions, or in terms of 'I.' *The references made by an indicator other than 'I' are ephemeral, and necessarily eliminable for those who make them.* Of course, the elimination of an indicator may very well introduce another one, as, for instance, when a man thinks something of the form "This is blue," and later on rethinks it as, e.g., "The object I saw *there* an hour ago was blue." Elimination is here a process of preserving information, not a process of analysis or of literal translation. By (I.6) we already know that there is no analysis of the indexical role (see chap. 4 above).[7]

(I.8) A person's uses of indicators are first-personal and eliminable for every other person.

3. Oo-Prefixes

Now we shall discuss some general properties of *oratio obliqua* to which we shall continuously refer in the ensuing investigation.

Cognitive acts or attitudes or dispositions are second-order tetradic relations involving a subject (person or self), a place, a time, and a proposition. Linguistic acts are second-order relations involving typically five or more relata: a speaker, one or more addressees, a place, a time, and a proposition. (I call them all second-order relations because one of the relata is a proposition.)

In a sentence formulating a proposition to the effect that a cognitive or linguistic relation obtains, we shall distinguish two parts: (i) an *oratio obliqua*, and (ii) an *oratio obliqua* prefix. *Oratio obliqua* is the clause that formulates or represents the propositional relatum of the cognitive or linguistic relation. A *strict oratio obliqua prefix*, or simply *strict oo-prefix*, is a clause that contains: (a) a cognitive or linguistic verb, (b) expressions denoting the nonpropositional relata, and (c) the word 'that' at the right-hand end. For example, in

(1) Grabbing the knife on the table Peter told Mary in the kitchen at 3 p.m. that he would kill her with it there.

the strict oo-prefix is 'Peter told Mary in the kitchen at 3 p.m. that.' In (1) 'Grabbing the knife on the table' is not part of the strict oo-prefix. Clearly, (1) is really the conjunction "Peter grabbed the knife on the table at 3 p.m. yesterday, and (he) said to Mary in the kitchen at 3 p.m. yesterday that he would kill her with it there." Now, a clause containing a strict oo-prefix and other expressions will be called an *extended oo-prefix*.

For the sake of brevity we shall sometimes represent an oo-prefix by the schema

$L[x, y_1, \ldots, y_n, p, t]$ (———),

where x is the speaker or thinker (arguer, knower, etc), $y_1, \ldots, y_n$ are the addresses, p the place, and t the time involved in the linguistic or cognitive relation. If the relation is cognitive, 'y_1', . . . , 'y_n' vanish. Here '———' indicates the place of the *oratio obliqua* involved.

Linguistic acts of the assertive kind, that is, whose objects are propositions, not sentences or noises, are dependent on cognitive acts. For example, to state or say or claim is at once to have the thought that something is the case. It is clear that a noise or mark by itself is not an indicator: It is one if and only if it carries with itself an indexical reference. Likewise, a word is not a name or description unless it carries within itself a nominal or descriptive reference that some speaker means it to carry. Thus, the roles which words or phrases or clauses discharge as vehicles of components of a proposition depend on the structural relations of these components *qua* components of the proposition in question. The structure of what is thought, the proposition, is the fundamental structure, and in principle one could think without using a language as a means of thinking.[8] Nevertheless, by the same token, even if one can think without using a language at all, the propositions one deals with in mere non-linguistic thinking have a structure which parallel certain structures of the complete sentences in which one would formulate one's thoughts, if one had a language.[9] We may suppose that in the case of a being who performs a noncommunicating cognitive act, for example, the having of the silent thought that it is raining, the object of his act is structurally analogous to the sentence 'It is raining.'[10] In particular, in silent cognitive acts that include references to particulars, these references can be put in one-to-one correspondence with the types and kinds of singular-referring expressions. Thus,

(I.9) To attribute a cognitive or linguistic propositional act to a person may very well be to attribute to the person in question purely indexical references.

Some cognitive relations are dispositional. A sleeping man, for example, may believe or know that the Earth is not flat. Here the disposition consists of a propensity to perform acts whose objects are analogous to sentences. We shall say that attributing a cognitive disposition to a person is to attribute to him *implicit* uses of sentences or words of certain types (without this implying a reduction of cognitive acts to linguistic acts). Now, a cognitive disposition may be exercised through different cognitive acts at very different times and places. Hence, to attribute a cognitive disposition to a person P is to attribute to P implicit uses of an indicator D, if and only if every possible exercise of P's disposition is unavoidably a use of D by P. By (1.5) and (1.6), this is wholly the case for P's use of the first-person pronoun. In brief,

(1.10) To attribute a cognitive disposition to a person P is to attribute to P implicit uses of an indicator D, only if D refers to a relatum, or place related to the place which is a relatum, of the cognitive acts through which the disposition is exercisable.

4. Indicators in Oratio Obliqua

By (I.1)–(I.2) a use of a genuine indicator refers directly to an entity, and does not depend for its reference on another expression. For example, the word 'he' is genuinely an indicator when it is used demonstratively in place of 'this' or 'that,' and it is an indexical description when it is short for 'this (that) man,' or something like 'that man with a beard.' 'He' is not indexical at all in the sentence 'Anthony came, after he called'; for here the word 'he' refers back to 'Anthony' and does not directly and by itself refer to Anthony. Similarly, the word 'I' is not an indicator in 'Mary told me that I am next in line.' With this sentence the speaker refers directly to himself by means of 'me'; the word 'I' in this case refers back to 'me.' Let us say that an *antecedent* of a pronoun or adverb in a sentence or clause is an expression of the sentence or clause to which the pronoun or adverb refers back, or with which it crossrefers, to pick up the latter's referent. Hence:

(1.11) Whether in *oratio recta* or in *oratio obliqua*, (genuine) indicators have no antecedents.

Suppose now that Privatus asserts of a dead friend of his:

(2) Once it occurred to Jones that I buried a letter here.

Privatus' statement is philosophically perplexing. It seems to attribute to Jones demonstrative references by means of 'I,' and 'here'; yet, quite palpably, neither could Jones ever refer to Privatus in the first-person way nor was he at the time of Privatus' assertions in a position to make any demonstrative reference at all. By (I.1), the demonstrative references of (2) are Privatus', not Jones's. Thus, we have a philosophical question: What exactly is the proposition that, according to Privatus, Jones once took to be true? That is, what exactly are the types of the references that, according to Privatus, Jones made to Privatus and to the place in question?

One thing is clear. In spite of their misleading position in the *oratio obliqua* of (2), the indicators of (2) serve to mark the positions occupied by some unspecified referring expressions in the sentence formulating the unspecified proposition that, according to (2), Jones once took to be true. Those referring expressions that Jones used were, of course, either

(a) single indicators; or

(b) names; or

(c) indexical descriptions, like 'this man,' 'my friend,' or 'five years ago today (now)'; or

(d) Leibnizian descriptions, that is, descriptions that contain no indicators.

The actual proposition that, by (2), Jones once took to be true can be one of eight different types, depending on which sort of reference Jones made to Privatus and the place in question. And now we must raise another question: Is Privatus' statement (2) definite enough on this point? And the answer seems to be that it is not: Privatus' statement (2) is simply the statement to the effect that *one* of the eight types of propositions allowed by the two positions occupied by indicators was taken by Jones to be true. That is, Privatus' statement (2) is to be conceived of as a disjunction of certain statements which we proceed to identify.[11]

So far, we know that the indicators of (2) are in a sense misplaced, and that in their positions Jones's references must be represented. This suggests that the preliminary scheme of the analysis of (2) is this:

(2′) Once it occurred to Jones about me and
    about this place that —— buried a letter in
                me

    —— ——,
    this place

where the subscripts indicate the antecedents of the expressions in the blanks.

Suppose that Privatus wanted to attribute to Jones purely indexical references. Hence, what we should put in the blanks of (2′) are precisely the quasi-indicators corresponding to the first-person and the place indicators. Thus, Privatus' statement would be more perspicuously put as

(3) Once it occurred to Jones about me and about this place that I* buried a letter here*.

Since we are mainly concerned with the typical logic of indexical reference, we may here lump together names and descriptions. Now, if Privatus wanted to attribute to Jones references by means of either names or descriptions, he would have had a hard time finding an appropriate idiom or locution in ordinary language. We shall, however, introduce a counterpart to quasi-indicators by means of a subscripted 'd'. Thus Privatus' statement analogous to (2), except that through it Privatus attributes to Jones references by means of names or descrptions, can be formulated in extended English as

(4) Once it occurred to Jones about me and about this place that I_d had buried a letter here$_d$.

Thus, the first step in the analysis of (2) is to take it as the disjunction of (3), (4), and the two other statements "Once it occurred . . . that I* here$_d$" and "Once it occurred . . . that I_d . . . here*."

Since names and descriptions, Leibnizian or indexical, attribute properties to the entities they refer to, it is natural to think that (4) is analyzable as

(4N) There are properties ϕ-ness and μ-ness such that: I am the only ϕ, this place (here) is the only μ, and once it occurred to Jones that the only ϕ buried a letter in the only μ.

There is a general way in which (4N) is the analysis of (4), namely, the general way in which when a man says "I am ill" other people transmit his information by saying "He is ill" or even "The man . . . is ill." This is the way in which there is one and the same property that both Smith and Jones attribute to Privatus when Jones identifies Privatus by the description 'the man I met three days ago' and Smith identifies Privatus by the description 'the man Jones met three days ago.' On the one hand these descriptions identify Privatus by means of the same property, considered in itself, independently of the ways it is conceived of by Jones or Smith or anybody else. On the other hand, each of these descriptions ascribes to Privatus that property, not merely as it is in itself, but as it appears to either Jones or Smith: 'the man I met three days ago' ascribes to Privatus that property from Privatus' first-person perpective, whereas 'the man Jones met three days ago' ascribes to Privatus the same property from a third-person perspective. By (I.5)–(I.7) we know that a first-person way of considering a certain property is irreducible to a third-person way of considering it, and clearly the latter is irreducible to the former. Since each of the descriptions explicityly mentions the perspective from which the given property is attributed, each description realy attributes a property-*cum*-perspective. Thus, in the general sense that a predicate denotes an attributed property, we can, and must distinguish between a *neutral*, or *non-perspectival* property and the *perspectival* properties through which the former is presented. (I owe this terminology to W. Sellars.) I will use the italicized word '*properties*' to refer to perspectival properties, and I will indicate with subscripts the person to whose perspective of the world a given *property* belongs. The unitalicized word 'property' will be used to refer to neutral properties or to neutral and perspectival properties indeterminately.

Since a person has to consider (neutral) properties in some way or other, we are never really dealing with properties naked, so to speak, of their perspectives. But as long as we deal with so-called extensional contexts only, we can enjoy the illusion that we are intellectually manipulating bare neutral properties. However, as soon as we move to the level of discourse about cognitive and linguistic relations, we must face up to the fact that we are in a partial egocentric predicament of properties.

This predicament creates the fundamental problem of the logic of communication: How to correlate another person's *properties* with our own and pass information across these correlations. The fundamental assumption regarding the possibility of communication is simply that such correlations can be achieved. And the exercise we are engaged in, viz., to determine the type of proposition that, according to Privatus, Jones once took to be true, is precisely an exercise in formulating some of the principles that allow the achievement of the communicating correlations.

In short, (4N) is, correctly, the *nonperspectival analysis* of (4). But since (4) is a nonextensional context, (4N) does not allow us to get hold of the precise statement that, according to Privatus, Jones once took to be true. The characteristic feature of (4N) is that one may know what properties ϕ_1-ness and μ_1-ness one should instantiate the quantifiers of (4N) into, without being in a position to produce the instance of (4N) that would be the straight report of it having occurred to Jones that such and such. To illustrate, suppose that

ϕ_1-ness $=$ man-met-by-Jones-on-July-1–1960-ness

μ_1-ness $=$ flowerbed-dug-by-Jones-ness

That is, let Privatus know that:

(5) There are properties ϕ-ness and μ-ness such: ϕ-ness $=$ man-met-by-Jones-on-July-1–1960-ness, μ-ness $=$ flowerbed-dug-by-Jones-ness, I am the only person who is ϕ, this place is the only one which is μ, and once it occurred to Jones that the only person who is ϕ buried a letter in the only place which is μ.

From (5) Privatus cannot conclude that:

(6) I am the only man met by Jones on July 1, 1960, this place is the only flowerbed dug by Jones, and once it occurred to Jones that the only man met by Jones on July 1, 1960, buried a letter in the only flowerbed dug by Jones.

The difficulty lies in the last conjunct "once it occurred to Jones that the only man met by Jones on July 1, 1960, buried a letter in the only flowerbed dug by Jones." Obviously, this may be false even though Jones did refer to Privatus and the place in question as possessors of these properties ϕ_1-ness and μ_1-ness when it occurred to him what it occurred to him according to Privatus' statement (2). For instance, it may have occurred to Jones what he would have reported by saying "The only man met by me on July 1, 1960, buried a letter in the only flowerbed dug by me." The crux of the matter is that in a proposition that a person takes to be true, or simply entertains, a property enters not merely as a neutral property, but as a property determined by the way in which the person in question grasps it or conceives of it. Thus, while Privatus' statement (5) presents the above properties ϕ_1-ness and μ_1-ness as they are grasped by Privatus, his statement (6) presents ϕ_1-ness and μ_1-ness both as grasped by Privatus, in the oo-prefix, and as grasped by Jones, in the *oratio obliqua*. This is why the inference from (5) to (6) is invalid.

Let us turn, then, to *properties*. Consider an expression containing no indicators or quasi-indicators that formulates a property. Clearly, there are four ways of considering or predicating the property in question:

(i)   the first-person way;

(ii)   the second-person way;

(iii) the third-person way involving third-person indicators;

(iv) the third-person way formulated by the given expression.

Let us use subscripts to signal these ways of considering properties, as follows: '$_1$' for (i), '$_2$' for (ii), '$_i$' for (iii), and '$_o$' for (iv). Thus, the property being-met-by-Jones-5-days-before-July-1–1965 determines the following *properties* from Jones's perspective, to be called *properties$_J$*:

(a) being a person met by Jones$_1$ 5 days before (July 1, 1965)$_i$;

(b) being met by Jones$_1$ 5 days before (July 1, 1965)$_o$;

(c) being met by Jones$_o$ 5 days before (July 1, 1965)$_i$; and

(d) being met by Jones$_o$ 5 days before (July 1, 1965)$_o$.

On the other hand, for Privatus it determines the *properties$_p$*:

(d) as above;

(e) being a person met by Jones$_2$ 5 days before (July 1, 1965)$_i$;

(f) being a person met by Jones$_1$ 5 days before (July 1, 1965)$_o$;

(g) being a person met by Jones$_o$ 5 days before (July 1, 1965)$_i$; etc.

Note that, by (I.1) and (I.8), *properties* (c) and (g) are quite different.

By our definition of quasi-indicators we know that quasi-indicators represent the uses of indicators in *oratio obliqua*. Thus, when a *property* ϕx-ness appears in *oratio obliqua*, we can represent it by means of an expression which results by putting quasi-indicators instead of the indicators in the expression denoting ϕx-ness. The resulting expression does not, of course, represent ϕx-ness *simpliciter*, but as it is considered by the one who makes the statement, and even perhaps as it is considered by a few other persons as well.

In general, let $P(i_1, \ldots, i_n)$ be a phrase that Jones uses (or can use) on a certain occasion O to formulate a *property$_J$*, where $i_1, \ldots, i_n$ are indicators that Jones uses (or can use) on O to refer to entities $E_1, E_2, \ldots, E_n$. Let $P(i_1/e_1, \ldots, i_n/e_n)$ be the phrase that results from $P(i_1, \ldots, i_n)$ by replacing each indicator i_k by the corresponding expression e_k, which is an expression that a man X uses (or can use) on O to refer to entity E_k. Clearly, $E(i_1/e_1, \ldots, i_n/e_n)$ formulates a *property* $_X$, and to indicate its correspondence with the *property$_j$* formulated by $P(i_1, \ldots, i_n)$, we shall call it a *property* $_{J/X}$. Similarly, let $P(i_1/q_1, \ldots, i_n/q_n)$ be the expression that results from $P(i_1, \ldots, i_n)$ by replacing each i_k by its corresponding third-person quasi-indicator q_k. In the next section we shall discuss this correspondence between indicators and quasi-indicators in detail. That there is such a correspondence is obvious from the fact that Privatus' statements (2) and (4) are not addressed to Jones, but are about Jones having taken a certain statement to be true, so that Privatus must have some technique (namely, the use of quasi-indicators) for representing in a third-person way Jones's uses of indicators (if any). We shall say that $P(i_1/q_1, \ldots, i_n/q_n)$ formulates a *property*$_{*J}$, that is, formulates someone's, here Privatus', *oratio-obliqua* way of considering the *property* $_J$ in question. Since the quasi-indicators q_k have nothing to do with Privatus, the *property*$_{*J}$ is really an inter-personal or inter-subjective version of the corresponding *property$_J$*, and while by (I.7) most *properties$_J$* must yield even for Jones to other *properties$_J$*, the corresponding *properties*$_{*J}$ are permanent: anybody can refer to them at any time, as we shall see in detail later on.

With this machinery we can give a deeper analysis of Privatus' statement (4):

(4) Once it occurred to Jones about me and about this place that I$_d$ buried a letter here$_d$.

A perspectival analysis in terms of *properties* is as follows:

(4P) There are *properties* ϕ_j-ness and μ_J-ness such that: I am the only person who
is $\phi_{J/I}$, this place is the only place which is $_{J/I}$, and once it occurred to Jones
that the only person who is ϕ_{*J} buried a letter in the only place which is μ_{*J}.

Note that since Privatus is in (4) referring to himself in the first-person way, the
property$_P$ related to ϕ_J-ness and μ_J-ness must yield the first-person schematic
symbols '$\phi_{J/I}$' and '$\mu_{J/I}$' representing properties and having adjectives as substituends.

Consider how Privatus' statement

(7) Jones believed that I buried a letter here.

By (7) Privatus attributes to Jones a cognitive disposition and, hence, only implicit references to him and to the place in question. These referencese are not
indexical, even if Privatus' statement (7) reports what Jones believed at a single
instant. Indeed, suppose that at a certain instant t it occurred to Jones out loud:
"He [pointing to Privatus] buried a letter here [pointing to the place in question],"
and suppose that Jones died at that very instant. In this case, Jones never exercised
the disposition which is his belief in anything but thoughts containing indexical
references. Yet, since these references are by (I.7) eliminable for Jones, the onsetting of his belief is precisely the onsetting of procedures of elimination, which
were never exercised, but were nevertheless acquired. Furthermore, even at instant t Jones had, dispositionally, i.e., as part of his belief, ways of referring to
the place and to Privatus other than by the use of single indicators. For instance,
he could have referred to Privatus by means of an indexical description such as
'this man,' 'the man over there,' 'the person I see on my right,' etc. Thus, I submit
that in the case of (7) the non-perspectival and the perspectival analyses are non-
disjunctive, as follows:

(7N) There are properties ϕ-ness and μ-ness such that: I am the only person who
is ϕ, this place is the only place which is μ, and Jones believed that the only
person who is ϕ buried a letter in the only place which is μ;

(7P) There are *properties* ϕ_J-ness, μ_J-ness, $\phi_{J/I}$-ness, and $\mu_{J/I}$-ness such that:
I am the only person who is $\phi_{J/I}$, this place is the only place which is $\mu_{J/I}$,
and Jones believed that the only person who is ϕ_{*J} buried a letter in the only
place which is μ_{*J}.

Evidently, the discussion of Privatus' statements (2)–(7) is applicable, *mutatis
mutandis*, not only to other statements by Privatus, but to any statement made by
any other person. Thus, we shall regard as established that:

(I.12) Indicators in *oratio obliqua* are eliminable for their users in terms of indicators in *oratio recta*;

(I.13) Indicators in *oratio obliqua* representing the propositional relata of cognitive or linguistic acts are analyzable non-perspectivally as well as perspec-

tivally. The procedures of analysis can be carried out one step at a time for each oo-prefix, as illustrated by (4N) and (4P), respectively;

(I.14) Indicators in *oratio obliqua* representing propositional relata of cognitive dispositions are analyzable non-perspectivally and perspectivally. The procedures of analysis can be carried out one step at a time for each oo-prefix, as is illustrated by the analysis of (7) as (7N) and as (7P), respectively.

5. Quasi-Indicators

The preceding discussion of indicators is not only a good background for, but has to be complemented by, the study of quasi-indicators.

(Q.1) Quasi-indicators do not make demonstrative references. They may even fail to make reference to single entities, for *they can play the role of variables of quantification*. For instance, in "Always everywhere a boy tells a girl that he* will love her* from then* on" the quasi-indicators 'he*,' 'her*,' and 'then*' are (also) variables bound, repsectively, by the quantifiers 'a boy,' 'a girl,' and 'always.'

(Q.2) Quasi-indicators have necessarily an antecedent to which they refer back, but they are not replaceable by their antecedents. Quasi-indicators are both referentially and syntactically dependent: They are syncategorematic expressions. And the sentences (clauses) that contain quasi-indicators without containing the latter's antecedents are also syncategorematic. An interesting example is provided by the following inference:

(8) While in Brown's office Jones knew that Smith was killed there*

hence

(9) Smith was killed there.

It is obviously valid, and sentence (9) expresses a complete statement in *oratio recta*, in which its 'there' can be replaced by its antecedent 'in Brown's office.' Hence, by (Q.2) 'there' in (9) is not an instance of the quasi-indicator 'there*.'

It might be thought that 'there' in (9) is precisely another occurrence of the word 'there*' of the premiss. It has to be the same quasi-indicator, it might be argued, since the above inference is validated by the rule.

(K.1) From a statement of the form "X knows that p" you may infer that p.

This argument is, however, invalid: (K.1) says nothing about detaching the sentence to the right of 'knows that.' (I have shown in He^{12} that (K.1) itself is a rule that cannot always be applied.) What the argument needs is a rule like

(K.2) If a sentence of the form 'X knows that p' formulates a statement that you accept, then you may detach the sentence (or clause) represented by 'p' and use it by itself, with no change of meaning or sense, to make the very same statement which it formulates as a part of the longer sentence 'X know that p.'

The word 'there' in (9) is, of course, an instance of the quasi-indicator 'there*,' which does appear in (8), if the inference "(8), hence (9)" is validated by (K.2).

Suppose, then, that Privatus believed (8) to be true, that while he himself was in Brown's office he made out loud that inference, and that

(10) While in Brown's office Privatus did not believe that Brown's office was there*.

While drawing the inference from (8) to (9) Privatus believed that both (8) and (9), that is, he believed that (while in Brown's office Jones knew that Smith was killed there* and Smith was killed there). Make now the assumption that the word 'there' in the conclusion (9) is the quasi-indicator 'there*.' Then since "X believes that p and q" entails "X believes that q,"

(10') While in Brown's office Privatus believed that Brown's office was there*.

Since (10') contradicts (10), the assumption is false. Since the use of 'there' in (9) as part of the inference "(8), hence (9)" is the same regardless of the truth of (10), we conclude that in no case is 'there' in (9) the quasi-indicator 'there*.' Therefore, the inference "(8), hence (9)" is not validated by rule (K.2), and (K.2) is *not* a universally valid rule.[13]

(Q.3) Quasi-indicators have an epistemological priority over indicators and indexical descriptions: a person's uses of indicators are not only eliminable for another person in terms of quasi-indicators, but the latter are the only linguistic expressions that preserve the full force of the former. This is clear from the discussion in section 4 above.

(Q.4) There are two types of quasi-indicators: (A) those, to be called *primary quasi-indicators*, whose antecedents belong to a strict oo-prefix to which they are subordinated, and (B) those, to be called *secondary quasi-indicators*, whose antecedents lie in no strict, but only in an extended oo-prefix. The former's antecedents denote structural elements of cognitive or linguistic acts, while the latter's antecedents denote entities external to cognitive or linguistic relations. The distinction is epistemologically important, as we shall see in (Q.8)–(Q.10). For example, suppose that Jones grabbed at time t the sharpest knife in the kitchen and said to Mary:

(11) I am going to kill you with this here now!

Privatus can naturally report the proceeding by asserting:

(12) Jones grabbed at t the sharpest knife in the kitchen and said to Mary that he was going to kill her with it there then.

From (11) and (12) we see that the word 'it' in (12) represents an actual use of the indicator 'this' by Jones, and it has as antecedent the occurrence of the phrase 'the sharpest knife in the kitchen' in (12); it is the quasi-indicator 'it*.' But the antecedent of 'it' is not a part of, while the antecedents of the quasi-indicators 'he,' 'her,' 'there,' and 'then' are parts of, the strict oo-prefix of (12).

Sentence (12) by itself contains a subtle ambiguity, analogous to the one we found in sentence (2) above. It can be used to make three different kinds of statement, depending on whether its 'it' is used to attribute to Jones a reference to the sharpest knife in question, which is (i) purely indexical, or (ii) descriptive, or (iii) one or the other, indeterminately. With the notation already introduced we can formulate these distinctions perspicuously as follows, where the dots indicate that the remaining parts of the sentence (12) are preserved:

(12.i) . . . it$_{*J}$ . . . ;

(12.ii) . . . it$_d$ . . . ;

(12.iii) Either (12.i) or (12.ii).

With the background furnished by statement (11) we know that statement (12) is the same as statement (12.i). As we shall see later on, (Q.8)–(Q.10), the quasi-indicator 'it*,' hence 'it$_{*J}$,' is unanalyzable. On the other hand, (12.ii) and (12.iii) are analyzable along the lines of the procedures illustrated in section 4 for the analysis of indicators in *oratio obliqua*.

By definition, 'it$_d$' in (12) expresses that by means of some description, indexical or otherwise, Jones referred to the knife referred to by Privatus as the sharpest one in a certain kitchen. Jones's description may, of course, be entirely different from Privatus'. In brief, we have here very much the same situation as we had in section 4 for the case of indicators. Thus, we also have a non-perspectival and a perspectival analysis of Privatus' statement (12.ii) as follows:

(12.iiN) Jones grabbed the sharpest knife in the kitchen, and there is a property ϕ-ness such that: that knife is the only thing which is ϕ, and Jones said to Mary that he* was going to kill her* with the only thing which is ϕ there* then*;

(12.iiP) Jones grabbed the sharpest knife in the kitchen, and there is a *property* ϕ_J-ness such that: that knife is the only thing which is $\phi_{J/I}$, and Jones said to Mary that he* was going to kill her* with the only thing which is ϕ_{*J} there* then*.

I have put the asterisks signaling the quasi-indexical role of the pronouns they attach to, in conformity with the definition of quasi-indicators and principles (1.9) and (I.10).

(Q.5) The chart below both establishes the third-person correlation between indicators and quasi-indicators appealed to in (2P), (4P), (7P), and (12.iiP), and summarizes previous results, like (I.7), (I.9), (I.10). The columns contain the following:

1. the type of entity X a person P refers to;

2. the indicator I by means of which P refers to X;

3. the type of second-order relation R that has as its relata P and the statement constituted by P's mentioned reference to X by means of I;

4. the eventual type of relation, i.e., disposition or occurrence, of R;

5. the third-person quasi-indicator Q that corresponds to I; and

6. the type of oo-prefix containing the antecedent of Q.

We use the following abbreviations:

C-cognitive relation; L-linguistic relation;
O-occurrence; D-disposition;
S-strict oo-prefix; E-extended oo-prefix

1	2	3	4	5	6
I. Self	first-person pronoun: 'I'	C, L	O, D	'he*'	S
II. Time	adverb of time 'now' (mainly)	C, L	$O, \frac{1}{2} D$	'then*'	S
III. Space:					
(a) near	adverb of place 'here' (mainly)	C, L	$O, \frac{1}{2} D^1$	'there*' 'here*'	S
(b) far	adverb of place 'there' (mainly)	C, L	O	'there*'	E
IV. Other Selves:					
(a) addressed to	second-person pronoun: 'you'	L	O	'he*'	S
(b) others	third-person pronoun: 'he'	C, L	O	'he*'	E
V. Objects	demonstrative pronouns: 'this,' 'that'	C, L	O	'it*'	E

In this table, we use $\frac{1}{2}D$ (half disposition) because implicit references to indicators are limited as required by (1.10). Moreoever, it should be noted that the quasi-indicator 'now*' has as antecedent the indicator 'now,' and similarly the quasi-indicator 'here*' has as antecedent the indicator 'here.'

By putting 'I*' instead of 'he*' in the next to the last column we can produce the first-person correlation between indicators and quasi-indicators, where 'I*' has the indicator 'I' as antecedent. Similarly, by putting 'you*' in place of 'he*' we obtain the second-person correlation, where, again, 'you*' has the indicator 'you' as antecedent.

The above table makes it apparent how the five (or seven) types of indicators compare with one another. It shows that each type of indicator is fully characterized by pairing a category mentioned in the first column with a pattern yielded by third, fourth, and last columns. For example, type V of indicator is fully determined by the pair (object: C-L-O-E); the first-person indicator[14] is fully determined by the pair (self: C-L-O-D-S). In these pairs, the category determines the only amount of classifying that indicators perform, and this by implication only, indirectly, so to speak, not by attribution. The pattern, on the other hand, merely indicates how wide is the range of use of an indicator. From this we may see immediately that the first-person indicator cannot be defined in terms of the other indicators: no combination of the latter has the wide range of the former.

At any rate, it is clear that

(I.15) The pairs of categories and patterns are both adequate conditions for defining the several types of indicator, and criteria for ascertaining the type of indicator to which a certain word of a given language belongs.

Let $S(E)$ be a sentence containing an occurrence O of an expression E, and let $S(E/E')$ be the sentence that results from $S(E)$ just by replacing O with an occurrence of E'. I shall say that O is *a proxy for E' in $S(E)$*, if and only if one and the same person using $S(E)$ assertively on a given occasion would make the very same statement that he would formulate by using $S(E/E')$ assertively on that occasion. I shall say that O is *a substitute for E' in $S(E)$*, if and only if the statement any person would formulate on a certain occasion by using $S(E)$ assertively is logically equivalent to the statement the same person would formulate by using $S(E/E')$ assertively on the very same occasion.

Quasi-indicators are substitutes for other referring expressions in some trivial cases, namely, in sentences formulating self-contradictions, necessary truths, or certain redundant statements. For instance, "—— & Peter believes that he* is ϕ, or ——" is tautologically equivalent to "——"; and replacing the explicit occurrence of 'he*' with any other referring expression does not destroy the equivalence.

(Q.6) An occurrence of a quasi-indicator is not a proxy or a substitute for an indicator or indexical description in some sentence of the form $(L[x, y_1, \ldots , y_n, p, t]$ (——)' or '$\sim L[x, y_1, \ldots , y_n, p, t]$ (——)'. This is obvious from our discussion of indicators in *oratio obliqua*.[15]

(Q.7) An occurrence of a quasi-indicator is not a proxy or a substitute for a name or a description containing no quasi-indicators, in some sentence of the form '$L[x, y_1, \ldots , y_n, p, t]$ (——)', or the form '$\sim L[x, y, \ldots , y_n, p, t]$ (——)'.

We can assimilate reference by means of names to reference by means of descriptions. On the one hand, many names apply to several objects, so that to guarantee uniqueness of reference they must be supplemented with a description. On the other hand, one acquires (or learns) a name for an entity either through a description or through a personal confrontation that gives a descriptional support to the name. (This assimilation is not necessary, but it simplifies the argument. The important thing is that reference by means of a name is not equivalent to reference by an indicator.) By (Q.6) we need not consider the case of descriptions containing indicators.

The following statement verifies (Q.7):

(13) On May 15, 1911, the German Emperor believed that it was raining then*.

Clearly, the German Emperor may have had no idea at all as to the date on which it was raining then*, and he may have also failed to have any other non-indexical description that uniquely characterized May 15, 1911. I cannot, however, muster a formal argument to show this. But a general argument for (Q.7) can be framed with the half of (I.3).

Let I be an indicator. Then by (I.3), there is at least one sentence $S(I)$ such that for no description D containing neither indicators nor quasi-indicators, the statement "$S(I)$" formulated by $S(I)$, if $S(I)$ is used assertively in circumstances C by some person X to refer to an object O, is not equivalent to the statement "$S(I/D)$" that $S(I/D)$ would formulate if assertively used by X in C to refer to O. Thus the statements "$S(I/D)$" and "$S(I)$" are both self-consistent. Now, let Q be the quasi-indicator that represents uses of I in *oratio obliqua*. Then by (Q.2), the clause $S(I/Q)$ is syncategorematic and expresses the statement "$S(I)$" only in a context of the form '$L[x, y_1, . . . , y_n, p, t]$ $(S(I/Q))$' or even a more inclusive one. Consider one of the statements formulated by a sentence of this form and call it "$OS(I/Q)$." This is a statement to the effect that the person X stands at some place p and time t in some cognitive (or linguistic) relation R to (some addressees and) the statement "$S(I)$." On the other hand, the corresponding sentence of the form '$L[x, y_1, . . . , y_n, p, t]$ $(S(I/D))$' formulates the statement, "$OS(I/D)$," that X stands at the same place p and time t in the same relation R to (the same addressees and) the statement "$S(I/D)$." Obviously, we can choose a name or some self-consistent description of the person X to put in the place of 'x' in the oo-prefix of the above sentences. Thus, we can choose statements "$OS(I/D)$" and "$OS(I/Q)$," which are contingent. Hence, by the principle (P) below it follows that the statement "$OS(I/Q)$" is not equivalent to the statement "$OS(I/D)$," for whatever description D that contains neither quasi-indicators nor indicators:

(P) If a statement formulated by a sentence of the form '$L[x, y_1, . . . , y_n, p, t]$ (——)' is contingent, then if it is equivalent to the corresponding statement of the form '$L[x, y_1, . . . , y_n, p, t]$ (. . .)', then the statement formulated by what fills the blank '----' is equivalent to the statement formulated by what fills the blank ' . . . ' provided both are self-consistent.

By (P), to believe that a certain proposition S is true is equivalent to believing that a certain proposition S' is true, only if S and S' are themselves logically equivalent. For example, believing that it is both raining and hailing is equivalent to believing that it is both hailing and raining, and, clearly, "it is raining and hailing" is equivalent to "it is hailing and raining."

It should be noted that if in the above reasoning the sentence expressing "$OS(I/Q)$" is categorematic, then Q is a primary quasi-indicator. On the other hand, if the sentence in question is syncategorematic, i.e., it formulates "$OS(I/Q)$" only by being concatenated with another clause, with which it forms a larger context C, then Q may be a primary or a secondary quasi-indicator. In the latter case (as we shall see later on) Q may be a substitute for some description variable in C. But this in no way affects its being substitute for no description containing no quasi-indicators in the smaller context that formulates "$OS(I/Q)$."

If "$OS(I/Q)$" is not equivalent to "$OS(I/D)$," then " $\sim OS(I/Q)$" is not equivalent to " $\sim OS(I/D)$." And since being a proxy entails being a substitute for the same expression in the same sentence, (Q.7) is fully established by the preceding argument.

6. Unanalyzability of Strict Quasi-Indicators

Variables of quantification are unanalyzable referring expressions. Thus, inasmuch as quasi-indicators sometimes function as variables of quantification, they cannot be analyzed in terms of names, indicators, or descriptions containing no quasi-indicators. But from (Q.6) and (Q.7) the stronger result follows that no quasi-indicator referring to a single entity is analyzable solely in terms of indicators, names, or descriptions (indexical or Leibnizian) that do not contain quasi-indicators. Furthermore the procedures discussed in section 4 for the analysis of indicators in *oratio obliqua* cannot produce an analysis of quasi-indicators. Consider, for example, Privatus' statement

(14) Jones thought at 3 p.m. yesterday that Paul was then* sick.

If we apply to (14) the procedure for non-perspectival analysis we find

(14N) There is a property ϕ-ness such that: the (time) $\phi = 3$ p.m. yesterday and Jones thought at 3 p.m. yesterday that Paul was sick at the (time) ϕ.

But (14N) and (14) can have different truth-value. For while (14) attributes to Jones a purely indexical reference to the time of his thinking, (14N) attributes to him a descriptive reference.

If we apply the procedure for a perspectival analysis we obtain:

(14P) There is a *property* ϕ_J-ness such that: the time which is the only $\phi_{J1} = 3$ p.m. yesterday, and Jones thought at 3 p.m. yesterday that Paul was sick at the only time which is ϕ_{*J}.

Again, (14) and (14P) can have different truth-values: it is possible that when Jones thought what Privatus reports, he just made either a purely indexical or a descriptive reference to the time of his thinking, but not both. In the case of (14P) there is the additional point that even if it were an analysis of the singular quasi-indicator 'then*' of (14), it would be an analysis in terms of the quasi-indexical variables 'ϕ_{*J}.' Thus, the perspectival procedures would constitute at best an analysis of singular quasi-indicators.

Now, a language or conceptual scheme through which the only self or person that can be conceived is the one who uses the scheme, obviously, does not allow for the conception of the contrast between two persons. Such a language does not allow for the contrast between first- and other-person statements, or between second- and other-person statements. Thus, whatever verbal and whatever pronominal forms are part of that language, they will simply fail to express the distinction among grammatical persons. Thus, we may suppose, for concreteness, that in such a language we only have what appears to be first-person statements of the form "I am ϕ." Yet the pronoun 'I' cannot refer in such statements to an entity which has general mental properties, that is, properties that do not necessarily have just one instance. For a language to have predicates that formulate such general properties is for it to allow the framing of statements which formulate the possibility that these properties be exemplified by several entities. Thus, the pronoun 'I' in the seemingly first-person statements of the type of language we are discussing has to refer to an entity of a category, namely, self, for which the language does not allow other members. Hence, I submit that the seeming first-person statements in question are really either (i) disguised strictly impersonal statements (like "There is a pain here," "There was a thought that it will rain," and "There was a belief that it would rain now"), or (ii) statements in which the entity the word 'I' refers to is simply the totality (and hence the only entity of its sort) of all the experiences, thoughts, etc, that constitute the user of the conceptual scheme in question.[16] I shall assume that perceptual thinking necessarily involves demonstrative reference.

On the other hand, a conceptual scheme that allows for the mere possibility of other thinking beings, which have perceptions but need not be aware of themselves, allows necessarily for the contrast either between first- and other-person statements, or between third-person statements about one entity and third-person statements about another entity. That is, the user of the scheme can at least consider statements like "This is a cow and X thinks that it* is pregnant," which attribute to the other thinking beings experiences and experiential judgments that involve the use of demonstrative reference. In brief,

(Q.8) A conceptual scheme that allows for the possibility of other perceiving thinking beings (even though their reality isn't affirmed in the scheme) is characterized by the possession of the unique and unanalyzable referring mechanism constituted by the secondary quasi-indicators discussed in (Q.4).

A person is not only a center of consciousness or a factory of thoughts and reasonings. A person is a center of self-consciousness. Thus, a conceptual scheme that allows even for the mere possibility of several persons (or self-aware selves) necessarily allows for: (i) the formulation of the contrast between first- and third-person statements, and (ii) the formulation of statements of the form "X thinks at place p at time t that he* is —— there* then*" and of the form "I think that I* am ——." Therefore

(I.16) A conceptual scheme that allows for the mere possibility of several persons (or self-aware selves) is characterized by the possession of the unanalyzable referring mechanism constituted by the first-person indicator, and

(Q.9) by the possession of the unanalyzable referring mechanism constituted by the primary first- and third-person quasi-indicators.

Finally, a conceptual scheme that allows for the possibility of communication necessarily allows for: (i) the formulation of the contrast between first- and second-person statements, and (ii) the formulation of second-person statements of the form "You believe that you* are ——." Hence,

(I.17) A conceptual scheme that allows for the possibility of communication is characterized by the possession of communication is characterized by the possession of the unanalyzable referring mechanism constituted by the second-person indicator, and

(Q.10) by the possession of the unanalyzable referring mechanism constituted by the primary second-person quasi-indicator.

7. Quasi-Indicators in N-Fold Oratio Obliqua

We proceed to discuss the quasi-indicators' counterpart of indicators in *oratio obliqua*, namely, the case of quasi-indicators subordinated to oo-prefixes which themselves occur in *oratio obliqua*. To start with, suppose that Privatus asserts

(15) In Brown's office Smith thought that in Brown's office Jones thought that a treasure is hidden there*.

Then we have a problem: to ascertain what exactly was Privatus' statement. His utterance has a noteworthy ambiguity. It may be brought out neatly by imagining Smith to be in Brown's office making the first-person statement corresponding to (15). He has a choice among:

(16) Here I thought that in Brown's office Jones thought that a treasure was hidden here;

(17) Here I thought that in Brown's office Jones thought that a treasure was hidden there*;

and

(18) Here I thought that here Jones thought that a treasure was hidden here.

In short, the ambiguity lies in that the quasi-indicator 'there*' in (15) may have as its antecedent either the second occurrence of 'in Brown's office' to the left of 'there,' which is in *oratio recta*, or the other occurrence, which is in *oratio obliqua*. In the former case Privatus' statement is the counterpart of (16), while in the latter it is the counterpart of (17). But there seems to be no natural way of expressing this distinction in English. It can be expressed, however, by means of some artificial improvement upon English, for example, by attaching to 'there*' a subscript that indicates the distance between it and its antecedent. Either the antecedent, as in the case of (15), lies in a strict oo-prefix P, or its lies in an extended oo-prefix P; thus, we can measure the distance between an occurrence of a quasi-indicator and its antecedent by counting the strict oo-prefixes up to P to which that occurrence is subordinated. For instance, Privatus' counterpart of (16) is, then:

(19) In Brown's office Smith thought that in Brown's office Jones thought that a treasure was hidden there*$_2$.

Privatus's statement which is the counterpart of (17) is:

(20) In Brown's office Smith thought that in Brown's office Jones thought that a treasure was hidden there*$_1$.

By (Q.2)–(Q.9), the 'there*' in (20) is not analyzable. But by (I.12) the indicator 'here' at the end of (16) is eliminable for the speaker, and by (I.10)–(I.11) the elimination conforms to the procedures illustrated in section 4. Since 'there*$_2$' in (19) represents the use of 'here' in (16), then 'there*$_2$' is eliminable for the speaker by the same procedures illustrated in section 4. Thus, Privatus' statement (19) is more perspicuously formulated *as the perspectival statement*.

(19P) In Brown's office Smith thought that there is a *property* ϕ_S-ness such that: the only place which is ϕ_S = *[Brown's office], and in Brown's office Jones thought that a treasure was hidden at the only place which is ϕ_{SIJ}.

It is easy to see that at this stage our subscript notation allows of a simplification (hereafter adopted) without diminishing its power to dissolve ambiguity. An expression of the form '$\phi*_{Jn}$' is a quasi-indicator such that (i) its antecedent lies n units to the left of it, in an oo-prefix P, and (ii) it represents J's uses of indicators, where 'J' stands for an expression both referring to person J and being the subject of the verb in the same oo-prefix P. Thus, we can drop the subscript 'J' from '$\phi*_{Jn}$', since by looking at the nth prefix to its right we can find both its antecedent and the expression 'J' stands for.

Now, it is a trivial exercise to construct parallel distinctions for each of the other quasi-indicators.[17] And if we regard the subscript notation as a characteristic feature of quasi-indicators, we can, then, conclude that

(Q.11) Quasi-indicators that are more than one unit removed from their antecedents are eliminable. That is, quasi-indicators of distance 1 are unanalyzable, but all other are analyzable in terms of those of distance 1.

Our subscript notation is, however, not yet fully adequate to eliminate the ambiguities of some sentences containing quasi-indicators. Consider, for example, Privatus' statement:

(21) In Brown's office Jones thought that Smith claimed there* that a treasure was hidden there*.

Clearly, the first 'there*' has 'in Brown's office' as its antecedent, and Privatus is not, by (21) ascribing to Jones the knowledge or even the idea that the place at which he was when he had the thought in question was precisely Brown's office. But the 'there*' at the end of (21) is ambiguous. No doubt, in some sense it also has 'in Brown's office' as its antecedent. But whose uses of the indicator 'here' does the second 'there*' represent? If it represents Jones', then the second 'there*' has 'in Brown's office' as its direct antecedent. If it represents Smith's, then its *immediate* antecedent is the first 'there*' and 'in Brown's office' is only its *ultimate* antecedent. Yet there is no normal way of expressing this distinction in ordinary language.

At this juncture I want to propose a notation that can be used as an auxiliary to English to make all the necessary distinctions that quasi-indicators in n-fold *oratio obliqua* allow. This notation will also serve the theoretical purpose of allowing the precise formulation of a fragment of the logic of quasi-indicators.

8. Notation for Quasi-Indicators

First, we unify the expression of all quasi-indicators by dropping the ordinary pronouns, adverbs, etc., used to express them, and simply indicate the underlying quasi-indexical role by means of '*'. Second, we prefix '*' to an occurrence O of the ultimate antecedent of the quasi-indicator whose expression we are framing. Third, we suffix to such occurrence O a subscript that indicates the distance between the quasi-indicator and its immediate antecedent. (We could drop '*' altogether and express the pure quasi-indexical role by the mere suffixation of the subscript. But we preserve '*' and suggest that it be read as 'he,' 'then,' 'it,' etc., as the case may be.)

With this notation we can unambiguously write the two interpretations of (21) as

(22) In Brown's office Jones thought that Smith claimed *(in Brown's office)$_1$ that a treasure was hidden *(in Brown's office)$_2$;

and

(23) In Brown's office Jones thought that Smith claimed *(in Brown's office)$_1$ that a treasure was buried *(in Brown's office)$_1$.

This exegesis of (21) satisfies (Q.10). Since the second 'there*' of (22) is at distance 2 from its antecedent, by (Q.10) it is analyzable, and its subscript '2' is an immediate indication of its analyzability. Similarly, the subscripts of (23) clearly convey that none of its quasi-indicators is analyzable.

Parallel examples show that the temporal quasi-indicator 'then*' has parallel ambiguities that can be dissolved by our notation. But the quasi-indicator 'he*,' when it represents a use of the indicator 'I', not, e.g., of the indicator 'this (man),' does not allow the ambiguity parallel to that of (21). Consider, for example

(24) Jones believes that he* believes that he* is sick.

If Jones were to make the first-person counterpart statement, he would say:

(25) I believe that I believe that I am sick.

In short, Privatus' statement (24) attributes to Jones belief in the truth of a first-person statement about somebody's being sick, at the same time that it attributes to Jones belief in the identity of that somebody to himself. Thus, in our notation (24) comes out as

(24A) Jones believes that *Jones$_1$ believes that *Jones$_1$ is sick.

Again, (24A) palpably shows that by (Q.10) neither occurrence of the quasi-indicator is analyzable. Here we have a distinctive feature of the primary quasi-indicator 'he*' that sets it apart from all other quasi-indicators.

The secondary quasi-indicator 'he*,' which represents uses of the personal indicator 'this (that),' allows of an ambiguity analogous to the one of (21). For example,

(26) John told of Mary that Brown would think of her* that she* had been appointed.

The occurrence of 'she*' expresses a demonstrative reference either by Brown, in which case it is '*(Mary)₁,' or by John, in which case it is '*(Mary)₂ with 'her*' as its immediate antecedent. Naturally, 'her*' is '*(Mary)₁.'

Our notation is also adequate to dissolve another type of ambiguity proper to linguistic verbs. For example,

(27) John told Paul that he* had been made a full professor.[18]

In this case 'he*' is ambiguous between a use of 'I' or a use of 'you' by John. These interpretations come, respectively, to be:

(28) John told Paul that *(John)₁ had been made a full professor,

and

(29) John told Paul that *(Paul)₁ had been made a full professor.

For simplicity of the formulation of general principles (P.A) below we shall consider every statement a person X makes or believes to be true, or merely entertains, as subordinated to a tacit strict oo-prefix of the form 'I think here now that.' This conforms with the egocentric characteristic of *properties* above discussed.

The preceding examples suggest that the general principle in operation is the following:

(P*.P) Let $\phi(*a_n)$ be an incomplete or syncategorematic clause such that: (i) it contains an occurrence O of $*a_n$, (ii) it does not contain the antecedent A of O, (iii) it is immediately subordinated to the oo-prefix P_n represented by '$L[b, \ldots]$', (iv) P_n is immediately subordinated to the oo-prefix P_{n-1} of the form '$L[c, \ldots]$', and (v) $n > 1$. Let a formula of the form "$F(u//v)$" denote the result of replacing all the occurrences of the term u under consideration in the formula $F(u)$ with occurrences of the term v not occurring in $F(u)$. Then $L[b, \ldots]\phi(*a_n)$ is analyzable as:

There is a *property* μ_c-ness such that: $*a_n$ is the only thing that is μ_c and there is a *property* $\mu_{c/b}$-ness such that $[Lb, \ldots]\phi(*a_n//\mu_{b/c})$.

Suppose that some of the occurrences Ox of $*a_n$ are the immediate antecedents of occurrences of $*a_1$, in a component of $\phi(*a_n)$ of the form $L[d, \ldots]\psi*a_1)$. Then $L[d, \ldots]\psi*a_1)$ is analyzable as:

There is a property $\nu_{b/d}$-ness such that: $*a_1$ is the thing that is $\nu_{b/d}$ and $L[d, \ldots]\psi*a_1//\nu_{b/d})$.

In general, I submit that

(Q.12) By $n - 1$ applications of principle (P*.P), we may analyze perspectivally every occurrence of a quasi-indicator $*a_n$ in a sentence $\phi(*a_n)$ in terms of the quasi-indicator $*a_1$.

By dropping the suffixes 'b' and 'b/c' of the predicate variables in (P*.P) we obtain a formulation of the non-perspectival principle (P*.N), and (Q.13) By $n - 1$ applications of (P*.N) we may analyze non-perspectivally every occurrence of a quasi-indicator *a_n in a sentence $\phi(*a_n)$ in terms of the quasi-indicator *a_1.

Notes

1. Part of this research was carried out under the National Science Foundation Grant No. GS-828.

2. Some of the main results of this paper are generalizations for all quasi-indicators of previous results obtained, in the terminology of (Q.4) below, for the very special primary quasi-indicator 'he*.' These previous results together with other complementary results are discussed in my " 'He': A Study in the Logic of Self-consciousness," *Ratio* 8 (1966): 130–57. It will be cited as "*He.*"

I owe the initial stimulus for these generalizations to my colleague Robert Sleigh, Jr., who on March 12, 1965, said to me that 'then' in "Jones believed at t that it was raining then" is like (the primary quasi-indicator) 'he*' in not being replaceable by its antecedent 't.' Peter T. Geach has really studied *He* and in correspondence has provided a sustained flow of encouragement, criticisms, and suggestions. George Nakhnikian read the first draft of this paper and pointed out several obscurities and errors. Wilfrid Sellars read the second draft and pointed out errors and obscurities and suggested improvements.

3. N. Goodman, *The Structure of Appearance* (Cambridge, Mass.: Harvard University Press, 1951), p. 290. However, Goodman's criterion for the selection is different: "a word is an *indicator* if (but, . . . , not necessarily only if) it names something not named by some replica of the word."

4. The latter should offer no major difficulty after both the study of "now" and"then" included here and the study of tenses by W. Sellars in "Times and the World Order,"in H. Feigl, M. Scriven, and G. Maxwell, eds., *Minnesota Studies in the Philosophy of Science* (Minneapolis: University of Minnesota Press, 1957). An important problem open in this area is the examination of difficulties (if any) raised by quasi-indicators for Quine's program of eliminating all singular referring terms in favor of predicates and variables of quantification. See his *Word and Object* (Cambridge: MIT Press, 1960), pp. 163, 170–86. The auxiliary notation introduced here can be easily formalized and, then, adjoined to a calculus of "knows" and "believes," such as Hintikka's in his *Knowledge and Belief* (Ithaca, N.Y.: Cornell University Press, 1963). For the need to supplement Hintikka's calculus with some such notation, see my review of his book in *The Journal of Symbolic Logic* 24 (1964): 132–34.

5. Cf. P. F. Strawson, *Introduction to Logical Theory* (London: Methuen, 1952), and cf. R. L. Cartwright, "Propositions," in R. J. Butler, ed., *Analytic Philosophy* (Oxford: Blackwell, 1962).

6. H. Reichenbach, *Elements of Symbolic Logic* (New York: Macmillan, 1947), p. 284.

7. For a penetrating defense of the unanalyzability and theoretical indispensability of indexical reference, see P. F. Strawson, *Individuals* (London: Methuen, 1959), pp. 117–20. See also the very interesting defense of indicators as singular terms by Manley Thompson in "On the Elimination of Singular Terms," *Mind* 67 (1959): 361–76, against Quine's thesis that all singular terms are eliminable. I hasten to point out that my theses (I.6)–(I.7) do not seem incompatible with Quine's. I am not (here at any rate) laying claim to the necessity of the unanalyzable indexical roles being performed by singular terms in Quine's sense, and Quine, for his part, does not claim that all indicators can be defined or analyzed away. Quine lets 'now,' 'then,' 'here,' and 'there' to remain uneliminated as general terms (*Word and Object*, p. 185), and he also allows that the attributive use of these indicators as general terms depends on pointing. If Quine's reduction holds, my claims in (I.6) and (I.7) must be construed as claims about the indexical general terms that Quine introduces.

8. I myself have argued for this possibility in "Lenguaje, Pensamiento y Realidad," *Humanitas* (Monterrey, Mex.: University of Nuevo León) 3 (1962): 199–217; I touch on the issue in "The Private

Language Argument," entry of *The Encyclopedia of Philosophy* (New York: Macmillan, 1967), VI, pp. 458–64.

9. This parallelism does not require that there be a component of a proposition *P* for every word or phrase of a sentence formulating *P*. The parallelism we need to accept is compatible with certain words or phrases being, e.g., mere grouping devices or scope signals like 'it is the case that.'

10. For theories about thinking based on the structural analogy between a proposition and the sentences expressing it, see Wilfrid Sellars, "Empiricism and the Philosophy of Mind," in *Minnesota Studies in the Philosophy of Science*, vol. 1 (Minneapolis: University of Minnesota Press, 1956), pp. 305–28, and P. T. Geach, *Mental Acts* (London: Routledge & Kegan Paul, 1956), chap. 14, 17, and 22.

11. This analysis of (2) occurred to me after George Nakhnikian pointed out an error in an earlier analysans candidate.

12. Toward the end of section 4.

13. Obviously a similar counter-example against (K.2) can be produced using 'then*' and 'it*.' In *He*, Section 4, appears the original argument of this type employing 'he*' qua representation of uses of the indicator 'I'.

14. Note that the first-person pronoun, which is also used as a quasi-indicator, is not being characterized here.

15. In *He*, Section 2, I examine several natural ways in which it might be thought that the primary indicator 'he*' could be construed as a vehicle for indexical reference.

16. For more details on the impersonal core of first-person statements, see P. T. Geach, *Mental Acts*, pp. 117–21, and my "Behavior and Consciousness," in *Studies in the Philosophy of Mind* (Detroit: Wayne State University Press, 1966), sections 9 and 10. In *Individuals*, p. 99n, Strawson formulates the much stronger principle that "the idea of a predicate is correlative with that of a *range of distinguishable* individuals" (my italics in 'distinguishable'), and I have criticized this principle in *La Dialéctica de la Consciencia de Sí Mismo* (Guatemala: University of San Carlos Press, 1960), pp. 45–50.

17. For the case of the primary indicator 'he*' see *He*, examples (18)–(20).

18. I owe this example to P. T. Geach, and with it the realization that it exhibits a peculiar kind of ambiguity.

Part III
A Semantic and Ontological Theory
for the Language of Experience: Guise Theory

13

Thinking and the Structure of the World *Discours d'ontologie*

*Il faut donc considérer ce que c'est que d'estre attribué
véritablement à un certain sujet.*

Leibniz, *Discours de métaphysique*, VIII

This paper formulates a basic system of ontology that has several interesting qualities: (1) it is suggested very strongly by the most naive and simplest consideration of certain perplexities involving psychological states: (2) the system does justice to several apparently conflicting insights that have been debated by many philosophers; (3) the system separates the a priori from the empirical elements of the world very nicely and neatly; (4) indeed, the system concentrates all the empirical elements of the world on two irreducible dyadic predicates; (5) for this reason the system seems to be a nice formulation of a conception of the world that was started by Plato, was envisioned by Leibniz, guided Frege, at least in part, and was defended by Meinong. The system appears, therefore, to have the historico-philosophical value of illuminating the long and important abstractist and rationalist tradition. I motivate its development with an initial discussion of a problem widely discussed nowadays. This is meant to honor those great metaphysicians by suggesting how contemporary their insights into the problems were, even if their solutions are not followed.

Among other things, the system accomplishes the following: (i) provides an account of possible objects; (ii) provides an account of predication; (iii) furnishes an analysis of ordinary particulars; (iv) preserves the fundamental feature of identity, namely, the identity of indiscernibles; (v) eschews representationalism; (vi) drops the dichotomy sense-referent, by making, so to speak, the sense of a single term its referent; (vii) explicates the fundamental connections among actuality, concreteness, and existence; (viii) characterizes the objectification of impossible individuals by thinking, (ix) provides an easy account of transworld identity, for those who like so-called possible-world semantics; (x) yields an account of trans-story identity for fictional entities; (xi) furnishes a new ground for the assimilation of sense-data and physical objects.

1. Ontological Data and Problems

1.1 Frege's Triad

As is well known, Frege was perplexed by the apparent truth of triples of propositions like this:

(1) Tom believes that the morning star is Venus.

(2) Tom does not believe that the evening star is Venus.

(3) The morning star = the evening star.

He could not understand how a thing a and a thing b can be really identical and yet differ in some property, for example, the property of being believed by Tom to be Venus. Frege insisted correctly, as Quine has done in recent years, that the indiscernibility of identicals is the central part and parcel of the concept of identity. As is also well known, Frege attempted to solve the perplexity of the triad (1)–(3) by claiming that the terms 'morning star' and 'evening star' are ambiguous, having in (3) one sense and one referent, and another of each in (2), or (1), respectively. I propose not to follow the details of his theory at this juncture.

There is, however, a naive solution to Frege's perplexity. Take (1) and (2) as the proof that (3) is false if '=' is taken to mean literal identity. On the other hand, (3) is true if it is a proposition about a relation weaker than identity. On this naive solution, Frege's (1) and (2) establish that the evening star and the morning star are really different entities. Of course, identity is governed by Leibniz's principle of the indiscernibility of identicals. Whatever is *genuinely identical* with the morning star is indeed believed by Tom to be Venus, if (1) is true.

This naive solution was briefly considered by Quine in his short essay, "The Problem of Interpreting Modal Logic,"[1] for the case of another similarly perplexing traid:

(4) It is necessary that the morning star be the morning star.

(5) It is not necessary that the morning star be the evening star.

(6) The morning star is the evening star.

Quine suggested, apparently tongue in cheek, that the consistency of (4)–(6) be explained by taking the 'is' of sentence (6), not as expressing honest-to-goodness identity, but a weaker relation, for which he proposed the name 'congruence'. He used the letter 'C' to represent perspicuously the 'is' of (6). Quine's purpose was, apparently, to discredit interpreted modal logic by showing how it involves the repudiation of material objects on the best interpretation.

It may be protested, however, that the view that the morning star and the evening star are not genuinely identical does not imply a repudiation of material objects. It is the *material* evening star which is not genuinely identical, a philosopher may hold, with the *material* morning star, even though they are congruent and, if you wish, are the same material object. But we won't pursue this discussion now.

1.2 Quine's Argument against Intensional Entities

Later on Quine was able to make a stronger attack against both modal logic and quantification into belief contexts than his accusation of repudiation of material objects. He discovered a persuasive argument to show that introducing intensional entities as the values of the variables of quantification does not resolve the original perplexity. This argument Quine has iterated several times. One of his earliest versions appears in *From a Logical Point of View*[2]:

> [if] A is any intensional object, say an attribute, and 'p' stands for an arbitrary true sentence, clearly
> (35) $A = (\iota x) [p \cdot (x = A)]$.

Yet, if the true sentence represented by 'p' is not analytic, then neither is (35), and its sides are no more interchangeable in modal contexts than are 'Evening Star' and 'Morning Star', or '9' and 'the number of planets'. [p. 153]

Quine is talking about modal contexts like (4)–(5), but his point is applicable to Frege's triad. Let A be the morning star, and let 'p' stand for any proposition about which Tom has absolutely no idea at all. The identity (35) should require that Tom believes that $(\iota x) [p \cdot (x = A)]$ is identical to the morning star, but since Tom has no idea of what 'p' represents, it is not the case that he believes this identity.

Obviously, Quine's argument must be met by denying that his (35) is true if '=' expresses genuine identity. But to defend this one must explain why this is so, and this requires a theory of both what exactly an individual is and what it is for an individual to have properties. In short, the naive solution to Frege's puzzle has to become sophisticated: There is really no naive solution without a theory of predication and of individuality: But before embarking in the formulation of one such theory, let us consider other puzzles that seem to require a solution very much like the naive solution suggested for Frege's perplexity. A solution common to all is definitely superior, by being systematic and not ad hoc.

1.3 Geach's Puzzle

In "Intentional Identity,"[3] Geach raised a nice problem. He presented it by means of an example about witches, which by non-existing make the puzzle somewhat more dramatic, but also misled some critics by suggesting to them that the puzzle pertains to fictional entities. A pedestrian illustration is this:

(7) John believes that there is a man at the door, and Paul believes that he [that man] is a burglar.

(8) But there is no one at the door.

The problem is precisely the existential quantifier 'there is a man', which in (7) appears in the scope of 'John believes' and yet binds the occurrence of the variable of quantification 'he [that man]' which appears in the scope of 'Paul believes'.

Clearly, the quantifier 'there is a man' cannot be placed at the beginning of (7) and be given the whole of (7) as its scope, if that quantifier is supposed to range over existing persons. To do so would conflict with (8). Thus, we have Geach's problem of identifying the entity which is the object of John's and Paul's beliefs. This problem remains even if the problem about the scope of the quantifier disappears.

One naive solution is this: Take the quantifier 'there is a man' to range not only over existing objects, but also over non-existing possible objects. This solution is like the one discussed in section 1 in that it introduces non-material objects in our ontological inventory. If in the case of Frege's triad we take the evening star to be an existing (material) object, which is the selfsame whether it exists or not, we can take the possible objects required for the solution to Geach's problem to constitute the same domain of objects required for the solution to Frege's perplexity.

1.4 Impossible Objects

We have talked about possible objects. But we must reckon with impossible objects as well. Geach's problem need not be the one created by two men thinking of a possible man. It can arise from two men thinking about impossible objects.

(9) John believes that there is a blue round square and Paul thinks that *it* is hollow.

To be sure, all kinds of solutions supported by their corresponding theories of predication and individuation can be constructed. The point here is that once we adopt the path of intensional entities for Frege's and Geach's puzzles, we should naturally go further in that path and consider Meinongian impossible objects.

1.5 Cross-Attitudinal References

The problem raised by Geach involves two thinkers. But the problem is more general. It appears in the case of just one person who has several different attitudes toward an entity and his attitudes form part of one unitary consciousness or mind. Consider, for instance,

(10) Benjamin believes that there is a fountain of life and he hopes to drink from it.

The quantifier 'there is (a fountain of life)' has to be the dominant operator so that it can bind references to the same entity both within the scope of 'believes' and within the scope of 'hopes'. So, we seem committed to introducing nonexisting objects once again as values of the variables of quantification. Patently, such nonexisting objects may very well be impossible, self-contradictory objects.

1.6 Reality and Thinking

Thinking is oriented toward the world, and often succeeds in hitting a real thing. A central problem is the nature and structure of that success. In particular, we must explicate how the very same entity that exists in the world is *exactly* what a successful episode of thinking is about.

1.7 Existence

Thinking is oriented toward the world, the existents in the world: To think of an object and to think of it as existing seem to be the same thing. Yet, somehow, thinking is impervious to existence. Thinking is quite as comfortable in the contemplation of the existent as in the contemplation of the non-existent. Thus, existence appears to be *both* a differentiating feature that some, but not all, objects of thought possess *and* a nonfeature at all incapable of differentiating one object from another. In traditional terms, existence is not a real predicate; yet it is not a logical or formal predicate, for existence, that is, the existence of material and mental things and events, is precisely the innermost core of contingency.

1.8 The Fundamental Problem

The nature of existence is a most serious problem. But there is underlying it the problem of the constitution of an object. The unity of a thing and its possession of properties is the primary philosophical problem. Does the unity of a thing consist of an underlying substrate? Or of something else? How do properties compose a thing? These questions include as a special case the way in which existence enters into objects or how existence accrues to objects. The fundamental problem is, therefore, the problem of the most elementary (and trivial) structural relationships among the basic categories of the world: Thing, Property, Predication, Existence, Identity, and Thought. It is the problem of the connection between Thinking and the Fundamental Structure of the World that appears to consciousness or, for that matter, that thinking itself creates. Which of these disjuncts is the case belongs to a *discours de métaphysique*, and goes beyond our present ontological (that is, phenomenologico-ontological) concern. (Phenomenological ontology is epistemologically prior to metaphysical ontology.)

2. The Abstractist Ontology: Informal Presentation

2.1 Ontological Atoms

In good old Platonistic style, the abstractist conception of the world takes properties by themselves, that is, separated from particulars, to be ultimate components of the world. There is a verbal issue as to whether quantifiers are properties. To avoid it, let us say that the ultimate components of the world are *Forms*, and these divide into *properties* and *operators*. The former are ranked into monadic, dyadic, triadic, . . . , in short, n-adic properties for any natural number n.

Among the operators are those that operate on properties yielding complex properties. Some, like non-vacuous quantifiers, diminish the n-adic rank of properties. Others, like logical connections, increase the rank of a property. Individuals are operators that diminish a property's rank, too. (Formally, the most elementary mechanisms of property composition can be neatly described by systems of quantification that use operators instead of variables, as, for example, in Quine's "Variables Explained Away."[4])

For convenience we shall use variables of quantification. Ontologically, we can regard the introduction of variables, let us call it *variabilization*, as the operation that transforms abstract properties into propositional functions, which are the concrete properties entering in the composition of individuals.

2.2 Individuals

There is one operator, let us represent it by braces, that operates on entities and forms sets. The primary sets are composed of concrete properties. Sets are abstract individuals.

Another operator, let us represent it by c, operates on sets of monadic properties (or propositional functions), whether simple or complex, and yields *concrete individuals*. From now on 'individual' means concrete individual. These are, *roughly*, Frege's senses of definite descriptions. For example, the round square is the individual c {being round and square}. The individual composed of the properties roundness and squareness is c {being round, being square}. They are different because the sets of properties composing them are different: the former is a unit set, the latter is a pair. There is, of course, an intimate connection between them, and we discuss it in section 2.6.

Suppose that, as it seems likely, the round square *was* Meinong's favorite impossible object. That is to say, consider the individual c {being Meinong's favorite impossible object}. This is, obviously, quite a different individual from the c {being round and square}. Thus, the italicized occurrence of the word '*was*' in the first sentence of this paragraph does not express genuine identity. We shall say more about identity below.

2.3 Meinongian Predication

An individual is in an obvious sense a cluster of properties. Most of them are finite clusters. Clearly whatever property Fness we consider, the Fer is F, and necessarily so, if 'is' is meant in the sense of ontological composition. Thus, Meinong's persistent claim that "the Fer is F" is analytically, or logically, true, is correct in the primary sense of 'is'.

Let us call the primary predication *Meinongian predication*, and let us represent it by expressions of the form "$a(F)$", where 'a' denotes an individual and 'F' a property. Thus, the proposition expressed by a sentence of such a form is true, if and only if the property denoted by 'F' is a member of the set of properties constituting the individual denoted by 'a'.

Many of us have an inclination to think that Mount Everest neither possesses the property of being an even number nor possesses the property of not-being an even number, even though the two properties seem to be mutually exclusive. This inclination is at bottom an intuition of the primary Meinongian predication. Evidently, for any property Fness we consider, many concrete individuals do not include in their constituting set of property Fness or its denial nonFness.

We also have an inclination to say that for any property Fness anything has Fness or has not Fness. That inclination is the intuition that in our confrontation with the world we also use another conception of predication. We discuss it below in section 2.5.

2.4 Identity

Genuine identity is as it is normally conceived to be. It is a very special dyadic relation, which is reflexive and is governed by Leibniz's Law of the indiscernibility of identicals. In short, we have the following two fundamental ontological princples:

Id.1. $x = x$

Id.2a. $(x = y) \equiv (x \ (F) = y \ (F))$

Entering into a fact is, of course, *not* a property. But identity requires the fact-indiscernibility of identicals. Let '$\sigma \ [a]$' express a fact, *simple or complex*, in which the individual denoted by 'a' enters and '$\sigma[a/b]$' the same fact with the individual denoted by 'b' entering in some positions in that fact instead of the individual denoted by 'a'. Then we have the law:

Id.2b. $(x = y) \supset (\varphi \ [x] \equiv \varphi \ [x|y])$

2.5 Actuality

Actuality, which accrues to concrete individuals, is most mysterious. It is the ultimate act, in Aristotle's sense, that contrasts act with potentiality, and lies wholly outside the realm of abstracta. (Note that as Plato observed, the realm of abstracta is so comfortable to the mind that it looks like its natural habitat.) Actuality must, of course, be at least obscurely and partially apprehensible. Otherwise, there would not even be a reference to a real world. Actuality has to be thinkable, and this means that there is a Form, a sort of property, under which it is conceivable. This suggests another form of predication, connecting a concrete individual with other properties, which do not constitute it. Now, the previous characterization of an individual makes an individual bounded, determined exactly by a set of properties which may be finite and, hence, is not even closed under logical implication. Thus, actuality must not only connect an individual to other properties not in it, but must connect them in an external way. Furthermore, this external way has to preserve the total individuality of each individual, namely, the individuality required by self-identity, that is, by Leibniz's Law.

Well, all these vague considerations gain body in the view that among the properties there is a dyadic relation, which I call *consubstantiation* or *co-actuality*. This is the *only* relation that connects different concrete individuals, and makes them both exist.

Let us represent consubstantiation with the symbol 'C*'. (The asterisk comes after the letter 'C' to indicate that we are dealing with an *a posteriori*, or contingent, relation. The fact that there is only one asterisk indicates that this is the fundamental, the number one, contingent relation: in a world deprived of thinking it would be the only one.) Thus, if '*a*' denotes the morning star and '*b*' the evening star, what is ordinarily meant by the sentence 'The morning star is the evening star', or by the sentence, 'The morning star is the same as the evening star', can be more perspicuously put as the fact that

$C*(a, b)$.

To explain the nature of consubstantiation better let us analyze some ordinary statements. Consider

(11) The Principal is bald.

Most likely a person making a statement by means of sentence (11) would not intend to assert the Meinongian statement

(11a) The Principal (baldness).

Most likely, such a person would be meaning to assert that the Principal exists and has baldness, not as an ontologically constitutive property, but as a contingent property. Thus his statement is more likely this:

(11b) There is an individual y such that: both $C*(y$, the Principal) and y (baldness).

Consider now a relational proposition:

(12) The Principal kissed the Art Teacher.

Once again, there are the Meinongian, *a priori* trivial propositions, which are palpably false:

(12a) The Principal (kissed-the-Art-Teacher-ness);

(12b) The Art Teacher (being-kissed-by-the-Principal-ness);

(12c) (12a) & (12b).

But more likely whoever uses sentence (12) to make a statement in practical life wants to convey some nontrivial information like this:

(12d) There is an individual y and there is an indivdual z such that: $C*(y$, the Principal) & $C*$ (z, the Art Teacher) & y (kissing-the-Art-Teacher-ness) & z (being-kissed-by-the-Principal-ness).

Consubstantiation is an equivalence relation within the actual. It conglomerates infinites of individuals. Thus, the old Platonic idea that actuality is community receives here one of its clearest expressions.

2.5.1 Existence

On the present ontological view, existence is analyzed as self-consubstantiation. Thus, we can introduce the linguistic abbreviation:

Def. x exists = def. $C^*(x,x)$

We also have the law, or axiom:

C*.1. $C^*(x,y) \supset C^*(x,x)$

2.5.2 Consubstantiation: Equivalence Properties

Because consubstantiation is an equivalence property within the realm of existents, indeed, the most important equivalence property from the point of view of the contingency of the world, the word 'is' expresses it. Thus, besides C*.1, we have the laws:

C*.2. $C^*(x,y) \supset C^*(y,x)$

C*.3. $(C,^*(x,y) \ \& \ C^*(y,z)) \supset C^*(x,z)$

2.5.3 Consubstantiation: Actuality Properties

Consubstantiation is governed by the law of consistence, i.e., that only logically compatible sets of properties determine actualizable concrete individuals.

C*.4a. $C^*(x,x) \supset (x(F) \supset \ \sim x \, (\sim F))$

C*.4b. $C^*(x,x) \supset (x(\sim F) \supset \ \sim x \, (F))$

In order to simplify the statement of the next laws of consubstantiation, let us introduce a simple convention:

> *Convention.* An expression of the form "$a[\varphi]$" is an abbreviation of an expression having the operator 'c' prefixed to an expression of the union of the set of properties making up the individual denoted by the sign a and the unit set whose member is the property denoted by the symbol φ. For example, if a is c{Round, Square}, a[Golden] is c{Round, Square, Golden}.

I shall refer to the individual denoted by an expression of the form "$a[\varphi]$" as the *φ-protraction* of the individual denoted by a.

The communizing character of actuality is spelled out by the following laws:

The Law of Contiguity:
C*.5. $C^*(x,y) \supset (y(F) \supset C^*(x,x[F]))$

The Law of Completeness:
C*.6. $C^*(x,x) \supset (C^*(x,x[F]) \ v \ C^*(x,x[\sim F]))$

The Law of Logical Closure:
C*.7. $C^*(x,x) \supset (C^*(x,x[F_1]) \ \& \ . . . \ \& \ C^*(x,x[F_n]) \supset C^* \, (x,x[G]))$,
   provided that "$F_1 \ \& \ . . . \ \& \ F_n \supset G$" is a theorem in standard quantificational logic.

The Law of Closure C*.7 is, of course, only the most general and fundamental law of closure there is. Laws of nature are specific laws of closure. The pattern of the law is the same throughout. All we need to change is the proviso, so that a certain formula be a theorem in some system of laws of nature, instead of being a theorem in quantificational logic.

2.5.4 Consubstantiation: Uniqueness

One of the errors of Meinong was to confuse the incomplete object The Circle with the property circularity. The latter is present in every existing circle, but the former is not. The entity The Circle is $c\{Circle\}$, that is, the individual which is only a circle. Hence if The Circle exists, there exists only one consubstantiation cluster in which circularity enters. Thus we have the law:

C*.8. $C^*(x,x) \supset (\forall y) (C^*(y,y) \mathbin{\&} (\forall F) (x(F) \supset y(F)) \supset C^*(x,y))$

If x exists, then whatever existent has Meinongianly all the properties x has Meinongianly is consubstantiated with x.

2.5.5 Consubstantiation: Compossibility

Some relations require that if a relatum exists so do the others. If the Principal kisses the Art Teacher, the Art Teacher exists and is in reality kissed by the Principal. On the other hand, if the Principal looks for the art teacher of his dreams, the latter need not exist. Thus, for *some* relations, 'u' and 'y' being variables bound by the individual or implicit in 'x' and 'y_i':

S.C*.9. $C^*(x,x[Ry_1, \ldots , y_i, u, y_{i+1}, \ldots , y_n]) \supset C^*(y_i, y_i [Ry_1, \ldots , y,x,y_{i+1}, \ldots y_n])$, for every $i = 1, \ldots , n$.

This law combines Leibniz's reduction of relations to qualities with Nino Cocchiarella's e-attributes, i.e., attributes that imply existence.[5]

2.6. Objectification or Consociation

Concrete individuals are objects of thought, and as such, they are all on equal footing, whether they are impossible, merely possible, or actual. Of course, some individuals are seldom thought of, and some will probably never be thought of. Those that are thought of enter in an empirical relatedness to a mind. And this relation requires analysis. The first thing to note about the objectification of an individual is that, as Meinong remarked, to think of an individual (an object in his terminology) is to confer upon the individual some sort of existence, even if the object is nonexistent, alas! even if it is impossible. Thus, objectification is like actuality, but it is not actuality. Hence, objectification must be analyzed as involving a special empirical dyadic relation by the symbol 'C**', where the letter 'C' signals again the community of being, the double asterisk signals the secondary character of the community in question, and their postposition to 'C' signals the *a posteriori* nature of the community. Let us call this relation *co-objectification* or *consociation*. Consider the sentence:

(13) Meinong used to think of the round square.

A partial ontological analysis of what (13) expresses is revealed by:

(13a) There is an individual x such that: x(being thought of by Meinong) & C^{**} $(x, c$ {being round and square}).

Naturally, (13a) does not analyze the way in which the individual Meinong enters into what (13) expresses. In the light of our discussion of actuality, presumably another part of (13) is:

(13b) There is an individual y such that: y (thinking of the round square) & $C^*(y,$ Meinong).

I submit that (13) is simply an abbreviation of

(13c) There are individuals x and y such that: x(being thought of by Meinong) & y(thinking of c {being round and square}) & $C^*(y,$ Meinong) & $C^{**}(x,$ c{being round and square}).

A fuller understanding of (13c), or (13), requires an understanding of the role of the proper name 'Meinong'. In section II.13 we say something about the roles of proper names.

Using a mixture of ordinary language and the notation introduced above in section II.5.3, we can abbreviate (13c) as follows:

(13c') C^*(Meinong, Meinong [thinking of the round square]) & C^{**}(the round square, the round square[being thought of by Meinong]).

Consociation is like consubstantiation, not only in being a dyadic external, genuine relation, but also in being an equivalence relation within its field. Thus, we have the laws:

C^{**}.1. $C^{**}(x,y) \supset C^{**}(x,x)$

C^{**}.2. $C^{**}(x,y) \supset C^{**}(y,x)$

On the other hand, consociation is not consubstantiation. It lacks the features of consistency, closure, contiguity, and completeness.

2.7. Conflation

Besides genuine identity or selfsameness, characterized in section II.4, there is another important a priori relation. It is like identity in that it deals with the internal constituents of an individual. But it has somewhat external character, being a genuine mechanism of a pervasive and *a priori* community of being. I call it *conflation*, and represent it by the symbol '*C'. It is, like identity, an unrestricted equivalence relation:

*C.1. $*C(x,x)$

*C.2. $*C(x,y) \supset *C(y,x)$

*C.3. (*C(x,y) & *C(y,z)) ⊃ *C(x,z)).

The law of internality that governs conflation is this:

*C.4. *C(c{ . . . , F, . . . G}, c { . . . , F & G, . . . }).

Law *C.4. and *C.1 together justify the trivial claim that the man who murdered both Napoleon and Caesar is the same as the entity that alone has just the following properties: first, is a man; second, murdered Napoleon; and third, murdered Caesar.

The following law may be called the "self-identity property of conflation":

*C.5. *C(x, c{x = −})
       which is *C(x, cy {x=y}), in a notation with variables instead of operators.

Law *C.5 establishes the conflation of each individual with the individual constituted by the property of being identical with the former individual. Obviously, the two individuals are different, since they have different properties as constituents. Their community is, however, trivial and profound; that is, they conflate.

Law *C.6 is the most obvious case of the general law of the *conflation of self-congruents*:

*C.6 *C(x, c{C(x, −)}), or *C(x, cy{C(x,y)}),
       where 'C' is either '*C', 'C*' or 'C**' or '=' or, for that matter, some other congruence relation that constitutes the community of being.

This law shows part of the redundancy of the relations of ontological congruence. Another part of such redundancy is captured by the law:

*C.7 *C(x,x[being C with x]),
       where 'C' is as in *C.6.

2.8. Existence Again

The special case of law *C.6 involving the relation *C is worthy of special mention. It lies at the center of the perennial disputes about whether existence is a predicate (that is, a property) or not. In the present ontological theory this issue receives a "yes and no" answer.

On one hand, existence is a property in that it is thought of through the property Form C*. It is a compound property in that it is the special monadic case of C* operated on by Reflexivity.

On the other hand, existence is not a property in that it is the contingency of the world underlying the property C*, but lying otherwise fathomless beyond the jurisdiction of the mind as the target of thought. Part of this fathomlessness of existence is captured by Law C*.6, of the completeness of co-actuality. Yet again, existence must be somewhat docile and accessible to a mind that is not to stop chasing it filled with the despair of failure. This partial docility of existence is captured by the other laws of co-actuality, especially the laws of consistency and closure. (Are these laws imposed by the mind itself to a somewhat complacent underlying reality?)

Existence is mysterious. It is rich and complex as shown by its laws; it is what in the end the whole of what thinking and acting is about. Yet it seems redundant and empty. As Kant put it, "the real contains no more than the merely possible."[6] More specifically, for any property Fness, the existing Fer is the same as the Fer. In the example that interested Meinong, the existing round square is the same as the round square. (I am not sure that Meinong clung fast enough to this sameness in his dispute with Russell.) This sameness, i.e., the fundamental redundancy of the property of existence, is partially captured by the special laws:

*C.6 $*C(x, \ cy\{C*(x,y)\})$

*C.7 $*C(x,x[\text{being } C* \text{ with } x])$

An alternative approach, which I find tempting, is to revise the notion of individual and require that $C*$ be a member of the set of properties constituting an individual. This would make existence more patently redundant.

2.9. The Meinong-Russell Debate on Existence

It may not be amiss to make some comments on the Meinong-Russell dispute concerning the existing round square. It will be recalled that Meinong claimed both that the round square is round and that it is square. Russell argued that Meinong's principle that the Fer is F yields contradictions. Russell's first argument was that it is a contradiction to say that the round square is both round and square. His second argument was that, by that principle, the existing round square, which we know not to exist, is existing; thus, we have another contradiction. Meinong's replies were as follows: (1) the law of contradiction applies only to the real, not to the merely possible or the impossible; (2) there is a difference between saying (a) the existing round square is existing, and (b) the existing round square exists.[7]

On point (1) the present ontological theory sides with Russell on one issue: the law of contradiction must prevail throughout the realm of truth. But it concedes a point to Meinong: it recognizes impossible objects. On point (2) Russell contented himself with saying that he did not see any difference between (a) and (b). However, the present ontological theory can formulate the difference and score a point for Meinong.

The sentence

(14)   The existing round square is existing.

can naturally be taken to express a proposition about Meinongian predication, so that it must be analyzed as:

(14a) the existing round square (being self-consubstantiated).

Of course, sentence (14) can be interpreted also as expressing a different proposition, namely, the one naturally expressible by sentence (15) below.

(15)   The (existing) round square exists.

Most likely (15) expresses a proposition about actuality, so that it must be parsed as

(15a) C*(the (existing) round square, the (existing) round square).

We can drop the parenthetical word 'existing' in moving from (15) to (15a) by virtue of Law *C.7. In any case, Meinong seems to be right in insisting on a distinction between two natural interpretations of (14) and (15). If our exegesis of his claim is correct, namely, that he meant (14) as (14a) and (15) as (15a), then he is right in holding that what (14) expresses is true while what (15) expresses is false.

Meinong did not proceed to explain his claim about the difference between (14) and (15) as the difference between (14a) and (15a). He went on to speak of a modal aspect in the thinking of the proposition expressed with (15). But this is an obscure doctrine.

2.10. Ordinary Material Objects and Counting

On the ontological view being developed here, the concrete individuals our definite descriptions refer to are the same whether they exist or not. Our concrete individuals are material entities when they are actualized. Thus, the term 'the present Queen of England' refers to the individual constituted by the property present-Queen-of-England-ness, or the propositional function of being a present Queen of England. That term does *not* refer, at least not in its primary and basic meaning or use, to the individual the wife of the present Duke of Edinburgh. Nor does the term 'the present Queen of England' refer in its primary meaning or use, to the set of all those concrete individuals consubstantiated with the wife of the present Duke of Edinburgh. Of course, this set of individuals is consubstantiated with the set of individuals consubstantiated with the present Queen of England. But the term 'the present Queen of England' does *not* even refer, in its primary meaning or use, to this latter set.

Yet there are occasions on which an utterance of the term 'the present Queen of England' may perhaps refer to the set of concrete individuals consubstantiated with the present Queen of England. If it really exists, such use of the term is derivative and rests on its primary and basic use. Clearly, the use of a term '*t*' as short for an expression of the form 'the set of concrete individuals consubstantiated with *t*' can be understood only on the assumption that the use of '*t*' in the unabbreviated description is both understandable and different from its abbreviated use. At any rate, when we count "The (present) Queen of England, the King of Denmark, the Emperor of Japan, the Duchess of Tuscany, the Dictator of Nicaragua, . . . ," we seem to be counting the sets of individuals consubstantiated with the individuals being listed.

It must be emphasized that the view we are expounding does *not* identify material objects with the sets of mutually consubstantiated individuals. Sets are always abstract individuals. Thus quantification over our concrete individuals *is* quantification over material objects, and quantification over sets of mutually consubstantiated concrete individuals is *not* quantification over material objects.

An ordinary material object is at its core an aggregate of properties, or propositional functions. Indeed, we may say that an ordinary object, material or otherwise, is a *bundle* of properties, including relational ones, to underscore the fact that it is not a mere aggregate or set of properties: the set has to be operated on by the concretizing operator *c*. Furthermore, an ordinary actual individual, material or not, is itself bundled up, i.e., consubstantiated, with an infinity of other individuals.

Thus, the present ontological theory sides with the bundle-of-universals theorists, but it parts company with those theorists who equate bundles with sets. Apparently our theory also differs from standard bundle theories in its account of bundlehood. Our theory also differs from the theory put forward by Plato in the *Phaedo*[8] that an ordinary object is a set of particulars that exemplify just one property. It also differs from the view often attributed to Stout, that an ordinary object is a agglomeration of particularized properties. (I often miss the distinction between a particularized property and a simple or perfect particular that exemplifies just one property.)

2.11. Leibnizian Individuals

From the laws of contiguity and consistency governing consubstantiation it follows that each individual, say the Fer, that exists determines a set of sequences of mutually consubstantiated individuals that culminate in one infinite individual, that is, one individual that is constituted by a maximal consistent set of properties. Such infinite individuals I call *Leibnizian concrete individuals*. Naturally, they are beyond the apprehension of finite minds. To apprehend a Leibnizian individual one must be able to contemplate the set of properties *in propria persona*, with all its members in full view. As Leibniz noted, such individuals (which he called *complete concepts*, for reasons beyond our present compass) are fitting objects for a divine understanding.

Also as Leibniz noted, given that a Leibnizian individual contains in its constituting set of properties *all* its relations to all other individuals, each Leibnizian individual contains in its inside the whole history of a possible world. Any two Leibnizian individuals mirror each other. A Leibnizian individual can belong to just one possible world.

Leibnizian individuals are wholly beyond our reach. Well, yes, they are beyond our *direct* reach. But they are indirectly accessible: They are *pointable*. Since sets of properties constitute the core of concrete individuals, there are *quasi-Leibnizian individuals* available to us. These are the individuals whose core is a property of the form *having all the properties of a certain Leibnizian individual*. Such quasi-Leibnizian individuals must perforce exist and be consubstantiated with actual Leibnizian individuals. For instance, consider the individual the present Queen of England. It is consubstantiated with the married present Queen of England, with the present Queen of England that is married and has a living husband and begat children who are living such that one of them is consubstantiated with (if you wish, is the same as) the Prince of Wales, and. . . . The sequence ends with the Leibnizian individual. I cannot present it here or anywhere else. But the quasi-Leibnizian c{being the Leibnizian culmination of the sequence of mutually consubstantiated individuals that begins with the present Queen of England} is consubstantiated with the Leibnizian individual at the end of that very sequence of individuals.

Quasi-Leibnizian individuals are rather cheap and obscure. But they are our only links with Leibnizian individuals. They provide us with guidance in our formidable task of lengthening our acquaintance with chains of mutually consubstantiated finite individuals.

We said above that when we are engaged in so-called counting material objects we seem to be counting sets of mutually consubstantiated individuals. Of course, we are. But we are also counting Leibnizian, as well as quasi-Leibnizian individuals. Thus when we count "The Queen of England, the King of Nairobi, the President of Venezuela, the Dictator of Portugal, . . . " we may take each of these definite descriptions as being used in a special sense as abbreviations for descriptions referring to quasi-Leibnizian individuals. This is perfectly fine. What is crucial to keep in mind is that the abbreviational uses, again, must be derivative and presuppose the primary use of referring to an individual having exactly the property being mentioned — Meinongianly.

Many Leibnizian individuals are material individuals. Thus, if we allow that there is an absolute space and time at which consubstantiated individuals consubstantiate, we might think that our ontology contradicts the principle of the impenetrability of matter. There is, of course, no such contradiction. This principle has to be analyzed in terms of individuals. What it says is that one region R of space cannot be occupied at a given time t by material individuals that are not mutually consubstantiated. But a Leibnizian individual, the finite individuals consubstantiated with it, and the quasi-Leibnizian individuals consubstantiated with them both, can, and must, occupy the same region of space at the same time.

Existing objects belong to semi-lattices of consubstantiations, at the apex of which semi-lattices lie Leibnizian individuals.

2.12. Time and Transubstantiation

There is no space here to discuss time and space. There are at this juncture two conceptions to explore. One is to internalize time and space to each cluster of consubstantiated individuals. Another is to treat them as an absolute framework within which existence unfolds. (They themselves do not exist in any case.) In such a view the clustering of consubstantiated clusters along a spacetime vector must be viewed as another contingent genuine relation: the transubstantiation of consubstantiation clusters.

2.13. Proper Names

There are several theories about how proper names refer to individuals and how they relate to definite descriptions. Many of the existing theories are built on the non-differentiation between the pure and strict reference of a name, that is, the reference made by the speaker, and the reference made by the hearers of a name. Obviously, names do not refer to anything by themselves. It is also obvious that mere pairings of names and entities, sometimes called semantical functions over, or interpretations of, a set of names, do not bestow any referential powers on names. The references expressed by a name are references made by the thinker who uses the name (see chap. 2 for a full account).

The view that I find congenial is this. (i) Sentences containing names of individuals do not express propositions (facts, or states of affairs), but propositional functions. (ii) A name has the logical role of a free variable of quantification, indicating the positions of an element of the proposition before the mind of the speaker, which element he is leaving unexpressed. (iii) A name also has the logical role of expressing that the element left unexpressed is a quasi-Leibnizian individual. (iv) A proper name has an intended causal role, namely, that the hearer's perception of the name will cause him/her to apprehend a proposition that converges with the proposition before the mind of the speaker. By *convergence* here I mean that the proposition P before the speaker and proposition P' before a hearer, in case the intended causality of the name is successful, have as components the same logical operations, the same copula and community relations, and differ at most, by having different individuals, but these individuals are consubstantiated, or consociated, or conflated, depending on which type of proposition the speaker intends. In short, P can be obtained from P' by replacing in it some occurrences of individuals with occurrences of appropriately congruent individuals, and the appropriateness of the ontological congruence is determined by the communication intentions of the speaker.

When I think of Leibniz I am thinking of one or more finite individuals, for example, the author of the *Discours de métaphysique*, or the inventor of the standard notation for the differential calculus, or of the man who was engaged with Clarke on a correspondence about time and space. At different times I undoubtedly think of different individuals within the same set of mutually consubstantiated individuals. When I say "Leibniz was a skillful diplomat" I am not revealing to my audience the individual that is the subject of the proposition I am thinking. My words reveal the propositional function "$C*(x,x[\text{being a skillful diplomat}])$." Hopefully my audience will be composed of persons who *have* the name 'Leibniz' in their language. But to have a name in one's language is nothing more than to be part of a causal network such that one's perceiving the name causes in normal circumstances the apprehension of a proposition having as a component a certain individual. Thus, if my audience has acquired the name, that is, has undergone the proper rearrangement of capacities so as to have the mechanism to react to my utterance by having thoughts about individuals congruent with the one I am thinking of, I do succeed in communicating by means of the use of the name. My hearer will, thus, think two propositions, just as I do. He thinks, say the proposition "C*(the author of the *Monadologie*, the author of the *Monadologie* [being a skillful diplomat])". And on believing that such author existed, he also thinks of the quasi-Leibnizian proposition "C*(the Leibnizian individual on which the author of the *Monadologie* culminates, the author of the *Monadologie* [being a skillful diplomat])".

On this view, proper names do refer, namely, to whatever individual the speaker is referring to when he uses the name. Also, since variables of quantification are essentially mechanisms of reference, proper names can be said to have a primary or essential referential role. A proper name has, on the other hand, a general sense, namely, a certain Leibnizian individual on which a certain ontological chain of consubstantiations culminates. This feature of the meaning of names also adds to the enhancement of their referential role. By referring to a quasi-Leibnizian individual they point, so to speak, to the Leibnizian individual that underlies all the individuals the speaker or the hearer is referring to during the act of communication. It is crucial, however, to fasten to the idea that sentences of the form "Name φs" do not express a proposition: what they express is neither true nor false: There are no propositions having as components special individuals not fully specified by descriptions to which names refer.

2.14. Propositions

On the present view propositions are exactly what are often called states of affairs. We do not need a representationalist duality between states of affairs and before-the-mind intermediaries. We are epistemological *realists*: The contents of thinking are states of affairs. Furthermore, facts are true propositions.

2.15. Concepts

The individuals of the present view are genuine individuals, and not so-called individual concepts. We think of individuals by having them before the mind. There are no Fregean senses or Carnapian concepts mediating between individuals thought of and thinking. Thought is always direct in its reference to objects, always successful in reaching an object, always transparent in its contents, always translucid in its reference. To think of the Queen of England is to apprehend the Queen of England (that is, to have the Queen of England before one's mind) in person, whether she exists or not. This realistic thesis is the only one that fits the conception of existence, clearly contemplated by Kant, according to which existence adds nothing to the content of what is thought of.

2.16. Frege's Sense-Reference Distinction

As is well known, Frege postulated two kinds of entity, senses and referents, partly under the pressure of representationalism, but partly under the pressure of so-called nondenoting descriptions. As you recall, his view of the meaning of a definite description D assigns to D two series of entities: its referents and its senses. If D appears in a sentence S embedded in *n oratio obliqua* constructions, then D has in S as referent and as sense the nth referent and the nth sense, respectively, of the preceding series. Frege simplifies his ontology by identifying the nth referent of D with its $(n-1)$th sense, for $n > 1$. Contrariwise, on the present ontological view all these "entities" are expunged. *Inexactly put*, on the present view the referent of a definite description D is its Fregean sense. But this is inexact, since Fregean senses are necessarily non-material, and they relate to their referents by something like *instantiation*, when the descriptions they are referents of denote. On our view, if a definite description D denotes, then what it denotes both exists and is, as Kant would have it, genuinely identical with the individual D refers to in any case.

On the present view, in the sentence

(16) My friend came, but while Jones believes that my friend came Martha does not believe that Jones believes that he came

the clause 'he came' has exactly the same sense in its three occurrences. Likewise, the two occurrences of the term 'my friend' and the occurrence of the pronoun 'he' all refer to a certain individual, the finite individual $c\{$being a friend of mine, $\varphi\}$, where φ is an ordered triple of a concrete individual, a place, and a time.[9] No doubt, whoever uses (16) assertively will most likely assume that such individual is consubstantiated with an infinity of individuals. But in any case the predicative nexus between that individual and the property of having come$_\varphi$ is the same throughout (16).[10]

The present ontological view, thus, restores (or preserves) the unity of *oratio recta* and *oratio obliqua*.

2.17. Negative Existential Propositions

The present ontological view, by treating existence as an external relation to concrete particulars, provides a simple solution to the problem of negative existential propositions. On this view, a definite description does not have a different meaning in sentences attributing a shape or color to the entity it refers to, from the meaning it has in sentences denying existence to such entity. Thus, consider:

(17) The tallest man of Brasilia likes strawberries

and

(18) The tallest man of Brasilia does not exist.

In both cases the definite description 'the tallest man of brasilia' refers to one and the same entity, namely, the obvious one: the tallest man of brasilia, whether he exists or not. The two sentences are, in their most natural meanings, partially analyzable as:

(17a) C*(the tallest man of Brasilia, the tallest man of Brasilia[liking strawberries]) and

(18a) It is not the case that C*(the tallest man of Brasilia, the tallest man of Brasilia).

Thus, the present view maintains the concreteness of ordinary individuals and maintains the unity of thought and speech about existence: The negation and the affirmation of existence are both about the same entities.

2.18. Singular Generalization

On the present view individuals can be generalized upon, whether they occur in propositions about psychological states or not. Thus,

(19) Anthony believes that the oldest spy is a spy

implies the singularly generalized proposition

(20) There is [*not*, of course exists in the sense of self-consubstantiation] a concrete individual x such that Anthony believes that x is the oldest spy.

Both (19) and (20) are ambiguous sentences, depending on whether the 'is' predicating spyhood is meant in the sense of the primary Meinongian copulation, or in the sense of consubstantiation. But this ambiguity does not alter the validity of the step from (19) to (20), provided that the same copulation is meant in both cases.

Sleigh and Kaplan have both objected to a move from (19) and

(21) The oldest spy exists.

to

(22) ($\exists x$) (Anthony believes that x is a spy).

Here the quantifier '($\exists x$)' is an *existential* singular quantifier.[11]

On the present view Quine's original intuition that (19) and (21) imply (22) is reinstituted. And this implication holds, regardless of the copula expressed by the 'is' before 'a spy'. Thus the implication of (22) by (19) and (21) involves two cases:

(I) (19a) and (21) imply (22a):
   (19a) Anthony believes that the oldest spy (being a spy)
   (21)   C*(the oldest spy, the oldest spy)
   (22a) There is an individual x such that: both C*(x,x) and Anthony believes that x (being a spy).

(II) (19a) and (21) imply (22b):
   (19b) Anthony believes that C*(the oldest spy, the oldest spy [being a spy])
   (22b) There is an individual x such that: both C*(x,x) and Anthony believes that C*(x,x [being a spy]).

What then of Sleigh's and Kaplan's arguments? For one thing, their arguments seem to be couched in terms of quantifiers that have as values strange entities that seem to be a cross between Leibnizian individuals and sets of self-consubstantiated individuals. They will probably call them "ordinary individuals". But the reader of the preceding sections will undoubtedly find them mysterious. It is not easy to determine what exactly their internal constitution is. For another thing, Sleigh and Kaplan both seem to think that quantifying into psychological contexts must attribute to the subjects special powers of identification. This idea has been fostered on a wholesale basis by Hintikka, indeed, that idea is one of the more fundamental ideas underlying his systems of epistemic and doxastic logic in his *Knowledge and Belief*,[12] as well as of his subsequent writings on the topic. Hintikka has forcefully argued that the logic of quantification into knowledge contexts is precisely the logic of knowing-who. Yet it seems to me that that idea can be resisted. Naturally, that idea has an important grain of truth at its basis. This grain of truth is this: there is a crucial difference in sense between

(23)   Anthony believes that there exists someone who is a spy

and

(24)   There exists someone whom Anthony believes to be a spy.

As Quine says, (24) conveys certain "urgent information" not conveyed by (23). But what his this information? The striking difference in information between (23) and (24) is the indeterminateness of (23) and the *determinateness* of (24). Evidently, (23) attributes to Anthony a belief about no one in particular, while (24) attributes to him a belief about a *particular person*. One is tempted to make the meanings of (23) and (24) more explicit by developing them as follows:

(23a) Anthony believes that there exists someone, *whoever he may be*, who is a spy

(24a) There exists someone, *namely* . . . , whom Anthony believes to be a spy.

The phrase 'whoever he may be' in (23a) suggests that according to (23a) Anthony need not have an answer to the question "Who is that person?" By contrast, one is dragged into thinking that (24a) and (24) must, perforce, differ from (23) and (23a), by requiring that Anthony have an answer to that question. If this is so, Anthony must, then, if (24) is true, have some way of identifying the spy in question.

I think that something like this seduction has exercised its power. Yet I propose to resist it *at all costs*. I will resist it even if the ontological view I have been developing cannot ultimately be defended. Undoubtedly, (24) has something to do with identification. But it is *not* identification by Anthony, but *possible* identification by whoever asserts (24). Note that the 'namely'-rider belongs *outside* the scope of the belief operator 'Anthony believes that'. Yet, it may be adduced, the indeterminateness of (23) that contrasts with the determinateness of (24) has to do, not with the speaker, but with Anthony. This is true. But this contrast is nothing other than the following:

(A) Each proposition normally expressible with (24) implies that there is a true proposition of the form "Anthony believes that α is a spy" for some singular term replacing 'α'.

(B) No proposition normally expressible with (23) implies that that there is a proposition of the form "Anthony believes that α is a spy", for any term replacing 'α'.

2.19. Knowing-Who and Subject's Identification

In English we attribute the power of identifying an individual by means of the locution 'knows who'. Undoubtedly, this locution is connected with 'knowledge'. But it is more complicated. It does not seem to me that knowing-that belongs to the propositional level and knowing-who to the quantificational one. It seems evident that there is a quantificational level of knowing-that. There is no time to enter into an examination of the view that equates quantification-into with possession by the subject of identification powers. I simply proceed to outline what seems to me a satisfactory view of knowing-who.

Knowing-who requires a relativized conception of knowledge-that. This is a relativization to a set of identification procedures. Let us use the letter 'w' to represent sets of identification procedures, and let us write 'Knows^w', to denote knowledge-that relativized to some such set w. Then, part of the analysis of knowing-who is this:

(K.C*) X knows^w who the φer is =
　　　　There is a property ψ-ness such that ψ-ness belongs to w and X knows
　　　　that C*(the φer, the φer[ψ-ness]).

(K.C.*) represents the analysis of the most empirical, ordinary part of knowing-who. There are other parts and they can be obtained from (K.C*) by replacing 'C*' with a sign for some other ontological congruence.

2.20. Fictional Entities

Fictional entities have always been a problem. I used to think that the best treatment of them consisted in supposing that for each story there is an intentional operator, like *It is thought that*, that would be implicitly enunciated in statements about fictional characters. Thus, for example, the sentence

(25) Don Quijote enjoyed his misfortunes

is true and must, on that view, be understood as short for

(26) In *Don Quijote*, Don Quijote enjoyed his misfortunes.

By assuming an implicit *story* operator one, on one hand, can reject the implication that there exists a man who is Don Quijote, and can, on the other hand, claim that all the words in (25) have their ordinary meanings. This second point is important, because some of us do *not* want to accept that the truth of (25) with its lack of existential commitment requires that in it 'enjoying one's misfortunes' has a special meaning.

Undoubtedly, there are story operators, as in (26). But this analysis of (25) does not suffice to elucidate propositions about fictional characters. For one thing, there are fictional stories about real persons and things. For another, there are statements that refer to characters across different stories. For example:

(27) Don Juan becomes more human and sensitive in the works of German writers than he ever was in the Spanish plays about him.

Here we need an individual, who, though nonexisting, is the subject of several stories, and who remains somehow the same while undergoing all sorts of changes. We have therefore, in the case of fiction, a problem analogous to the one discussed above in sections 1.3–1.5.

The story operator approach is, however, correct in pointing out that stories are creations of minds, so that a story is simply a set of propositions contemplated by a storymaker. Thus, the connection between the propositions making up a story is nothing but the connection created by thinking, and the unity of a fictional character is, therefore, nothing but the unity of a *chain of consociations*. Once it is created by an author, a chain of consociations constituting a certain fictional character remains available for public examination on a piece of writing or in the memory of a storyteller. Thus, (25) above, which of course rests on (26) for its truth, is

(25a) C**(Don Quijote, Don Quijote [enjoying his misfortunes]).

Clearly, the original Don Quijote is just the chain of consociations created by Miguel de Cervantes, but he has gained other consociation links in different authors or critics. Don Quijote himself, like any other outstanding fictional hero, developed throughout *Don Quijote*: among other things, he became more tolerant and more appreciative of other dimensions of human nature, besides those of being a foe, being a friend, and being an object of injury or protection. This development cannot, naturally, be transubstantiation, but it is something analogous. We may call it *transconsociation*. This is the phenomenon described in (27) above.

It is important to fasten to the fact that psychological attitudes and acts, whether massive enough to constitute the creation of a story or not, involve consociation (and transconsociation), and not consubstantiation (or transubstantiation). Consider (19) and (21) above again:

(19) Tom believes that the oldest spy is a spy;

(21) The oldest spy exists.

Consider the property of being such that Tom believes that he is a spy, i.e., the property *Tom believes that* u *is a spy*. Undoubtedly this property is possessed by the oldest spy. But this possession is, obviously not Meinongian predication. But it is not consubstantiation either: it is consociation. Thus, (19) and (21) fail to imply, together or separately, that C*(the oldest spy, the oldest spy [Tom believes that u is a spy]). They imply together, and (19) implies by itself, that

(28) C**(the oldest spy, the oldest spy [Tom believes that u is a spy]).

Remember that consociation is not governed by the laws of closure or consistency or transitivity.

3. Properties: A Metaphysical Glimpse

We have assumed that properties are the building blocks of the world and of the framework of possible and impossible objects sustaining it. Aside from nominalistically inclined philosophers, that central assumption has been challenged by other philosopers also belonging to the abstractist tradition. They think that ordinary properties are too concrete, that the properties we find in the world are in fact complexes of some more basic contents of the world. They may even add the Kantianesque thesis that the properties we find are products of the interaction of the mind and Reality, and that other Minds would find, or actually find, analyses for our properties. Others hold that there are no absolute atoms, so that whatever "metaphysical atoms" a creature may find, at his level of penetration, another creature can find them to be complex.

We cannot discuss such claims here. (We are not doing metaphysics here, only phenomenological ontology.) But we can remark that the structure of the world developed in Part II is compatible with the claim that the properties assumed there are complexes of metaphysical micro-entities. Indeed, the same type of analysis could be applied to properties so that they turn out to be special sets of proto-properties, and the same for these. Likewise, our consubstantiation lattices and consociation chains may indeed form more complex entities as well. Thus, the ontological scheme of section 2 of this chapter is compatible with the metaphysical claim that, given the type of minds we have, we zero in at a certain level of metaphysical complexity in a hierarchy of being that is infinite in every direction.

We also leave it open whether the ontological structure development above is merely a picture, a *façon d' imaginer*, which is at most a barren epiphenomenal by-product in the midst of the interaction of humans' exercises of their complex capacities to throw noises to one another. This is a nominalistic metaphysics liberal enough to recognize the fact of consciousness.

The system of Part II interweaves the insights of the great historical figures mentioned in Part I or in Part II. Naturally, the fundamental assumption of the system, namely, its Platonism, has been steadily challenged throughout the history of philosophy by Nominalists and Materialists (or Physicalists). We cannot engage here in an attack of Nominalism. This is a perennial issue, and perhaps it is not amenable to a total solution. Perhaps we are condemned to see the two types of metaphysical nature always fighting with each other in an avoidable historical dialectic through which clarifications and developments of the two types of view must take place. Perhaps in this case philosophical progress consists in seeing more cleary and more of each of the two main conceptions of the world.

4. Conclusion

The ontological scheme unfolded in section 2 of this chapter conforms to the data deployed in section 1. It solves the puzzles discussed there as well as the problems mentioned in section 2 itself. The reader can assure himself that this is so. [Later on concrete individuals were called *individual guises*.]

Appendix

Raul Orayen[13] has objected to my account of our ordinary counting of objects in *Thinking and the Structure of the World*. Typically we do not count individual guises as such. Thus I proposed to construe the use of singular terms in counting as denoting either Leibnizian guises or consubstantiational systems. Neither proposal is satisfactory. But the situation is somewhat more complex.

Orayen seems to take it for granted that an operation of counting always delivers a number, which from outside, we may call the *consubstantiational maximum* of the situation. If this is so, then there is slight disagreement between us. There are occasions in which we count individual guises, which are consubstantiated (that is, exist), but in no way do we pursue a consubstantiational maximum. In fact, at the maiden presentation of *Thinking and the Structure of the World*,[14] Jonathan Cohen proposed an example of the following sort:

> A janitor reports that he has seen four persons walk up and down the stairs, but also that he is not sure how many of them are exactly the *same* person, thus, perhaps—he says—just three different persons have walked up and down the stairs. [My italics.]

In Cohen's example the number 4 is the number of very partial systems of guises, certainly not maximal, that the janitor has counted. The sense of 'same' is, of course, that of consubstantiational sameness.

The janitor's last words contain the key to the solution of the counting problem. He hypothesizes the maximal number of consubstantiational systems most likely to be involved in the walkings of that day. The janitor counts individual guises, in any case, but he counts them in accordance with certain constraints. In particular, the janitor counts objects, through counting guises representing them such that: (i) the counted guises belong to a type of a special interest, and (ii) these guises are distinct, diverse, with respect to some criterion appropriate to the context of speech or thought.

Typically in the normal contexts of daily life we are interested in counting individual guises that are diverse in their not being consubstantiated. In such cases the excellent problem posed by Orayen is this:

(O) Can we formulate a question whose answer is a number obtained by means of a counting procedure that, in Orayen's words, from an "external point of view of Guise Theory," is a procedure for counting consubstantiational systems, *one by one* — even though in Guise Theory such systems are not amenable to singular reference?

Now, within the Guise Theory of *Thinking and the Structure of the World* the answer I should have given to the basic counting problem is the following question schema:

(Q*) What is , with respect to the property Fness, the cardinality of a class A of individual guises such that:
  (i) $\forall g$: if g is in A, then $C^*(g, g[\text{Fness}])$;
  (ii) $\forall g'$, g'': if g' & g'' are both in A,
         then $-C^*(g', g'')$;
  (iii) $\forall g'$: if $-(g'$ is in A) & $C^*(g', g'[\text{Fness}]$,
         then $\exists g(g$ is in A & $C^*(g', g))$?

Patently, the criterion of diversity relevant to the counting situation is encapsulated jointly in the class A of guises and in the property Fness.

In *Thinking and the Structure of the World* there is a partially reductionist talk about ordinary massive objects to talk about individual guises. As in (Q*) above, there is no expression that refers to such objects in a unified way, but only expressions referring to sets of guises. On the other hand, in *Identity and Sameness*[15] quantifiers ranging over such objects are allowed. Because of the infinity of such objects no singular reference to them is allowed. That is, those quantifiers cannot be instantiated into genuine individual constants. Let us use the letters 'm', and 'n', with subscripts if necessary, as variables of quantification for such massive objects, that is, infinite consubstantiational systems of individual guises. We can introduce a categorial predicate, say, M, to represent the whole domain of such quantification. Then Orayen's problem (O) allows in the account of *Identity and Sameness* of a succinct solution, to wit:

(Q**) How many M's (of type G) are F?

Now, we count also nonexisting guises, and sets of such guises related by other sameness relations, for example, conflation, consociation, and even transconsociation. Indeed, we even count mixed sets of conglomerates of existing with conglomerates of nonexisting guises. For instance, we may plan to build, say, twenty houses and succeed in building only twelve. An example proposed by Michael McKinsey runs as follows. An art and history teacher may expound on the adventures of some three Arthurs, two of which are real and one mythical.[16] In those cases we can introduce counting questions in either the style of (Q*) or the style of (Q**). The studious reader may want to experiment by himself.

Notes

1. W. V. O. Quine, "The Problem of Interpreting Modal Logic," *The Journal of Symbolic Logic* 12 (1947): 43–48.

2. W. V. O. Quine, *From a Logical Point of View* (New York: Harper & Row, 1963), p. 153.

3. P. T. Geach, "Intentional Identity," *The Journal of Philosophy* 64 (1967):627–32.

4. W. V. O. Quine, "Variables Explained Away," *Selected Logic Papers* (New York: Random House, 1966).

5. Nino Cocchiarella, "Some Remarks on Second-Order Logic with Existence Attributes," *Noûs* 2 (1968): 165–75.

6. I. Kant, *Critique of Pure Reason*, A599.

7. For a summary of the dispute and bibliographical references see R. Chisholm, "Editor's Introduction," *Realism and the Background of Phenomenology* (Glencoe, Ill.: The Free Press, 1960), p. 9ff.

8. See H.-N. Castañeda, "Plato's *Phaedo* Theory of Relations," *Journal of Philosophical Logic* 1 (1972): 467–80.

9. For a discussion of indexical reference that can be accommodated to the present ontological view see H.-N. Castañeda, "Indicators and Quasi-indicators," *American Philosophical Quarterly* 4 (1967): 85–100 [chap. 12 above]; "On the Phenomeno-logic of the I," *Proceedings XIVth International Congress of Philosophy* (Vienna: Herder, 1968), vol. 3: 260–66; and "On the Logic of Attributions of Self-knowledge to Others," *The Journal of Philosophy* 65 (1968): 439–56.

10. For a clear awareness of the problem of the copula in *oratio obliqua* once one introduces so-called individual concepts as the referents of definite descriptions in *oratio obliqua*, see Wilfried Sellars, "Some Problems about Belief," in D. Davidson and J. Hintikka (eds.), *Words and Objections: Essays on the Work of W. V. O.Quine* (Dordrecht: D. Reidel, 1969), p. 193.

11. See Robert C. Sleigh, "On Quantifying into Epistemic Contexts," *Noûs* 1 (1967): 28; and David Kaplan, "Quantifying In," in D. Davidson and J. Hintikka (eds.), *Words and Objections* (Dordrecht: D. Reidel, 1969), p. 220. See also W. V. O. Quine, "Reply to Sellars," ibid., pp. 337ff, and Quine, "Reply to Kaplan," ibid., pp. 341ff. In these replies Quine accepts the invalidity claim made by Sleigh and Kaplan.

12. J. Hintikka, *Knowledge and Belief* (Ithaca, N.Y.: Cornell University Press, 1962).

13. This is the only criticism Raul Orayen addresses to Guise Theory in his excellent paper "Objetos no existentes," which he presented at the Third International Philosophical Colloquium of the National Autonomous Univeristy of Mexico, August 24, 1982.

14. At the 1972 Autumnal Congress of Philosophy of the University of Victoria.

15. Hector-Neri Castañeda, "Identity and Sameness," *Philosophia* 5 (1975): 121–50.

16. Cited in Hector-Neri Castañeda, "Reply to Tyler Burge: Reference, Existence, and Fiction," in James E. Tomberlin (ed.), *Agent, Language, and the Structure of the World* (Indianapolis: Hackett, 1983). For more discussion on our experiences that involve counting of and quantification over mixed sets of different structures of individual guises, see Hector-Neri Castañeda, "Objects, Existence, and Reference: A Prolegomenon to Guise Theory," *Grazer Philosophische Studien* 25/26 (1985/86): 3–59.

14

Method, Individuals,
and Guise Theory

1. Summary of Plantinga's Criticism of Guise Theory

In his "Guise Theory,"[1] cited as *GT*, Plantinga raises grave issues about philosophical method and the nature of theories. He also deals deeply with crucial
problems about the nature of the objects we can think of. The context of his illuminating discussion is Guise Theory. The essay is a powerful and brilliant pair
of studies: one, an excellent summary exposition of Guise Theory (I have only
one caveat); the other, a penetrating and instructive critique of this theory. The
critique is tough, detailed, and purportedly devastating. Succinctly put, Guise
Theory "is fundamentally mistaken" (*GT*, p. 43). He argues for this by developing
intricate subarguments for each of the following theses:

(I) Guise Theory is erected on a grave methodological error concerning the
data/theory contrast;

(II) There is no evidence for Guise Theory;

(III) Guise Theory is too proliferative of entities;

(IV) Guise Theory suffers from a vicious infinite regress;

(V) Guise Theory needs additional sameness copular relations;
and

(VI) Guise Theory presupposes Aristotelian predication.

Obviously, (I)–(VI) constitute a most impressive indictment of Guise Theory,
asking for capital punishment. The verdict on each count is, however, "Not
guilty." Yet the trial is a blessing: It brings forth the vitality of Guise Theory and
even enriches it.

Naturally, not all the charges are equally injurious. For instance, (V) simply
urges further development of Guise Theory, and in no way can it be predicted

that the required developments will cause any damage to the theory. Concerning objection (III), the proliferation of entities is not bad if it does not postulate entities lacking explanatory functions. To ascertain whether this is so or not, we must go outside the theory and see how it fares with experience. At this juncture Plantinga's objections (I) and (II) intrude.

To objection (II) the only decent response is to deploy some relevant data. Here we are in the fortunate but naughty position of having insufficient space to discuss all the evidence for Guise Theory. But some data suffice. In response to objection (I), we clarify some aspects of philosophical theorizing. Because Plantinga does not appreciate fully the depth of my commitment to philosophical pluralism, he distorts my view of the contrast, and the connections, between data and theory.

Plantinga's objection (IV) is, on the surface, the most noxious of them all. The appropriate punishment for a theory abetting a vicious infinite regress is destruction. But Plantinga's claim that Guise Theory feeds an infinite regress within its bosom is a trivial consequence of the particular way in which he argues for objection (III). This includes the lemma that guises generate micro-guises, and these generate their own sub-guises, and so on. Hence, Plantinga's arguments for (III) is the main testimony – the *pièce de résistance* – in his case against Guise Theory. Therefore, we must and *do* examine it very carefully. The examination establishes that Plantinga's argument imports two foreign theses into Guise Theory, theses the rejection of which is an integral component of Guise Theory. The testimony provided by that argument is, therefore, inadmissible in the court trying Guise Theory.

Plantinga's claim (VI), that Guise Theory presupposes Aristotelian predication, is utterly fascinating. I would like to know what Aristotelian predication really is. In some texts Plantinga seems to suggest that Aristotelian predication involves substrates; but Guise Theory shuns substrates. In other passages he seems to take Aristotelian predication as predication not reducible to class membership. In this sense, the predication of Guise Theory is Aristotelian at least five times over.

Let us proceed now to the pleasurable details.

2. Methodology: Data versus Theories: Theoretical Pluralism

Plantinga takes me to task for my view of how theories relate to data. He claims the following:

(i) "But this contrast between data and theory is problematic and unclear in extreme." [*GT*, p. 57.]

(ii) "Castañeda sometimes speaks as if the distinction between theory and data is *absolute*." (P. 57, Plantinga's italics.) "What we have, rather than a distinction between data and non-data is, relative to a given person *S* and a given problem, a continuum ranging from propositions that *S* is very strongly inclined to accept to those he has at best a weak inclination to accept." [*GT*, p. 59.]

Here, in spite of Plantinga's intimation to the contrary, we are in total agreement. Indeed, I have added another dimension of relativity to the contrast between data and theory: that it is, besides, relative to research goals. The significance of this has to do both with the inherent obscurity of the data/theory contrast and, because of that, with philosophical pluralism. Let us take a glimpse into these most important methodological issues.

Plantinga discusses my "Philosophical Method and the Theory of Predication and Identity" (1978, to be cited as *Method*). In it I separated the three singular statements below as data:

(1)   Before the pestilence Oedipus believed that the previous King of Thebes was dead;

(2)   It is not the case that: before the pestilence Oedipus believed that Antigone's paternal grandfather was dead;

(3)   Antigone's paternal grandfather was the *same* as the previous King of Thebes.

I contrasted (1)–(3) with the following theoretical generalizations:

(ID)   If x is genuinely or strictly identical with y, then whatever is true of x is true of y, and vice versa.

(T)   The matrix 'Before the pestilence, Oedipus believed that —— was dead' expresses something true of a person referred to by a term of the form 'the such and such' just in case the sentence obtained from that matrix by filling in the blank with the term in question is true (or expresses a truth).

(S)   The sameness of (3) is genuine or strict, though contingent identity. [*Method*, p. 191.]

I considered two factors for the distinction: the singularity of (1)–(3) vs. the generality of (ID)–(S), and the wide acceptance of (1)–(3) as obvious facts. But I was not intent in claiming that (1)–(3) were absolutely datanic (to use Plantinga's word) whereas (ID)–(S) were absolutely theoretical. The data/theory distinction is relative to the purpose of research. I wrote:

> Thus, in principle we have *three* initial types of theory that can be, and *must* be, developed. . . . Furthermore, the theories must be *developed*. It is utterly irresponsible, philosophicaly speaking, simply to say, for instance, that the principle of identity (ID) does not apply to belief sentences. The assertion cannot be taken seriously except as a statement of the initial direction in which a theory solving the paradox of reference is to be channeled. [*Method*, pp. 191–92; the italics in 'three' are new.]

Contrary to Plantinga's contention, for me neither has (T) been an absolute datum; nor has it been more secure than (ID) or (S). Nor have I ever held that (ID) and (T) are data, whereas (S) is just a suspicious assumption. As I said then, *ALL three* propositions are in exactly the self-same boat; both as data and as initial theoretical steps. This methodological non-dogmatic, democratic attitude toward what to count as data has no limit. That is why each type of theory *MUST* be developed fully – not merely to the simple level of rejecting one or another generalization. I went on:

> The greatest philosophical illumination appears when different comparable theories are contrasted. . . . Each theory contains a large amount of conventions . . . reality is not fully categorized *per se*, independently of our conceptual scheme. Thus, experiencing the world through different theories . . . can be the only procedure for discarding the local features of each of the categorizations, and for approaching, in the experience of their contrasts, an experience that is as neutral with respect to our conventions or stipulations as this is feasible: we may perhaps reach by that method an ultimate set of *structural invariances*. . . . [Ibid., p. 192.]

In the work cited, I gave the name *dia-philosophy* to the study of such structural invariances or partial isomorphisms between most comprehensive theories. (See *On Philosophical Method*, referred to as *OPM*, for a fuller discussion of dia-philosophy.)

Plantinga castigates me for taking (T) and (ID) as absolute points of departure for Guise Theory. This is not justified on at least three counts. *First*, I do not take them in that paper as data, on equal footing with the three singular propositions (1)–(3). *Second*, I treat democratically each of the three general principles as a candidate for rejection for the development of a theory. *Third*, each of the theories that such rejection originates must be developed. Thus, I have no objection at all to Plantinga's alternative theory centered on Aristotelian predication. Indeed, I welcome it because in dia-philosophical exercises it may help reveal some structural invariances.

Plantinga is completely correct in claiming that the contrast between data and theory cannot be made simply in terms of the generality of (ID)–(S) and the particularity of (1)–(3). It is certainly open to a philosopher to start building another theory of semantics, reference and objects by taking only some of the statements (1)–(3) as data. The short of it is that there is no criterion for absolute data. The answer to the question about what we should take as data is simply this: take alternatively different sets of statements as data and build as *many* comprehensive theories as you can. (See *OPM*, pp. 55–56.) The problem is, of course, that comprehensive theories are hard to build, and few philosophers can build several of them. We have to specialize and cooperate. We need other philosophers' theories to contrast with ours, hoping that the experience of the contrast be an illuminating dia-philosophical experience. Now:

> Philosophers tend, naturally, to work on fashionable problems and within fashionable points of view. This is reasonable because the fashions have the virtue of mobilizing a large amount of needed cooperation. [*Method*, p. 193.]

We can all become wise by studying the products of the fashions of our time. But if one is to enjoy the complementary wisdom of a nonfashionable vision, one has to build up that view by oneself. This is the ultimate reason why I have taken (1)–(3) as empirical data and (ID) and (T) as the initial general tenets on which to erect for myself one nonfashionable view, namely, Guise Theory. It is non-fashionable because it rejects (S).

Now, Plantinga and I disagree about the connection between theory and data. For theoretical pluralism, the connection from the data to theory is not deductive. Plantinga, on the other hand, apparently believes that the data for Guise Theory should imply that the connection is deductive. Just reflect on this tantalizing criticism:

> But suppose Castañeda is right; suppose that we *can't* think of an explana-
> tion of the truth of (10) that doesn't involve nonexistent objects. [A] It
> wouldn't *follow* that we ought to accept an explanation that *did* involve such
> objects. Couldn't we say instead that we don't know just how to construe
> (10)? [B] But the fact is that there are plenty of ways of explaining the truth
> of (10). [*GT*, p. 64; the italics in 'follow' and the labels are mine – H-N.C.]

According to Planginga's [A], certain phenomena I consider as data for Guise Theory are ruled out because they do not imply the thesis of Guise Theory they suggest. I most definitely disagree with this highly-demanding criterion for theory support. It leads to a strong version of *epistemological foundationalism*, which does not appeal to some of us.[2]

Yet Plantinga goes on to assert [B]. This is bewildering. He intimates that Guise Theory is in bad shape because there are alternative accounts. But if they are alternative accounts, *none* of them is implied by the data. Why should they, or any one of them – say, Plantinga's preferred view – be in any better shape than Guise Theory? As far as I can see, we must choose either scepticism about *all* theories, or some strategy for allowing theories not related to their data by logical implication. My own liberal, pluralistic view is that *all* the alternative accounts are in exactly the same position. That is why we need *more, much more* data to elicit preferences among the alternatives, and that is why all the alternatives viable at a certain stage should be developed into comprehensive theories.

In brief, the fact that certain data allow two or more different theories to illuminte them is *never* a proof that those data are not evidence for *each* of the theories in question.

Because the connection between data and theory is not deductive, data do not relate individually to a theory. Data are not islands unto themselves: they belong within *Gestalten*. Consequently, their evidential value grows both with their size and with their patterns. Clearly, a refutational policy that isolates each datum from the others can be utterly misleading in the assessment of a theory. (Just consider the case of the critic who objects to a thesis Q claiming that no adequate evidence for Q has been given; each reason given fails to entail Q: one reason being P, another being "If P, then Q.")

3. Evidence for Guise Theory

I assume that from here on we are liberated from the methodology that requires theories to be deductive consequences of their data. Thus, we can appreciate both the significance of the support each datum in its own peculiar way gives to Guise Theory, and the special power of the different patterns in which the data combine to support it.

As Plantinga himself notes, the best data for a theory are the different puzzles and paradoxes to which it provides a solution. The way in which Guise Theory provides a solution to the Paradox of Reference is the primary topic in the several papers in Part I and in my responses to them in Tomberlin 1. Other puzzles and paradoxes are discussed in these studies. Thus, the evidence for Guise Theory is pretty strong. (Of course, we hold fast to the fact that data provide evidence, i.e., support, for different and even incompatible theories.) A good idea of the comprehensiveness and the power of Guise Theory can be gleaned by a summary of the wide range of puzzles and paradoxes it unifies and illuminates. Here is an incomplete chart of such data:

1. *Puzzles about existence*

   (a) Moore's puzzle about existing tigers;
   (b) Moore's puzzle about the meaninglessness of the existence of tigers;
   (c) Kant's puzzle about existence adding nothing to the content of an object;
   (d) Kant's puzzle about the identity of what is thought of and what exists in the case of veridical thought.
   (e) The puzzle of the denials of existence.

2. *Puzzles about thinking*

   (a) Imperviousness of thinking to existence;
   (b) The Paradox of Reference;
   (c) Geach's puzzle about cross-reference through several persons's beliefs;
   (d) The puzzle about cross-references in one person's propositional and practical attitudes;
   (e) The impact of imaginary beings in daily life;
   (f) The thinkability of contradictions.

3. *Puzzles about properties and propositions*

   (a) The contrast between neutral and perspectival properties;
   (b) Ephemeral propositions and indexical reference;
   (c) Facts and their manifestations to mind;

4. *Puzzles about predication and property-having*

   (a) Contrast between predication of the form 'is F' and reference of the form 'The F thing';
   (b) Difference between predication and quantification;
   (c) Contrast between predication of a physical property and predication of a psychological one;

(d) The tension between the necessity of "The FG thing is F" and its falsity when the FG thing does not exist;

(e) The possession of properties by mythical and fictional heroes.

5. *Puzzles about sameness*

   (a) Contrast between necessary and contingent identity;

   (b) Contrast between identity and material composition;

   (c) Conflict between identity and theoretical sameness;

   (d) The Paradox of Analysis;

   (e) The Puzzle about the subject of change;

   (f) Difference between identity and having properties.

6. *Puzzles about individuals*

   (a) The problem of the nature of individuation;

   (b) The problem of the ground of differentiation;

   (c) Contrast between objects and objects *qua* such and such or objects under descriptions;

   (d) Objects and demonstrative reference;

   (e) Objects and attributions of reference;

   (f) Objects and their perceptual presentations;

   (g) Objects and their doxastic presentations;

   (h) Objects and the communication of reference.

7. *Ontological puzzles about perception*

   (a) Discrepancies between physical and perceptual spaces;

   (b) Seeing double;

   (c) Illusions;

   (d) The finitude and incompleteness of what is perceived;

   (e) The generality of what is perceived, e.g., color without particular shade, numerosity without a particular number;

   (f) Contrast between conceptual and perceptual;

   (g) Perceptual discrimination by attending to what is perceived.

8. *Fiction in experience*

   (a) The culturization of fiction;

   (b) Historical truths and real objects in fiction;

   (c) Ideal entities in science;

   (d) Unactualized objects that have been carefully planned;

   (e) (See 2.e).

9. *Ontological puzzles about practical thinking*

   (a) The first-person character of intentions and volitions;

   (b) The sameness between the agent's self and his body;

   (c) The essential third-person demonstrative character of intentional action;

   (d) (See 1.e).

10. The unity and homogeneity of all experiences
   (a) The same concepts are required for waking experience, scientific experimentation, and dreams;
   (b) The same individuals can be perceived, imagined, hallucinated about, dreamt, or thought of.

4. Plantinga's Wedge between Identity and True-of

Plantinga claims that there is no evidence for the following central tenet of Guise Theory:

(PP.GT) *Prism Principle of Guise Theory*: An ordinary object is a system of (infinitely) many guises.

And he is certainly right in his favorite sense of 'evidence' that requires that the evidence or data imply (PP.GT). But we operate under a weaker concept of evidence.

Plantinga develops, however, a direct attack upon the Guise Theorist's right to use (T) and its generalization (T*) below as an inceptive tenet in his argument for (PP.GT):

(T*) "F(−)" is an English sentence matrix with a blank *for a referring term*; "F(a)" is the result obtained by putting a in the blank. We say that what "F(a)" expresses is true of the individual denoted by a if "F(a)" expresses a truth. [*Method*, p. 197; the italics are new.]

N.B. (T*) is a generalization of (T), discussed above. In both the quotation marks function as Quine's quasi-corners.

Plantinga's strategy against (T*) is to connect (T*) with (ID) and draw a serious hiatus between (ID), as a linguistic principle of substitution, and the principle of identity:

(II) For any objects x and y and any property P,
      if x is identical with y
      then x has P if y has P.

His tactic is to deploy some proposed counter-examples that conform to (II) but not to (ID), to wit:

(19) '——' contains the letter 'm';

(20) It is necessarily false that there is a spy in North Dakota shorter than ——

(21) The mayor of Minot believes that —— is meaner than any other man in North Dakota;

(22) '——' contains just four letters.

Examples (19) and (22) are cute, but strange. (T*) is a principle about sentence matrices of English, with genuine semantic blanks, open for their appropriate fillers, namely, singular referring terms. Now, on one reading of (19) and (22) they contain no blanks. The standard philosophical convention is this: single quotes construct a name of the expression a token of which they enclose. This is the convention Plantinga himself uses in (19) to provide a name of the letter 'm'. This name has a physical design part of which is the design of the letter 'm', but the letter, understood semantically, does not occur. As Quine has remarked, 'cattle' does not include the word 'cat', but only a physical mark of similar geometric design.

Thus, sentences (19) and (22) express falsehoods. Neither is a sentential matrix with a genuine semantic blank. Their common grammatical subject is the name '——', which has neither an 'm' nor four letters.

Now, the above convention on quotation marks, together with that governing Quine's corners, which preserve the semantic blanks, open for singular referring expressions, is the one present in (T) and (T*).

I conclude, therefore, that Plantinga's argument (pp. 61–62), which depends so heavily and exclusively on example (22) does not touch (T*), and, *a fortiori*, casts no doubt on the evidence for Guise Theory.

What about (20) and (21)? They are also innocuous. However, they raise valuable methodological issues. That is why I am very much surprised that Plantinga did not discuss them at all, preferring to rest his case against (T*) on example (22).

Plantinga seems to be assuming a principle like this:

(NP.Int) A [so-called] intensional context "F(−)" expresses no property of the object denoted by the term a even if the resulting sentence "F(a)" expresses a truth.

Clearly, the matrices (20) and (21) are typical examples of intensional contexts. Here I will confine my discussion to (21). Consider a referring term, e.g., 'Ken Wolterstorf's oldest brother'. Let us suppose that it is the name of the shortest spy in North Dakota, about whom the Mayor of Minot has the requisite belief, so that (21.A) below is true:

(21.A) The mayor of Minot believes that Ken Wolterstorf's oldest brother is meaner than any other man in North Dakota.

Plantinga allows (*GT*, p. 59) that we take (T*) as a definition of *true of*. Hence, we can move from (21.A) to:

(21.B) It is *true of* Ken Wolterstorf's oldest brother that the mayor of Minot believes that he is meaner than any other man in North Dakota.

But he won't allow that (21.C) expresses a truth:

(21.C) Ken Wolterstorf's oldest brother has *the property* that the mayor of Minot believes that he is meaner than any other man in North Dakota.

What hinges on this refusal and on the insistence on contrasting (21.B) with (21.C) in truth-value? It is not clear by itself; it all depends on one's *theory of properties*. Such a theory must connect with a theory of predication (that is, what it is to have a property) with a theory of individuation, and with a theory as to how psychological states in one person P that are allegedly about an object O connect with O, since O gains no property by P having those states toward it. Once (NP.Int) creates a hiatus between (ID) and (II), heavy theorizing is required to connect what we think about with ourselves and with our thinking. Naturally, because of my dia-philosophical pluralism, I favor and urge such a complex theorizing.

On the other hand, it is easy and natural to suppose that when P believes that O is beautiful or cheap, O gains a property, a relational property, to P. That belief grounds actions on P's part toward O, rather than to another entirely different object O'. It seems as if there has to be some natural connection, a relation between O and P, to explain why. On the natural assumption, this type of explanation gets a nice easy start. The natural assumption provides, furthermore, an excellent *general principle* which by being so encompassing can aid in our search for understanding the large structures of the world and experience. The natural assumption makes (ID) an important special case of (II). It is a *special* case given that (ID) applies to sentences in English, and presumably there are infinitely many properties that are not expressible in English. (For an argument for this see *Thinking and Doing*, p. 37.) It is an *important* case because it captures the maximal range of identification that can be expressed in English. By including both so-called extensional and so-called intensional properties, (ID) provides the *strictest* condition for identity — strict identity — that we can specify in English for all expressible properties taken singly. By covering both sorts of properties the principle provides a fundamental structural bridge between the mental and the physical, and between minds.

These are some advantages to construing (ID) under the wings of (II), as in Guise Theory. But, once again, it is a *theoretical* option whether, or not, one assumes (NP.Int), that so-called intensional contexts do not express properties. Note, dia-philosophically, how the views contrast. Whereas a theory adopting (NP.Int) complicates the connection between thinking or thinker and object thought of, it expects to maintain a single world of ordinary objects to which we can make singular, not only general, references. On the other hand, Guise Theory maintains a simple connection between contents of thought and the objects in the world, but it does — I own — complicate the world. It would be illuminating to compare in full detail the shifts in complexity and simplicity and their varying patterns. Shouldn't we in the end reach two empirically equivalent world views with wonderfully instructive isomorphisms?

5. Things That Do Not Exist

Another central tenet of Guise Theory is this:

(P.GS) *Principle of Guise Subsistence*: There are guises that do not exist—but all subsist in, belong to, the domain of thinkables.

Again, Plantinga's attack on (P.GS) is partly grounded on his general criticism of the distinction between data and theory. This comes out sharply in his first round of criticism of my use of the following datum:

(10) Benjamin believes that there is a fountain of life and he hopes to drink from it.

I commented as follows:

> The quantifier 'there is (a fountain of life)' has to be the dominant operator so that it can bind references to the same entity both within the scope of 'believes' and within the scope of 'hopes'. So we seem committed to introducing nonexisting objects once again as the values of the variables of quantification. ["Thinking and the Structure of the World," p. 8; p. 238 above.]

Plantinga charges as follows:

> But there is something objectionable to this procedure. I suggested earlier that it's not always obvious what's *data*; but I should have thought that the truth of
>
> (26) there are no things that don't exist
>
> has every bit as strong a claim to datanic status as does the truth of Castañeda's (10). [*GT*, p. 63.]

Now, the following points should be clear from the preceding discussion of method and the connections between data and theory:

(i) Sentences like (10) are part and parcel of living ordinary language. Many of them are proffered with the patent intention to assert something true, and many hearers regard such acts as successfully expressing truth. Such sentences and their use provide inexcludable data. Another true example that must be considered is this:

(11) There are two papers on Frege's view on numbers that I planned and made extensive notes for, but will never be written—they will never exist.

(ii) The grammar of sentences (10) and (11) is clear, and so are their meanings.

(iii) The data do not imply any theory.

(iv) Of course, Plantinga is *completely right* in bringing his sentence (26) as part of the data. By my lights it is just as "datanic" as (10) and (11) are.

(v) Sentence (26) must be subjected to exegesis, just as much as sentences (10) and (11).

(vi) If there is a conflict between data (10)–(11) and datum (26), then different alternative types of theory are at least initially feasible. *I* cannot, nor do I wish to, claim that (10) and (11) preclude the development of any theory that Plantinga may have in mind. I believe that Plantinga agrees with this. But I also hold, but I suspect without Plantinga's comfortable support, that likewise, the mere existence of sentence (26) expressing in some of its uses an important truth does not *ipso facto* invalidate any theory built on (10).

(vii) Furthermore, if there is a conflict between (10)–(11) and (26), then the two types of theory *must* be erected—for dia-philosophical illumination.

(viii) I do take seriously both (26) and (11) as data. Their conflict is itself an important datum. Obviously, since both (11) and (26) express patent truths, either 'exist' or 'there are' has a different domain in (11) from the one it has in (26).

(ix) The preceding resolution of the conflict is an elementary satisfying piece of wisdom. It leads to Guise Theory.

In sum, first, not only has Plantinga not blunted the force of datum (10), but second, he correctly and helpfully insists that datum (26) must also be taken into account. Here is one of those cases in which the evidence of a complex of data is much greater than the mere sum of the evidence of each of the data.

6. Plantinga's Argument for the Alleged Fission of Guises

Plantinga's claim that a vicious infinite regress infects Guise Theory hinges on the following contention:

The same reasoning will drive us to suppose that for guises of any level m there are guises of level $m + 1$; and guises of level m will be semi-lattices composed of guises of level $m + 1$. [*GT*, p. 66.]

Here is Plantinga's argument in full for this contention:

[A] . . . on Guise Theory, as we have seen, an ordinary individual such as *my willow tree* [my italics—H-N.C.] fractionates into a vast horde of simpler entities. . . .

[B] [1] Thomas, for example, believes that c{omniscience, omnipotence, being wholly good} contains omnipotence in its core; [2] he doesn't believe that Anselm's favorite guise *is* c{omniscience, omnipotence, being wholly good}, . . . [3] Anselm's favorite guise *is* c{omniscience, omnipotence, being wholly good}.

[4] There is thus a triadic sieve that distinguishes c{omnipotence, omniscience, being wholly good} from Anselm's favorite guise: following Castañeda we shall have to suppose that the first isn't strictly identical with the second.

[C] And of course there are as many entities as you like thus related to c{omniscience, omnipotence, being wholly good} (call it 'G1' for short).

[D] [1] Sam believes that G1 includes omniscience, but [2] doesn't believe that the second member of the ordered pair $<G_0,G_1>$ contains omniscience in its core. Hence, [3] G_1 is not strictly identical with the second member of the ordered pair $<G_0,G_1>$, [4] even though (as we ordinarily put it) G_1 *is* [Plantinga's italics] the second member of the ordered pair $<G_0,G_1>$.

[E] Similary, Sam doesn't believe that the third member of the ordered triple $<G_0,G_2,G_1>$ contains omniscience in its core; and so on. . . . .

[F] Corresponding to G_1 there are the members of the set {the second member of $<G_0,G_1>$, the third member of $<G_0,G_2,G_1>$}; call them 'M_2', 'M_3', . . .

[G] Following Castañeda's reasoning, we shall have to see M_2, M_3, and their colleagues as distinct; each will consist of a (unit) set of properties operated on by an operator.

[H] And aren't M_2, M_3, . . . related to each other in *precisely the way* [my italics – H-N.C.] in which, on Guise Theory, the guises of an ordinary object are related to each other?

[I] [1] The various guises of the ordinary object *my willow tree* are related by being guises of that object; [2] they are *consubstantiated* [my italics – H-N.C.]; [3] that is, they are all 'appearances' of the same substance (ordinary object), or ways in which it is presented.

[J] By parity of reasoning the same will have to be said for M_2, M_3, . . . ; they are all appearances of a certain guise, or ways in which that guise is presented.

[K] Perhaps we should say that M_2, M_3, . . . are *conguisiated*. Guises, therefore, have guises.

[L] And just as there are semi-lattices of guises which are ordinary objects, so there will be semi-lattices of guise-guises call them 'ordinary guises'. [*GT*, pp. 65–66; my labeling.]

This is a deep-searching and utterly impressive argument. Indeed, it is a brilliant piece of philosophical skulduggery.

Plantinga means his argument [A]–[L] to be an internal attack against Guise Theory using nothing but the tenets of Guise Theory. Nevertheless, as we shall soon see, at crucial junctures the argument imports assumptions that contravene Guise Theory.

7. Plantinga's Fission Argument: The Importation of Improper Singular Terms and the Neglect of Oedipan Sieves

The very first step [A] of Plantinga's argument smuggles in a principle foreign to Guise Theory. There he *takes* the guise he describes as "my willow tree" to have guises. Yet this is precisely an instance of the very first level of guises for which his general conclusion is to be proven. Of course, Plantinga is not so uncouth as to *say* "the guise *my willow tree*"; he says, instead, both at [A] and at [I]. [1]: "the ordinary object *my willow tree*" (*GT*, p. 66.) This does not look question-begging.[3]

Plantinga *should* have applied the technique of *Oedipan Sieves* to the expression 'my willow tree' (with or without underlining—just as he correctly applies it to the terms he introduces as step [B]. The principle requiring the application of the technique to all singular terms holds universally in Guise Theory. What 'my willow tree" denotes in each occasion of its use as a singular-referring expression is an individual guise, on the self-same footing as any other guises with which it is related by some sameness relation. Within Guise Theory it cannot be singled out as the kingpin of the whole set. The same holds for the guises introduced at step [I].[1].

By not being able to make singular reference to so-called ordinary objects, we cannot subject such entities to the prismatic effect of Oedipan sieves. They do not break into subguises under Oedipan sieves.

In brief, at steps [A] and [I].[1], when he treats the term 'my willow tree' as a singular term for a non-guise, Plantinga's argument imports into Guise Theory a wholly foreign enemy agent. When he neglects to apply Oedipan sieves to 'my willow tree', he imports a second, related foreign enemy agent. This consists of an invidious alien restriction for the selective application of the Principle of Oedipan Sieves.

8. Plantinga's Fission Argument: The Importation into Guise Theory of an Inimical Asymmetric Aspect-of Relation

At step [J] of his argument, Plantinga imports yet another principle, the likes of which do not occur in Guise Theory. Here Plantinga adopts a principle that allows him to take the different guises he calls 'M_2', 'M_3', . . . to be "aspects of a certain" guise, namely, G_1. But why "aspects"? Why aspects of G_1? Why not consider G_1 an aspect of M_2, and M_3 an aspect of M_4? Why not treat G_1 and M_1 (for i = 2, 3, . . .) as aspects of each other? Clearly we need both a criterion of being an aspect of and an argument for the anointing of G_1 as the kingpin of all those guises. Furthermore, both the criterion and the argument must be valid in Guise Theory.

Plantinga claims that M_2, M_3, . . . are aspects of G_1, but not vice versa, on the mere ground that the Oedipan sieves he applies show that they are different. But the asymmetry of being an aspect-of *cannot* be gleaned from Guise Theory. Note how the Oedipan sieves behave *symmetrically* with respect to the terms, and the guises, to which they apply.

Plantinga is absolutely correct in his claims at steps [C]–[E]. The guises he calls G_1, M_2, M_3, . . . are indeed not strictly identical to each other, as he very nicely establishes by means of Oedipan sieves. That they are different is also immediately evident from the difference in their cores. Obviously, from these differences it does not follow that G_1, or, for that matter, some M_1 is the substrate or kingpin guise of which the others are "aspects". At this juncture Plantinga's argument is not entirely translucid to me. Apparently his derivation that M_2, M_3, . . . are "aspects" of G_1 depends on his claim [D].[4]. This contains the following premise:

(30*) c[omniscience, omnipotence, being wholly good]is
       c[the second member of the ordered pair $< G_0$,
       c[omniscience, omnipotence, being wholly good] $>$].
       Abbreviation: G_1 *is* M_2.

The scrutiny of this premise may be instructive. What does '*is*' mean in sentence (30*)? Remember that Plantinga is attempting to find an *internal* difficulty in Guise Theory. We are, therefore, concerned with both: (i) the meaning or meanings of sentence (30*), and (ii) the representation of such meanings in Guise Theory.

Plantinga's underlining of the copula '*is*' at [D].[4] signals that he intends it to mean identity. Guise-theoretical strict identity, however, won't make (30*) come out true. Thus, on such an interpretation (30*) is of no use in deriving within Guise Theory the wished-for fission of guises. Doubtlessly, as Plantinga's underlining of '*is*' reveals, (30*) is short for:

(30**) G_1 is the same as M_2.

Let us turn to Guise Theory to ascertain which sameness relations can provide a true interpretation of (30**). A brief investigation delivers the following results:

Chart 1

(1) INTERNAL PREDICATION: not applicable: no;

(2) IDENTITY: G_1 is $= M_2$; $G_1 = M_2$:   no;

(3) CONFLATION: G_1 is$-$*C M_2; *C(G_1,M_2):   yes;

(4) CONSUBSTANTIATION: G_1 is$-$C* M_2; C*(G_1,M_2):   ?

(5) CONSOCIATION: G_1 is$-$C** M_2; C**(G_1,M_2): yes, indexed;

(6) TRANSUBSTANTIATION: G_1 is$-$T* M_2; T*(G_1,M_2):   no

Evidently, the strong identity Plantinga finds in (30*) is conflation. Charts similar to the above can be constructed for the other premises of Plantinga's argument:

(31.1) G_1 is M_2; (31.2) G_1 is M_2; (31.3) G_1 is M_3; . . .

Plantinga does not stop to consider that all the sameness relations are *symmetric*. There is simply no way *within* Guise Theory to single out G_1 as the anchor

or substrate or kingpin guise of which all other guises conflated (or consubstantiated, or consociated) with it are to be aspects. Furthermore, given that G_1 is conflated with M_2, M_3, . . . and conflation is transitive, all guises G_1, M_2,
M_3, . . . are in the very same boat. They are *democratically* at the self-same
level.

9. Internal Predication and Copulational Symmetry

Guise Theory is a paean for copulational symmetry. In it internal predication is
a dissonance crying out for dissolution. One uniform symmetrization of copulation in Guise Theory is to reduce internal predication to strict identity, as follows:

(IP.Id) c{ . . . }(F) = $_{Analysis}$ c{ . . . } = c{F, . . . }.

The objection to this is that (IP.Id) identifies trivial analytic propositions that
some philosophers may want to differentiate from each other. For example, some
feel that (let us call it datum D.DiP) the proposition *The present Queen of England
is a queen* is not strictly identical to the proposition *The present Queen of England
is of England*. By (IP.Id) they are.

Another view reduces internal predication to conflation, replacing in (IP.Id)
'=' with '*C'.

One approach that both preserves the conflational reduction and conforms to
datum D.DiP involves a drastic revision of Guise Theory. It takes guise cores to
be, not merely sets of monadic properties, but *ordered* sets of properties. Let us
call this new theory < Guise > Theory.

Some philosophers will object that on < Guise > Theory the class of individual guises is greatly enriched. For me the new guises are objectionable only
if they are gratuitous, with no explanatory role. I concede that datum D.DiP is
too modest to justify by itself the introduction of < Guise > Theory. There is,
however, the much more important datum that *thinking is sequential*. Consider
a very large (unordered) set A of monadic properties. According to simple Guise
Theory, A determines just one individual guise. Let a person Jim think believingly that cA is−x F (in some sense x of 'is'). Thinking is sequential. Hence, Jim
will have to think of cA by considering each of the properties in A in some order.
Clearly, he may in the same period think disbelievingly that cA' is-x F, where
A and A' merely differ in the order in which Jim's thinking goes through A. Here
we have, then, an Oedipan sieve that differentiates between the individuals cA
and CA', as well as between the propositional guises that cA is F and that cA'
is F. (On propositional guises see "Perception, Belief, and the Structure of Physical Objects" (1977), part 2.)

Naturally, the guises are conflated. That is, *C(cA,cA'), and *C(that cA is
F, that cA' is F).

Our thinking is symbolic. Yet the preceding schematic Oedipan sieve is neutral
concerning a reduction of the sequential character of thinking to the sequential

character of our running through the strings of symbols that are our means of thinking.[4]

10. Plantinga's Vicious Infinite Regress

Plantinga argues that, because of a vicious infinite regress, on Guise Theory no reference is possible. The argument is a mathematical induction having as its base premise a thesis that indeed figures in Guise Theory, namely, that singular reference is not to so-called ordinary objects but to individual guises. This is precisely the thesis violated by Plantinga's steps at which he takes 'my willow tree' to denote a nonguise. It seems that both the Guise-theoretical principle and its violation play their alloted roles in the internal attack against Guise Theory.

Plantinga's argument for the vicious regress depends essentially on his contention that guises fission into sub-guises at every level. But we have seen that guises do not fission. Hence, Plantinga's vicious infinite regress in Guise Theory remains a non-existent entity. (This is a singular reference.)

11. Additional Forms of Predication

Next Plantinga offers some propositions that he claims cannot be formulated in Guise Theory. This is an excellent challenge. The theory must be tested against experience and extended wherever necessary. Challenges to extend are, of course, not objections; but nice extensions do invalidate objections.

Before we consider Plantinga's challenges I want to concede that Plantinga and William Richards have convinced me that consociation is *not* transitive.

Plantinga's first challenge is the claim that (34) below cannot be represented in Guise Theory, because it contains a mode of predication not now recognized in the theory:

(34) The round square is hard to grasp.

This is an excellent example. Now, (34) is ambiguous, and some questions must be decided before we parse it.

To begin with, on one construal, 'it is hard' is a modality. Let (34) mean something like:

(34.a) For every person x and every proposition p: if p includes the round square: Hard (C*(x,x[——understands that p]).

The copula 'includes' has to be added to Guise Theory. It is a kind of part-whole relationship between propositions. Perhaps the laws governing such a part-whole relation may yield a conflation of the form: *C(the {round, square}, the {round, square, being a constituent of p(. . .), the {round, square}}). There is work to be done here.

The Guise-theoretical sub-theory pertaining to second- and higher-order predication is still underdeveloped. Perhaps the just-mentioned part-whole constituency must be added as a new sameness copular relation. Represent it with **C, to signal a priori constituency. Then we would have: redness is a constituent of the proposition that p: **C(redness, redness[that p]). The categorial or classificatory higher-order predication, like "Redness is a color" I treat as class-membership.

Plantinga's next challenge is represented in his sentence:

(35) c{being a willow tree, being in my back yard} has just two properties.

This challenge has also been posed by others. My answer is still conflation. But I must say much more. Plantinga has shown that underlying (35) is a very serious problem. A Leibnizian guise must have as its core a set L that recopilates all the properties anywhere in a guise core in the consubstantiational structure with L as its apex. Therefore, unless the predication in (35) is handled with extreme care, the core of L will include the property having two properties (from the subject guise in (35)), the property having three properties (from other guises in the semi-lattice under L), and so on. Hence, every existing Leibnizian guise would be contradictory.

The parsing of (35) must meet several conditions:

(i) the numerical property of the finite guise still has to be involved in an *a priori* predication – since non-existing guises exemplify such properties;

(ii) the subordinating Leibnizian guise must include and have all such properties – given its recopilational nature;

(iii) such properties must not be dangling in the core of any guise that subordinates a lower guise with numerical properties in its core;

(iv) the second-order character of such numerical properties must be brought forth in the account of their predication.

Obviously different solutions are in principle available. One solution is to specify each numerical property fully, indicating the set which instantiates it, as follows:

(35.a) c{being a willow, being in my backyard} is − *C c{having two properties (being a willow, being in my backyard), being a willow, being in my backyard}.

This is a conflational statement. Perhaps sometimes in daily life we make consubstantiational statements analogous to (35.a), in which 'is − C*' replaces 'is − *C'.

Apparently, then, (35) does not require an extension of Guise Theory. Even its ambiguity can be handled with the present resources. But Plantinga is completely justified in his righteous chastising of me for having limited myself, in the passage he quotes, to a narrower conception of conflation than the one that catches *all a priori* equivalences.

Plantinga next brandishes some embellishments of (35). They are his sentences (37) and (38). They can be handled along the lines proposed for (35).

Then Plantinga tosses the following challenge:

(39) c{being a willow, being in my backyard} is a node in the Leibnizian individual in which the willow in my backyard culminates.

What does (39) really mean? As far as I can see, (39) means nothing else than:

(39.a) There is a Leibnizian individual L such that: c{being a willow, being in my backyard} is $-C*$ L.

The last challenge Plantinga hurls is this:

(41) The property of being pink is in the core of some existent individuals.

I am not confident I have fully grasped Plantinga's intent here. There are two straightforward interpretations of (41), depending on whether 'The property' is a sign of a categorical variable or a classificatory predicate. Their representations in Guise Theory are also straightforward:

(41.a) There are existing individuals x such that x(being pink).

(41.b) $\exists g$ ($C*(g, g)$ & (being pink ϵ PROPERTY) & g(being pink)).

(N.B: The parentheses around a property expression to the right of a singular term signal internal predication.)

12. Copulas, Saturation, and Types of Property

Plantinga's penultimate challenge is the representation of:

(40) The operator c is abstract.

This is an exciting example. The operator c is the individuator: the operator that forms guises out of sets of monadic properties. Here we have the problem of Frege's concept Horse. I follow Frege in distinguishing saturated from unsaturated entities. Thus, the *predicative* entity (or aspect of experience or of reality) denoted by a predicate expression, for example, 'tall', I take to be different from the corresponding *individual* tallness. The former is unsaturated, the latter not. The logical connectives represent unsaturated structural aspects; predication (whether it is, as most philosophers hold, of just one type, or is manifold, as Guise Theorists maintain) is the most unsaturated of them all.

Given those Fregean differences, the underlined expressions in the following list of sentences represent related aspects of reality, just as the capitalized expressions represent another family of related aspects.

(42.1) Charles IS *friendly*.

(42.2) Charles HAS *friendliness*.

(42.3) HAVING relates Charles and friendliness.

The verb 'HAS' contains both the copula in its inflection and a relational predicate in its stem; 'HAVING' drops the copula and is a noun. (Perhaps we should put

'HAVINGNESS' instead of 'HAVING'.) The point is that the bottom aspect of reality is what the mere copula denotes; fully unsaturated, massive and unarticulated reality; next is the predicative aspect represented by 'HAS', which is a grade less unsaturated; then the corresponding individual denoted by the noun. This saturation consists partly in the capacity of the entity to function as a subject in a proposition: the capacity to be involved directly with copulas.

Let us return to Plantinga's (40). The expression 'the operator c' is a singular term. It denotes that particular individual corresponding to what the expression 'c' expresses in a well-formed term in a sentence. (This is essentially what the definite article 'the' expresses in its use as a prefix forming singular terms.) The latter, not being an individual, has no guise core. The individual has a core, namely, the singleton of the property being C. This property *corresponds* to, but is not the same as, the fully unsaturated individuator. This preceding sentence is paradoxical. Because of the unsaturation we have here an ontological difference so fundamental that it is perspicuously shown but badly described.

In brief, Plantinga's (40) exhibits, naturally, the Fregean "paradoxicality" of unsaturation. The following is a tentative analysis using conflation:

(40.a) c{being C} is − *C c{being C, being C ϵ ABSTRACT}.

The Fregean paradoxicality of unsaturation is not so much a paradox, i.e., something calling for dissolution, but a characteristic mark of non-individuals. There is a great lot to be said about these matters. For instance, inarticulated, sensitive consciousness seems to be connected with the grade of consciousness that goes with the apprehension of a copula − not by itself, of course, because of its unsaturation, but in the context of apprehending a proposition. This connects immediately with the apprehension of a figure against a background, whose ground is presented to sensitive consciousness. Further, there is vague unarticulated consciousness of causation that is characteristic of practical, especially intentional, volitional thinking. (See *Thinking and Doing*, chap. 10, section 3, and "Perception, Belief, and the Structure of Physical Objects and Consciousness," part 2; see also William Richards's work.)

13. Plantinga's Aristotelian Predication

To conclude his study Plantinga discusses this fascinating claim: "the Guise Theorist is obliged to presuppose the Aristotelian notion of predication in stating his own theory." (p. 73.) Both the claim and the argument are intriguing but bewildering. For one thing, he says so little about Aristotelian predication. Moreover, as he says, his argument for that claim "is hard to articulate clearly" (*GT*, p. 73).

Several things seem to me to be going on in Plantinga's argument. At one place the Guise Theorist is described as "presupposing a mode of property possession that isn't to be analyzed in terms of a membership relation" (*GT*, p. 74). Clearly, in this sense Guise Theory contains a predication that is Aristotelian five times over. Neither identity, nor conflation, nor consubstantiation, nor consociation, nor transubstantiation (the forms of predication, besides set-membership, so far introduced in Guise Theory) are reducible to set membership.

I cannot tell what Aristotelian predication is from his discussion of examples. The first example is:

(42) The thing that is the meanest man in North Dakota, and conflated with my willow tree (call it 'MNW'), *is* conflated with my willow tree. (My italics.)

Plantinga acknowledges that (42) is true in Guise Theory if the italicized 'is' represents internal predication. But he contends:

> . . . I should think that the Guise Theorist would want to hold that (42) is false, that MNW doesn't really have a core equivalent to that of my willow tree; . . .
>
> What is going on, I think is this: the Guise Theorist is *implicitly* [my italics—H-N.C.] presupposing that there is *another* [Plantinga's italics] mode of property possession involved here, one in which MNW does not have the property of having a core equivalent to that of my willow tree; and that other mode . . . is what counts . . . and *this mode . . . is Aristotelian property possession.* [*GT*, p. 73.]

Plantinga is absolutely correct in claiming that the Guise theorist holds that sentence (42) expresses something false on some ordinary interpretation. Here Plantinga underestimates the Guise Theorist when he construes him as holding this position only implicitly. The Guise Theorist is explicitly committed to *at least five* different copulas. Hence, he finds at least five initial different interpretations for the italicized 'is' of (42). Clearly, identity is ruled out. We have, thus, the following chart with interpretations and truth-values:

True: (42.i)   MNW is-i conflated with my willow tree;

False:(42.C*)   MNW is-C* conflated with my willow tree;

False:(42.C**)   MNW is-C** conflated with my willow tree;

False:(42.*C)   MNW is-*C conflated with my willow tree;

False:(42.T*)   MNW is-T* conflated with my willow tree.

Which of the four senses of '*is*' expresses Plantinga's Aristotelian predication? Or is his predication something else? But how do we presuppose something else? Plantinga's last examples (44) and (45) give rise to similar perplexities.

Plantinga chides me for having published (in 1974) that internal predication is the "primary" sense of 'is'. He construes me as implying some kind of reduction of the other forms of predication to internal predication. The thought of this has never entered my mind. I am very little interested in reductions. My bent of mind is to see hierarchical structures everywhere. Thus, I tend to speak of something as primary or fundamental, even as more or less fundamental than something else, depending on the roles the things in question play in the hierarchical structures encompassing them. But having lower order in a hierarchical structure does not imply reducibility.

Plantinga is wholly right in opposing the reduction of some basic forms of property possession to set-membership. Furthermore, he is also right in chastising me for saying that internal predication is "primary." Indeed, as we saw in section 9, internal predication is reducible in <Guise> Theory.

14. Conclusion

Guise Theory is acquitted of all of Plantinga's charges. It has, however, undergone valuable revisions. Thanks to Plantinga's deep-searching and thorough critique, Guise Theory is now healthier and better equipped to handle the world before it. This is particularly so in its new version <Guise> Theory.

The ontology and the semantics of <Guise> Theory account nicely for the temporally sequential character of thinking and speaking. <Guise> Theory constitutes a better model of the Kantian idea that all our references take place within experience and language. This new theory is more complex than its predecessor. But the examination of the large patterns of experience reveals that things are indeed more complex than they appear to be when we focus on small bits of the world.[5]

Notes

1. References to "Guise Theory" by Alvin Plantinga, in Tomberlin I, pp. 43–77, will be indicated by *GT*, followed by page number.

2. *GT*, p. 64; italics in *follow* and the labels are mine – H.-N.C.

3. *GT*, p. 66.

4. On some issues pertaining to language as a means of thinking, see "Castañeda on Private Language" by Carl Ginet, in Tomberlin I, pp. 271–86.

5. For additional discussion of Guise Theory see the materials mentioned in note 12 to chap. 1, page 17.

Index

Author Index

Adams, Arthur, 155
Adams, Margaret, 155
Adams, Robert M., 144–46, 152, 156, 158, 174
Albritton, Rogers, 10, 116, 144–45, 146–51, 153
Almog, Joseph, 10, 17, 61
Alston, William, xv
Anscombe, Elizabeth, 61
Aristotle, 53, 103, 241, 262–64, 281–82
Augustinus, Aurelius, 12, 16
Aune, Bruce, 61
Avellaneda, Alonzo Fernandez de, 96

Bach, Emmon, 132, 136
Baker, G. P., 15
Baker, Lynne R., xv
Bally, Charles, 136
Barness, Hazel, 67
Barwise, Jon, 13, 16
Bello, Andres, 117, 124
Benacerraf, Paul, 10, 129
Bergman, Greta, 21–29, 34–36, 42, 49–51, 53, 60–61
Bergson, Henri, 173
Bismarck, Otto, 70–71
Black, Max, 61, 174–75
Boër, Stephen E., 80–87
Brand, Miles, 16, 87
Bratmann, Michael, 16, 61, 87
Burge, Tyler, xiv, 8, 15, 33, 51, 53–58, 61, 148–49, 261
Butler, Ronald J., 230

Caesar, Gaius Julius, 246
Carnap, Rudolf, 252
Cartwright, Richard L., 230
Castañeda, Carlos, 40
Castro, Fidel, 93–99, 189
Cervantes Saavedra, Miguel de, 96, 185, 202, 257
Chisholm, Roderick, xv, 10, 16, 61, 67, 93, 126–27, 129–30, 205, 261
Chomsky, Noam A., 184
Chopin, Frederic, 86
Clark, Romane, 17, 174
Clarke, Samuel, 251
Cocchiarella, Nino, 204–5, 244, 261
Cohen, Jonathan, 259
Columbus, Christopher, 91, 93–95, 98–101, 189
Columbus, Diego, 100
Columbus, Fernando, 100
Copernicus, Nicholas, 161
Cramer, Konrad, xiv, 15, 174
Curie, Marie Sklodowska, 78

Davidson, Donald, 61, 87, 261
Descartes, René, 160, 162–63, 165, 173–74, 208
Dewey, John, 8
Donellan, Keith, 47, 58

Edwards, Paul, 15, 108
Evans, Gareth, 80

287

Subject Index

Hector-Neri Castañeda, the Mahlon Powell Professor of Philosophy at Indiana University since 1974, was founding editor of *NOÛS* in 1966, and is a past president of the American Philosophical Association (Western Division). He has contributed over 150 essays to periodicals and anthologies, edited three anthologies, and written eight books. His philosophical work covers a wide variety of areas, including action theory, practical reasoning, moral philosophy, history of philosophy, philosophy of mind, language, and perception, theory of knowledge, metaphysics, and ontology. His recent books are *The Structure of Morality* (1974), *Thinking and Doing: The Philosophical Foundations of Institutions* (1975), *Human Action* (1976), *On Philosophical Method* (1980), and *Sprache und Erfahrung* (1982). His views have been revised, developed, extended, and strengthened in his replies to criticisms in three honorific volumes: *Agent, Language, and the Structure of the World: Studies Presented to H-N. Castañeda With His Replies* (edited by James E. Tomberlin, 1983), *Hector-Neri Castañeda* (also edited by Tomberlin, (1986), and *Das Denken und die Struktur der Welt, Castañedas epistemologische Ontologie in Darstellung und Kritik* (edited by Klaus Jacobi and Helmut Pape, 1989).